COUNSELING IN A DYNAMIC SOCIETY:

Opportunities and Challenges

Edwin L. Herr

AMERICAN
COUNSELING
ASSOCIATION

5999 Stevenson Avenue
Alexandria, VA 22304-3300

(AACD became the American Counseling Association on July 1, 1992)

American Counseling Association
5999 Stevenson Avenue
Alexandria, VA 22304

Cover Design by Sarah Jane Valdez

Printed in the United States of America

Library of Congress Cataloging-in-Publication Data

Herr, Edwin L.
   Counseling in a dynamic society.
   Bibliography: p.
   1. Counseling.   I. American Association for
Counseling and Development.   II. Title.
BF637.C6H43   1989   158'.3   89-6473
ISBN 1-55620-062-5

CONTENTS

PREFACE

The purpose of this book is to examine major categories of social and economic change likely to affect the purposes for, the techniques of, as well as the settings for counseling in the remainder of this century. The book is not about the counseling process per se. It is not about theories of counseling and their implications for practice. Rather, it is about the environment, the social and economic contexts in which individual behavior is shaped and the provision of counseling occurs. Stated differently, it is about the interactions between economic, social, and political environments, individual behavior, and the form and substance of counseling.

A central premise of the book is that the United States is in a transition in which it is undergoing significant transformations in its institutions, behavioral metaphors, and psychological structures. As these elements of the social structure change so will the ways by which people negotiate their personal identity and live out their self-concept. The book attempts to synthesize a wide-ranging, multidisciplinary literature that outlines changes in the larger society, changes that have or are likely to have direct implications for individual behavior and for counseling responses. It provides counselors, counseling psychologists, other mental health practitioners, and counselor educators an overview of the individual problems, their antecedents and behavioral elements, and their contexts about which "helping professionals" must be knowledgeable in a rapidly changing society.

The book is also incomplete. The changes described here are constantly in a dynamic state; they are systems in flux. Therefore, any book that attempts to capture these changes is likely to be in search of a series of moving targets. It is also likely to be less than encyclopedic in its treatment of the subject. The major and minor challenges discussed here are each the substance of multiple books and articles rather than chapters or paragraphs. Thus, the examination here is selective and, indeed, may miss some social, economic, political, or psychological trends that another writer would have legitimately included and given prominence. It is hoped, however, that the serious

ix

reader will find the book's bibliographic references a source of opportunities to carry this book's level of analysis to more extensive and specialized levels.

The book's content is presented in eight chapters. The chapters and their content are briefly described in the following paragraphs.

As chapter 1 suggests, the content of counseling, with whom the counselor works, and the degree to which counseling is seen as a vital and important sociopolitical institution derive from major social, economic, and political themes that affect individual and group psychology. Thus, the images, beliefs, narratives, and realities that compose national macrosystems also have ripple effects through the other subsystems—community, school, work place, family—in which people interact with institutions and individuals to negotiate their identity, their sense of purpose, their meaning.

In chapters 2 through 5 we examine four major challenges that promise to have great future influence on individual behavior and on the perceptions of how counselors should interact with the settings and populations they serve. These are not new challenges in an absolute sense. The seeds, if not the substance, of each of these four challenges already are affecting the psychological environment of the United States and stimulating new conceptualizations of how, where, and when counseling and related interventions should be implemented.

The first of the four challenges that seem likely to have the greatest effect on the counseling profession into the 21st century concerns the ripple effects of the shifting economy and the transformation of the occupational structure in association with the pervasive effects of advanced technology. The second challenge comprises the implications of changing family structures, the gender revolution, and child-rearing practices. The third challenge is the growing pluralism of traditions, languages, ethnicity, and race that is the rule, not the exception, in contemporary America. Group definitions such as majority and minority are undergoing rapid change, and by the year 2000 will describe an America of substantially different racial composition than is true of the 1980s. Hence the implications for and the practices of counseling will need to be increasingly responsive to cross-cultural issues. The fourth challenge has to do with the changing definitions of "at-risk" populations. Traditional concepts of psychological vulnerability and the etiology of such vulnerability are increasingly seen through the lenses of stress, anger, crisis, and transition and not simply as psychopathology or deficits. Therefore, mental health problems and other challenges to counselors are viewed as dynamic and as encompassing a larger proportion of the population that can profit from counseling interventions.

Chapter 2 addresses specifically the complex issues that relate to the implementation of advanced technology. The economic climate, international competitiveness, educational content and delivery, the forms of work organization, the processes of career development, underemployment and unemployment, stress levels, the psychology of change, and many other areas of daily and national life are being affected by the myths and the realities of advanced technology. Clearly, the actual and perceived implications of advanced technology affect and are affected by the other three challenges examined in chapters 3, 4, and 5: families, pluralism, and being "at risk."

Chapter 3 treats the dramatic shifts in family structures and the sex revolution; this challenge is perhaps less well defined in its effect than is true of the first challenge, the shifting economic climate and advanced technology. However, just as the increasing adaptation of advanced technology is transforming the occupational structure and all of its corollaries, the revolution in family structures and sex roles is transforming the nuclear and intact traditional family into a large number of family patterns. In so doing it is altering forever many of the historical sex role divisions that have differentiated the roles of men and women. These matters have in turn altered child care practices, changed the demographics of the work force, and put at risk in some cases the personal identities of both men and women.

The third challenge, the focus of chapter 4, is even less clear in its effect on counseling than the previous two, but a challenge it will be nevertheless. Because America has been for at least 3 centuries a land of immigrants, it has declared itself a melting pot of differences in traditions and languages into a common culture and set of beliefs. Although such national purposes remain intact, it also has become increasingly obvious that America is a land characterized by pluralism and regional differences in "world views," traditions, values, and related matters. The rise in concern for cross-cultural counseling, multicultural sensitivity, and other such matters is one symbol of the growing recognition of an attention to such pluralism. The implications of cultural differences within the American population, however, are probably more profound than has commonly been acknowledged in counseling, in individuals' information processing, in values and belief systems, in communication, and in other arenas. Chapter 4 discusses some of these implications.

Chapter 5 addresses the concepts embodied in the term "at risk," who can be so characterized, and the factors that put children, youth, and adults at risk. As is true in chapters 2 through 4, perspectives will be provided about the role and content of counseling in responding to the challenges described.

Chapter 6 departs to some degree from the format established in chapters 1 through 5. It focuses not on challenges external to counseling or on the social, economic, and political mechanisms that shape individual behaviors, but on some of the emerging theoretical and other paradigm shifts. These describe how the content and processes of counseling should shift to respond effectively to the challenges, settings, and populations described elsewhere in the book.

Chapters 7 and 8 return to the intent of the first five chapters and discuss recurring and emerging challenges that are less pervasive or more vague in their implications for counseling than the four major challenges discussed in chapters 2 to 5. The challenges described in these chapters vary across settings, populations to be served, and professional issues. They differ also in the level and form of speculation selected "futurists" project about trends likely to grow in importance for counselors in the next decade.

Permit me to thank Dr. Stanley Cramer, my long-time friend and colleague, for reading the first draft of this manuscript and making helpful comments about it. I also appreciate the support and word-processing expertise of Marsha Bierly, Karen Homan, and Judy Kauffman. They have been valued colleagues in bringing this book to completion. Finally, I thank my wife and children, Pat, Alicia, Amber, and Christopher for their love, understanding, and goodwill during the course of this project.

—Edwin L. Herr
State College, Pennsylvania

CHAPTER 1

THE CONTEXT OF COUNSELING

A central premise of this book is that neither counselors nor the problems people bring to counselors exist in a vacuum. In all nations of the world in which mental health services, counseling, guidance, or related processes are available to citizens, these services and their practitioners perform sociopolitical functions. Depending on the specific nation, the resources to support counseling, the definitions of which groups should be served, the conceptions of mental health or illness, the settings in which counseling is provided, and the configuration or substance of counseling services are likely to be classified, articulated, and provided, directly or indirectly, through funds and policies implemented by federal, state, or local governmental units. In accordance with the political, economic, and social characteristics of a given nation, the focus of counseling is related to expectations beyond those defined by some set of professional guidelines. As a result, counseling services often differ in purpose and content across national boundaries and across cultures.

Counseling services can be provided to meet the needs of a nation to better identify and distribute human capital, to treat what national policies define as particularly troublesome segments of the population (e.g., the mentally ill, the violent, the unemployed), or to facilitate human development and self-actualization. Obviously, these targets or functions of counseling are not mutually exclusive. There is overlap in the techniques used and in the dynamics of each of these functions. The overarching point, however, is that the pro-

1

vision of counseling services, who provides them to whom, where they are provided, the purposes for which they are provided, and the outcomes expected are not wholly random. Rather a complex set of legislative and fiscal interactions—mediated through the political processes, the nation's current developmental status, and the stability of the social metaphors with which a nation identifies (e.g., informed individual freedom of action vs. the socialist personality; service to the state vs. collectivist fealty to the group)—affects what counselors do and why.

In historical terms, the implementation of counseling services has been uneven across the world. This has been so primarily because nations must reach particular levels of industrialization, information, occupational and psychological diversity, and resource availability to require formal organizations of mental health or other therapeutic services designed to facilitate individual behavioral development as sanctioned within that national context (Herr, 1985). Counseling services, then, must be understood and appreciated as sociopolitical processes shaped by the legislation and policies of a specific nation and by the cultural dimensions that prevail. Of particular importance are such elements of culture as "the nature and rigidity of the class and caste structure, the value system, the relationship of the individual to the group, and the nature of the enterprise system" (Super, 1985, pp. 12–13). These elements vary from nation to nation and within nations. But, whatever the combination, they are the mediators of the opportunity structure for different groups of people; of the available career paths and mobility factors; of the social metaphors that are translated into policy and into achievement images portrayed by the mass media; of contingencies or reinforcements that shape the individual's cognitive structures, habits, and information-processing mechanisms; of the in-groups and the out-groups of the society; and of expectations for institutional or personal loyalties. Regardless of its specific focus, the social structure of a particular community or nation creates the circumstances in which people develop as human beings, as workers, as parents. The social structure shapes the possibilities for choice, determines the knowledge available to people about their opportunities, and reinforces the acquisition of specific types of behavior. It is within their physical, social, and cultural environments that people negotiate their personal identity, belief systems, and life course. Such political, social, and economic contexts in which individuality is framed and is lived out change across nations, communities, and families, across racial or socioeconomic groups, and, certainly, across time.

The Transactional Nature of Human Behavior

The transactional nature of counseling relative to the environment in which it is located is seen in the behavior that people bring to counselors. The content of counseling, the dilemmas people experience, and the substance of the problems with which they have to cope do not typically arise without external triggering events. In large measure, the personal questions for which people seek help are really functions of how they view current social or occupational expectations and opportunities for personal choice, achievement, social interaction, self-initiative, prestige, role differentiation, autonomy, and many other matters. The resulting anxieties, information deficits, or indecisiveness people experience is the content that concerns counselors and related professionals. These dilemmas and conflicts frequently manifest themselves in mental health problems such as depression and in interpersonal dysfunctions within the family or in the work place. These problems become the concerns of counseling and also form the interactive layers of anxiety and confusion in which such concerns are wrapped. These must be disentangled in the counseling process.

Watzlawick, Beavin, and Jackson (1967) effectively described the interaction of context and behavior as they discussed pathological communication and paradox in issues of mental health:

> . . . a phenomenon remains unexplainable as long as the range of observation is not wide enough to include the context in which the phenomenon occurs. Failure to realize the intricacies of the relationships between an event and the matrix in which it takes place, between an organism and its environment, either confronts the observer with something 'mysterious' or induces him to attribute to his object of study certain properties the object may not possess. Compared with the wide acceptance of this fact in biology, the behavioral sciences seem still to base themselves to a large extent on the monadic view of the individual and on the time-honored method of isolating variables. This becomes particularly obvious when the object of study is disturbed behavior. If a person exhibiting disturbed behavior (psychopathology) is studied in isolation, then the inquiry must be concerned with the *nature* of the condition and, in a wider sense, with the *nature* of the human mind. If the limits of the inquiry are extended to include the effects of this behavior on others, their reactions to it, and the context in which all of this takes

place, the focus shifts from the artificially isolated *monad* to the *relationship* between the parts of a wider system. The observer of human behavior then turns from an inferential study of the mind to the study of the observable manifestations of relationship. (p. 21)

Watzlawick et al. (1967) then focused upon the importance to the individual of communication as a primary mediator of individual existence. To wit:

The environment, then, is subjectively experienced as a set of instructions about the organism's existence, and in this sense the environmental effects are similar to a computer program; Norbert Weiner once said about the world that it may be viewed as a myriad of 'To Whom It May Concern Messages.' . . . Thus, the impact of the environment on an organism comprises a set of instructions whose meaning is by no means self-evident but rather is left up to the organism to decide as best it can. (p. 258)

To understand human behavior and the potential of counseling is to understand that people live in various social, cultural, political, and economic "environments." These environments exert influence or apply limits to the conception of sex and family roles, the achievement images likely to be nurtured, the cognitive and interpersonal styles employed, the resources available, and the forms and comprehensiveness of information provided. The mixes of environments through which people move and negotiate their identity are affected by birth order, place of origin, socioeconomic status, history, and many other factors. Such environments are not static. They are constantly changing, and individuals are under constant pressure to receive, interpret, and act upon messages related to personal behavior that emanate from these environmental mixes.

Effects of Change on Individual Behavior

Drucker (1981), among other observers, noted that within the last decade there have been

. . . genuine structural changes in the social ecology, most pronounced perhaps in population structure and population dynamics in the developed countries; but also in the role and performance of old, established and seemingly stable social bodies, such as governmental agencies or boards of directors, whether of businesses, hospitals, or universities; in the interface between sciences and society; and in fundamental theories that are still widely taught as 'revealed truths.' (p. vii)

Of major interest to the counselor is how changes in the social ecology affect individuals and what the nature of such interaction is.

Toffler (1970), almost two decades ago, indicated that changes in the "social ecology" affect the behavior of people exposed to rapid changes in institutions and values. Toffler coined the term "future shock" to describe the shattering stress and disorientation individuals experience when they are subjected to too much change in too short a time. He believed that future shock is manifested in a great range of stress-related problems that have become the foci of much of the research and literature addressed to counselors in the last quarter of the 20th century. He spoke of stress-related physical illness, the deterioration of individual decision making under conditions of "overchoice," the spreading use of drugs, outbreaks of vandalism and undirected violence, apathy, and other forms of social irrationality under the excessive change and stimulation of future shock. Toffler suggested that people have an "adaptive range" below and above which "the individual's ability to cope simply falls apart" (p. 344).

In an echo of the observations of Watzlawick et al. described earlier, Toffler contended that:

> Rational behavior, in particular, depends upon a ceaseless flow of data from the environment. It depends upon the power of the individual to predict with at least fair success, the outcome of his own actions. To do this, he must be able to predict how the environment will respond to his acts. Sanity, itself, thus hinges on man's ability to predict his immediate, personal future on the basis of information fed him by the environment. (p. 350)

But, Toffler again contended that the more rapid the change and the more novel the environment, whether one talks in terms of "culture shock" or "future shock," the more information the individual must process in order to make effective, rational decisions. When the limits of individuals' ability to process information are exceeded, they are likely to manifest sensory or information overload or decision stress. Such overstimulation causes people to feel increasingly harried, tired, and out of control. In turn, people are likely to cope with these conditions by denial, overspecialization, reversion to previously successful adaptive behavior that is no longer relevant or useful, or attempts to unrealistically simplify what is being experienced. "Overstimulation can also lead to confusion, disorientation, or distortion of reality; to fatigue, anxiety, tenseness, or extreme irritability; to apathy and emotional withdrawal'' (p. 348).

Every mental health specialist—counselor, psychologist, social worker—has seen the signs in individual behavior that Toffler so prophetically predicted. The issue, however, is how practitioners interpret such signs. Do they attribute such behavior to mental illness and psychopathology, or to problems of living instigated by environmental overstimulation, excessive novelty, and difficulty in decoding and processing the multitude of information from the multiple environments people occupy—environments that are themselves in flux? Either way, the question of how individuals and environments interact and under what conditions should be at the heart of any therapeutic alliance between counselors and clients.

Individuals and Environments in Dynamic Interaction

A major premise confronting counselors is that people are in dynamic interaction with their environment. According to Kleinman (1988), ''In the anthropological vision, the two-way interaction between social world and person is the source of thought, emotion, action. This mediating dialectic creates experience. It is as basic to the formation of personality and behavior as it is to the causation of mental disorder'.' (p. 3). Vondracek, Lerner, and Schulenberg (1986) described such interaction as follows: ''Dynamic interaction means that the context and the organism are inextricably embedded in each other, that the context consists of multiple levels changing interdependently across time, and that because organisms influence the contexts that influence them, they are able to play an active role in their own developments'' (p. 37).

These observations affirm that individual-environmental transactions are reciprocal. Each affects the other. To understand individuals' behavior, it is typically necessary to understand the effects of their past and present contexts on their present perceptions of events, possibilities, or their own characteristics. Most people do not operate in uncontrolled, impulsive, or spontaneous ways. Rather they operate in accordance with prior experiences, rules, and guidelines that have shaped their present behavior.

The phenomenological axiom that Syngg and Combs (1949) espoused 40 years ago—that people behave as they perceive—is a powerful construct with implications for humanistic, behavioral, and cognitive approaches to intervention. In essence, this concept indicates that people learn to interpret or perceive the same event or cue differently and that people also bring different behavioral repertoires from which they select responses to similar cues. Thus, people can view the same event, interpret it differently, and behave in response to it in opposite ways with widely varying levels of emotion, intensity, and stress. Whereas one person may perceive a particular event as threatening, another can essentially disregard it as unimportant or benign. The reasons for such individual variability in perceptions and responses are complex and are found in both the individual's history and how that history is played out in current behavior.

Variations in Individuals' Perceptions

A 1987 issue of *Psychology Today* with a cover story about "life flow" declared on the cover that "We are each unique, but each a child of our times" (*Psychology Today, May 1987*). Such a statement affirms that a major aspect of individual-context interaction has to do with when one was born and what that means for one's values and belief systems, and one's pessimism and optimism about economic opportunities and other life possibilities. Neugarten and Neugarten (1987), among other researchers, found that the economic and psychological emphases of different historical periods and the accompanying social expectations affect how "cohorts" of people—those born in the same year or time period—progress through their lives. People's perceptions and expectations are shaped by the social context in which they are born, raised, and live.

One only has to conjure up the contrasts evoked by considering how Americans who have lived through the Great Depression of the 1930s, the patriotism and common cause of the Second World War, the social activism of the 1960s, or the material enthusiasms of the yuppie generation of the 1980s would be likely to differ in their interpretation and approach to possible life opportunities. Their views of the "social clock"—the hypothetical timetable people use to determine when it is appropriate to get married, have children, establish themselves in a work role, become middle-aged or old—are likely to differ, creating varying stereotypes of appropriate and inappropriate behavior, and otherwise patterning their lives. The degree to which one's life pattern tends to be in accord with the social clock of one's cohort has much to do with how one anticipates and acts on the inevitable transitions from adolescence to adulthood and one's various parental, family, work, and social roles. Thus, the timing of life transitions, the ways one is expected to cope with them, and their importance are imposed upon individuals by the society's institutions. But the content and importance of transitions also shift across time. Therefore, the expectations or psychological boundaries that guide one generation's behavior are not likely to be the same for the next. As a result, how different cohorts of people interpret and act upon their society is likely to differ, as are the values and commitments they manifest.

One illustration of how environments change over time in their content and, therefore, in the messages they send individuals is reflected in the ongoing transformation of work values and work ethics in this nation. Yankelovich (1981) compared American life themes of the 1960s with those of the 1980s. These are adapted in Figure 1. The point is that as work meanings shift, so do the psychology and the behavior of the workers. These individuals, in effect, march to different "drumbeats."

Thus, one can view any population as constituted of people acting out different individual scripts, patterns, or scenarios shaped by social, psychological, economic, and technological conditions with which they were more or less imprinted by their family, birthplace, and period of origin. These conditions are experienced differently from family to family, region to region, community to community, and time to time. As such conditions vary, they reflect the decrease of some opportunities and life styles and the increase or emergence of others. New social belief systems or value sets ebb and flow as people try to negotiate their personal identity and the rules by which they "expend their lives." Available achievement images, interpersonal behaviors, and related phenomena differ across time and place as well as across groups. They are differently processed, reinforced, and lived out from one socioeconomic group to another, from one cultural group to another, and from one national group to another (Peabody, 1985).

The context for one's life pattern and personality is also a function of one's birth order among siblings in a family. Parental models of child rearing and available resources are likely to change with time, creating different "environments" for children born and raised at different times within the same family. As parents cope with their own development, or their entrance into or relief from substance abuse or physical illness, their child-rearing practices may create a different environment for children reared at different points along such a continuum.

The examples cited above are intended to show that the course of one's development is dependent on when one is born; how many others are growing up at the same time and competing for resources or opportunities available (either within a family or a larger community); how sex roles are defined in one's historical time; the rigidity

FIGURE 1
Trends in the Work Ethic in the 1960s and the 1980s

1960s	*1980s*
The Good Provider Theme The breadwinner—the man who provides for his family—is the real man.	*Reduced Fear of Economic Insecurity* For most people economic security continues to dominate their lives. But today people take some economic security for granted. A substantial minority say that they are now prepared to take certain risks with their own economic security for the sake of enhancing the quality of life.
The Independence Theme To make a living by working is to "stand on one's own two feet and avoid dependence on others."	
The Success Theme Hard work always pays off.	*Economic Division of Labor Between the Sexes* The economic discipline that maintained the rigidity of sex roles in the past has weakened.
The Self-Respect Theme Hard work of any type has dignity whether it be menial or exalted. A man's inherent worth is reflected in the act of working.	The idea of women working for self-fulfillment rather than economic motives gains wider acceptance all the time. *The Psychology of Entitlement* A broad new agenda of social rights is growing, and a psychological process is developing whereby a person's wants and desires become converted into a set of presumed rights. *The Adversary Culture Challenges the Cult of Efficiency* The average American has begun to wonder whether too great a concern with efficiency and rationality is not robbing life of the excitement and pleasure desired. *The Changing Meaning of Success* An increasing number of people are coming to feel that there is such a thing as enough money. A "big earner" who has settled for an unpleasant life style is no longer considered more successful than someone with less money who has created an agreeable life style. People are no longer as ready to make sacrifices for economic success as they were in the past.

From "The Meaning of Work" (pp. 33–34) by D. Yankelovich. In J. O'Toole, J.L. Scheiber, and L.C. Woods (Eds.), *Working, Changes and Choices*, 1981, New York: Human Science Press. Reprinted by permission from E.L. Herr and S.H. Cramer, *Career Counseling and Guidance Through the Life Span: Systematic Approaches*, 3rd ed. (p. 48), 1988, Glenview, IL: Scott Foresman.

with which the roles of children, adolescents, or adults are demarcated and conveyed; and the sharpness, singularity, and focus of the dominant cultural beliefs about achievement, sex roles, success, happiness, individual versus collective progress, interpersonal interactions, and related phenomena. Therefore, whether one is born as part of a "baby boom" or "baby bust,"; in a time of "women's liberation" and enlightened or repressive attitudes toward racial minorities; in a time of economic depression or abundance; in a family that is intact and healthy or disintegrating; or in a socioeconomic stratum characterized by hopefulness and minimal economic barriers or the opposite are all elements of both the psychological and the literal "opportunity structure" with which people cope and interact as they form their personal values, interests, and personal plans of action. These elements are also the seedbeds for feelings of self-efficacy, self-esteem, and purposefulness, or their lack. As such these contextual-individual interactions become the mechanisms that influence what psychological issues are likely to arise at what points of history, for what groups, and whether or not they are likely to be brought to counselors or other "helpers."

Perspectives on Environmental Effects on Individuals

As is true in virtually any attempt to understand individual-environmental interaction, there are multidisciplinary "windows" through which one can view such phenomena. One window is that of social psychology. At least two notions are useful from such a perspective. One is that of collective personality; the other is that of collective consciousness. Collective personality consists of the collective sensations people share in a society; collective consciousness consists of the reflections and reactions people share in dealing with these common sensations (Sennett, 1977).

Collective Personality and Collective Consciousness

To take the point further, collective personality is the ability of people to interact with each other, to share sensations, and to perform common actions by virtue of their belief that they share an essential likeness. Whether the collective personality is really a typical person or a caricature of a collective profile of what a society would like its members to resemble is debatable. But, whether exaggerated or not, the collective personality represents what people in a particular society recognize as the common characteristics of the image they share when they speak of an "American," an "Arab," a "worker," a "woman," "we," and "them." In the sense of our use of the term "social metaphor" at various points in this book to describe the images societies create about themselves, social psychologists would argue that societies differ not only in social metaphors but in the cast of characters and the personality types they create to play them out.

Collective consciousness is the group consciousness of people exposed to the common, if contradictory, impressions of history. Collective consciousness is "like the wax upon which the forces of society leave their imprint" (Sennett, 1977, p. 69). Social psychology is the study of and the testimony to the perception that social conditions can influence emotional experience. Thus, two broad areas of inquiry occur in social psychology. One deals with the kinds of images groups form of themselves (collective personality) and the kinds of symbols and values groups share because of their social interactions (collective consciousness) (Sennett, 1977, p. xix). Inherent in such notions is the acknowledgment that different nations, societies, and cultural groups provide different social and psychological conditions for their people and information having varying levels of clarity. Also implicit in such perspectives is the view that personal enmities, fears and hopes, prejudices and illusions, sympathies and antipathies, convictions, articles of faith, and principles are shared in a particular nation, society, or cultural group but that these differ from one such collectivity to another. These realities are at the base of cross-cultural counseling as well as, in global terms, of diplomacy, political negotiation, and conflict resolution.

Reich's Morality Tales

Reich (1987) suggested that American history is composed of several "morality tales" or parables that underlie the collective consciousness of Americans. This is a realm of values, purposes, and visions to which individual behavior is frequently referred in the mass media, biographies, official pronouncements, art, literature, and politics. The body of metaphor or morality tales that characterize any nation, ethnic, or racial group can be used to mobilize public action or to shape individual aspirations and behavior. Morality tales and social metaphors help groups define their uniqueness and to understand who they are and what they are for themselves or others. As nations and societies move through their own stages of development, different aspects of their social metaphors receive more or less emphasis. Nations define their problems in relationship to the prevailing notions of who they are, their origins, and their destiny. Reich suggested that American history and its uniqueness are rooted in four cultural parables. They are briefly discussed below.

The mob at the gates. As a function of the flight from older cultures, its immigrant heritage, America has become "a depiction of a beacon light of virtue in a world of darkness, a small island of freedom and democracy in a perilous sea" (p. 8). This morality tale suggests that Americans are uniquely blessed, the proper model for other people's aspirations, the hope of the world's poor and oppressed. Such a view also suggests that America must constantly be on guard against the mob at its gates, lest the forces of darkness overwhelm it.

The triumphant individual. This parable is one of the little individual who works hard, takes risks, believes in him- or herself, and eventually earns wealth, fame, and honor (p. 9). This parable celebrates self-reliance, rugged individualism, the loner and maverick, plainspokenness, getting the job done, determination and integrity, and uncompromised ideals. Perhaps more than any other tale Americans have incorporated as truth is that of the triumphant individual and its portrayal in the heroic literature, films, and the symbolism of the Statue of Liberty.

The benevolent community. This parable depicts the willingness to reach out to others in need, to provide a helping hand, a fair deal, and foreign aid to the less privileged. The image is one of philanthropy, local pride and self-help, generosity, and the nurturance of community.

The rot at the top. The fourth of America's parables or morality tales reflects its rejection of central authority and the privilege of aristocracy. It is suspicious of powerful elites in which the common people must be alert to corruption, decadence, irresponsibility, and conspiracy against the broader public. From the time of the Founding Fathers to the present, the possibility of the abuse of power has been at the center of governmental checks and balances and the subject again of plays, stories, and movies in which the poor but honest man or woman takes on the corporate giant or the big bully and wins.

Whether or not each of these morality tales is appropriate in a period of global interdependence, international competition, and growing group, rather than individual, action is beside the point. These parables give a sense of uniqueness and meaning to our national lives, to our dreams and hopes. They sanction and reinforce some behaviors and reject others. In some ways, these metaphors represent the ideal, what the nation might be, rather than what it is. In such contexts, these morality tales represent tensions between the real and the ideal. They rebuke selfishness, narcissism, dependence, pretension, and they provide standards by which to examine gaps between aspiration and perceived reality. They represent the content of conversations about the symbols, ideals, and ways of feeling that matter to the members of particular cultures (Bellah, Madsen, Sullivan, Swidler, & Tipton, 1985). The American metaphors of individualism, success, freedom, and justice are unique aspects of the building blocks of social character, just as different concepts are important in other cultures.

Individual and Social Interaction

Somewhat analogously to the social psychology notions of collective personality and collective consciousness discussed earlier, Fromm (1962), also discussed the interaction of individual and social character. In his view, societies differ in their structural elements and objectives. Therefore:

> . . . it is the function of the 'social character' to shape the energies of the members of society in such a way that their behavior is not a matter of conscious decision as to whether or not to follow the social pattern, but one of *wanting to act* as *they have to act* and at the same time finding gratification in acting according to the requirements of the culture. In other words, it is the social character's function to *mold and channel* human energy within a given society for the purpose of the continued functioning of the society. (p. 79)

Societies, then, differ in both the content of social character (e.g., in the United States, the behavioral components of the four morality tales described above) and in the methods by which social character is produced (e.g., childhood training, the content of schooling).

Fromm (1962) argued, for example, that societies apply different filters to reinforce what comes to collective consciousness as appropriate behavior or "social character." This includes the subtleties and nuances of national language; the logic (e.g, Aristotelian, paradoxical, inductive-deductive) that directs the thinking of people in a particular culture; and the social taboos that "declare certain ideas and feelings to be improper, forbidden, dangerous and which prevent them from reaching the level of consciousness" (p. 121). The social taboos may be overt, as in cultures where right and wrong are clearly delineated and one is exposed to public shame or intense personal guilt if taboos are violated, or less clear, and possibly contradictory, leading to diffuse anxiety in some individuals (Reisman, 1961). The social taboos and their structuring of what should be also can capture by inclusion or exclusion the national rhetoric and cultural parables described previously. Fromm called these "national ideologies" and compared them for the United States and the Soviet Union in the following paraphrased fashion: For Americans—we are religiously free; we are individualists; our leaders are wise; we are good; our enemies (whoever these happen to be at the moment) are bad; our parents love us and we love them. For the Soviets—we are Marxists; we are socialists; socialism expresses the will of the people; our leaders are wise and work for humanity; our profit interest in society is a socialist profit interest and different from the "capitalist" profit interest (p. 123).

The point of this analysis of individual and social interaction is that nations, societies, and subgroups provide the environment for varied perceptions of reality, information processing, and personal identity and behavior. Individual behavior then is not simply a function of intrapsychic forces, needs, and drives, but of complex interactions, transactions, and negotiations between individuals and the multiple environments they occupy.

Multidimensionality of Environments

To understand better the interaction of individuals and environments as the precipitators of counseling problems, it is useful to consider several other notions. One of these is that the environments people occupy are multidimensional. One's "life space" is more properly thought of as "life spaces" that vary in their expectations for individual behavior and the influences or limits they impose on such behavior. Such life spaces can be positive or negative or, indeed, benign with regard to their effects on individuals. As Gibson (1979, 1982) suggested, environments also can be viewed as providing "affordances"—objects, events, people—that can provide information, stimulation, or opportunities to those who can perceive such affordances. The contingency term in such a notion is "can perceive." Although one might argue that it is theoretically possible to formulate a taxonomy of affordances available in different environments and how these might pertain to different individual needs or perceptual systems, it is likely that many individuals will not profit from such affordances because they are not open to the possibilities, fear they cannot fulfill the expectations required, or are preoccupied with other matters that narrow their perceptual field.

Although not using the terminology of affordances per se, Bandura (1982) talked about the importance of fortuitous or chance occurrences affecting life paths through the reciprocal influence of personal and social factors. He contended that the personal determinants of the effects of chance encounters are the entry skills, emotional ties, values, and personal standards individuals bring to the encounter. He suggested that the social determinants of the effects of chance encounters include the rewards likely to be associated with the encounter; hearing a particular lecture, reading a particular book, unexpectedly witnessing a particular event on television; the openness of the environment, or of the individual to changing one's life path. These personal and social determinants also may predispose people to use or not use "affordances." Bandura suggested that different groups or individuals furnish different symbolic environments and that for these reasons and others, some chance encounters "touch people only lightly, others leave more lasting effects, and still others branch people into new trajectories of life" (Bandura, 1982, p. 749).

Person-Environment Fit

Historically, several lines of theoretical inquiry have been devoted to person-environment transactions or fit. They include such perspectives as those of Murray and Kluckhohn (1956) who stated:

> A human being does not grow up in a vacuum: his development is determined not only by the physical environment as the biologist proved, and by the family environment as Freud proved, but, as the massive data collected by the cultural anthropologists showed, by the larger societal and cultural institutions . . . (p. 4)

Stern, Stein, and Bloom (1956) contended over three decades ago that to understand behavior one must study both the individual and the environment. More specifically they stated:

> Behavior represents an ongoing field process. It is the resultant of the transaction between the individual and other structural units in the behavioral field. For convenience, these other units may be referred to collectively as the *environment*. This environment provides a continual source of actual and potential stimulus demands and consequences. (p. 35)

Murphy (1947, p. 867) in his "situationism" construct maintained that human beings respond as situations require them to respond.

Whatever their biological diversities, if capable of learning, they will take on the attributes for which the situation calls. Given a changed situation, there is a changed role and consequently a changed personality.

The line of thinking termed "field theory" is concerned with the interaction between the individual and the stimuli present in the environmental context within which he or she is operating at a given moment. This thesis does not negate the fact that individuals have certain biological differences and inherited propensities; it simply minimizes their importance in view of the present stimuli confronting the organism. An example of this is the belief held by Snygg and Combs (1949) that "all behavior, without exception, is completely determined by and pertinent to the phenomenal field of the behaving organism" (p. 15). Out of the phenomenal field, Snygg and Combs differentiated a phenomenal self, which includes all those parts of the phenomenal field the individual experiences as part or characteristic of him- or herself. The phenomenal field, then, consists of the totality of experiences of which the person is aware at the instant of action; one behaves as one perceives.

Lewin (1951) also applied the concepts of field theory to a wide variety of psychological and sociological phenomena. He considered the person and his or her environment as interdependent regions of "life space," Lewin's term for the total psychological field. The principal characteristics of Lewin's field theory can be summarized as follows: (a) behavior is a function of the field that exists at the time behavior occurs, (b) analysis begins with the situation as a whole from which the component parts are differentiated, and (c) the concrete person in a concrete situation can be represented mathematically. Lewin defined the field as "the totality of coexisting facts which are conceived of as mutually interdependent" (p. 240). Hall and Lindzey (1957) stated that "Lewin's theory was one of those that helped to revive the conception of man as a complex energy field, motivated by psychological forces, and behaving selectively and creatively" (p. 253).

Mathewson (1955), at approximately the same time, contended that ". . . no individual can be understood apart from his field. And the field must necessarily include both inner and outer phases or states, or in other words, a complex of interrelated socio psychological forces" (p. 132). In an even earlier classic view, Murray (1938) argued that it was possible and advisable to classify an environment in terms of the kinds of benefits (facilitations, satisfactions) and the kinds of harms (obstructions, injuries, dissatisfactions) that it provides.

Murray (1938) distinguished between environmental characteristics (reinforcements, norms, expectations), which he labeled *press*, and individual *needs*. His research examined the degree to which specific needs might be gratified or satisfied in particular environments. He also distinguished between *alpha press*, what objective or scientific inquiry suggests are the actual reinforcements or expectancies in an environment, and *beta press*, the subject's own interpretation of the environment as he or she perceives it. Murray called the process of the individual's recognizing what is "being done" to him or her at the moment (that says "this is good" or "this is bad") *pressive perception*. Murray saw this process as definitely egocentric, giving rise almost invariably to some sort of adaptive behavior. Furthermore, Murray believed that the power of a stimulus situation (which may be considered in our terms as an "affordance," a chance encounter, or an environment) does not depend on pressive perception but, instead, on *pressive apperception*: beliefs that "the environmental conditions may do this to me (if I remain passive)" or "I may use the object in this or that way (if I become active)." Murray further believed that because the individual is a historical creature, pressive apperception is a consequence of past experiences conjured up as a result of the present image and which, through integration, determines behavior. In Murray's view, if the individual "apperceives" a stimulus or a constellation of stimuli as harmful, or the present environment as uncongenial or unsatisfying, the individual will engage in adaptive behavior designed to permit the person to leave or otherwise diminish the environmental effects.

Holland (1966, 1973, 1985) advanced the notions of Murray and others into a theory of personality types interacting with different environments. Much of his research has been devoted to developing concepts and structures by which to understand and predict the behavior of individuals in different types of work environments. Holland's concepts have been concerned primarily with the career implications of person-environment fit, but the conceptualizations have wider applicability to social and educational environments.

Basically, Holland takes the view that an individual's personality is a product of both heredity and environment. As an outcome of early and continuing influences of genetic potentialities and the interaction of the individual with his or her environment, there develops a hierarchy of habitual or preferred methods for dealing with social and environmental tasks. The notion of "modal personal orientation" attempts to describe the most typical way in which an individual responds to an environment.

Holland explicated the notion that individual choice behavior is an expression of personality. Therefore, because people inhabiting specific environments, occupational or educational, have similar personality characteristics, their responses to problems and interpersonal relations are likely to be similar. Thus, people seek those environments that permit expression of their personality styles.

The heart of Holland's theory lies in four assumptions promulgated in 1973 and several secondary assumptions used to refine and extend his theory in 1985. First, the 1973 assumptions:

1. In our culture, most persons can be categorized as one of six types: realistic, investigative, artistic, social, enterprising or conventional.
2. There are six kinds of environments: realistic, investigative, artistic, social, enterprising and conventional.
3. People search for environments that will let them exercise their skills and abilities, express their attitudes and values, and take on agreeable problems and roles.
4. A person's behavior is determined by an interaction between his personality and the characteristics of his environment. (Holland, 1973, pp. 2–4)

In 1985, Holland provided several additional assumptions that extend the four basic assumptions addressed above. They include the following:

- *Consistency*. Some types of persons or environments have more relationship to each other than to others. Thus, "degrees of consistency or relatedness are assumed to affect vocational preference" (p. 4).
- *Differentiation*. "The degree to which a person or an environment is well defined is its degree of differentiation. . . . Personal identity is defined as the possession of a clear and stable picture of one's goals, interests, and talents. Environmental identity is present when an environment or organization has clear, integrated goals, tasks and rewards that are stable over long time intervals" (p. 5).
- *Congruence*. "Different personality types require different environments. Incongruence occurs when a type lives in an environment that provides opportunities and rewards foreign to the person's preferences and abilities—for instance, a realistic type in a social environment" (p. 5).

Microsystem, Mesosystem, Exosystem, and Macrosystem

Bronfenbrenner (1979) provided a different, although complementary view of environment and individual interaction through his conceptual lens. In essence, he defined an individual's environment as composed of four interconnected systems that affect psychological growth. Each of these four structures is conceived of as being a part of the next largest system, starting from the most intimate, in individual terms, to the largest and most encompassing. These four systems, beginning with the one exerting the most direct, developmental effect on the individual's psychological growth, include the *microsystem*, the *mesosystem*, the *exosystem*, and the *macrosystem*.

The *microsystem* would be represented by one's family, one's school or peer group, and one's work place. It is composed of the interpersonal relationships, goal-directed activities, and system-defined roles and expectations an individual experiences most directly from his or her context or environment. As defined by Bronfenbrenner: "A microsystem is a pattern of activities, roles, and interpersonal relations experienced by the developing person in a given setting with particular physical and material characteristics" (p. 22). Encompassed in such a system are activities carried on by an individual alone, with others, or by others directed toward the individual. Of major importance are the dyadic relationships in the family system between a parent and child or between siblings, as well as the larger systems of interactions in a total family unit or a peer group. Also at issue are the role expectations engendered and reinforced within the microsystem. Recent research on the children of alcoholics, on children of disrupted families, on children used as family scapegoats, and on the effects on children of being in the position of leaders or followers in peer groups conveys the importance of the microsystem for psychological development, and indeed as a target for counseling intervention.

The *mesosystem* is seen as linking microsystems with the content—molar activities, interpersonal relations, and role transitions—spilling from one system to the other, particularly the mesosystem to the microsystem. According to Bronfenbrenner, a mesosystem is "a set of interrelations between two or more settings in which the developing person becomes an active participant" (p. 209). Thus, what is happening to a child in school or a parent in a work place is likely to affect the family environment; but, perhaps the more important element is the notion of "multisetting participation." In each setting (home, school, work place, social network, church, community agency), the individual is likely to experience different demands, expectations, norms, and emotional stimuli. Often the public life at the work place is very different in intent and psychology than are the demands of the private world of marriage or child rearing experienced in the nuclear family. These settings come into serious conflict when the residual effects of one setting affect performance or happiness in the other (e.g., the unhappy worker who berates his wife or children at home). At times it becomes difficult for people to discriminate which behavior is appropriate in which environment.

It is also possible, according to Bronfenbrenner, to think of mesosystems in sequential terms. As one moves from one ecological transition to the next (school to work, job to job, employment to retirement), such notions as "intersetting communication" and "intersetting knowledge" reflect how or whether experience and information is useful as the individual attempts to employ it from one setting to the next. What are the effects of value shifts on behavior from one setting to another, from one time to another? As Bronfenbrenner has cogently observed, "Development is enhanced to the extent that, prior to each entry into a new setting . . . the person and members of both settings involved are provided with information, advice, and experience relevant to the impending transition" (p. 217). The question is, of course, how and where do people get information about the likely effects of their transition from one mesosystem to another, the new behaviors required, or the new perspectives that need to be gained? Counseling is one such place. But, counseling frequently also is employed because people have experienced faulty or ineffective transitions from one mesosystem to another. In such cases, people need to understand what has gone awry, how to acquire the new images or skills required by the mesosystem transition, how to be more flexible or discriminating in the behaviors they implement in the new setting, how the mesosystems involved are congruent or incongruent in their expectations and demands, and to what degree prior experience is useful in the current situation.

The third system Bronfenbrenner defined is the *exosystem*. Exosystems encompass the indirect effects upon children and adults of what is happening in a parent's or spouse's system. As Bronfenbrenner defined, exosystems consist "of one or more settings that do not involve the developing person as an active participant but in which events occur that affect, or are affected by, what happens in that setting" (p. 273). Thus, it is assumed that there are causal links between the content of exosystems, external events, and the content of microsystems. The logic is straightforward. For example, if a parent experiences sudden unemployment in the work place, the child will suffer. The child is obviously not an active or direct participant in that work place, but the economic and psychological turmoil the parent experiences will undoubtedly change the characteristics of the family environment, or the microsystem. It may also change the mesosystem interaction of the child. To illustrate, the effect of the exosystem, the parent's work place, upon the child's microsystem may be a reduction of the family's economic viability to such an extent that the planned transition of the child from school to college is no longer viable. The child may need to go directly to work to help sustain the family and, therefore, postpone or change the sequential nature of mesosystem transitions from school to college to work, to one of school to work to college, or to one of school to work. Obviously, a whole series of personal identity, information, skills, values, communication, and interpersonal matters has been altered for the child as an indirect effect of the parent's experience in the exosystem.

Not all indirect effects from the parent's work place are negative or as visible as the example just used. Rather, the point is that such matters as the parents' discretionary time, social status, autonomy, vacation time, work content, and relations with supervisors may manifest themselves in parental expectations about the children's initiative and independence, views of punishment, expectations about education or part-time work, emphases on income or interpersonal orientations, and so on. These in turn will affect the characteristics of the child's microsystem and will be incorporated in the child's values and behavior.

The *macrosystem* is seen as the most encompassing of the ecological systems. It contains the other three systems and is the purveyor of the major cultural beliefs, the morality tales, and the historical traditions or influences of a society. It is the source and sustainer of the social metaphors by which national images of identity are defined and organized, by which ideologies about sex-roles, admired personality traits, and appropriate behavioral sanctions are created. It is also the source of "cohort effects"—the major political, social, policy, and economic contexts that shape personal images of opportunity, security, risk, style, and other matters that affect personal development.

Conclusions

Chapter 1 has examined the premise that neither counselors nor the problems that clients bring to counselors exist in a political, social, or economic vacuum. Rather, both the form and substance of counseling and of client problems are seen as products of complex transactions between individual behavior or the characteristics of counseling and the larger social context in which they are located.

Given the above premise the notion was explored that counseling services in different nations or, indeed, with different population subgroups are likely to vary. A variety of theoretical positions from social psychology, sociology, and differential psychology were examined in an effort to describe some of the mechanisms of individual-environmental transactions from the intimate level of microsystem effects to the national level of macrosystem effects. Particular attention was paid to how social metaphors, national morality tales, and cultural parables affect the psychological climate of a nation or a group, concepts of appropriate behavior that ensue, and shifts in these perspectives over time.

Questions of significance to counselors are how do families, communities, and subpopulations influence the behavioral expectations that individual clients hold for themselves? Are these expectations consistent or contradictory? Does the client perceive these expectations with accuracy? In chapter 4, the reader will explore the cultural diversity and pluralism that characterize contemporary America. In that chapter, it will be apparent that although there are social metaphors and cultural traditions of significance to American history, there are also particular social metaphors and cultural traditions of importance to the many ethnic and racial groups that compose the pluralistic American population. Both the so-called majority and minority cultures are heterogeneous in their values and in their traditions. One cannot substitute the ''Afrocentricity'' of Black Americans for the history and ''world view'' of Hispanic Americans or Asian Americans. The sets of values, traditions, and ''world views'' distinguishing each group are diverse and important in their shaping of individual behavior; they are not interchangeable simply because, in the common parlance, each of these groups is labeled a minority group. Although people in each of these culturally diverse groups can identify with the aspirations and possibilities of the larger American view of freedom, success, and justice, the ways of their participation in that agenda are mediated by the systems of reinforcements, expectations, and behavioral sanctions intimately tied to the characteristics of their family, race, ethnic group, and sex.

Chapter 2 is intended to help the counselor consider the effects of advanced technology and the shifting economic climate in the United States upon different groups of youths and adults. Advanced technology also spawns metaphors and mythology. Counselors need to help clients understand these effects upon both the psychology of choice and the opportunity of structure.

The remaining chapters of the book will explore other forms of individual-environmental transactions as these are affected by changing family structures, changing demographics of the population, and factors that put clients at risk in terms of psychological, career, or behavioral vulnerability. In each of these areas there are matters of substance and of mythology about which counselors need to be knowledgeable. Finally, in each of the chapters that follow, connections will be drawn between the likely effects on clients of the challenges discussed (e.g., advanced technology, shifting family structures, cultural diversity, risk factors) and how counseling and counselors do, can, or should respond. It is intended that analyses of these challenges will help counselors and other readers understand more fully the complexity of the effects of these phenomena upon client behavior, the comprehensiveness of the responses required, and the fundamental importance of counseling in American society in transition.

References

Bandura, A. (1982). The psychology of chance encounters and life paths. *The American Psychologist, 37*(7), 747–755.

Bellah, R.N., Madsen, R., Sullivan, W.M., Swidler, A., & Tipton, S.M. (1985). *Habits of the heart: Individualism and commitment in American life.* New York: Harper & Row.

Bronfenbrenner, V. (1979). *The ecology of human development.* Cambridge, MA: Harvard University Press.

Drucker, P.F. (1981). *Toward the next economics and other essays.* New York: Harper & Row.

Fromm, E. (1962). *Beyond the chains of illusion.* New York: Simon & Schuster.

Gibson, J.J. (1979). *The ecological approach to visual perception.* Boston: Houghton-Mifflin.

Gibson, E.J. (1982). The concept of affordances in development: The renascence of functionalism. In W.A. Collins (Ed.), *The concept of development.* The Minnesota Symposium of Child Psychology. Vol. 15. (pp. 55–81). Hillsdale, NJ: Erlbaum.

Hall, C.S., & Lindzey, G. (1957). *Theories of personality.* New York: Wiley.

Herr, E.L. (1985). International approaches to career counseling and guidance. In P. Pedersen (Ed.), *Handbook of cross-cultural counseling and therapy* (pp. 3–10). Westport, CT: Greenwood Press.

Holland, J.L. (1966). *The psychology of vocational choice.* Waltham, MA: Blaisdell.

Holland, J.L. (1973). *Making vocational choices: A theory of careers.* Englewood Cliffs, NJ: Prentice-Hall.

Holland, J.L. (1985). *Making vocational choices: A theory of vocational personalities and work environments.* (2nd ed.) Englewood Cliffs, NJ: Prentice-Hall.

Kleinman, A. (1988). *Rethinking psychiatry: From cultural category to personal experience.* New York: Free Press.

Lewin, K. (1951). *Field theory and social science: Selected theoretical papers.* New York: Harper.

Mathewson, R.A. (1955). *Guidance policy and practice.* (Rev. ed.). New York: Harper.

Murphy, G. (1947). *Personality.* New York: Harper.

Murray, H.A. (1938). *Explorations in personality.* New York: Oxford University Press.

Murray, H.A., & Kluckhohn, C. (1956). Outline of a conception of personality. In C. Kluckhohn (Ed.), *Personality, nature and society.* (2nd ed.) (Chapter 1). New York: Knopf.

Neugarten, B.L., & Neugarten, D.A. (1987). The changing meanings of age. *Psychology Today, 21*(5), 29–34.

Peabody, D. (1985). *National characteristics.* Cambridge, England: Cambridge University Press.

Psychology Today. (1987, May). 20th Anniversary Issue, *21*(5).

Reich, R.B. (1987). *Tales of a new America.* New York: Vintage Books.

Reisman, D. (1961). *The lonely crowd.* New Haven, CT: Yale University Press.

Sennett, R. (1977). *The psychology of society: A selected anthology.* New York, Vintage Books.

Stern, G.G., Stein, M.I., & Bloom, B.J. (1956). *Methods in personality assessment.* Glencoe, IL: Free Press.

Super, D.E. (1985). Career counseling across cultures. In P. Pedersen (Ed.), *Handbook of cross-cultural counseling and therapy* (pp. 11–20). Westport, CT: Greenwood Press.

Syngg, D., & Combs, A.W. (1949). *Individual behavior.* New York: Harper & Row.

Toffler, A. (1970). *Future shock.* New York: Bantam Books.

Vondracek, F.W., Lerner, R.M., & Schulenberg, S.E. (1986). *Career development: A life-span developmental approach.* Hillsdale, NJ: Erlbaum.

Watzlawick, P., Beavin, J.H., & Jackson, D.D. (1967). *Parameters of human communication: A study of interactional patterns, pathologies and paradoxes.* New York: Norton.

Yankelovich, D. (1981). The meaning of work. In J. O'Toole, J.L. Scheiber, & L.C. Woods (Eds.), *Working, changes and choices* (pp. 33–34). New York: Human Science Press. Adapted from Herr, E.L., & Cramer, S.H. (1988). (3rd ed.) Career counseling and guidance through the life span: Systematic approaches (Table 2.2, p. 48). Glenview, IL: Scott Foresman.

CHAPTER 2

ADVANCED TECHNOLOGY: ECONOMIC, EDUCATIONAL, AND PSYCHOLOGICAL EFFECTS

If one were to define a contemporary social metaphor of the United States, building upon and refining the historical narratives and morality tales described in chapter 1, it would undoubtedly include such words as dynamic, free, ordered, complex, powerful, resilient, self-conscious, scientific, and technological. Certainly in the final decade and a half of the 20th century, America would give prominence to those last two words, science and technology, as crucial to this time in the nation's history. They are words that have been associated with strength, power, and leadership in the world community. To some degree, they define the assumptions on which rest the nation's economic policy and its attempts to be internationally competitive. As such, these words, although not interchangeable, have become part of the macrosystem by which the nation's beliefs, traditions, and values are translated into narratives, stories, rhetoric, and images that affect individual behavior and organizational forms.

Just as individuals change their self-concepts over time and space, so do nations. Each decade or so, a new set of terms surfaces and becomes popularly accepted as descriptive of the current national or social reality.

For 30 years or more, various observers have characterized the United States as a postindustrial society. They have argued that massive joblessness was about to occur as a result of automation and mechanization in the work place. However, for most of this period, neither massive nor particularly prolonged unemployment occurred. Rather, the cyclical rises in unemployment reflected temporary factors rather than underlying structural changes in the economy.

Many names have been given to the structural transition represented by the term *postindustrial society*. Toffler (1980), after rejecting many attempts to name the changes the United States is now undergoing—such as space age, information age, electronic era, global village, technetronic age, super-industrial age—suggested that the magnitude of the present and foreseeable upheaval and transformation is so great that it constitutes a parallel to the two major waves of change that have shaped most of the world's history: first, the agricultural revolution and second, the industrial revolution. The result is the "Third Wave" of civilization which, among other features, is highly technological and anti-industrial (p. 10).

Whether or not the current transformations in the content, process, and organization of work are equivalent to the effects of the agricultural and industrial revolutions is debatable (Roscak, 1986), but the effects of science and technology in America are wide-ranging and profound. They also are interactive with other important changes in the American and global economies. A glimpse of the magnitude of such changes is inherent in a major study, entitled *Technology and the American Economic Transition: Choices for the Future* (Office of Technology Assessment, Congress of the United States, 1988), which begins with the following observations:

> During the next two decades, new technologies, rapid increases in foreign trade, and the tastes and values of a new generation of Americans are likely to reshape virtually every product, every service, and every job in the United States. These forces will shake the foundations of the most secure American businesses. (p. 3)

The report then outlines further some of the promises of technology in the work place:

> Technology can replace many of the most tedious, dangerous, and dehumanizing tasks while creating jobs that require more intellectual and social skills. Machines are likely to plant seeds, weave cloth, fabricate metal parts, handle routine paperwork, enter data, and perform a vast number of

other repetitive tasks more efficiently and more productively than people. By default, the majority of jobs created in the economy could be those requiring human, and not machine-like skills: designing; tailoring products and services to unique customer needs; teaching; caring; entertaining; promoting; and persuading. Ironically, one result of sophisticated technology may be a work force whose primary task is dealing with people—as customers or as colleagues. (p. 3)

Given the vast potential of advanced technology to transform the American work place, before turning to its specific implications for human behavior and counseling, the next several sections of this chapter will examine the characteristics of the growing relationships between science and technology, the definitions and content of high or advanced technology, and some of the myths and realities associated with such processes.

The Interaction of Science and Technology

Although science and technology are not the same processes, they are intricately linked in the sense that in contemporary industrialized societies there would be little technology without scientific discovery. Indeed, under current conditions of international competition and corporate economic rivalry, industry in the United States is increasingly poised to translate scientific ideas into forms of technology that can be applied and exploited commercially. As a result, the historic time lag between scientific discovery and its translation into technological forms that can transform the home, the health care system, or the work place is growing shorter. As new science creates new technology, it also creates new tools for research that keep shortening the cycle from knowledge breakthroughs to their applied technological roles in society, and these in turn initiate new questions, new problems to be solved, new configurations of science, new technologies, and a constant repeating of these interactions as each of the sciences contributes its particular insights to the social need for information and technological application.

Judson (1985) addressed some of the important trends in science as these begin to shape the future. He stated:

Perhaps the most general and one of the most interesting trends is that until recently the scientific revolution and its technological consequences have affected our external or physical environments, whereas in what is to come we can look increasingly for effects on what can be called our internal environment, the social environment. The shift will manifest itself in many ways. To begin with, the physical, geographical planet is filled in and filled up—ever more thoroughly explored 'and mapped, now increasingly catalogued for exploitation, mined and harvested, and, of course, populated. The world is becoming ever more urban, ever more exclusively human. Thus, the timing is fortunate. The shift from the external environment to the internal, social environment is paralleled by a shift in attention from the highly developed physical sciences to the sciences of social interaction—demography through the neurological basis of behavior through social psychology, all still in their infancy. (pp. 33, 36)

Judson's remarks are important for a number of reasons. First, they accent the fact that science operates on many different problems simultaneously and that science is composed of a variety of bodies of knowledge that vary in their maturity and unity of perspective. The natural sciences—physics and chemistry, for example—tend to be older in their theoretical and empirical bases than does biology. However, in contrast to the adolescence of biology, compared to the maturity of physics and chemistry, psychology is infantile as seen in historical terms. Thus, the questions posed by science tend to change as science itself evolves into its differentiated disciplines and into hybridization—e.g., geochemistry, bionics, neuropsychology—that will increase in the future as two or more disciplines are brought together to comprehend complex problems (e.g., the interaction of developmental biology with neurobiology and with perceptual and cognitive psychology to understand how language and other information processing mechanisms evolve and function).

A second important implication of Judson's remarks is that scientific breakthroughs are unpredictable in their timing, but, when they happen, their effects are not simply linear and evolutionary; they are likely to be exponential and revolutionary in their transformation of how we think about certain problems or respond to them. Thus, the search for and accomplishment of scientific breakthroughs become international matters of politics, competitiveness, and resource allocation as each nation tries to find a scientific edge that, in turn, gives it a technology different from that of another nation. That edge might be sought in agriculture, in space weapons, in computers, or in myriad other arenas that have potential for carrying with them power, control, economic growth, or other geopolitical outcomes (O'Neill, 1983).

A third implication of Judson's observations is that people live in both external and internal environments. Historically science has been most attentive to comprehending and mastering the physical environment. The internal environment, mind and emotions, tended to be left to the philosophers and the artists as arenas not susceptible to scientific or empirical inquiry. In the past century, as psychology has become independent of philosophy and spawned its own subdisciplines and empirical methodologies, the internal environments of cognition and emotion, mental illness and normal development, and the antecedents to behavior and behavior modification have come under the increasing scrutiny of scientists who probe the organic and the social, cultural, and psychological effects upon individual and group behavior.

These observations do not suggest that all counselors must become scientists in order to understand the effects of advanced technology on their clients. They do imply, however, that in a society in which the images and effects of science and technologies are so pervasive, it is important that counselors develop at least a personal "metascience"— an understanding of the language and trends in science that are related to the emergence of advanced technology, and the likely effect that such trends will have on either the external or internal environments of their clients. More will be said about this matter later in this chapter. For now, however, it is useful to acknowledge some of the scientific areas that are on the cutting edge of developing breakthroughs likely to alter individual opportunities and environments in the future.

Trends in Science and Technology

The appendix provides an analysis of 25 discoveries that were described in *Science 85* in 1985 as capable of changing our lives. These discoveries are arrayed across such areas as the following:

Biomedical sciences. The genetic mapping of the egg as it is transformed into an organism; gene therapy; drug therapy; breeding plants resistant to diseases and of higher nutritional quality in order to increase farm productivity; creating cancers in order to understand what causes them and how treatments may be developed; making replacement body parts from super-strength composite materials; making computer-driven prostheses.

Physical science. Revisions in the theory of gravity, integration of these revisions with quantum mechanics, and new speculations about the geometry of space and matter; new space telescopes that can study galaxies billions of years old, compare their formation and change, and more accurately measure distances from earth to other galaxies for purposes of space travel and other interstellar research.

Evolutionary science. Research in fossil data to examine changes in species related to habitat changes; the practical effects of transferring genes between species to improve the productivity of animals or plants for foods.

Mathematics. The use of computers to graphically display geometric or mathematical formulae, and to apply experimental mathematics to both linear and nonlinear dynamic systems—e.g., electrical fields, quantum theory, weather, fluid dynamics; the development of new concepts of geometry and dimensionality and their combination with new mathematical formulae to construct models of symmetry in the universe, physics, and number theory.

Neuroscience. Research studies linking genes, cellular and molecular biology, brain chemistry, and behavior are beginning to map the origins and mechanisms that trigger or sustain basic emotions, drives, and behaviors from the level of genes and molecules to specific nerve circuits and brain systems. As a result treatments are emerging to enhance certain types of outcomes (e.g., memory) and inhibit others (e.g., depression, aggression). In addition to modifying the application of psychotherapy in mental disorders that are basically organic or chemical, scientists are creating new drugs to treat neurological, psychiatric, as well as genetic disorders.

These major categories of scientific breakthroughs are complemented by other, more specifically technological breakthroughs. They include *parallel computers.* In order to increase dramatically the speed and capability of computers, one alternative is to harness multiple microprocessors to work simultaneously on many parts of a complex task. In so doing, the architecture and use of parallel computers is close to the point when a billion calculations per second will be possible for a computer system. There are many other important technological breakthroughs as well, for example, the wedding of *fiber optics* and *microcircuit chips.* Theoretically, the use of light wave communications through glass fibers would permit the total scope of current telephone traffic in the United States to be carried on a single fiber. *Space transportation* in the near future will require new propulsion systems (e.g., solar power, electric and magnetic thrusts, nuclear power) and larger vehicles made of extremely light, advanced structural materials so that the economics of carrying equipment, satellites, and people can be made less costly and more internationally competitive. Many of the emerging needs for light-weight, strong, heat-resistant materials go beyond the capability or the availability of natural resources. Thus, new *composite materials* are being developed from polymers, carbon, and other sources to form synthetic fibers, plastics, and other materials that are stronger and lighter than steel or ceramics. They also require less fuel to make than do steel and related materials. *Ceramic science*, by using such raw materials as sand and clay and fabricated synthetic materials, is providing new materials for manufacturing, building, medicine, electronics, transportation, and other areas. For example, ceramic materials that are strong, light, anticorrosive, and sensitive to changes in temperature, humidity, pressure, and sound intensity are being used in computers, electrical insulators, optical communications, cutting tools, engine parts, capacitors, as well as for electronic, optical, mechanical, or medical purposes.

Many additional categories of technological breakthroughs fuel and extend the application of "advanced technology." One of these is *microchip technology*. The development of lighter, smaller, faster, more powerful "superchips" capable of storing 10 million bits of information per chip, an area much smaller than a fingernail, is a subject of intense international competition. Such engineering challenges include the ability to interconnect millions of tiny circuits and transistors on a single chip and to locate hundreds of integrated circuit chips in spaces smaller than the diameter of a human hair. Another important technology in the production of drugs and vitamins, fuels, fertilizers and pesticides, plastics and adhesives, and every synthetic fiber is that of *catalysts*. Catalysts create specific and predictable chemical reactions necessary to the selective production of novel and complex chemical products: advanced drugs, plastics, fibers, composite materials, and fuels.

An overarching technology that empowers the accelerating conversion of scientific knowledge into advanced technology is *computer software*. The computer as an electronic tool is guided in its operations by a script, typically called software, which represents the program of action the computer executes. Until now, much effort has been expended in miniaturizing computers—making their internal components smaller, more powerful, and less expensive. The next decade will likely bring dramatic changes in computer software. Included will be the use of natural language (e.g., English) to make software easier for users to understand and to implement. Software also will be constructed to extend the representation of information on the screen—e.g., 3D graphics, speech generation and recognition, and music synthesis. A further outcome will be constructing software able to engage in some learning and artificial intelligence, to increase the qualitative capability of computers as a complement to the quantitative changes of the past several decades.

Undoubtedly, the scientific and technological discoveries reported here are not exhaustive of all the scientific-technological connections that are shaping the occupational structure of the present and future. Residual breakthroughs from past decades presently are shaping the architecture of advanced technology, just as the 25 discoveries identified in 1985 will shape it in the future. For example, in 1982, the National Science Foundation suggested that major emerging technologies include computer science, biological engineering, electronics, electro-optics, energy, materials, and miscellaneous processes (See Figure 2). The application of these technologies is to occur in such areas as communications, agriculture, chemicals, health care, mineral extraction, transportation, development of energy sources, construction, defense, and education as well as consumer goods and services.

The Growth of a Global Economy

Other views of important technologies also are likely to affect the types and content of work available in this nation and others. For example, O'Neill (1983), an analyst of Japanese industrial success as well as other forms of world-wide competition, indicated that six major marketing opportunities, in essence six major technologies, will affect world competitiveness over the next decade or so. He cast those technologies against three interacting criteria that are directly involved in the global economic competition, particularly between Japan and the United States. These criteria are: "They must serve individual human beings better than the older technologies they replace; they must be more efficient in their use of energy; and they must be more benign to the planetary environment" (p. 13). After interviewing industrialists in Japan, North America, and Europe about emerging technologies that both meet these criteria and are likely to effect major changes in national economies, he concluded that they include microengineering, self-replicating robots, genetic reconstruction, magnetic flight or levitation, personal aircraft, and large-scale construction in space. The United States does not lead in the conception and implementation of any of these technologies, although this nation has reasonable advantages in the areas of microengineering, genetic reconstruction, and

FIGURE 2
Emerging Technologies

Computer Science

Artificial intelligence
High-level language
Digital signal processing
Speech synthesis
Speech recognition
Speech understanding
Digitization
Packet switching
Computer-aided design
Robots
Expert systems

Biological Engineering

Recombinant DNA
−Insulin (Human)
−Gene therapy
−Interferon
Hybridoma
Tissue culture
Enzymes
Growth hormones/vaccines
Food supplements
Embryo transfer
Micropropagation
Aquaculture
Fermentation
Soil-free cultures
Irradiation

Electronics

Microprocessors
Memory devices
Logic arrays
Sensors
Production equipment
Josephson junctions
VLSI lithography
Gallium arsenide
Bubble memory
Transponders
Earth stations
Microwave

Electro-optics

Lasers
Displays
Fiber optics
Optical disc
Optical computers
Semiconductor lasers

Energy

Photovoltaics
Nuclear fusion (hybrid)
Synfuels
−Methanol
−Ethanol
Fuel cells
Solar hot water
Advanced fission
Geothermal

Materials

Polymers
Thin films
Superconductors (cryogenic)
Metal matrix alloys
Ceramics
−High-temp/structional
−Fiber reinforced
−Metallic glasses
−Solid electrolytes
Metals
Cutting/forming
Assembly
Test and inspection
Bearings
Brazing alloys
Pressure vessels

Miscellaneous

Ultrasound
Surface properties
Membrane technologies
Supercritical fluids
Controlled atmosphere
Ocean mining

From *Counseling Youth for Employability: Unleashing the Potential* (p. 3) by E.L. Herr and T.E. Long, 1983, Ann Arbor, MI: University of Michigan, ERIC/CAPS. Adapted from the National Science Foundation, 1982.

personal aircraft. With the exception of magnetic flight, where Europe and Japan are far ahead in its use in fast trains, the United States may be able to compete successfully in the production and application of such technologies. Whether or not the United States becomes a leader in the production of these technologies, there will be little choice but to participate in their adaptation.

Inherent in O'Neill's observation is the fact that the effects of advanced technology are global in character. As Rumberger and Burke (1987) stated:

> Today the countries of the world are much more interdependent and are a part of a growing global economy. New technological developments spread much more quickly throughout the world, affecting developed and developing economies alike. In fact, one basic feature of the new global economy is that developing countries, such as Taiwan and South Korea, now can compete in international markets for very technically sophisticated products like computers and automobiles. (p. 3)

One implication of these observations is that national economies are rapidly disappearing and are being integrated into a global or world economy. In order for this to occur, however, technology becomes critical at every step of international trade, production, and communication as raw materials, labor forces, and ideas are integrated into world systems of commercial interaction.

Whether or not a global economy becomes the dominant economic structure in the future, continuous interaction between national and international economies must grow. The effects of such transformations and the importance of technology therein also are evident in a recent study of the economic forces that will shape and reshape American jobs and industries from now until the year 2000 (Hudson Institute, 1987). The most important trends have been described as:

- Continued integration of the world economy;
- Further shifts of production from goods to services;
- The application of advanced technologies to most industries;
- Faster gains in productivity, particularly in services;
- Disinflation or deflation in world prices; and
- Increased competition in product, service, and labor markets. (p. 1)

Another consideration worthy of mention in the development of advanced technology is its effect on the language of work. Clearly, the technologies described in Figure 2 and throughout this section on trends in science and technology create a new vocabulary of career and personal identity. This is the language of career counseling, job training and retraining, worker recruitment, and mobility in the future. It is a language with which counselors, counseling psychologists, and other career guidance specialists must become familiar.

Many other perspectives on new technologies might be cited as well (e.g., Battelle Research Corporation, 1982). On balance, however, they tend to overlap with what has already been identified. The important point here is not to list all possible emerging technologies, because these are in a dynamic state, but to consider somewhat more precisely the meaning of the terms "high" or "advanced" technology.

Advanced Technology: Some Definitions

There are various ways to define advanced or high technology; these terms are typically used interchangeably. But, first, it is useful to consider the meaning of technology itself. Gerwin (1981) suggested that: "Technology refers to the means utilized to accomplish a task. It may be manifested in machine processes, computer programs and other explicit procedures, but also in performance programs stored in individual memories" (p. 5). In a broader sense, technology refers to all the ways people use inventions and discoveries to satisfy needs and desires. From early history until the present, human beings have been in a constant age of technology as they have invented tools, machines, materials, and techniques to make work easier or to cope with new physical or social challenges. Thus, technology includes both primitive and advanced techniques and tools applied to problems related to physical survival, industrialization, or other purposes.

In essence, there is not one technology but many technologies that stem from different settings, disciplines, applications, or categories of problems. As described earlier in this chapter, there are industrial, medical, social, computer, materials, agricultural, and many other technologies. In historical terms, not all technology is based on science. Certainly, early humans developed tools and techniques to make things happen without having the benefit of science to help them know why they happened. Increasingly, however, science and technology have become inseparable, particularly in areas now defined as advanced or high technology.

High technology typically refers to the "most sophisticated, esoteric, and often the most recently advancing technological knowledge, skills, and hardware applications" (Dyrenfurth, 1984). Minshall (1984) applied the term "high technology" both to work places and processes:

- High technology signifies high-growth occupational areas in which technological applications are rapidly changing job knowledge and skill requirements in terms of an arbitrary percentage of a worker's useful working life.
- High technology refers to (1) products, processes, and applications stemming from the latest scientific and technological developments, (2) utilization of high-level machine intelligence and information decision capability, and (3) the extension of human manual and intellectual capacities through the use of computer technology and the application of sophisticated physical principles. (pp. 29–30)

Castells (1985) provided a somewhat different view of high or advanced technology. His perspectives probe the underlying characteristics of advanced technology:

Two features are characteristic of the stream of technological innovation under way. First, the object of technological discoveries, as well as of their applications, is *information*. What microelectronics does is to process and eventually generate information. What telecommunications do is to transmit information, with a growing complexity of interactive loops and feedbacks, at increasingly greater speed and at a lower cost. What the new media do is to disseminate information in a way potentially more and more decentralized and individualized. What automation does is to introduce preinformed devices in other activities. And what genetic engineering does is to decode the information system of the living matter and try to program it. The second feature concerns the fact that the outcome is *process-oriented rather than product-oriented*. High technology is not a particular technique, but a form of production and organization that can affect all spheres of activity by transforming their operation in order to achieve greater productivity or better performance through increased knowledge of the process itself. (pp. 11–12)

Effects of Advanced Technology on Work and the Occupational Structure

The effects of the emerging technologies described previously, however exotic they seem, have profound implications for the work force. They are changing the jobs available, the characteristics of such jobs, as well as the broader economic climate. In so doing, they are changing the contexts, content, and vocabulary with which counselors and clients must process problems and the anxieties that result from work-related questions. More about the latter implication will be said. For now, it is important to consider some of the specific effects of advanced technology.

First, emerging technologies are changing our economy from one rooted in the so-called "smoke stack" or "sunset" industries to one characterized by an increasing proportion of "sunrise" industries. The first is composed of high-volume, standardized production of durable goods (e.g., automobiles, steel, rubber, furniture). These are typically large, centralized, management-driven, capital- and labor-intensive industries. The second, the so-called "sunrise industries" are those that deal much more with generating information and services and applying advanced technology to goods production. Such industries are increasingly concerned with precision and customized manufacturing. They also are characterized by generating or applying information to the services or products they handle, fabricate, or develop. Both sunset and, to a larger extent, sunrise industries are characterized by machines operating machines (e.g., computer-controlled machine tools, the use of robots); bioengineering (e.g., the development of biological organisms to achieve industrial processes—devour pollution, create new medicines, etc.); and the wedding of computers or laser optics to communications and other industrial processes. These high technology applications are, in turn, changing the processes of banking, retailing, warehousing and inventory control, transportation, agriculture, and production. Thus, they are changing the nature of work, where it is located, the amount of work available, and the types of training or education required to engage in high technology occupations.

Education and training related to advanced technology. Hull and Pedrotti (1983) identified six educational implications common to all high technology occupations:

1. They require a broad knowledge of math, computers, physics, chemistry, electricity, electronics, electromechanical devices, and fluid flow.
2. They involve heavy and frequent computer use, including knowledge of practical applications of programming.
3. They change rapidly and require lifelong learning.
4. They are systems-oriented and involve working with systems that have electronic, electromechanical, electrical, thermal, optical, fluidic, and microcomputer components.

5. They require a fundamental understanding of a system's principles, as well as practical skills in designing, developing, testing, installing, troubleshooting, maintaining, and repairing the system.
6. They require substantial employee flexibility and adaptability. (pp. 28–31)

Whether or not a worker is directly involved in a high technology occupation, the pervasive application of advanced technology throughout the occupational structure is demanding higher educational skills. Part of this phenomenon is related to the fact that automation of work is easiest in low-skilled jobs; eliminating many unskilled and semi-skilled jobs through technology increases the average education or training required in the remaining jobs or in the emerging occupations.

Such an analysis is somewhat simplistic because many jobs still require only a minimum education. In the future occupational structure, however, more and more unskilled jobs will be eliminated and an increasing premium will be placed on higher levels of reading, computation, communication, and problem-solving or reasoning skills. An increasing number of employers are extending their conception of basic skills to include self-discipline, reliability, perseverance, accepting responsibility, and respect for the rights of others (U.S. Department of Education/U.S. Department of Labor, 1988). These latter skills are increasingly being defined as "general employability skills" in the United States and as "industrial discipline" in Britain (Herr, 1984). They are important across the spectrum of work and are, in that sense, "very elastic" in their application. These general employability skills do not substitute for the basic academic skills noted above, but they clearly are mediators of how effectively such academic skills will be practiced.

According to a joint publication of the U.S. Department of Education and the U.S. Department of Labor (1988), "New technology has changed the nature of work—created new jobs and altered others—and, in many cases, has revealed basic skills problems where none were known to exist" (p. 3). New technology, then, has intensified national cries for educational reform and stimulated the need for literacy audits among workers and the need to introduce basic skills training directly into the work place where such audits show that it is needed.

For 10 years or more studies have documented the lack of basic skills of many American workers, implying that the national goals of remaining internationally competitive and being able to adapt advanced technology to the work place are in jeopardy. For example, studies (Knowles, 1977) have indicated that approximately 40% of the American adult population is coping inadequately with typical life problems (e.g., getting work, holding a job, buying products, making change, managing its economic life, and parenting). Other studies speak more directly to deficits in basic academic skills that reduce productivity among workers. One national study of employers found that 30% of those surveyed reported that secretaries have difficulty reading at the level required by the job; 50% reported that managers and supervisors are unable to write paragraphs free of grammatical errors; 50% reported that skilled and unskilled employees, including bookkeepers, are unable to use decimals and fractions in math problems; and 65% reported that basic skills deficiencies limit the job advancement of their high school graduate employees (Center for Public Resources, 1983). In another example, the New York Telephone Company, in a major recruitment effort, found that from January to July 1987, only 3,619 of 22,880 applicants passed the examinations intended to test vocabulary, number relationships, and problem-solving skills for jobs ranging from telephone operator to service representative (U.S. Department of Education/U.S. Department of Labor, 1988).

The findings reported here suggest that the effects of advanced technology ''ripple'' throughout many of the society's institutions, but, clearly, a functionally literate work force is a fundamental requirement to successfully implement advanced technology. Such findings also suggest that the pressure on both youth and adults to possess basic academic skills will necessitate that counselors diagnose problems stemming from inadequate basic academic skills and broker or encourage remedial programs.

The changing mix of jobs. Interacting with the changing educational and training requirements of high technology occupations is the changing mix or proportion of jobs in the occupational structure. As suggested above, a major trend in the evolving configuration of jobs in the economy is the likelihood that machine systems and robots will replace many of the low-skilled and semi-skilled production jobs now held by poorly educated or untrained workers. Carried to its furthest extremes, such a condition is perceived by some observers as potentially leading to a two-tiered occupational structure represented by a small elite of scientists, engineers, and managers, and a large cadre of low-skilled operatives (e.g., drivers, custodial personnel, receptionists, sales personnel) who tend the machines and perform assembly or support roles that are not feasible for machine applications. In such a scenario, middle management and skilled workers per se would not be necessary as a middle tier. Although a two-tiered occupational structure is not likely in the near future, it is clear that the applications of advanced technology have altered the mix of jobs available in modern America.

For example, today over 50% of the U.S. labor force are white collar or information workers, ranging from executives, managers, analysts, and programmers to teachers, designers, illustrators, and sales representatives, to copywriters, statistical clerks, and secretaries. Clerical workers constitute the largest single class of employees in the U.S. labor force—about 20% of all employed people. Since 1950, industrial work has fallen from around 38% of the labor force to about 18% in 1984. Just as the large decrease in agricultural employment over the last 25 years has been accompanied by a large rise in agricultural output so, too, has the decrease in industrial employment been accompanied by a continuing and accelerating rise in industrial output, signifying a long-term shift from labor-intensive to capital-intensive production. The latter reflects the growing effect of the application of technology to production (e.g., numerical-controlled machine tools, computer-aided design and manufacture, robotics). Finally, since 1960, service work has risen from about 18% of the labor force to nearly 30% and has led many to call the likely U.S. economy of the future a service-based economy (Hudson Institute, 1987).

From another perspective, by 1982, only 3% of the labor force of the United States was engaged in agriculture (and an undetermined proportion of these workers are involved in agribusiness, which does not typically occur on farms or involve direct production of agricultural commodities), less than 30% was engaged in the production of non-agricultural goods (mostly manufacturing), and 70% was engaged in service occupations (defined in the broadest sense to include all enterprises not engaged in the production of goods—mining, manufacturing, and construction—or agriculture) (Ginzberg, 1982). Since 1981, 19 out of 20 new jobs have been in the service sector. Up to two thirds of the new jobs since 1978 have been in three groups of occupations: business services, retail trade (including restaurants), and health care (World Press Review, May 1988). Another relevant statistic about the changing mix of American jobs by industry is the fact that 5 million experienced workers lost their jobs between 1981 and 1986 because of plant closings or lay-offs; half of these workers had worked in manufacturing, where 1 job in 8 was eliminated (Office of Technology Assessment, 1988, p. 39).

As projected from 1986 to the year 2000, it is expected that the service-producing industries will provide 20 million new jobs. Of these, 49.8% will be distributed among health, business, legal, educational, social, and personal services; 24.1% in retail trade; 8.1% in finance, insurance, and real estate; 8% in government; 7.6% in wholesale trade; and 2.4% in transportation, communications, and public utilities (U.S. Bureau of the Census, 1988, p. 380).

Several other trends are embedded in this discussion of the changing characteristics of the occupational structure. One is that the terms *manufacturing* and *service* are themselves losing meaning. By the year 2000, the definition of these two apparently opposite terms will have little relationship to the definitions of these terms in 1985. For example, the auto worker on an assembly line in 1980 was still performing the same tasks auto workers had performed for the past quarter century. By 1990, however, the widespread use of robots for welding, painting, shaping, and moving automobiles through an assembly line will have begun to change the role of the assembly line worker to that of a programmer or maintenance-service worker. Though employed in the manufacturing part of the automobile industry, the "production" worker will produce service, not cars. He or she will increasingly handle information, not raw materials or tools per se. As we will discuss in a moment, even in "high tech" industries that produce advanced technology or in "technology intensive" industries that apply high technology to production or services, many more workers are in support roles—secretaries, maintenance workers, security personnel, copy center operators, equipment mechanics, motor pool operatives and drivers —than directly employed in production or direct service.

Another trend reshaping the American occupational structure is that of transferring what had been American manufacturing jobs overseas. In the March 11, 1985, issue of *Business Week*, the headline story was "America's High Tech Crisis, Why Silicon Valley is Losing its Edge." (Wilson, 1985). The President of Dataquest, Inc., a market research firm specializing in high technology was quoted as stating that "American industry is becoming a distribution economy and we haven't even noticed we are in trouble." Americans design products, then move the actual production overseas where labor costs are cheaper. In a short time, others imitate our development and sell the products we designed back to us. To illustrate such points, the article goes on to indicate the distribution of costs for an IBM Personal Computer, built largely from pieces made overseas. For example, the manufacturing cost for an IBM PC, including a printer, is quoted as $860; $625 of that sum is spent in Japan, Singapore, and Korea for components assembled and distributed in the United States. In the same issue of *Business Week*, other information suggests that because of the breakup of AT & T and the federal deregulation of the communications industry in this nation, America experienced a

31% rise in imported communications equipment in 1984; similar shifts in increases in imported goods are occurring in cellular mobile telephones, computer chips, and semiconductors, among other goods. Such examples illustrate that advanced technology is a world-wide phenomenon. It has become a focus of world-wide competition and has stimulated American corporations to purchase a larger amount of goods from overseas manufacturers, altering the type of jobs available in this nation and increasing the trade import/export deficit, thus creating pressures on the economy. These observations reaffirm that America is deeply enmeshed in a global, not a national economy.

The Social Psychology of Work

In addition to changing the mix of jobs, advanced technology, particularly computers, has also changed the social psychology of work. The implementation of computers has redefined the social role of workers, changed the relationships among workers in organizations, and changed the flow and exchange of information within organizations. For some workers the installation of computers in the work place has engendered more autonomy, but for others it has created new forms of monitoring worker productivity, exerting social or organizational control, and altering employee and management relationships (Jackson, 1987). In these instances, computer monitoring of worker output may reduce worker pacing of work, decrease autonomy, increase conforming behavior rather than self-initiative, alter social relationships and communication, and stimulate worker reactions against technology or attempts to circumvent it. Depending how computers are designed and implemented in a particular work setting, they can either "deskill" the worker or enhance the worker's role, or they can change a worker's role from one of high-task involvement to one of monitoring and troubleshooting what the computer does. Such shifts in workers' roles and self-perceptions in relation to computer technology may be positive or negative, enhancing or demeaning.

One application of computers to work that received considerable early enthusiasm is telecommuting. In such a situation, also called the "electronic cottage," a worker with a computer terminal at home could perform tasks without being required to be at a central work location daily (Toffler, 1980). Supposedly, such an arrangement would reduce, if not eliminate, the travel from home to work each day, make child care and parenting at home more feasible, and provide other benefits to people involved in telecommuting. However, available research data suggest that because telecommuting essentially isolates workers and removes them from the social relationships most people consider important at work, many workers find that the positive features of telecommuting are offset by the negative effects of isolation or the inability of some workers to structure their work at home. Certainly, not all telecommuting workers view the situation as negative. Those who have high-demand, essentially irreplacable skills, who can control the pace and style of their work, and who work at home for personal growth reasons may find telecommuting a positive and exciting opportunity. For others, however, the widespread application of telecommuting is likely to foster less optimistic and positive views.

Computers also can alter the flow and the amount of information as well as how it is presented and communicated. As such the computer can redistribute power in an organization, change decision-making assumptions and processes, and alter specific individual and organizational communication patterns. "When workers use electronic mail the nature of their interactions shifts. Terminal users lack the nonverbal communication clues, have few norms of interaction, and have developed a communication which is more content centered" (Jackson, 1987, p. 258).

Much more can be said about how technology, particularly computers, modifies work environments, communications, and social relationships. In many ways, such issues of social technology are only now becoming the focus of research. Undoubtedly, however, counselors dealing with workers who are experiencing techno-stress, feelings of isolation, deskilling, or other behavioral manifestations will want to explore in depth the growing literature on computers and the social psychology of work.

A further, less visible trend associated with advanced technology worldwide is a major process of urban-regional restructuring of job availability and population location. The implementation of high or advanced technology frequently alters the environments in which jobs are located and causes some population shifts. Castells (1985), in studying such phenomena internationally suggested a model of high tech manufacturing and its likely locations. The following observations describe this model:

1. Because high tech industries are science-based and knowledge-intensive, they need close connection to major universities and research units, as well as to a large pool of technical and scientific labor.

2. Given the dependence on government markets, . . . high tech activities tend to cluster historically in regions where the military has established its testing sites.

3. High tech companies are generally characterized by a strong anti-union feeling in their managements. Not so much because of traditional economic reasons such as wages or benefits, but because of the fears of bureaucratization and slowness in an industry that requires constant flexibility and innovation. . . . Thus, areas with a strong union tradition will tend to discourage high tech location, all other things being equal.

4. The risk (and promise) of investment in this new field requires the existence of venture capital in the region that is both a function of a high level of wealth and of an entrepreneurial culture oriented toward nontraditional financial markets.

5. The process of production in high tech in general, and in microelectronics in particular, is highly discrete and can be easily separated in time and space between its research and design, fabrication, assembly and testing functions. Given the very different requirements of each function, especially for labor, it follows that there is a hierarchical division of labor across space, and the need for all activities to be located in a good position in a communication network. (p. 13)

These characteristics suggest that the location of high tech manufacturing is not a random event. Rather, the geography, the demographics, and the political environment of a location has much to do with its suitability for high tech manufacturing. Other issues in the location of high tech industries deserve mention as well. For example, depending upon the type of advanced technology involved, geographic locations must also have the appropriate "infrastructure" (e.g., water, sewer systems, transportation networks, electricity) in place to satisfy the needs of a particular industry. In many parts of the United States, because of zoning, inadequate resources, or lack of planning, the infrastructure available is unsuitable to the placement of industries that emphasize advanced technology. Again, whereas some geographic problems can be offset by the linkages across decentralized management or production units that advanced communication technologies provide, political, union, and tax structure considerations, the availability of suitable pools of workers, or other matters may preclude implementing high tech manufacturing in a particular area. As such circumstances evolve, regional differences across the nation increase rather than decrease the likelihood that people in particular regions will experience major differences in occupational opportunities, quality of life, education and training, and other disparities. These conditions stimulate migration within and across national boundaries, urban congestion and stress, potential widening of gaps between rich and poor, erosion of family and community support systems, and changes in family structures. These conditions engender a dilution of feelings of personal responsibility for one's fate, a blurring of behavioral sanctions that tend to control individual behaviors, and other conditions that create a seedbed of mental health and career development problems of major importance to the shape and substance of counseling services. More will be said about these matters shortly.

The Occupational Structure

However one defines "advanced" or "high technology," it seems clear that it will be a pervasive factor in the future transformation of the American society. Whether we term what is now happening within the economy, the international environment, and the national rhetoric a function of the Third Wave, as does Toffler, or the Next American Frontier, as does Reich (1983), it is clear that the occupational structure of the future will not be what has prevailed in the past. The environment in which work takes place and the possibilities for work will change. The context for employability will change. And the effects of those changes will vary from one group of youth and adults to another.

One of the problems with the current transitions in the occupational structure is understanding the timing of the changes in work that are likely to occur as well as predicting the occupations likely to emerge, decrease, or vanish. Current perspectives on these matters as they appear in the popular press tend to disagree with available research studies. Although the onslaught and the effects of advanced technology in the future are likely to be dramatic, counselors and other mental health specialists have an obligation to help their students or clients keep such matters in perspective. For example, Levitan and Johnson (1982) reminded us that although we have the technology to transform the work place and to incorporate mechanization of work in great magnitude, even with tax incentives the costs of such dramatic shifts will be enormous and beyond the capability for many firms. Many employers will have to find ways to compete in the marketplace other than by incorporating new or advanced technologies simply because they are available. This reality is likely to cause many firms to give new and creative attention to the use of human resources, which in turn will provide new opportunities for counselors in business and industry.

In a somewhat similar vein, Hunt and Hunt (1983) argued that the mass media are guilty of massive exaggeration about the effects of robotics on employment and potential unemployment. They state that "Futurists and others compete for media attention with wild projections of the impact of robotics—800,000 people making robots, 1.5 million technicians maintaining robots, and millions of workers displaced—with little or no consideration of the practical issues involved" (p. 165). In short, Hunt and Hunt, like Levitan and Johnson (1982) reminded us that "there are physical, financial, and human constraints on the rate of change in manufacturing process technology as it is actually applied" (p. 173). In contrast to the views of many futurists, their research suggests that until 1990 there will be a growth rate of about 30% to 40% in robotics usage, or roughly 50,000 to 100,000 units in 1990—that will eliminate over that period of time 100,000 to 200,000 jobs and create 32,000 to 64,000 new jobs. These views are reinforced by recent Bureau of Labor Statistics data that show that in the United States, high technology occupations as a group will account for only 7% of all new jobs between 1980 and 1990. Of the 20 occupations expected to add the most jobs in the economy during this period, not one is related to high technology. Indeed, the five occupations expected to produce the most new jobs are all in low-skill areas: janitors, nurses' aides, sales clerks, cashiers, and waiters (Levin & Rumberger, 1983). Most of these jobs do not have extended career paths or paths that intersect with high tech occupations.

Another important perspective is reflected in how "high technology" is defined by the Bureau of Labor Statistics and how its effects on the labor force are foreseen. According to the Bureau of Labor Statistics, "high technology" is used to refer to those industries where technology is being rapidly exploited, or the state of the art in product development is rapidly changing because of scientific or technological breakthroughs. For example, industries utilizing electronics or biochemistry often are characterized as "high tech." Actually, there are two categories of industries dealing with technology: those that are by nature of their processes and purposes truly "high technology" and those that are "technology-intensive." There are other occupations in which high tech is not a major factor in its own right. These differences are determined in part by (a) research and development expenditures as a percentage of gross product originated and (b) percentage of scientists, engineers, and technicians in the total employment. Said another way, high technology industries are those that consider their major business to be the creation of high technology; technology-intensive industries are those that significantly employ high technology products even if they do not themselves create such products.

Workers in technological occupations, when counting those employed in any industry regardless of its state of technology, accounted for 3.4% of total wage and salary workers employed in 1980. This proportion is expected to increase to 3.7% in 1990. Another way to look at this material is to indicate that technological occupations composed about 15.8% of total employment in high technology industries in 1980. This proportion is expected to increase to 17.9% in 1990. These statistics and others imply that because high technology industries and high technology occupations compose a relatively small proportion of total employment and are not expected to grow significantly faster in employment than the rest of the economy, it is not likely that high technology industries on a national basis will absorb large numbers of unemployed and dislocated workers. The point is that although new jobs and occupations are created by the growth of advanced technology, these jobs may expand at a rapid rate but numerically they will account for a relatively small proportion of new job growth. A telling illustration of the point is Carey's (1981) analysis of the 20 occupations with the largest absolute growth in employment from 1979 to 1990. As depicted in Table 1, not one of the 20 occupations offering the largest number of job opportunities during this period can be considered an example of a high technology or advanced technology occupation. Most of the occupations portrayed are in service delivery.

More recent projections of the occupations that will account for the greatest job growth from 1986 to 2000 alter Carey's earlier projections; these are shown in Table 2.

Even in these revised data to the year 2000, however, high technology occupations do not contribute prominently to employment growth in the economy. Only three occupational areas—computer programming, computer systems analysis, electrical and electronic engineering—can be considered to be high tech; the remaining 24 tend to be in service occupations, which are not easily automated, with only four exceptions, and these do not require a college education.

Such a trend toward service occupations and away from manufacturing occupations is becoming increasingly pronounced. Projections of employment trends by the U.S. Bureau of Labor Statistics (Personick, 1985) indicate that "almost 9 out of every 10 of these new jobs will be added in a service-producing industry (transportation, communications, public utilities, trade, finance, insurance, real estate, miscellaneous services, and government). The remainder are projected to be goods-producing jobs (manufacturing, construction, mining, and agriculture)" (p. 26).

TABLE 1
Twenty Occupations With Largest Absolute
Growth in Employment
1978–1990

Occupation	Growth in Employment (in Thousands)
Janitors and sextons	671.2
Nurses' aides and orderlies	594.0
Sales clerks	590.7
Cashiers	545.5
Waiters/waitresses	531.9
General clerks, office	529.8
Professional nurses	515.8
Food preparation and service workers, fast-food restaurants	491.9
Secretaries	487.3
Truck drivers	347.6
Kitchen helpers	300.6
Elementary schoolteachers	272.8
Typists	262.1
Accountants and auditors	254.2
Helpers, trades	232.5
Blue-collar worker supervisors	221.1
Bookkeepers	219.7
Licensed practical nurses	219.7
Guards and doorkeepers	209.9
Automotive mechanics	205.3

From "Occupational Employment Growth Through 1990," by M.L. Carey, 1981, *Monthly Labor Review, 104*, p. 48.

As suggested previously, the continuing dilemma for people exploring job entry and for those considering retraining is to balance the search for occupations among those that have the largest number of job openings, those that have a small number of jobs but the fastest growing opportunities, and those that are declining in opportunity. Tables 3 and 4 provide the projections of the U.S. Department of Labor for the fastest growing occupations and the fastest declining occupations for the period 1984 to 1995 (Silvestri & Lukasiewicz, 1985).

In reference to the data in Tables 3 and 4, several additional trends are noteworthy. According to the U.S. Department of Labor projections on which the data are based, the following trends are likely:

TABLE 2
Occupations Accounting for More Than
Half of Total Job Growth
From 1986 to 2000

Occupations	Numerical Growth, 1986–2000	% Growth, 1986–2000
Sales workers, retail	1,201,000	34
Waiters and waitresses	752,000	44
Registered nurses	612,000	44
Janitors and cleaners	604,000	23
General managers and top executives	582,000	24
Cashiers	575,000	27
Truckdrivers	525,000	24
General office clerks	462,000	20
Food counter and related workers	449,000	30
Nursing aides, orderlies, and attendants	433,000	35
Secretaries	424,000	13
Guards	383,000	48
Accountants and auditors	376,000	40
Computer programmers	335,000	70
Food preparation workers	324,000	34
Teachers, kindergarten and elementary	299,000	20
Receptionists and information clerks	282,000	41
Computer systems analysts	251,000	76
Cooks, restaurant	240,000	46
Licensed practical nurses	238,000	38
Gardeners and groundskeepers	238,000	31
Maintenance repairers, general utility	232,000	22
Stock clerks, sales floor	225,000	21
Clerical supervisors and managers	205,000	21
Dining room attendants and related workers	197,000	26
Electrical and electronic engineers	192,000	48
Lawyers	191,000	36

From "Projections 2000," by E. Abramson, 1987, *Occupational Outlook Quarterly, 31*, p. 32.

TABLE 3
Fastest Growing Occupations, 1984–1995
(Numbers in Thousands)

Occupation	Employment		Change in employment 1984–95		Percent of total job growth 1984–95
	1984	1995	Number	Percent	
Paralegal personnel	53	104	51	97.5	.3
Computer programmers	341	586	245	71.7	1.5
Computer systems analysts, electronic data processing (EDP)	308	520	212	68.7	1.3
Medical assistants	128	207	79	62.0	.5
Data processing equipment repairers	50	78	28	56.2	.2
Electrical and electronics engineers	390	597	206	52.8	1.3
Electrical and electronics technicians and technologists	404	607	202	50.7	1.3
Computer operators, except peripheral equipment	241	353	111	46.1	.7
Peripheral EDP equipment operators	70	102	32	45.0	.2
Travel agents	72	103	32	43.9	.2
Physical therapists	58	83	25	42.2	.2
Physician assistants	25	35	10	40.3	.1
Securities and financial services salesworkers	81	113	32	39.1	.2
Mechanical engineering technicians and technologists	55	75	20	36.6	.1
Lawyers	490	665	174	35.5	1.1
Correction officers and jailers	130	175	45	34.9	.3
Accountants and auditors	882	1,189	307	34.8	1.9
Mechanical engineers	237	317	81	34.0	.5
Registered nurses	1,377	1,829	452	32.8	2.8
Employment interviewers, private or public employment service	72	95	23	31.7	.1

From "Occupational Employment Projections: The 1984–1995 Outlook'' by G.T. Silvestri and J.M. Lukasiewicz, 1985, *Monthly Labor Review, 108*, Table 4, p. 52.

TABLE 4

Fastest Declining Occupations,
1984–1995
(Numbers in Thousands)

Occupation	Employment		Percent decline in employment
	1984	*1995*	
Stenographers	239	143	−40.3
Shoe sewing machine operators and tenders	33	22	−31.5
Railroad brake, signal, and switch operators	48	35	−26.4
Rail car repairers	27	21	−22.3
Furnace, kiln, or kettle operators and tenders	63	50	−20.9
Shoe and leather workers and repairers, precision	43	35	−18.6
Private household workers	993	811	−18.3
Station installers and repairers, telephone	111	92	−17.4
Sewing machine operators, garment	676	563	−16.7
Textile machine operators, tenders, setters, and set-up operators, winding	279	235	−15.7
Machinery maintenance mechanics, textile machines	26	22	−14.8
Statistical clerks	93	81	−12.7
Industrial truck and tractor operators	389	342	−11.9
Central office operators	77	68	−11.5
Farm workers	1,079	958	−11.2
College and university faculty	731	654	−10.6
Farm and home management advisers	27	24	−9.6
Extruding and drawing machine setters and set-up operators, metal and plastic	28	25	−9.1
Pressing machine operators and tenders, textile, garment and related	116	106	−8.8
Postal service clerks	317	290	−8.5

From "Occupational Employment Projections: The 1984–1995 Outlook" by G.T. Silvestri and J.M. Lukasiewicz, 1985, *Monthly Labor Review*, *108*, Table 5, p. 53.

- Compared with an overall 15 percent total increase for employment, the needs for executive, administrative and managerial workers are likely to increase by 22 percent.

- Professional specialties are expected to increase by 22 percent. These include computer-related occupations, engineering, and health specialties.

- Technicians and related support workers are expected to grow by 29 percent.

- Salesworkers are projected to increase by about 20 percent.

- Administrative support workers, including clerical, are expected to grow slower than average because of computerized office equipment and office automation, although as a group this largest of occupational areas will add 1.8 million jobs and reach 20.5 million workers by 1995.

- Service workers, except private household workers, are projected to continue to grow faster and to account for more job growth than any other broad occupational group, accounting for 3.3 million of the 16 million new jobs added between 1984 and 1993.

- Precision production, craft, and repair occupations are projected to grow by about 12 percent compared to the growth of total employment of about 15 percent.

- Operators, fabricators and laborers are projected to increase by only 7 percent compared to total employment growth of about 15 percent.

- Farming, forestry, and fishing workers are expected to continue to decline because of productivity growth in agriculture. (Silvestri & Lukasiewicz, 1985, pp. 42–43)

Data such as these need to be considered from several perspectives. One is that projections are not absolute realities. Political decisions, economic downturns, war, and other events can alter the trends identified here. Also, even in occupations that are declining there are still opportunities. People retire, die, or take other occupations, thereby creating vacancies for people who really want to be in a specific occupation. Thus, even if the long-term future of a particular occupation is less favorable than that of another occupation, these are relative matters that do not suggest an absolute lack of opportunity in a particular industry or occupation.

One example of the above phenomena is that as this book is being written (late 1988), some of the national rhetoric about a postindustrial society is changing. An increase in manufacturing jobs is occurring, and there is some general enthusiasm for ''reindustrializing America'' as opposed to allowing all durable goods and heavy industries to be moved to other nations. Likewise, some political observers are expressing concern that the infrastructure of America—the roads, bridges, sewer systems, and water resources—is in a state of decay and must be restored. If political decisions and resource commitments are made to reindustrialize or to correct the decay in the infrastructure, the obvious results will be major increases in many types of skilled and semi-skilled jobs in construction and in manufacturing. Although such decisions may not reverse the long-term trends toward service jobs or a service economy, they would certainly alter the supply-demand situation for certain skills and occupations for a decade or more.

What is apparent in the trends reported here is that employment opportunities will continue to grow in virtually all occupations from 1984 to 1995. So-called declining industries, those where the proportion of total employment is expected to decline in the future, will actually have more workers in 1995 than in 1984. New jobs will continually be added to the economy, with the result that the civilian work force is expected to grow from 114 million to 129 million by 1995, and to 131 million by 2000. Jobs requiring more education and more complexity, however, will grow more rapidly than occupations requiring minimal education and training. To a large degree, such phenomena reflect the effects of advanced technology, computerization, and automation on the content of work and the requirement for skills that are not easily automated. Another important statistic is that women will account for more than three fifths of the growth in the labor force from 1984 to 1995. This attests to the rapid growth of two-worker families in America as well as a growing propensity of all women, regardless of marital status, to enter the job market. This development will be further explored in the next chapter.

Recent data from the U.S. Department of Labor (Hudson Institute, 1987) describing the work force in the year 2000 show the following:

- The population and the work force will grow more slowly than at any time since the 1930s (p. xix.). This slow growth rate will tend to slow down the nation's economic expansion and will shift the economy more toward income-sensitive products and services (e.g., luxury goods and convenience services). It also may tighten labor markets and force employers to use more capital-intensive production systems.

- The average age of the population and the work force will rise, and the pool of young workers entering the labor market will

shrink (p. xix). This projection will probably motivate employers to seek ways to keep older workers employed longer
and increase efforts to automate some of the jobs now performed
by young workers.

- More women will enter the work force (p. xx). Almost two
thirds of the new entrants into the work force between now and
the year 2000 will be women, and 61% of all women of working
age are expected to have jobs by the year 2000.

- Minorities will constitute a larger share of new entrants into
the labor force (p. xx). Blacks and other minorities will make
up 29% of the new entrants into the labor force between now
and 2000, twice their current share of the work force.

- Immigrants will represent the largest share of the increase in
the population and the work force since the First World War
(p. xx).

In combination, these demographic changes will mean that new
workers entering the work force between now and the year 2000 will
be different from those who now occupy it. Minorities, women, and
immigrants will make up more than five sixths of the net additions to
the work force between now and the year 2000.

What is not apparent in these statistics is what these trends mean
for individuals and groups. What does it mean for exploration and job
seeking? Even though the economy as a whole may be experiencing
only a 5.3% unemployment rate, individuals who haven't found work
are 100% unemployed. How does being in this position affect mental
health and self-perception? What are the implications for counselors
of the effects of advanced technology on the mythologies and the
realities of the occupational structure?

Advanced Technology, Occupational Transformations, and Human Behavior

In the first part of this chapter we examined the myths and realities
of advanced technology as a social metaphor for contemporary society
and as a stimulant to occupational transformation. However, opinions
about the rapidity and the extent to which advanced or high technology
will alter the content, requirements, and opportunities for work differ.
But, as an overarching concept, it seems clear that the major problems
associated with advanced technology are not scientific or technical

problems; they are human problems and problems of "social technology."

There can be no doubt that the scientific and technological creativity is available throughout the world to build newer and more complex machine-machine systems, to miniaturize computer technology, to wed microelectronics and information processing, to alter the way work is done, to mechanize or robotize work, and to amend the interactions between people and machines. Similar changes occur in the biosciences, where we are rapidly achieving ability to do things biologically in a controlled manner: to build biological organisms to accomplish specific industrial tasks; and to modify plants and animals through genetic engineering and significantly increase our understanding of human biological and biochemical processes. As a function of the latter changes, the whole concept of people's working life span of the future may be different. Some observers believe that people will be provided the nutrition, the medicines, the artificial organs, or the joint replacements to retain their full mental and physical capacities into their 60s, 70s, and 80s. The traditional working life—leaving school or college at 18 to 25, working for 30 to 40 years, and retiring for 5 to 10 years will change. Instead people will probably take a more flexible approach to multiple careers—working at two, three, or four careers, not merely changing jobs or occupations during their working lives—thus people of the next century may return to school several times for training in a new field at ages as late as 60 or 70. At each of the transition points relating to multiple careers or the significant life events shaping such possibilities, the needs for values clarification, training and retraining, exploration, decision making, information, planning, support, and encouragement are likely to intensify.

The above observations make clear that the process of technological change and occupational transformation throws a long shadow. Be they viewed through bioscientific, chemical, or technical lenses, the effects of technological change and economic transitions on each individual in the society of the future will probably be dramatic even if these individuals are not themselves in technological occupations. Such effects also are likely to be different for every youth or adult subgroup of the population. For some people the effects of technological change and occupational shifts will be primarily psychological; for others the effects will be direct and literal.

For children and youth, the combined effects of urbanization, large work organizations, and changes in the occupational structure will impede the process of exploring opportunities and gathering information. As more and more work occurs behind fences and in large organizations controlled by safety, liability, and governmental regulations, it is increasingly difficult for youth to observe and participate intimately in direct observations of work. For a growing number of occupations, simulations, reading descriptive material, and interviews with workers rather than direct experience in the work place are the only exploratory opportunities available. When such problems are confounded by rapid shifts in education and training requirements, basic skills needed, and job content, informational sources tend to lag behind and complicate exploration.

For many adult workers, the main issue accompanying technological change in the work place is obtaining appropriate retraining. What the incentives and the opportunities for retraining are become important questions to such workers, as do concerns about what they should retrain for. Other personal questions concern the degree to which people need to be retrained. Do they need 15% new skills or 100% new skills? Are any of their existing job skills sufficiently elastic to be useful in their new occupations? What are they? How do they recognize and reinforce them? Rather than be retrained, should they seek employment in another location where they might be able to use their current skills? If they become retrained, how will this affect the career path available to them?

Some subgroups of adult workers are likely to have additional questions about their potential vulnerability. For example, women may be disproportionately affected by the effects of technology, particularly information technologies, on clerical work. In both the United States and Canada, clerical work has replaced domestic service as the primary form of female employment (Protti, Shulman, & Kirby, 1985). Aging workers are likely to be concerned about whether their employers will expend the funds to retrain them or whether they will be released. For some minority group members, the issue may be how to retain whatever economic gains they already have made. How do they avoid heightened vulnerability in a time of economic and occupational transition?

For occupationally dislocated adults, the issue may be how to cope with the physical effects of stress-related diseases as well as the psychological trauma associated with the lack of identity, purpose, or income accompanying unemployment. How will these adults cope with the feelings of victimization, grieving, and helplessness that accompany the loss of self in unemployment? How will they acquire basic skills, which recent data indicate that 20% to 30% of occupationally dislocated workers lack (Cyert & Mowery, 1987)?

For other groups, particularly the least educated and new immigrants, the issue will be whether they can cope at all—will they be permanently unemployed in the wake of skill changes and work habits they cannot acquire? Clearly, many new immigrants and poorly educated workers are likely to experience multidimensional problems: functional illiteracy in English; emotional, communication, or interpersonal problems that constrain their employability; dependency on government welfare programs or other types of income transfer that must be replaced by skills of independent living and responsibility for oneself and one's family; substance abuse; low self-esteem; child or spousal abuse; marital discord; lack of transportation; inadequate financial or nutrition management skills; or poor industrial discipline.

For the groups identified above and others, the effects of technological change in occupations will influence the security they feel about themselves and their society; the achievement motives they are likely to pursue; and feelings about their ability to master the opportunities available. The concerns about which such people seek help are functions of how they view current occupational or social expectations and opportunities for personal choice, achievement, social interaction, self-initiative, prestige, role differentiation, and other matters. All of these concerns are likely to change as the choice environment or possibility structure perceived by the individual is altered by the application of new technology. The resulting anxieties, information deficits, or indecisiveness people experience is the content with which counselors and related professionals are concerned. As suggested later in the chapter, such content may interact with other mental health issues such as depression, panic attacks, and antisocial behavior.

Recent data suggest that the emerging structure of the U.S. economy may add new kinds of risk to workers' health and safety:

> Stress resulting from working conditions has become a major health hazard, resulting in stress-related absenteeism and medical expenses that may cost between $50 and $75 billion annually. In addition, alcoholism and drug abuse may be related to job-induced stress. The National Institute on Drug Abuse has estimated that U.S. firms lose $33 billion per year due to employee drug abuse. . . . While uncertainty in the American economy has often been greater, pressures can increase in periods of rapid change. Rapid change in working environments and management practices can lead to stress. Many new office jobs result in increased responsibility without increased authority—a combination that easily leads to stress. Increased use of electronic surveillance equipment may also contribute to stress. (Office of Technology Assessment, 1988, pp. 390–391)

Such content is not static. It is constantly changing because of changes in the occupational structure, the larger society, and the "life spaces'' of clients themselves. Perhaps the major concern for counselors is how their clients perceive what is happening to them and how they feel they can cope with it. How do they label and interpret what they are experiencing? Do they label the stresses associated with change in the work environment as personal inadequacy? Do they label changes in work opportunities as purely economic phenomena, or rather the playing out of long-range and pervasive changes in the occupational structure itself? Do they see courses of potential action, or do they feel controlled and captured by the onslaught of forced automation and technological adaptation about which they can do nothing?

As suggested in chapter 1 and reinforced in this chapter, counseling is at the intersection, the junction of individual-environment interaction. It does not occur in a political, social, or economic vacuum. As such, it represents a switching mechanism between individual needs and skills and the freedom of choice, available information, and opportunities offered by a particular society or, indeed, a particular locale or work organization. Counseling also represents a mechanism to broker training and retraining opportunities for many workers, both those who are dislocated and those who are interested in enriched occupational opportunities in the future. Counselors can help workers differentiate among forms and structures of employment inside and outside of established labor markets, in government training schemes, in emerging small collectives of workers (who are willing to engage in contract work for firms for which such specialized work may not be economically feasible if their own labor force is used), in entrepreneurial behavior, and in self-employment. Counseling within or outside of business and industry can help workers who are dislocated, unhappy, maladjusted, underemployed, and unemployed with information, support, encouragement, or skill-building approaches that can facilitate hope, reduce feelings of social isolation and unworthiness, and provide stress reduction and management.

Counselor Needs in a Dynamic Occupational Environment

Within the individual-environment interactions, stimulated by the ripple effects of the science and technology described above, the emotional aspects of life intensify under the influence of rapid change, and the educational and occupational structures become different and more diversified. Work organizations change. Choice environments change. Social metaphors change. As a result, a series of needs, implications, and issues for counselors emerges.

At the most superficial levels, information about emerging technologies and their effects is important. Counselors working with people affected by technological change need to know about changing requirements of the work place for different skills and types of employability. Counselors will need to think of person-job fit in new work forms in which entrepreneurial and cooperative behavior is maximized. It will be important to know about those occupations that are most vulnerable to the replacement of human workers by mechanization and about new occupations being created, the skills they require, and how to train for them. Counselors will need to know about the elasticity of skills as people try to move from occupation to occupation, which in turn are variously affected by technological shifts.

But counselors must guard against allowing themselves or their clients to assume that the world of work will suddenly be transformed into something that has no resemblance to the present. Although new technologies will create many new occupations in the future, the availability of such occupations will be uneven in the timing of their emergence and, therefore, many present occupations will continue to have job openings into the foreseeable future even as the numbers of such opportunities may decrease. Indeed, however different in work mode or use of technologies the occupations of the future may be, current occupations will in many cases serve as the foundation for future occupations. For example, a gene splicer is still likely to be a biologist with a specialty in genetics. A fiber optics technician will probably be related to the physicist of today. Environmental engineers can be specialists in air pollution control, radiological health, solid wastes, industrial hygiene, sanitation, water pollution control, or environmental safety compliance. But they are still engineers and their conceptual integrity will likely be rooted in much of what is known today. Although many new occupations will spring from the ranks of existing occupations, it is also likely that there will be expansions in the mergers of intellectual disciplines and in the growth of hybrid occupations such as today's biochemists, geophysicists, and bionicists.

Furthermore, although emerging data suggest that adaptations to microelectronics, information technologies, and other forms of advanced technology do require qualitative differences in worker skills, this does not mean that old skills will become obsolete. For example, in Japan, surveys of employees engaged in adapting microelectronics to the work place have found that workers are required to adapt to changes in working conditions by acquiring a variety of new skills that build on conventional skills. Only 15% of the Japanese enterprises surveyed mentioned the necessity of new skills to replace present skills (Watanabe, 1984). From a psychological standpoint, it is a different matter entirely to learn additional skills than it is to start over from essentially a zero point. Japan's experience suggests that the latter is not the rule even in highly sophisticated microelectronics adaptation. The communication of such insights by counselors to workers and to potential workers will become increasingly important.

The implications for counselors that stem from the effects of advanced technology in the work force are not confined to needs for different kinds of information about emerging occupations and job content. Counselors also need to rethink how changes in advanced technology affect different groups seeking work. For example, counselors will need to be sensitive to how changes in the employment environment affect slow learners, the learning disabled, and the mentally handicapped. Will such people experience reduced choices and more vulnerable personal identities as a result of employers' or policymakers' assumptions that the only work skills needed in a high tech society are intellectual and problem-solving skills? Counselors will obviously hold important roles as advocates for such populations as interpreters of both the myths and realities of advanced technology, and of the characteristics of learning disabled or mentally disabled workers. Counselors will not only have important roles in helping individual handicapped clients to make meaningful transitions to employment, but also in helping employers to foster job redesign, realistic employment and training policies, and work environments that provide opportunity and dignity for the mentally handicapped.

Another population of growing concern to counselors are the physically disabled. The positive effects of science and technology, particularly medical science, are especially apparent in this population. Forty years ago, a spinal cord injury at the neck resulting in quadriplegia typically meant death within days or weeks because of kidney failure or infection. Now because of medical advances, a 20-year-old with quadriplegia can expect to live to age 62 (over 82% of one's expected life span without injury). But what about this person's quality of life, opportunities to work, dignity, and self-respect? As the disabled grow in proportion to the total population because of the advances of medical science, their well-being and effective participation in the work force will constitute new counseling challenges (Vachon, 1987).

Counselors increasingly will be required to consider the effects of advanced technology at the social level as well as at the individual level. Important questions are rapidly emerging about family changes that may result from using the home as a work place because of telecommuting, the opportunities to conduct one's business (e.g., sales, accounting, inventory control) from home through computer networking, and the decentralization of the work place. Other questions relate to the effects of changes in work times from 9 a.m. to 5 p.m. to virtually anytime during the 24-hour clock when people who have computers at home want to work. And what will be the effects upon the balance of work and leisure and family configurations occasioned by flex-time, more dual-career families, and shifts in role differentiation between the sexes? Some of these issues will be addressed in the following chapter. But these are only a few of the types of questions and information requirements associated with the pervasive advances of technology in the society. Other areas need to be considered as well.

As a result of the increasing mechanization of work, more discretionary time is likely to be available for most individuals, although this will vary across the occupational structure. During the past century the average weekly hours of work have decreased from 60 to 40 hours and are now approaching 37 hours per week or less in some industries. These are typically defined as hours at the work place. As such, they obscure the fact that in many of the professional and technical occupations, because of the information handling and abstract aspects of work, the boundaries between working and not working become blurred. Nevertheless, time off the job will probably grow for many segments of the work force because of the increases in productivity achieved through technological adaptation. A major point of interest to counselors is that such leisure time is not an unmixed blessing to people; its availability differs among people and their ability to use leisure time without experiencing additional stress or conflict also varies widely.

As early as the 1950s, mental health specialists were concerned that leisure time and its use were problematic for many. A.R. Martin, a chairman of the Committee on Leisure Time and Its Use of the American Psychiatric Association made the following observation:

> We must face the fact that a great majority of our people are not emotionally and psychologically ready for free time. This results in unhealthy adaptation which finds expression in a wide range of sociopathologic and psychopathologic states. Among the social symptoms of the maladaptation to free time are: low morale, civil unrest, subversiveness, and rebellion. (Martin, quoted by Theobald, 1966, pp. 55–56)

The importance of leisure counseling or education for the constructive use of leisure as a significant professional counseling activity will need to grow as advances in the adaptation of technology continue to affect the balance of work/nonwork time for larger segments of the population.

Brought on by advanced technology, the era of overchoice, which Toffler (1970) described as the result of rapid value and social shifts, is likely to continue to spawn stress-related diseases (what some other observers have labeled techno-stress), depression, apathy, and an increase in interpersonal violence. As a result, there will be a growing understanding that problems of dislocation and unemployment breed both physiological trauma and psychological disorders. (The specifics of such relationships will be explored in the next section of this chapter.) Indeed, the behavioral and psychological correlates of techno-stress and future shock may be exacerbated in the future as awareness increases that the nation is really pluralistic in life styles, languages, values, and belief systems and that such heterogeneity will expand dramatically in the future. A shifting racial and ethnic balance assaults the traditional views many citizens hold of common purpose, language, and motive systems in ways that affect the manner and contexts in which work is done. Chapter 4 will suggest that America has never been as homogeneous in languages, traditions, and beliefs as the "melting pot" metaphor suggests, and that the new reality of "pluralism" requires amendments to how work is viewed, structured, and rewarded in the future. Bilingualism among workers in the future is likely to be more generally prized. Growing interdependence among workers in different settings and with different backgrounds is likely to increase the need for greater attention to conflict resolution, effective communication, and interpersonal skills development in all types of occupations and settings. Counselors will need to understand and be prepared to work with the problems generated by such situations.

A major future issue is that careers are likely to be defined to include not only vertical but horizontal movement in recognition of the need to provide increased opportunities for people to develop new skills, solve different problems, and work with a variety of colleagues without necessarily being promoted within an organization in the traditional sense. Thus occupational mobility will probably be viewed not only as competitive but also as complementary (Tyler, 1978). Such a shift will affect the types of assessment and the kinds of measures necessary in career or employment counseling. New conceptions of work will prize employees' adaptability as well as higher levels of communication, problem-solving, and analytical skills. The generalist who can handle ideas and is flexible and teachable will probably be more prized in the future.

In the future counselors and other career guidance specialists may work in a field-based way with teams of workers to deal with work adjustment "in situ," at its source, rather than in some abstract or vicarious fashion. Some prototypes already exist. For example, in

Portage, Ohio, in one demonstration project, economically disadvantaged youth were involved in work teams assigned to community projects such as building a park or renovating a public building. Full-time counselors served on each team and worked with participants in every project. This tactic permitted counselors to use work as a form of behavior modification and to provide counseling immediately as problems arose at work (Herr, 1978). Obviously, such techniques can be applied in other work situations. Counselors are increasingly employed directly in business or industry, or as contracted specialists to assist employees who have been referred because of work-related or other problems that interfere with their work and productivity (e.g., chemical dependence, family relationships, bereavement).

The Counselor in the Work Place

Because of a network of factors—the effects of advanced technology, corporate mergers, changing demographics of the work force, trends toward later retirement, growing worker concerns about the quality of life, economic competitiveness—the view of workers held by business and industry is undergoing change. Workers are being seen increasingly in holistic terms, as people who do not leave their family and personal problems at the door when they enter the work place, nor leave work problems in the office when they go home. Thus, terms such as *employee-assistance programs, human resource development*, and *career services* are rapidly entering the vocabulary of business and industry. Workers increasingly are seen as corporate resources to be nurtured, not used up and cast away; as human capital that needs its own preventive maintenance in the forms of education, training, counseling, information about mobility within the firm, and help in preparing for such opportunities rather than being encouraged to hop from one job to another across corporations. Employers have learned that hiring and firing workers costs money, time, and productivity. Loyalty of the work force is at issue just as is the reputation and the public perception of the corporation locally. Closing plants precipitously, laying off workers without regard for their welfare, and fostering high levels of employee turnover bring social costs to the corporation as well as disruption and stress to the lives of the affected workers. In such contexts, more and more corporations are trying to mix "high tech" with "high touch," the latter being a notion of providing workers opportunities for personal growth, for further education, and for matching their talent, knowledge, experiences, and abilities to emerging opportunities in the corporation. "High touch" encourages internal mobility and provides challenge. Corporations can no longer be content with personnel management but must grow in their emphasis on personnel development. As Naisbitt and Aburdene (1985) indicated, powerful trends are at work to transform the business environment and to compel companies to "reinvent" themselves. One of these major trends is "the shift in strategic resources from financial capital in the industrial society to human capital in the information society" (p. 13).

Examining the most effective companies in the United States reveals that their techniques are not simply altruistic; they have come to realize that the employee's growth and the company's growth are compatible and mutually nourishing (Naisbitt & Aburdene, 1985, p. 54). In implementing such concepts, various companies are engaging in such people-oriented approaches as:

- Getting more of the most experienced, senior people out of their offices and working with younger talent;
- Instituting flexible hours;
- Creating an intellectually stimulating environment;
- Organizing travel/learning experiences;
- Awarding sabbaticals to creative people;
- Structuring jobs holistically to stretch, develop, and integrate new skills;
- Moving people laterally to develop well-roundedness;
- Recreating the role of manager as that of coach, teacher, and mentor;
- Redesigning management to include networking and employee/management sharing of responsibility; and
- Rewarding and nurturing creativity, independent thinking, and the entrepreneurial spirit within workers at all levels of the organization. (Naisbitt & Aburdene, 1985, pp. 54, 56)

Some companies are engaged in an intensive analysis of the fit between new technologies and the companies' organizational context. Such ideas, called "sociotechnical systems design," are concerned about how management must change and how interrelationships among workers must be altered to integrate new technologies successfully (Davis, 1986).

Such procedures may seem utopian but they are being implemented in many of the most progressive of America's corporations, and other firms are following their lead. Certainly such change is uneven. Not every employer understands or implements such perspectives, and in many situations workers continue to experience less than enlightened personnel procedures. Even in the most progressive firms, changes in management, in supervision, and in views of workers require time, reconfiguration of resources, and new information and support systems for workers and supervisors alike. It is in such environments that the roles of counselors and counseling psychologists become increasingly important.

For example, Leibowitz, Farren, and Kaye (1986) contended that a major change is taking place as the focus shifts from career planning programs for individual employees to the broader area of career development within organizations (p. xiii). Such programs are vital, in the authors' judgment, to provide "an organized, formalized, planned effort to achieve a balance between the individual's career needs and the organization's work-force requirements" (p. 4). But, such programs can also provide mechanisms to support changes in business organizations that are fluid and developing. It is for these reasons that career development as an area of expertise is likely to grow in importance as it plays a flexible and pivotal role in an organization's issues, concerns, and directions. One area of growing importance to which career development programs can offer support is "transformational management." Such a role would include helping "employees and managers move from traditional formal structures to the less structured approaches of matrix management and temporary work relations; by educating employees to cope with life crises, role transitions, and other types of change; and by designing programs to, for example, overcome obsolescence and help employees enrich their jobs" (p. 275).

Whether in contemporary or futuristic terms, counselors in business and industry can anticipate involvement in a wide range of activities that fall under the rubric of "career" but tend to push the limits of such a term beyond its traditional meaning. For example, Griffith (1980) found that the ranking of career services provided by 118 of the Fortune 500 companies conformed to that presented in Table 5.

Walker and Gutteridge (1979) reported on the career planning practices they found in a comprehensive survey of 1,117 firms to which some 225 firms replied. Their findings (presented in Table 6) indicate that although career planning practices in industry are wide-ranging, they tend to be more informal than systematic.

A variety of other surveys and opinions suggest how and why counselors and counseling psychologists should be involved in industry. Leonards (1981) spoke of the appropriateness of counseling psychology to be involved in industry because of industry's emphasis on working with healthy personalities. Leonards suggested that among the roles of counseling psychologists would be counseling for resolution of midcareer issues, for retirement planning, and for specific career development concerns. Osipow (1982) also suggested a broad

TABLE 5
Rank of Career Development Services Offered by 118
Corporations to all Employees by Frequency

Rank	Service	Frequency n(%)	Median Years Offered
1	Support for external training	98(83.1)	8
2	Alcohol/drug counseling	67(56.8)	6
3	Retirement planning	66(55.9)	5
4	Support groups for minorities/women	56(47.5)	4
5	Job separation counseling	51(43.2)	6
6	Career exploration	35(29.7)	3
7	Career ladders	25(21.2)	3.5
8	Teaching of advancement strategies	17(14.4)	2
9.5	Personal financial planning	12(10.2)	3
9.5	Family/marital counseling	12(10.2)	2

From "A Survey of Career Development in Corporations" by A.R. Griffith, 1983, *Personnel and Guidance Journal, 58.* Reprinted by permission.

range of contributions that counseling psychologists can make in an industrial setting. They include:

1. Helping employees and managers identify hazards in work;
2. Training people to identify their work styles (especially those that might be deleterious to them) and teaching them how to change them;
3. Clarifying the effects of repetitive work on people;
4. Clarifying the effects of transfers to new locations, especially if forced;
5. Helping relieve stresses and strains of the two-career family;
6. Helping relieve stresses experienced by people employed in boundary spanning roles (e.g., jobs that require employes to "split" allegiances);
7. Helping relieve stresses in people with high interpersonal demands in their jobs;
8. Preparing employees for retirement;
9. Helping supervisors deal effectively with the process of job evaluation;
10. Helping with the special problems of entrepreneurs;
11. Helping employees deal with the problems of job loss;
12. Helping with the special problems of small business people;
13. Helping with the special problems of professionals;
14. Counseling employees in health care issues;
15. Counseling to encourage self-help and self-care; and
16. Performing family counseling.

Clearly, counselors as well as psychologists have roles to play in such areas as:

- Educating first-line supervisors and managers to current perspectives on job satisfaction, work motivation, and work performance;
- Providing information to workers about career paths, career ladders, and the avenues and requirements for mobility within the organization;
- Classifying workers with respect to their technical skills and their psychological needs in an attempt to maximize person-job fit with regard to content, supervisory style, and related factors;
- Conducting workshops and seminars for workers designed to increase their understanding of their educational opportunities, their employability skills, and their understanding of the organizational characteristics with which they interact;

TABLE 6
Career Planning Practices in Industry*

Practices	Doing	Planning	Discontinued	Never Done
Informal counseling by personnel staff (n=222)	197(88.7%)	11(5.0%)	1(0.5%)	13(5.9%)
Career counseling by supervisors (n=217)	121(55.8%)	38(17.5%)	0	58(26.7%)
Workshops on interpersonal relationships (n=213)	104(48.8%)	26(12.2%)	5(2.3%)	78(36.6%)
Job performance and development planning workshops (n=210)	89(42.4%)	46(21.9%)	0	75(35.7%)
Outplacement counseling/related services (n=212)	79(37.3%)	4(1.9%)	4(1.9%)	125(59.0%)
Psychological testing and assessment (n=211)	74(35.1%)	17(8.0%)	40(19.0%)	80(37.9%)
Workshops and communications on retirement preparation (n=212)	71(33.5%)	51(24.1%)	0	90(42.5%)
Testing and feedback regarding aptitudes, interests, etc. (n=208)	68(32.7%)	20(9.6%)	28(13.5%)	92(44.2%)
Referrals to external counselors and resources (n=209)	61(29.2%)	8(3.8%)	8(3.8%)	132(63.2%)
Training of supervisors in career counseling (n=212)	53(25.0%)	67(31.6%)	2(0.9%)	90(42.5%)

Career counseling by specialized staff counselors (n = 210)	43(20.5%)	16(7.6%)	2(1.0%)	149(71.0%)
Individual self-analysis planning (n = 211)	33(15.6%)	39(18.5%)	2(0.9%)	137(64.9%)
Assessment centers for career development purposes (n = 213)	31(14.6%)	37(17.4%)	8(3.8%)	137(64.3%)
Life and career planning workshops (n = 210)	24(11.4%)	36(17.1%)	2(1.0%)	147(70.5%)

*Bases of percentages vary with responses. Nonresponses are excluded from percentage calculations. From *Career Planning Practice: An AMA Survey Report* (p. 11) by J.W. Walker and T.G. Gutteridge, 1979, New York: American Management Association. Reprinted by permission.

- Consulting with managers about job redesign and work enrichment schemes;
- Providing support groups for workers in various types of transitions (e.g., new jobs, geographical relocations, overseas transfers, shifting family structures, etc.); and
- Providing individual counseling about work behavior and career development.

It is important to reassert here that different groups experience the stresses and strains of the modern work place in different ways and respond in many forms. Emotional problems, problem drinking, mental health issues, and family dysfunction all contribute to absenteeism, industrial accidents, excessive use of sick leave, low productivity, and termination. So do feelings of powerlessness and being plateaued in one's career mobility. Counselors have contributions to make in resolving each of these sets of problems as they learn the language of industry, apply their skills to the problems of adults in transition, and create mechanisms by which workers can acknowledge and respond to an environment that demonstrates that it cares.

The descriptions of the effects of advanced technology and other shifts in the economic environment upon work and workers earlier in this chapter and in the next section accent the reality that personal adjustment and work adjustment exist in a symbiotic relationship. The work place becomes an environment in which both positive and negative, healthy and unhealthy, good and bad outcomes are stimulated; an environment in which conflicts, thwarted aspirations, and emotional baggage from one's life outside the work place is brought into the work place to filter and shape one's life as a worker. Therefore, career counseling, career assisting, and career intervention in the future will be a much more complex blend of development and remediation, of education and skill facilitation.

But, it would be inappropriate to argue that the only place where counselors and clients will be affected by advanced technology and economic shifts is the work place. Counselors in schools and universities as well will have expanded roles to play in preparing youth to anticipate and prepare for the changes in the work environment and opportunity structure that have been depicted throughout this chapter.

Counselors in Schools and Universities

Indeed, within the educational reform movements of many nations, attempts are under way to make schooling more career-relevant.

Students need help with understanding themselves as well as understanding available opportunities and necessary skills to plan and prepare for work more systematically and purposefully. As the industrialized and developing nations have entered developmental phases in which the relationships between education and work are seen as taking on new and interdependent forms, they have developed approaches to infuse academic subject matter with career development concepts. The following now are widely available: decision-making courses and experiences; required courses on the principles of technology to help students envision the effects of advanced technology in the work place and in the occupational structure; career resource centers; expanded contacts between schools and the larger community; work study, work shadowing, and work experience schemes; apprenticeship opportunities; and other career-related mechanisms in communities, schools, and work places.

In the United States and several other nations there has been a major shift over the past decade from the availability of career counseling or career guidance in schools as a random, one-on-one support process to career counseling or guidance as a program that is accountable for specific educational or career-related outcomes. National guidelines and competence statements have been developed to identify the content of these systematic career guidance programs. As a result, major advances have been made in identifying career guidance goals, identifying career guidance resources, and evaluating career guidance outcomes. In general, these comprehensive career guidance programs have been built around what might be described as career development curricula that translate theory and research in career development into curriculum materials designed for use with individuals, small groups, or classroom-size groups. These materials are delivered in career guidance workshops, group approaches, self-directed modules, or in conjunction with computer-assisted approaches. Most career guidance programs are built around specific clusters of career development tasks described in the literature to be most significant at different chronological life periods or at particular transition points. They may involve content designed to stimulate planning, exploration, information seeking, decision making, and self-knowledge. They may involve content designed to facilitate *work context skills* (e.g., skills related to the psychological aspects of the work situation—employer-employee relations, supervisor-worker relations, interpersonal skills, willingness to follow rules, adaptability, punctuality, pride in work, self-discipline, efficiency); *career management or guidance skills* (e.g., job search and interview strategies, constructive use of leisure, personal economics skills, self-knowledge, job knowledge, the use of exploratory resources); and *decision-making skills* (e.g., systematic methods to process information, predict and weigh alternatives, clarify values, examine risk-taking styles, project action consequences) (Herr, 1982).

Such programs are being modified to accommodate the needs of different types of populations. Many of these programs are addressed to young people who are experiencing major problems in the school-to-work transition. This issue is a particularly important one because of growing knowledge about the characteristics and issues inherent in this transition. For example, research findings show that as a group, young workers enter the labor force gradually rather than abruptly upon the completion of school. A period of trial-and-error experimentation typically precedes complete assimilation into the labor force. Large numbers of teenagers and young adults combine school and work before completing the transition. This process is made possible largely through the opportunity for part-time employment. However, a growing body of research indicates that beyond a predictable period of trial and experimentation, "joblessness among out-of-school teenage youth carries with it a hangover effect. . . . Those who have unfavorable early labor market experiences are less likely than others to have favorable subsequent experiences, education and other background characteristics held constant. Obviously early labor market experiences are related to subsequent measures of labor market success. They cannot be treated as though they were benign phenomena which simply 'age out' " (Adams & Mangum, 1978). Other research describes "thwarting conditions" that may pose work entry problems for youth (Haccoun & Campbell, 1972). These include two broad classes of problems: (a) those that deal with job performance problems; and (b) those that deal with job entry, career planning, and management problems. Additional research has suggested that those who adapt to work effectively must successfully adjust to five different areas: performance, organizational, interpersonal, responsibility, and affective aspects (Ashley, Cellijni, Faddis, Pearsol, Wiant, & Wright, 1980). Each of these conditions or challenges can be addressed specifically in comprehensive career guidance programs.

The studies reported here as well as others have indicated that frequent unemployment and other poor labor market experiences during the early years have a damaging effect on work continuity and adjustment later—in part because periods of unemployment represent loss of work experience, information, and skills that may put an individual at a competitive disadvantage in the eyes of an employer and also may have an injurious effect on attitudes toward work. The most serious problems in this regard are found among youths who are both out of school prematurely and out of work. In addition, the major transition problems are frequently experienced by certain groups of minority and other economically disadvantaged youth. Thus, the youth population is composed of subpopulations that vary in their ability to master the movement from school to work. Although the reasons are diverse, the need for comprehensive programs of career counseling and career guidance tailored to the needs of these diverse groups is critical and complex.

A series of national reports has emphasized the need for career guidance and for career counseling to be combined with other activities to address the complex problems that socially and economically disadvantaged youth in a rapidly changing economy face. For example, the Business Advisory Commission of the Education Commission of the States (1985), in a national report dealing with the growing problem of alienated, disadvantaged, disconnected, and other at-risk youth recommended "new structures and procedures for effecting the transition from school to work or other productive pursuits. . . . Young people today need more and better guidance than ever before" (p. 26). The report goes on to specify the need for coordinated programs including career counseling, financial assistance, summer jobs, cooperative education options, and role models if such at-risk youth are to be reconnected to schooling and to work. The Research and Policy Committee of the Committee for Economic Development (1985), in a major report dealing with business and the public schools, strongly recommended that schools provide exploratory programs to assist in career choice, job search, and general employability and employment counseling. The National Alliance of Business (1984), in a major analysis of the nation at work, particularly regarding relationships between education and the private sector, argued for more school-to-work transition programs including job placement assistance, career counseling, cooperative career information activities with business, and counseling about vocational-technical program alternatives to college degree programs (p. 8). Many of the recommendations of the reports cited above have been echoed and extended in a recent report, entitled *The Forgotten Half: Non-College Youth in America* (W.T. Grant Commission, 1988). This report argues that bridging the gap from school to work should include a mix of action programs. Among them should be monitored work experience, community and neighborhood service, redirected vocational education, incentives (guaranteed postsecondary and continuing education, guaranteed jobs, guaranteed training), career information and counseling (career information centers, parents as career educators, improved counseling and career orientation, community mentors and community-based organizations), and school volunteers.

The National Commission on Secondary Vocational Education (1984) in its report, *The Unfinished Agenda,* contended in behalf of guidance services in schools that systematic programs of interest and aptitude assessment, career planning, and occupational information designed to facilitate student curriculum choices must be available to all students. In addition, it argued that counselor functions need to include cooperative activity with teachers, the use of group guidance techniques, computer-assisted guidance, comprehensive career information systems, and related methods designed to provide career guidance to all students.

Although much more deserves to be said about the importance of comprehensive guidance services in secondary schools and in collaboration with community agencies and business and industry in an age of advanced technology, let us turn very briefly to the need for career guidance and counseling in colleges and universities. Research studies of college student populations continue to indicate that at least one half of college populations feel a need for assistance with career planning or career choice. As a result, career services in higher education have become more comprehensive in their offerings, and these tend to be tailored to the different needs of young and older students, reentry women, and other nontraditional populations. The era of offering placement services to students only at the end of the college experience has given way to a sequential *process* of career counseling that begins in the first year of college and builds in a sequential manner through the senior year. This process is designed to help students relate job opportunities to majors; to explore their career interests, values, and abilities; to obtain information; to talk to a counselor about career plans; to learn how occupations can affect their future way of life; to gain knowledge of people and places on campus that can help in career planning; to plan college courses that will give more flexibility in choosing among different occupations; and to obtain help in choosing work study, cooperative education, or part-time work that will provide applications of their majors and career exploration.

In broad terms, comprehensive career guidance programs in higher education are providing increased cooperation between academic departments and a central staff of career specialists who provide career advising, career planning, and career counseling. Typically, colleges and universities have used five major approaches in delivering career guidance: (1) courses, workshops, and seminars that offer structured group experiences in career planning, decision-making, and job access skills. Frequently, the topics include occupational information, resume preparation, interview preparation, study skills, values clarification, time management, assertiveness training, decision making, issues faced by special groups, and the career development of women. Increasingly these courses, workshops, and seminars use computer-assisted career guidance programs as adjuncts by which students can explore and clarify self-characteristics, opportunities, and majors; (2) individual counseling; (3) peer counseling; (4) group counseling; and (5) placement.

As both school counseling and career services in higher education are shaped and reshaped to reflect the changes in work places and in the requirements of work, they must fully integrate the vocabulary, the content, and the differentiation between myths and realities related to the effects of advanced technology discussed throughout this chapter.

The Counselor and the Unemployed

In the final analysis, advanced technology, changes in worker skill requirements, and shifts in the organization of work will leave in their wake the unemployed. There tend to be limits in all societies to what can be achieved to eliminate unemployment. People in such circumstances frequently experience multiple barriers to employment or re-employment as well as problems that seem intractable. As unemployment rates decrease, people with the most difficult problems become visible as formidable challenges for counselors in schools, in community agencies, and in work places.

The transitions in the occupational structure described in this chapter will cause the psychological and transitional consequences for the unemployed to be a continuing concern for counselors in many settings, whether they work directly with the unemployed, or with their children or other family members. In the least, counselors will need to be more knowledgeable about the different types of unemployment, the factors that cause it, who is likely to be affected and why, and how the victims of unemployment can be helped to extricate themselves from such circumstances. A simplistic or unidimensional view of unemployment causes counselors to contend that their profession will reduce unemployment. Although counseling is likely to increase the employability of individuals and, through various schemes of person-job matching, reduce the actual time of unemployment, in fact counseling is only incidentally able to create jobs that do not already exist. Thus counselors must not overpromise or create false assumptions among the public or policymakers about what counseling and related services can and cannot do.

Having identified such caveats, however, it is still important to recognize that although the unemployed are not homogeneous in their characteristics or reasons for unemployment, several broad principles can be articulated in working with them. First, counselors will need to help the unemployed understand and anticipate the psychological facets of unemployment, particularly the relationships between jobs, joblessness, and mental health. A growing literature is becoming available about the physiological problems and disease associated with unemployment and economic uncertainty. Also highlighted is the relationship between unemployment and low self-esteem, mental illness, family discord, and spouse and child abuse. Lichtman (1978), among others, observed an irrational willingness—perhaps even a need—for people to blame themselves for social processes for which they are not responsible. Counselors need to help people develop a transactional understanding of mental health that explores the fact that some problems come from personal, internal dysfunctions, but that many, if not most, are provoked and maintained by external factors such as unemployment, which overwhelm some people but not others. Those who are overwhelmed tend to blame themselves for circumstances they could confront and cope with, though not necessarily control.

Thinking about counseling as a form of preventive therapy or "stress inoculation" is fraught with problems. First, counselors might tend to blame the victim of social circumstances for having negative attitudes or for having chosen unemployment voluntarily or as part of a particular social group. In addition, some clients have the need to either stigmatize or glamorize unemployment as a life style. Clients must be assisted to gain perspective on unemployment but not to accept it as personally inevitable or as a condition from which they cannot escape.

Second, counselors must help people examine the range of community resources available in the event of unemployment or in order to avoid it. They need to help people see themselves as part of a system—not as social isolates. This requires being aware of services provided by church, education, or social welfare groups as well as those offered by governmental units or the private sector. It is in this context that counselors can help the unemployed to see themselves as social beings operating within a system of social institutions designed to provide experience, skill development, livelihood, and well-being. As the unemployed understand these perspectives, their ability to be active rather than reactive and socially conscious rather than individually isolated is likely to be enhanced.

Third, counselors need to recognize that those who experience unemployment are likely to need more than support. They are people who will probably have multiple problems to deal with: transportation, racial discrimination, lack of basic skills, poor industrial discipline, family discord, and drug or alcohol problems. Thus, people need to be helped to understand the interactive effects of such problems with the condition of unemployment. Counselors can provide basic skill training in many of these areas and information about others. But counselors also can serve as advocates for job needs to employers, community groups, and governmental bodies. In this role, counselors can aspire to be catalysts to stimulate the development of programs designed to create jobs, stimulate self-employment, and otherwise reduce unemployment.

As these three principles suggest, counselors have many roles to play with the unemployed. Among them are those suggested by Pryor and Ward (1985):

- Reduce the psychological effects of unemployment;
- Help in job search and improve the chances of obtaining employment;
- Assist people to survive unemployment; and
- Explore alternative forms of employment.

Pryor and Ward also recommended that in discharging such roles, the following techniques be used: relaxation training, systematic desensitization, assertiveness training, modeling, using video role play to increase self-presentation skills at job interviews and other situations, psychological assessment, job search skills, and coping with living on unemployment benefits (pp. 4–14). Borgen and Amundson (1984) emphasized additional techniques: effective listening, job search support groups, retraining, reassessment of self and values, early notification of job loss, and early and coordinated intervention for those about to be unemployed.

The concern for the unemployed is becoming more urgent as research studies demonstrate the linkages between work, mental health, and physiological well-being. Some of the findings that are particularly important for counselor consideration include the following:

- Unemployment tends to be associated with a rising incidence of mental illness, suicides, imprisonments, child abuse, spouse abuse, chemical dependency, and violence (Pryor & Ward, 1985). Other studies have shown that unemployment, fewer hours worked, and business failures is each strongly linked with an increased death rate among those affected; in essence, job loss can lead to early death (Brenner, 1973). Further data indicate that the experience of unemployment spills over to family members and that spouses report more depression, anxiety, and interpersonal problems as the period of unemployment continues (Shelton, 1985).

- Extensive research in Canada (Borgen & Amundson, 1984) and in the United States (Schlossberg & Leibowitz, 1980) clearly links the experience of unemployment to the experience of grieving and bereavement as originally defined by Kübler-Ross in 1969 and to the role of victim as described by Janoff-Bluman and Frieze in 1983. Thus, in the first instance, occupationally dislocated and unemployed people are likely to go through the stages of denial, anger, bargaining, depression, and acceptance as do those who have lost a loved one. In the case of involuntary unemployment, one loses a part of one's self-concept and the esteem, livelihood, and status that accompany being employed; the grief process addresses such a reality. In the second instance, the unemployed frequently experience psychological reactions similar to those of people who find themselves in the role of victim as a result of rape, incest, disease, or crime. The emotional reactions include shock, confusion, helplessness, anxiety, fear, and depression. Prolonged unemployment frequently is characterized by periods of apathy alternating with anger, sadness, sporadic optimism, few habits of regular structured activities, few meaningful personal contacts, and ominous feelings of victimization, lack of personal power, and low self-worth. None of these characteristics coincide with an ability to readily resume a constructive role in the work force without counseling or psychological assistance. Such people need at least some type of job-search support group to reduce their isolation, receive encouragement, develop more effective job search methods, reassess their interests and abilities, and consider alternate career paths. School counselors may have a major role in helping students understand what their parents are experiencing. As discussed in chapter 1, such situations require counselors and their clients to consider the interactive effects of the macrosystem, the mesosystem, and the microsystem in creating the stresses and strains that both unemployed workers and their family members experience.
- Assumptions that early unemployment is a transient matter that simply "ages out" is not correct. Unless young people attain some early success in the labor market, they are likely to be doomed to a life of jagged unemployment because of problems of lack of credibility with employers, lack of information relevant to effective job access and adjustment, and a lack of identity as a worker. All of these deficits put them at risk compared to their age cohorts unless they benefit from fairly

dramatic and systematic intervention both in terms of economic programs and counseling programs. Schools, employers, and community agencies will need to assume greater responsibility in the future for systematic attention to developing among all youth the necessary knowledge, attitudes, and behaviors that make for an effective school-to-work transition. Meeting such a goal will probably require significant expansion of comprehensive career guidance programs.

- Less obvious, perhaps, than the individual effects of psychological adjustment and stress-related disease that accompany unemployment are the social costs involved. These are the costs of lost worker productivity as well as the costs of providing needed social services to deal with the psychological problems stemming from long-term unemployment. Increases in mortality rates, suicides, imprisonments, mental illness, and child or spouse abuse cost money. Estimates suggest that each percentage point of unemployment costs the government billions of dollars in lost revenue and in the costs of providing needed social services to alleviate psychological problems. In 1982, for example, lost productivity from unemployment was estimated to cost the nation $19 billion, unemployment benefits $9 billion, and other financial assistance $6 billion, for a total of $34 billion for the year (Trippett, 1982). Hesson (1978) estimated that the amount of loss to the gross national product by the year 2000 would be $7 trillion if unemployment in this country remained above 6.5% until the end of the century.

The Counselor and the Underemployed

What is frequently missed in discussions of the unemployed are those who work but are underemployed. International labor statistics define underemployment as a condition where a person's employment is inadequate in relation to specified norms or alternative employment (International Labor Office, 1976). These statistics also identified two types of underemployment: visible and invisible.

- *Visible underemployment* reflects a condition where an inadequate amount of work exists. That is, the individual works fewer hours than is normal or desired, and would accept additional hours.
- *Invisible underemployment* relates to conditions associated with low income, low productivity, and underuse of personal skills.

O'Toole (1977) referred to underemployment as working at less than one's full productive capacity. He suggested that in many jobs a worker's unused potential represents a waste of personal capacity and commitment; the result is that the worker experiences alienation and estrangement from his or her interests, needs, and capacities. The personal and social distress associated with underutilization of talent and skills creates frustration and morale problems that can be a form of "social dynamite" in their negative effects upon work settings or the larger society. At the least, people who feel that they deserve a better job than they hold suffer from status conflict (O'Toole). Under conditions potentially on the horizon as advanced technology is used to replace middle management, clerical, semi-skilled, and unskilled labor, highly qualified workers often "bump" slightly less qualified workers from their jobs and push them further down the status hierarchy. As higher levels of skills and capabilities are unused and highly qualified people are underemployed, they are likely to be dissatisfied with their job. In such instances, they have great potential for occupational and social pathology (Herr & Long, 1983).

The implementation of advanced technology in the economic structure has created a new form of underemployment that is only now becoming visible. As the mix of occupations available changes from manufacturing to service industries, and as changes in the organization of work require the displacement of middle-managers and others, the quality of life and the earning power of those affected change. For example, the service industries tend to pay roughly two-thirds of the annual salary paid in manufacturing industries. Therefore, if a steelworker suffers displacement and finds a job in a service occupation (such as electronics repair), the former steelworker, although still employed, is likely to experience a significantly lower wage and quality of life. A laid-off steelworker who finds a job in the electronics components industry is likely to take a pay cut from $13.50 an hour to $7.50 an hour (in 1983 dollars). Coupled with the loss of seniority rights and the probability of reduced benefits packages, the result is a substantial drop in the standard of living. Similar if not greater disparities are found between former automotive industry or mining workers and the emerging occupations available to them (Steinberg, 1983). Research by Flaim and Sehgal (1985) on 5.1 million displaced workers during the years 1979 to 1983 added further concern about such transitions. Most of these displaced workers had lost jobs in heavy industries. This research showed that after 3 years, only 30% of the displaced workers had been employed in equivalent jobs; nearly 30% had had to take a pay cut of 20% or more, and for nearly half it was

20%; 40% had found no job, and only 25% of these were still looking for work; dominant in the latter group were women and Blacks. A related statistic is that since 1980, the United States has lost more than a million production jobs paying an average of $13 per hour. Simultaneously, the number of lower-paying jobs has increased. Since 1980, 5.5 million new jobs in the service and retail areas were created, paying an average wage of around $7 per hour (National Commission on Jobs and Small Businesses, 1978, p. 7). Another study by the American Society for Development and Training of Unemployed Middle-Managers found that roughly a third of those over 35 find jobs paying less than those they previously held. It takes most of these individuals 5 years to regain their previous salary levels (Rochell & Spellman, 1987, p. 7).

Rochell and Spellman (1987) contended that as advanced technology increasingly pervades the work places of the nation, "For those who want to work and have the skills, technological displacement is not likely to mean unemployment so much as lesser employment—a shift to what work is available—generally at lower pay" (p. 82). They go on, "the American working population faces a difficult and contradictory situation. Work will be available, but not necessarily the work people are prepared for and, it appears, not at the wages they are conditioned to expect" (p. 90).

The concern about a lowering of the quality of life and reduced earnings for many Americans is at the heart of the concern for a two-tiered work force mentioned earlier in this chapter, and a growing distance between the haves and the have-nots of society. The concern is exacerbated by a perception that many occupations are being "deskilled." As the computer is taking over middle-management and clerical tasks for which workers were formerly well paid, former job descriptions are typically downgraded and compensated at a lower level. Indeed, existing studies suggest that instead of increasing skill requirements, new technologies often replace the skills workers require to perform their jobs (Rumberger, 1987, p. 91). Another phenomenon that contributes to this downshifting of the quality of life is the growing use of free-lancers and part-time workers employed in small businesses or at home to do specific types of subcontracting for larger businesses. Frequently, these part-time workers get no benefits and must work several part-time jobs to meet their financial obligations. These workers lose much of the control to define their jobs and to participate in decisions about job design or other matters. Although not all free-lance and part-time work is at a low level, much of it is parallel to the routine, menial, and tedious work of the severely fragmented assembly line of past history. In any case, part-time work or work at home may increase job autonomy but also increase psychological displacement from the work place, co-workers, and the other elements of work that lead to self-esteem and affiliation.

Underemployment and the resulting deskilling, lack of control, downgrading of status, significant reductions in the quality of life, major changes in job content and one's knowledge of it, part-time rather than full-time work, and diminished status and self-esteem will not affect all workers nor all industries. But the indicators are clear that as certain skills in the work place are assigned to advanced technological devices, individuals who previously practiced those skills will be affected and potentially underemployed.

Counselors, then, will have a major role in working with the underemployed similarly as with the unemployed. Counselors will need to provide support, psychological assessment, and assistance to people in reevaluating their self-concepts and needs. Counselors will be asked to help develop avenues other than working to seek self-identity, perform leisure counseling, and help people explore retraining and alternative career paths.

Conclusions

Chapter 2 has attempted to illustrate the comprehensive transitions and, indeed, transformations in work that are occurring and that will accelerate in the United States during the remainder of the 20th century and beyond. The wedding of science and technology has influenced the social institutions, work places, and opportunity structures in the United States by the resulting effects of advanced technology, international competition in a global economy, changing skill requirements, and demographic shifts in the work force.

The effects of advanced technology are not isolated or confined to the content of work. They affect where work is done, when, by whom, and for what purposes as well as the levels of stress and anxiety that accompany rapid and wide-ranging change. Thus, in the last analysis, the implementation of advanced technology in society is not a technical matter; it is rather a matter of human perceptions, skills, and flexibility; a matter of social technologies designed to accommodate the psychological, physical, and educational demands to different groups of youths and adults attempting to explore, choose, prepare, retrain, or adjust to work in a condition of dynamic flux.

The implications for counselors in an age of advanced technology are many. The challenges represented by clients seeking information and support, insight and action planning, and assistance with exploration and adjustment will encourage counselors to become more comprehensive in techniques used, more programmatic in the use of psychoeducational models, and more cognizant of the connections between career counseling and behavioral health. In such contexts, counselors will become brokers of information, maximizers of opportunity, developers of skills, and collaborators and mentors for larger proportions of the population than they have traditionally served.

References

Abramson, E. (1987). Projections 2000. *Occupational Outlook Quarterly, 31*(3), 17–27.

Adams, A.V., & Mangum, G. (1978). *The lingering crisis of youth unemployment.* Kalamazoo, MI: Upjohn Institute for Employment Research.

Ashley, W.L., Cellijni, J., Faddis, C., Pearsol, J., Wiant, A., & Wright, B. (1980). *Adaptation to work: An exploration of processes and outcomes.* Columbus, OH: National Center for Research in Vocational Education, The Ohio State University.

Battelle Research Corporation. (1982). *Special Report IV: Identification of high-technology industries.* Columbus, OH: Battelle-Columbus Division.

Borgen, W., & Amundson, N. (1984). *The experience of unemployment: Implication for counselling the unemployed.* Scarborough, Ontario: Nelson Canada.

Brenner, M.H. (1973). *Mental illness and the economy.* Cambridge, MA: Harvard University Press.

Business Advisory Commission. Education Commission of the States. (1985). *Reconnecting youth.* Denver, CO: Author.

Carey, M.L. (1981). Occupational employment growth through 1990. *Monthly Labor Review, 104*(8), 42–55.

Castells, M. (1985). High technology, economic restructuring and the urban-region process in the United States. In M. Castells (Ed.), *High technology, space, and society* (Chapter 1). Beverly Hills, CA: Sage.

Center for Public Resources. (1983). *Basic skills in the U.S. work force.* Corporate Roles in Public Education Project. Washington, DC: Author.

Cyert, R., & Mowery, D. (1987). *Technology and employment.* Washington, DC: National Academy Press.

Davis, D.D. (1986). *Managing technological innovation.* San Francisco: Jossey-Bass.

Dyrenfurth, M.I. (1984). *Literacy for a technological world.* Columbus, OH: National Center for Research in Vocational Education, The Ohio State University.

Flaim, P.O., & Sehgal, E. (1985). Displaced workers of 1979–1983: How well have they fared? *Monthly Labor Review, 108*, 3–16.

Gerwin, D. (1981). Relationships between structure and technology. In P. Nystrom & W.H. Starbuck (Eds.), *Handbook of organizational design* (Chapter 1). New York: Oxford University Press.

Ginzberg, E. (1982). The mechanization of work. *Scientific American, 247*(3), 66–75.

Griffith, A.R. (1980). A survey of career development in corporations. *Personnel and Guidance Journal, 58*(8), 537–543.

Haccoun, R.R., & Campbell, R.E. (1972). *Work entry problems of youth: A literature review.* Columbus, OH: Center for Vocational Technical Education, The Ohio State University.

Herr, E.L. (1978). *Work focused guidance for youth in transition: Some implications for vocation education research and development.* Occasional Paper No. 43. Columbus, OH: The National Center for Research in Vocational Education.

Herr, E.L. (1982). Career development and vocational education. In H.F. Silberman (Ed.)., *Education and work* (Chapter 6). Chicago: University of Chicago Press.

Herr, E.L. (1984). Links among training, employability and employment. In N. Gysbers (Ed.), *Designing careers: Counseling to enhance education, work and leisure* (Chapter 3). San Francisco: Jossey-Bass.

Herr, E.L., & Long, T.E. (1983). *Counseling youth for employability: Unleashing the potential.* Ann Arbor, MI: University of Michigan, ERIC/CAPS.

Hesson, J.E. (1978). The hidden psychological costs of unemployment. *Intellect, 106,* 389–390.

Hudson Institute. (1987). *Workforce 2000. Work and workers for the 21st century.* Indianapolis, IN: Author.

Hull, D.M., & Pedrotti, L.S. (1983). Meeting the high-tech challenge. VOCED, *58*(3), 28–31.

Hunt, H.A., & Hunt, T.L. (1983). *Human resource implications of robotics.* Kalamazoo, MI: W.E. Upjohn Institute for Employment Research.

International Labor Office. (1976). *International recommendations on labour statistics.* Geneva, Switzerland: Author.

Jackson, L.A., Jr. (1987). Computers and the social psychology of work. *Computers in Human Behavior, 3*(3/4), 251–262.

Janoff-Bluman, R., & Frieze, I. (1983). A theoretical perspective for understanding reaction to victimization. *Journal of Social Issues, 39,* 1–17.

Judson, H.F. (1985). Paradoxes of prediction. The shape of science to come. *Science 85.* Sixth Anniversary Issue, *6*(9), 32–36.

Knowles, M. (1977). The adult learner becomes less neglected. *Training, 14*(9), 16–18.

Kübler-Ross, E. (1969). *On death and dying.* New York: Macmillan.

Leibowitz, Z.B., Farren, C., & Kaye, B.L. (1986). *Designing career development systems.* San Francisco: Jossey-Bass.

Leonards, J.T. (1981). Corporate psychology: An answer to occupational mental health. *Personnel and Guidance Journal, 30*(1), 47–51.

Levin, H.M., & Rumberger, R.W. (1983). *The educational implications of high technology.* Palo Alto, CA: Institute for Research on Educational Finance and Governance, Stanford University/U.S. Department of Labor.

Levitan, S.A., & Johnson, C.M. (1982). *Second thoughts on work.* Kalamazoo, MI: W.E. Upjohn Institute for Employment Research.

Lichtman, R. (1978). Jobs and mental health in a social context. *Center Magazine, 11*(6), 7–17.

Martin, A.R., quoted by R. Theobald. (1966). Cybernetics and the problems of social organizations. In C.R. Deckert (Ed.), *The social impact of cybernetics*. New York: Simon & Schuster.

Minshall, C. (1984). *High technology occupational trends*. Columbus, OH: National Center for Research in Vocational Education, The Ohio State University.

Naisbitt, J., & Aburdene, P. (1985). *Re-inventing the corporation*. New York: Warner Books.

National Alliance of Business. (1984). *A nation at work: Education and the private sector*. Washington, DC: Author.

National Commission on Jobs and Small Businesses. (1987). *Making America work again: Jobs, small business and the international challenge*. Washington, DC: Author.

National Commission on Secondary Vocational Education. (1984). *The unfinished agenda*. Columbus, OH: National Center for Research on Vocational Education, The Ohio State University.

National Science Foundation. (1982). *Emerging issues in science and technology, 1981*. Washington, DC: Author.

The new jobless. (1988, May). *World Press Review, 35*(5), p. 46.

Office of Technology Assessment. U.S. Congress. (1988). *Technology and the American economic transition: Choices for the future*. Washington, DC: U.S. Government Printing Office.

O'Neill, G.K. (1983). *The technology edge: Opportunities for America in world competition*. New York: Simon & Schuster.

Osipow, S.H. (1982). Counseling psychology: Applications in the world of work. *The Counseling Psychologist, 10*(3), 19–25.

O'Toole, J. (1977). *The reserve army of the underemployed*. Washington, DC: U.S. Office of Career Education.

Personick, V. (1985). A second look at industry output and employment trends through 1995. *Monthly Labor Review, 108*(11), 26–41.

Protti, R., Shulman, N., & Kirby, S. (1985). *Microelectronics and human resources*. Symposium on Microelectronics and Labor. Tokyo, Japan: National Institute of Occupational Research.

Pryor, R.J., & Ward, R.T. (1985). Unemployment: What counselors can do about it. *Journal of Employment Counseling, 22*(1), 3–17.

Reich, R.B. (1983). *The next American frontier*. New York: Times Books.

Research and Policy Committee. Committee for Economic Development. (1985). *Investing in our children, business and public schools*. New York: Author.

Rochell, C.C., & Spellman, C. (1987). *Dreams betrayed: Working in the technological age*. Lexington, MA: Heath.

Roscak, T. (1986). *The cult of information: The folklore of computers and the true art of thinking*. New York: Pantheon Books.

Rumberger, R.W. (1987). The potential impact of technology on the skill requirements of future jobs. In G. Burke & R.W. Rumberger (Eds.), *The future impact of technology on work and education* (Chapter 5). New York: Falmer Press.

Rumberger, R.W., & Burke, G. (1987). *The future impact of technology on work and education.* New York: Falmer Press.

Schlossberg, N., & Leibowitz, Z. (1980). Organizational support systems as buffers to job loss. *Journal of Vocational Behavior, 17,* 204–217.

Shelton, B.K. (1985). The social and psychological impact of unemployment. *Journal of Employment Counseling, 22*(1), 18–22.

Silvestri, G.T., & Lukasiewicz, J.M. (1985). Occupational employment projections: The 1984–1995 outlook. *Monthly Labor Review, 108*(11), 42–57.

Steinberg, B. (1983, November 28). The mass market is splitting apart. *Fortune,* pp. 9–10.

Toffler, A. (1970). *Future shock.* New York: Bantam Books.

Toffler, A. (1980). *The third wave.* New York: Morrow.

Trippett, F. (1982, January 18). The anguish of the jobless. *Time,* p. 90.

Tyler, L.E. (1978). *Individuality.* San Francisco: Jossey-Bass.

U.S. Bureau of the Census. (1988). *Statistical abstract of the United States.* Washington, DC: Author.

U.S. Department of Education/U.S. Department of Labor. (1988). *The bottom line: Basic skills in the workplace.* Washington, DC: U.S. Department of Labor.

Vachon, R.A. (1987). Inventory-2 future for individuals with work disabilities: The challenge of writing national disability policies. In D.E. Woods & D. Vandergoot (Eds.), *The changing nature of work, society and disability* (Chapter 4). New York: World Rehabilitation Fund.

Walker, J.W., & Gutteridge, T.G. (1979). *Career planning practice: An AMA survey report.* New York: American Management Association.

Watanabe, A.M. (1984, March 20). *Influences of microelectronics on education and training programs and career guidance in Japan.* Paper presented at the annual convention of the American Association for Counseling and Development, Houston, TX.

Wilson, J.W. (March 11, 1985). America's high-tech crisis: Why Silicon Valley is losing its edge. *Business Week, 2883,* 56–67.

W.T. Grant Commission. (1988). *The forgotten half: Non-college youth in America. An interim report on the school-to-work transition.* Washington, DC: Author.

CHAPTER 3

THE CHANGING AMERICAN FAMILY

Just as science and technology have fostered systems by which a society rewards and shapes its educational and occupational opportunity structures, societies evolve metaphors and related ideologies that encompass sex roles and family structures. The latter through narrative, image, and social policy tend to identify and provide incentives to sex-role differentiation, family responsibilities, child care, and the education and work environments that accommodate such policies.

It is now likely, however, that changes in family structures and their implications for counseling are occurring more rapidly and profoundly than national ideology can capture. Thus, in addition to the comprehensive influence of advanced technology on social institutions and individuals described in the previous chapter, a second major challenge for counselors in virtually all settings is the complex nature of the forms of relationships now subsumed under the term *family*. The nostalgic and traditional view of the typical American family unit in which mother, father, and two children coexist in a well-ordered, stable, and loving relationship, the father being the unquestioned bread-winner and the mother the nurturant care-giver, is rapidly fading. Indeed, the nuclear family unit, rather than being the most common family pattern, is rapidly becoming the exception. As a result, both the stresses and strains within families and the changing forms of family life have become increasingly exposed to scrutiny in the mass media and in the professional literature of counseling.

Because of this scrutiny, the fragility of families as well as their fundamental importance to the social fabric are being rediscovered.

Some families encourage health and wholeness; others cause stress and pain. The effects of either environment shape both childhood and adulthood, and growing national awareness of these effects is stimulating concerns about the needs for strengthened families as enclaves of love, support, discipline, and spirituality. Questions about the role of parents in sex education, career development, and the teaching of social values of honesty and responsibility are becoming regular features in the popular press as well as in learned treatises.

The reasons for the rapid and comprehensive changes in the family structures of the United States are diverse (Sundal-Hansen, 1985). A major one is certainly economic. Because of worker dislocation, inflation, diminishing levels of financial support for higher education, a devalued dollar, and related trends, it has become necessary for most families to have two incomes in order to maintain their quality of life. Thus, two-earner and dual-career families have become the rule rather than the exception. The sex revolution is another factor. As women's access to nontraditional educational and occupational opportunities has increased, women have been entering the professions and technical occupations in unprecedented numbers. Many have chosen to delay marriage or parenting until they have established themselves in careers. For others, the sex revolution has meant a blurring of traditional sex roles, resulting in equal partnerships in marriage and in work in which both husband and wife have full-time jobs to which they are committed for reasons of career mobility and advancement, and in support of which they share household responsibilities and child raising. In some instances, although still rare, the wife may be the major economic provider and the husband the "househusband," primary care-giver, and homemaker. Throughout the remainder of this chapter, a number of new family structures are described that are products of divorce, separation, and widowhood; same-sex orientations; or temporary arrangements.

The increased attention to these shifting family structures and their roles in society has parallelled shifts in how families are viewed in psychology and counseling. The disciplinary lenses through which the behavioral objectives of counseling interventions are viewed also are shifting. We see a movement away from a psychology that attributes all power and all deficits to internal states and to individual decision making and action. In its place there is an affirmation or reaffirmation that people live in collectivities, in environments that reinforce, shape, and model some behaviors and not others. These views acknowledge that one cannot understand human behavior only through a psychology of individual action. The perspectives of sociology, economics, political science, and anthropology are needed to understand fully the triggering mechanisms—individual-environment transactions—that are the seedbeds for values, interests, and self-concepts, and which provide the alternatives the individual has for playing out roles. These perspectives validate the importance of seeing families as *systems* of relationships, roles, and power for our subsequent concern about stresses and structures. Thus, the family is seen frequently as composing both the context and content as well as the instrument for counseling. The family structure defines the actors who need to be involved in counseling as well as the context in which roles and relationships are played out. The stresses and strains the family unit, whatever its structure, experiences are frequently the presenting content for counseling.

As perspectives on the family as a *system* of roles and relationships have evolved in Western psychology, an additional shift in counseling theory and practice has become apparent. There has been a gradual drawing back in psychological literature from the definition of personal maturity as the ability to be independent from the family, to be one's own person, a person whose decisions are self-centered and egocentric. We have gradually come to learn, as Eastern psychology has long known, that to be free one must be responsible to others; to be mature is not necessarily to be without gratitude to others or consideration for their needs; to acknowledge the importance of family members to each other is not a sign of weakness, but of strength.

For these reasons and others, the characteristics of the American family as an economic and a social unit, as a molder of values, and as a seedbed for identity are inexorably moving from the back burner to a position of central attention as models of counseling for the future are being defined and studied. Against such introductory comments, this chapter will explore four major topics:

- The demographics of family change;
- Perspectives on current and emerging family structures;
- An overview of family stresses; and
- Some implications for counseling.

The Demographics of Family Change

As in so many articles and speeches, it has become almost commonplace in the popular press to list in some terse fashion proportions and percentages of change in the American population whether by age, sex, race, income level, number employed, or other social indicators. In one way or another, these demographic variables are relevant to understanding the complexity of the stresses and structures that describe the family in America. Some examples of major demographic characteristics pertinent to changing American families follow.

First, according to the U.S. Census Bureau definition of the family as "two or more persons living together and related by blood, marriage, or adoption," 1980 Census figures indicate that there are approximately 58 million families in the country (Lou Harris and Associates, Inc., 1981, p.8). Over the next two decades, the definition of family may be, and probably will be, changed to "two or more people joined together by bonds of sharing and intimacy" (Family Service America, 1984, p. 7). Obviously, such a change in the definition will enlarge and shift the focus of the concept of family. Regardless of whether or not such a definition takes form, many other demographic variables help us to recognize the pluralism of factors now associated with families. For example:

- The number of married couples who decide to have children has declined; completed family size decreased from 2.4 children in 1970 to 1.7 in 1984 among Whites and from 3.1 to 2.2 children among Blacks (National Center for Health Statistics, 1986a).

- The number of two-income career marriages has increased.

- The number of married couples who postpone having children to extend their careers has risen.

- Greater numbers of unmarried couples are living together, although they represent only a fraction (less than 3%) of all couples living together.

- The proportion of never-married women has risen rapidly, especially among young adults, reflecting delayed marriage. The median age at first marriage among women in the United States rose from 20.6 in 1970 to 22.8 in 1984 (National Center for Health Statistics, 1987.)

- Nearly 4 in 10 marriages end in divorce.

- By 1978, the proportion of children under the age of 18 with two working parents had risen to 50%; one working woman out of nine was the sole support of her family. In 1985, nearly half of all women with children under age 18 were in the labor force, compared with less than 40% in 1970 (Hayghe, 1986).

- Attitudes about women working—and about the job of homemaking—have undergone profound changes. The proportion of women in the work force, particularly wives and mothers, has increased dramatically. Now nearly one half of all married women work outside the home and most have children under 18. Only 3 out of 10 women are full-time homemakers.

- Working mothers bear particular burdens and pressures. Two out of three family members say they do have enough time for themselves, and one in two working women agrees; it is working mothers who most emphatically say they do not have time for themselves—by 63% to 36% of working mothers polled (Louis Harris and Associates, 1981).

- Perceived changes in the quality of parenting are a greater source of worry than the issue of working parents alone. According to a Louis Harris Survey in 1981, almost twice as many family members feel that the effect of both parents working outside the home has been negative (52%) as compared to those who feel it has been positive (28%) for families. However, most feminists and many working women who stress the positive effects feel that the fulfillment for women working outside the home, added financial security, improved family communications, and independence for children outweigh the negative effects on the family.

- In 35% of American households with children at home, parents now supplement their own child care with other child-care arrangements. Nearly half of these households have other family members helping to care for their children, and 23% use paid help in the home. Fewer than one in five households use a day care center. Indeed, only about 10% of working mothers have day care facilities available to them.

- The number of U.S. households rose by 58% between 1960 and 1983, with nontraditional households accounting for most of the increase (Glick, 1984, p.205).

- Whereas the number of households containing married couples with children rose by only 4% from 1960 to 1983, one-parent households increased by 173%, and households composed of unmarried couples by 331%. In 1983, households maintained by married couples constituted 6 in 10 U.S. households (Glick, 1984, p.205).

- Lone parents living with their children represent nearly 1 in 10 households. Almost all of these parents are women—of whom two thirds are separated or divorced, one quarter have never been married, and fewer than 1 in 20 are widows (Glick, 1984). Families headed by women now account for 8.5 million, or about 15%, of the families in this country (Harris and Associates, 1981, p. 204).

- Since 1960, the number of children living with two parents has declined by nearly one fifth, and the number living with one parent—generally the mother—has more than doubled. Most of the children in single-parent households are in transition between residing with two natural parents and residing with one natural parent and one stepparent, because the large majority of divorced and never-married mothers eventually marry (Glick, 1984, p. 204). Around 75% of divorced people remarry, half within 3 years (Family Service America, 1984). By 1990, single-parent and remarriage families will constitute 45% of all families (Visher & Visher, 1982).

- Today, the nuclear family consisting of a husband wage earner, a wife homemaker, and two or more dependent children, which was once held up as typical and normal, accounts for less than 10% of all households (Family Service America, 1984).

- Divorce rates for first marriages are now between 40% and 50%. The incidence of divorce increased from about 14 per 1,000 married women in 1970 to nearly 22 per 1,000 in 1984 (National Center for Health Statistics, 1986b).

- Changes in marital status from 1965 to 1980: divorced, 2.9%–6.2%; widowed 9.0%–8.0%; single, 14.9%–20.1%; married, 73.2%–65.7% (U.S. Bureau of the Census, 1981).

- The rise in divorce rates between 1960 and 1980 may explain up to 17% of the rise in labor force participation of women during that period (Johnson & Skinner, 1986).

- By the year 2000, more people are expected to be living in a second marriage than in a first marriage (Duberman, 1975).

- By 1990, 30% of *all* children will be in single-parent families, and half of *all* children will have spent some time in a single-parent family before reaching age 18. At present, almost half of all Black children and a fifth of Hispanic children are being raised in single-parent families (Family Service America, 1984, p. 101).

- Recent U.S. census data suggest that the very norms of childhood are being redefined. In 1955, 60% of American households consisted of an employed father, a mother who remained at home, and two or more school-age children. Thirty years later, in 1985, such a family made up only 7% of U.S. households. With the major increase in two-earner families, dual-career or otherwise, estimates now place the number of children who come home from school to an empty house at 4 million. It has been projected that by 1990 there may be 6 million such children due to the influx of more mothers into the labor force (Turkington, 1983). These are the so-called "latchkey children" about whom there is increasing concern that lack of adult supervision will lead to sexual precocity, vandalism, chemical dependency, and other social problems.

- As suggested above, one of the most dramatic changes in family structures is the growing norm of children living with one parent; 59% of the children born in 1983 will live with only one parent at some time before reaching age 18. Many one-parent families consist of teenage mothers who are barely removed from childhood themselves. Of the 3.3 million births annually, approximately 700,000 are to adolescents. Such single-parent family structures, usually female-headed, are the new poverty pockets of the nation. One child in five under age 19 and one child in four under age 6 is poor. Black and Hispanic children living in female-headed households are at the greatest risk of growing up in poverty. Because of the higher rates of poverty and the large number of female-headed households among minority groups, it is likely that the rate of childhood poverty will continue to grow.

- Teenagers bear nearly 20% of all babies born in the United States, more than half of which are to unwed mothers, accounting for 44% of all births to unmarried women (Children's Defense Fund, 1982).

- Estimates are that 1.3 million children under age 5 are living with an adolescent parent, and that public aid to teenage parents and their children will consume over $16.65 billion annually ("Studies Target Teen Pregnancy," 1986, p.1).

- Whether related directly to changes in family structures and stresses or not, teenage homicide since 1950 is up by more than 200% for Whites and by 16% for non-Whites; teenage suicide is up by more than 15% since 1950; arrests for teenage crime for those 18 to 24 years old are up from 18% since in 1960 to 34% in 1980; and teenage unemployment since 1961 is up by 35% for non-Whites and 60% for Whites (Education Commission of the States, 1985). Certainly related to the changes in family structures and family stresses is another set of statistics: those that reflect current levels of violence in the family with either child abuse or spouse abuse at issue. For example, the

National Center on Child Abuse and Neglect estimates that approximately one million children are maltreated by their parents every year; of these 100,000 to 200,000 are physically abused, 60,000 to 100,000 are sexually abused, and the remainder are neglected. Each year more than 2,000 children die in circumstances that suggest or are clearly indicative of child abuse or neglect (Barnett, Pittman, Ragan, & Salus, 1980). Another national study reported that 1.8 million children were receiving public services as of March, 1977, and that abuse and neglect were the primary reasons that nearly 250,000 of these children needed professional assistance (Shyne & Schroeder, 1978).

• The data about spouse abuse are somewhat suspect in terms of how much and what type of such violence actually is reported. However, available estimates suggest that one third of all married couples engage in spouse assault (Straus, Gelles, & Steinmetz, 1980), which would involve some 15 to 20 million married couples. Other statistics indicate that more than one fourth of all American couples experience at least one violent incident sometime during their relationship, one sixth experience such an event every year, and 1 couple in 10 engages in extreme physical abuse (Barnet et al.).

What has been described above is the substance of a major transformation in the attitudes about and the characteristics of family patterns in the United States. These changes are dramatic and wide-ranging in their implications for family roles, sex roles, and child development in contemporary society. As subsequent sections of this chapter illustrate, statistics tend to mask the tensions, stresses, and problems inherent in the magnitude of shifts in both the macroenvironment and the microenvironment in which family interaction patterns, parenting roles, expectations for family success, and child-rearing are conceived and played out.

Changes in Family Structure

Inherent in the demographic shifts in American families are the outlines of both the changes in family structures and the stresses to which they must adapt. A brief analysis of the current characteristics of family structures will provide a useful context for subsequent analyses of changes in these structures.

In considering family structures, it is somewhat difficult to get beyond the notion that there are acceptable alternatives to the traditional, intact nuclear family, what Goode (1970) called "the classical family of Western nostalgia." It further follows that it is perhaps equally difficult to realize that the family, whatever its form, is a cultural creation, the specific characteristics of which vary across societies and across time as the needs for family units change under the pressures of societal shifts in values and opportunity. Such a view is reflected in the contrasts between the institutional family, dominant in past generations, and the companionate family that is evolving today.

The institutional family

> . . . brings a woman and a man together primarily on the basis of their interdependence and their abilities to perform certain complementary functions. If love, companionship, sexual satisfaction, mutual respect, and happiness are found in marriage, then it is a bonus rather than as a marital right. . . . The institutional family is oriented toward survival, the accomplishment of tasks having to do with production/reproduction, socialization of the young, sexuality, and other functions. (Glazer-Malbin, 1978, p.11)

The insitutional family was predominant in the agrarian society several generations ago when the family lived together and family members worked together to produce goods and perform services. Children were born and raised to promote family survival without much reliance on people outside the household even though neighbors, kin, and the church did have an influence. In the institutional family, *formal* social relationships predominate, and social interaction is constrained by role expectations. The father is the head of the household and principal breadwinner, and the mother and certainly the children are in different and typically less powerful roles.

The change from the institutional to the companionate family has evolved as technological changes and the organization of urban-industrial society have decreased or changed the functions family members used to perform for each other. As production of goods and services increasingly moved out of the home to the work place and as birth control was more widely practiced, many of the reasons for traditional family units changed in focus.

In the companionate family structure, personal social relationships rather than formal social relationships and obligations prevail. Although many of the institutional functions previously performed in the home are now performed outside the home, mass society tends to bring with it impersonalization and other assaults upon interpersonal needs that the family can counteract in its increasing emphasis upon companionate rather than institutional concerns. In such a context, sexual equality and the women's movement's emphasis on new life styles and role modifications can be played out; the desires for personal growth, closeness, and intimacy can find support; and the needs for privacy, property, commitment, safety, and security in an interpersonal enclave can be addressed.

It is obvious that the institutional family and the companionate family each has tensions and frustrations. In the former, perhaps, the stultifying limits of authoritarianism and rigid role expectations were the major source of family problems; in the latter, the vagueness and ambiguity of interpersonal relationships and personal expectations create stress. Neither of these family forms is necessarily good or bad, nor as absolute or discrete as suggested here. Rather, they both represent the cultural expression of how family structures vary as broader social changes shape and reshape their character and utility.

Although it is not appropriate to make direct comparisons between the institutional and companionate description of families and what general systems theory and its various proponents have described as relatively open or closed systems, it is useful to note similarities between these concepts. The terms ''open and closed'' refer to the boundaries of a family system and the effects on the quality and degree of interaction within the family and between it and the larger environment. The more open the system, the greater the degree of independence and autonomy individual family members experience and the greater their ability is to function in a self-directed manner. The more closed the system, the greater is the difficulty in differentiation, individualism, and separation the individual members experience. The manner in which the family invokes its rules influences the members' perceptions of what is expected, what is appropriate, and what is possible. It also reflects the degree to which a family can deal with critical corrections, changes, and stresses (Herr & Best, 1984).

Clearly the trend in family structures over the past decade or two has been toward increasing pluralism in the forms they take. As compared to the conventional, intact nuclear family, the family forms that have shown the greatest increase are those directly related to increases in divorce (single-parent and stepfamilies), dual-work and dual-career families, single-person households, and couples living together in cohabitation without the legal sanctions of marriage (Macklin, 1980). Combined with some of the evolving nontraditional family forms, there is a growing trend toward individual freedom of choice with regard to participation or, indeed, nonparticipation in family structures of diverse organization and purpose. Such involvement or noninvolvement and the type of family structure involved entail different forms of stress and different needs for counseling and therapy.

Nontraditional Family Structures

As might be assumed from the demographic shifts that affect families and their members, the word *nontraditional* is used frequently in the professional literature to describe current and evolving family forms. In many discussions of the topic, nontraditional is defined "as all living patterns other than legal, lifelong, sexually exclusive marriage between one man and one woman, with children, where the male is the primary provider and ultimate authority" (Macklin, 1980, p. 175). Macklin's review of family forms in the United States clearly shows that the majority of the households cannot be characterized as traditional nuclear families. Rather, such family forms as single-parent or dual-career families, persons living alone, and households consisting of nonrelated individuals have grown steadily in number and in proportion to the whole. Undoubtedly, each of these family forms has its own set of stresses. We will hold that discussion until we deal a bit more fully with family structures themselves.

Macklin identified some nine categories of family forms or life styles other than the traditional form defined above. In some cases categories have several variations. Her findings are useful in describing such family structures. Related research pertinent to Macklin's categories also is included.

Nonmarital Cohabitation

Although it is still a numerically small proportion of all couple households, roughly 3% or 2.7 million people in 1979 and approximately 2.3 million in 1989, the number of unmarried people living together as a household has more than doubled since 1979. It seems that nonmarital cohabitation is not replacing marriage, but is instead delaying marriage because most people, approximately 90% in such arrangements, intend to marry at some time, although not necessarily to their current partner. Indeed, most cohabiting relationships either terminate or end in marriage after a relatively short period of time, 6 months to a year or so. Thus, the absolute number of people who have cohabited at some point in their lives is larger than of those who cohabit at a particular point in time. Indeed, several researchers have found as many as five types of nonmarital cohabitation, varying from temporary and casual conveniences to permanent alternatives to marriage

(Petty, 1975). Available research about reported overall satisfaction, communication, sexual satisfaction, decision making, or division of labor has shown few differences between cohabiting and married couples except in the area of commitment.

Voluntary Childlessness

Current estimates show that approximately 10% of all women who ever marry are childless, with about 5% (or 50% of childless married women) choosing not to have children voluntarily. The present tendency to delay marriage and childbearing, and the related tendency of women who have not had a child by age 30 to forego childbearing permanently, suggests that family forms in which childlessness is voluntary and permanent are likely to increase to about 10% of women who ever marry (Veeners, 1979). Veeners found two major groups of voluntarily childless couples: those who are motivated by the disadvantages of parenthood and the responsibilities of raising children, and those who do not dislike children, but rather choose not to have them because of other interests or life styles in which children would be impediments.

The Binuclear Family: Joint Custody and Coparenting

A particularly interesting trend is that of the binuclear family. In this structure, divorce is not seen as a dissolution of the family, but rather a process that reorganizes and redefines the family. From such a process of redefinition, new models of divorcing families have emerged in which adults continue to practice their parental roles even though the spousal unit has been terminated. The notion of the "binuclear family" (Ahrons, 1979) views the child as part of a family system composed of two nuclear households (with varying degrees of cooperation between the two and time spent in each), with or without the parents sharing legal custody (Macklin, 1980, p. 179). Ahrons's classic longitudinal study of divorced parents who have been awarded joint child custody has shown that the kind of relationship developed by divorced parents who continue to share childrearing functions is an important factor in determining the effect of the divorce on the child.

The Stepfamily

Families in which one or both of the married adults have children from a previous marriage living permanently with them, traditionally

called stepfamilies, increasingly are being referred to as ''reconstituted'' or ''blended'' families. Such family structures now compose
about 10% to 15% of all households in the United States.

The most common stepfamily is composed of a mother, her children, and a stepfather. Research on such configurations tends to show
that stepfathers, compared with fathers in intact families, rate themselves more negatively as fathers and, unlike their wives and stepchildren, rate their stepchildren's happiness as being lower than do
natural parents, even though other national research has found few
differences between children raised in stepfather families and in intact
familes (Wilson, Zurcher, McAdam, & Curtis, 1975). Indeed, some
research (Duberman, 1975) has found that stepmothers are less likely
than stepfathers to establish good relationships with stepchildren and
have close relationships with young stepchildren. Here, as in most
family forms, there is need for much more empirical research rather
than relying on primarily personal and clinical experiences. In particular, there is a need for analyses of the structural and functional differences among the different types of stepfamilies (e.g., families
reconstituted because of widowhood rather than divorce, stepfamilies
with young children as compared with those with adolescents).

Open Marriage/Open Family

The terms ''open marriage'' and ''open family'' have become
frequent symbols of alternative family structures in the last decade.
''Open marriage'' is descriptive of relationships with realistic expectations, respect for personal privacy, role flexibility, open and honest
communication, open companionship, equality of power and responsibility, pursuit of identity, and mutual trust (O'Neill & O'Neill, 1972).
There is little research on the prevalence of open marriage as a family
form. Available research does suggest, however, that the number of
such marriages is probably small because of the ego development,
personal security, and commitment to personal growth such a life style
demands. One study (Wachowiak & Bragg, 1980) reported that open
marriage is associated with fewer children, less frequent church attendance, and younger age.

''Open marriage'' as a life style tends to be seen as similar to
''open family.'' The latter tends to emphasize flexible role prescrip-
tions across age and sex, clear communication with extensive negotiations and decision by consensus, open expression of emotion, and
mutual respect (Macklin, 1980, p. 180). Again, however, there are

few data suggesting the degree to which "open family" has become a major life style in the United States.

Extramarital Sex

"Open marriage" and "open family" as family life styles do not equate to the freedom to engage in extramarital sex, although this may be part of the equation in a particular family unit. Nevertheless, there are family structures in which extramarital sex, comarital (where two or more married couples share the same domicile and share sexual favors across couples) or sexually open marriages tend to affect the form family communication and roles take. Data do suggest that for middle-class, educated samples the rate of reported extramarital sex has increased, particularly for women; in general, women who work or volunteer outside the home report higher rates of extramarital sex. Data do not suggest, however, that extramarital sex is necessarily indicative of a poor marital relationship; rather, its significance tends to vary with the stage of marriage and is different for men and women.

Within the practice of extramarital sex, there are different degrees of openness among spouses. Some family structures include "swinging" and "sexually-open marriage."

Swinging has been defined as legally married spouses sharing coitus and other forms of erotic behavior with other legally married couples in a social context defined by all participants as a form of recreational convivial play (Gilmartin, 1977, p. 161). Macklin (1980, p. 182) indicated that the best estimate is that approximately 2% of the present U.S. population has engaged in swinging or wife swapping with about three quarters dropping out each year. Where mutual agreement between spouses exists on the appropriateness of the life style, marriages do not seem to be helped or harmed by swinging but, for those who have dropped out and become ex-swingers, problems such as jealousy, guilt, competing emotional attachments, and fear of discovery by children and neighbors seem to be major issues.

Sexually open marriage is characterized by a mutual decision of the married couple to permit one or both partners to have openly acknowledged independent sexual relationships with partners who maintain their own residences (Macklin, 1980, p. 182). Available research indicates that participants use such life styles as ways to allow both the freedom for personal growth and the security of committed relationships. Problems participants experience tend to revolve around the need for continuous accommodation and negotiation, jealousy and feelings of possessiveness, loneliness, conflicts over use of free time, and the difficulty of integrating such a life style into a broader social network.

Same-Sex Intimate Relationships

Just as research shows it to be true for other family structures, there is no one homosexual life style. Indeed, according to the research of Bell and Weinberg (1978) at the Institute for Sex Research, the great majority of male or female homosexuals are in stable couple relationships that bear many similarities to those of heterosexual couples. Although there is increasing interest in the homosexual relationship as a variant family form, with primary focus on the couple or spousal unit, data about the prevalence of such units, the extent of commitment or openness of life style, psychological reactions, and other behavioral aspects await more systematic inquiry.

Multi-Adult Households

Terms such as *multilateral marriage, commune* and *intentional community, affiliated family*, and *expanded family* are variations on family forms in which more than two adults are involved in child-rearing and, perhaps, sexual relationships with more than one adult in the family unit. For example, the Constantines (1973, p. 49) described multilateral marriage as consisting of "three or more partners each of whom considers himself/herself to be married (or committed . . .) to more than one of the other partners." Such units typically consist of four adult partners and their children from preexisting conventional marriages. Generally, the bonds between spouses that existed prior to the multilateral marriage continue as the primary bonds and survive the dissolution of the multilateral units.

There seem not to be reliable data on the number of multilateral family units in the United States. However, as one turns to communes or intentional communities as a family form, estimates as of 1975 were that 45,000 such communities with 755,000 residents existed at that time (Conover, 1975, cited in Macklin, 1980). Zablocki's study (1977) of 60 urban communes indicated that many of these were formed to provide social support for the individual or single parent. Most communes that survive tend to have a high degree of social organization. Thus, individual family units tend to experience a shift in the locus of social control from themselves to the communal organization and a loss of control over their life space or territory as well as control over their partners. Although parents receive help with parenting, they tend to lose the ability to make and enforce rules that differ from the community norms. Children seem to do extremely well in such communities as they gain expanded adult relationships, rule makers, and rule enforcers. There is little evidence of major emotional damage among children in such arrangements.

Stresses in the Family

As reflected in the multiplicity of family structures that now exists in the United States, there are many potential points of stress within and among such structures. Such stresses can be viewed in both macro- and micro-terms as the sources of stress are identified and analyzed.

If one takes the big picture, the macro view of family stresses, there is much to say. Since World War II the United States has experienced wave after wave of significant value shifts. Among them have been those dealing with equality and equity, accountability, quality of life versus material quantity, religion, entitlement, sex roles, sexual preference, sexual freedom, women's awareness, and minority pride. Values in transition obviously have affected social perceptions of family units and perceptions of individuals' place within families.

Shifting values have affected families' commitments to endure and have caused confusion within families about responsibilities, rights, and the appropriate set of values. Some social indicators suggest that value shifts and other changes in society are creating much higher expectations for the family than those held by previous generations. Expectations about sharing, intimacy, and emotional support may be set at too high a level of expectation to be sustained by many people forming families (Family Service America, 1984, p. 10).

The Macroenvironment

In many of the stresses identified above, there is an implicit, if not explicit, concern about how the macroenvironment affects families. Streib and Beck (1980) pointed out the importance of the effects of bureaucracy, pension provisions, service programs, and changes in medical care provisions as elements that bring about family stresses, particularly among older families. Obviously, the macroenvironment, the family-bureaucracy linkage, also can be analyzed in terms of many other areas of potential stress: the home-school relationship, social service-pregnant adolescent linkage, employer-alcoholic family member relationship, or the legal system-divorcing parent linkage. In each of these relationships, the macroenvironment provides a context of stressors that tend to affect different families in different ways.

The macroenvironment, for families as well as for individuals, is the source of images, reinforcements and, certainly, policies at the federal, state, or local levels that affect how families are viewed, the limits of appropriate behavior or structure, or how child abuse or spouse abuse is identified and treated. Such policies and the services they provide are, in turn, responses to the various macrolevel social trends that constitute broad categories of stressors on families.

Family Service America in 1983 surveyed its 270 affiliated family service agencies in the United States and Canada to obtain a contemporary inventory of family concerns or stresses. They received responses from 189 agencies serving more than 700,000 families. The concerns that emerged include the headings that follow in paraphrased form (Family Service America, 1984, pp. 72–77). Where relevant, related research is added to the findings of Family Service America.

Unemployment, along with its corollaries, was found to be the problem most frequently addressed by the agencies. As recent psychological research reported in the previous chapter has come to show (Brenner, 1973; Liem & Rayman, 1980; Borgen & Amundson, 1984), unemployment is not only an economic phenomenon, but rather one that is related to physiological stress and stress-related diseases, a rise in suicide and mental illness, spousal and child abuse, chemical dependency, depression, and many other manifestations. Because of its profound effects, unemployment ripples throughout a family, touching every member in one way or another.

Single parent problems are also of major concern to family service agencies. Inherent in such circumstances are feelings of personal vulnerability, frequent poverty, issues of child care, time management, guilt, and personal stress.

Although the largest number of single parents are women, there are also single custodial fathers. Custodial fathers seem to have fewer resources than their female counterparts in the areas of family, peer, and community assistance (Tedder, Scherman, & Sheridan, 1984). Whereas female single parents have major emotional and economic problems to cope with in relation to child-rearing, single fathers also experience difficult times adjusting to their new roles because of the lack of community and personal support, lack of information, loneliness, and poor coping skills in an unfamiliar situation. Some research has indicated that meeting the emotional needs of their children is the area of most concern to single fathers, but other research suggests that taking care of the physical needs of the children is the major difficulty. Tedder et al. in their review of the literature indicated that other concerns also tend to be of particular importance to single fathers: "finding good supervision, care, and protection for their children, obtaining information about rearing daughters in a motherless home, knowing what constitutes normal development in children, having the skills to perform homemaking tasks or finding a housekeeper" (p. 181). In addressing such concerns, the research of Tedder et al. found that support groups with an information-giving/discussion format were useful in helping single fathers deal with the divorce adjustment process. Thus they were able to achieve greater feelings of self-worth, greater separation from their former partners, and lowered feelings of anger toward their former partners.

Rise in family violence accompanies periods of economic instability and is a frequent presenting problem for families. Very young marriages, single-parent stress, unemployment, teenage pregnancies, and alcohol abuse each may trigger child or spouse abuse as family systems bear the brunt of frustration and anger its members experience.

Incest less hidden becomes an increasing issue for those adults who were abused as children, those who now abuse their children, and children now being abused. As public understanding about this problem grows, its frequency as a family stressor becomes increasingly evident. As more becomes known about the prevalence and the long-term effects of incest, it is evident that it is a widespread family problem. Estimates are that 9% to 16% of all women experience incest before age 18 (Finkelhor, 1979). Incest, as a form of child abuse, includes any type of sexual activity that occurs between a child and a parent, stepparent, sibling, extended family member, or surrogate parent figure (Sgroi, 1982). Depending upon the age of the child and the circumstances surrounding the incestuous relationship, many children exposed to such abuse experience the range of emotional reactions described in the literature on victimization—shock, confusion, helplessness, anxiety, fear, and depression (Janoff-Bluman & Frieze, 1983).

The aftermath of such traumatic experiences in one's life lead Briere (1984) to describe a post-sexual-abuse syndrome, common among incest victims, which includes such chronic symptoms as dissociation, anxiety, isolation, sleep disturbances, anger, sexual dysfunction, substance addiction, and self-destructiveness. In many instances, incest victims—like victims of rape, spousal abuse, and similar situations—

experience significant guilt, shame, low self-esteem, problems with intimacy, inability to trust, and other psychological phenomena. Although the actual events that cause such feelings may be repressed or the links between the experience of incest and the psychological effects may be blurred, the intensity of the psychological and behavioral reactions that persist across time are likely to lead many incest victims to counseling to resolve the conflicts in their emotional life.

Research (e.g., Josephson & Fong-Beyette, 1987) has suggested that counselors can be helpful to incest victims, and that factors related to initial disclosure and exploration of incest are client readiness, direct questioning by the counselor, positive counselor reactions to initial disclosure, and such counselor characteristics as being accepting, validating, encouraging, and knowledgeable about addressing incest experiences in counseling. "It is recommended that counselors acknowledge and validate the significance of the incest. Incest should be identified as an important trauma that is related to clients' current life difficulties. Perceiving incest clients as survivors who developed complicated coping skills that were actually adaptive to their early environment can help these clients see themselves as survivors rather than as sick or helpless victims" (Josephson & Fong-Beyette, p. 478).

A shrinking government role in assisting families or in providing services for families results in greater difficulty in locating and using such services, in personal frustrations, and in the exacerbation of the need for legal, medical, and mental health services for many families.

Divorce and remarriage may be increasingly open options to many, if not most, people, but they do not occur without psychological and physical costs. Problems of custody of and access to children after divorce; children becoming pawns in hostile divorce proceedings; issues of childrearing and discipline in stepfamilies; and questions of identity, divided loyalties, conflicting role expectations, and adjustment to new partners all intensify the difficulties of resolving problems of marriage and remarriage. Linkages also have been made between suicide rates and divorce, suggesting that divorce alters kinship systems, thus decreasing the regulation of the individual ego and increasing the propensity toward suicide (Wasserman, 1984). Other research has demonstrated that all members of a family affected by divorce, including children, have lower mental health and general health ratings than people in intact families. Children who have experienced family disruption and divorce also rate lower in social and academic performance. Finally, this research finds a complex interdependence among divorce, parental stress, children's stress, children's performance, and family physical health (Guidubaldi & Cleminshaw, 1985).

Growing evidence shows that divorce and separation entail developmental problems for children of all ages (Robson, 1987). As a result of divorce and separation, it is estimated that 40% to 50% of children born in the 1980s will spend some time in a single-parent home, and that about 25% of all children will be part of a remarried family (Hetherington, 1979). About 47% of second marriages eventually end, and children again face a readjustment in family patterns.

The effects upon children of divorce are not favorable. Robson's (1987) summary of the literature on the topic suggests the following: Children of divorce are overrepresented in psychiatric populations; they show higher rates of delinquency and antisocial behavior, neurotic symptoms, depression, conduct disorders, and habit formations such as sleep disturbances than do children in intact homes. In nonclinic populations, the children of divorce also demonstrate significant maladaptations as compared with children from intact families. "The children are more dependent, disobedient, aggressive, whining, demanding and unaffectionate. . . . [They] have generalized feelings of anxiety and helplessness and lower self-esteem. They perform less well on a variety of social and adjustment indices" (p. 2).

Robson (1987) also reported that children at different ages from infancy through college react to divorce and separation in ways that affect their development. For example, "children under age 5 tend to regress in their development, showing feeding difficulties, toileting problems including soiling, smearing, and enuresis and frequently disturbed sleeping patterns" (p. 3). These children also frequently manifest intense separation anxiety—fear of being left alone or being abandoned by both parents. Anger, fear, depression, and guilt are commonly seen in children of divorce at preschool and kindergarten ages. School-aged children (ages 6 to 8) may deny the separation or difficulties with it, but they also may exhibit depression and anxiety. They may be extremely hard to control and often have temper tantrums. They may use tactics such as refusal to go to school or noncooperation as ways to try to get parents back together again. Older school-aged children (ages 9 to 11) may experience loyalty conflicts between parents and become overly dependent on one or the other parent. They may demonstrate shock, surprise, denial, incredulity, and disbelief. They may come to reject one parent as they become enmeshed in the custody battle and, indeed, reject those parts of their life that were particularly associated with that parent (e.g., participation in sports). They experience a decrease in self-esteem and in their social and academic functioning.

Adolescents (ages 13 to 18) sometimes take on so many responsibilities for siblings or for household chores that they are forced to mature too quickly. Thus they lose their adolescence and do not resolve the normal adolescent developmental tasks expected of them. Adolescent girls who have experienced the absence of a father through separation may change in their interaction with men, seeking attention and acting out sexual behavior. Lacking intact parental guidance and discipline, adolescents may experience mental health problems, weak judgment, poor interpersonal relationships, and difficulty in perceiving their life in the future. College students (ages 18 to 22) experience stress, changed interactions with their parents, anger, worry about their parents' future, anxiety about their own future marriages, and feelings of loss of a family home. Such findings were supported by Lopez's (1987) comprehensive analysis of the effect of parental divorce on college student development.

Robson's (1987) analysis suggests that the younger the child when divorce or separation occurs, the more vulnerable and the more disturbed future behavior will be. Nonetheless, it is clear that children at all developmental ages are affected by such experiences and the residual of the feelings and cognitions associated with divorce and separation endure for an extended period of time, perhaps throughout adulthood. Indeed, in an analysis of two large national studies conducted 30 years apart, Kukla and Weingarten (1979) concluded that coming from a non-intact family of origin affects psychological well-being in adulthood. They further concluded that children of divorce are more likely to experience vulnerability to stress, weaker investment in the parental role, and more instability in their own marriages.

Remarriage families is a term that is frequently used as a synonym for an array of new terms in the American vocabulary: *blended, recoupled, reconstituted, merged*, and *reorganized* families (Hayes & Hayes, 1986). Typically, such marriages include at least one of the parents who has been previously married and probably has children. Indeed, both parents may previously have had children who may now be a part of a blended or reconstituted family. Such arrangements bring with them a variety of psychological issues that are different from those likely to be experienced in first marriages. In remarriages, either or both spouses still may be mourning the loss of the first relationship, trying to understand what went wrong, trying to establish who was to blame, experiencing problems of self-acceptance and acceptance of new roles and responsibilities, renegotiating roles and relationships with family and friends, and transforming the relationship with the former spouse (Garfield, 1980). But, in addition, one or both spouses may also be coping with the transition from single-parent status to newly remarried status, with the expectations their remarried status brings. The latter may involve dealing with new stepchildren or worrying about how one's own children are going to cope with a new stepparent. They are trying to create a set of relationships for which there is no history.

For the children, remarriage also can be fraught with dilemmas and confusion. At the least, remarriage disrupts the cognitive and social world of a child who had been living with a single parent after having lived in an intact, nuclear family. The reconceptualization of who one is within this new mix of a stepparent, a parent who is now the spouse of a new parent, and possibly a new set of stepsiblings; new grandparents; a changed relationship network; and perhaps a new geographic location takes time and energy for any child even when the outcome is positive. Obviously the child, like the parent, still may be mourning the loss of the previous family constellation or a previous parent and may feel anger, jealousy, guilt, apprehension, conflicting loyalties, abandonment, powerlessness, and many other emotions that are neither vocalized nor clearly understood.

Hayes and Hayes (1986) suggested that remarriage families have at least four general categories of concerns with which counselors can help: roles and relationships, feelings and fantasies, rules and regulations, and external forces. Within these categories of concerns are the implications that remarriage families have to create a history, a set of traditions, that is uniquely their own; that roles each family member plays must be negotiated, clarified, and supported; that expectations, realities, or fantasies must be sorted out and worked through; that a shared strategy of discipline must be put in place; and that systems by which the remarriage family has contact with the absent, former spouse(s) and how children interact with the separated parent(s) become very important. Hayes and Hayes (pp. 6–7) indicated that in working with remarriage families, counselors can help in the following ways:

- Encourage family members to relinquish myths they may hold about the remarriage family;
- Help members to understand the entire family system, its differences from their past families, and the involvement of non-family members in the system;
- Teach members more effective communication skills;
- Help members, especially children, to mourn the loss of previous relationships and encourage the development of new relationships;

- Provide a forum in which members can work out their relationships with one another and with quasi-kin, especially the absent parent;
- Offer structured programs of parent training and lists of readings that family members can use as self-instructional devices;
- Inform members of the latest research findings and clinical evidence that may be helpful to them in the reorganization process;
- Identify the tasks of parenting and the relationships that are necessary to enact those roles; and
- Run groups for remarriage parents in the community or for stepchildren in the schools.

Blurred male and female roles continue to cause conflict and confusion in many families. Matters of dependence and independence, role expectations, women entering the work force and men being unemployed, and responsibilities in dual-career families for child care and homemaking represent major sources of stress in many family units.

One of the issues of blurred male and female roles is the matter of balancing sex and work roles. Whether married or single, women and men must negotiate a personal identity in which views of sex role and views of self as worker are compatible. Cook (1985) described this balancing process as requiring consideration of self-perceptions of masculine and feminine personality characteristics; attitudes about ideal self and ideals for other people; distinctions between behaviors and skills a person possesses and those he or she actually is willing to use in various settings; and perceptions of environmental demands and rewards for behavior. Each of these categories may involve discrepancies or conflicts for particular individuals in one or more areas, leading to feelings of incompatibility between sex roles and work roles. These conflicts in turn may lead to dissatisfactions with the compromises required to resolve sex-role/work-role discrepancies, confusion, or distress. In such instances, counselors have important roles to play in assisting individuals to identify their conflicts and to bring into better balance their perceptions of the various aspects pertinent to sex roles and work roles.

The inability to balance role behavior in the family and in the work place has been found to foster severe depression in both employed women and in homemakers. At the root of these problems are disagreements within the family about roles and dissatisfaction with the tasks women feel required to undertake in the home. Whereas depression and dissatisfaction are present for both employed women and homemakers who experience such role disagreements with their husbands, employed women exhibit less severe depression apparently because of the offsetting economic and intrinsic benefits from work. Homemakers have no similar outlet or compensating mechanism for their feelings of dissatisfaction and depression (Keith & Schaefer, 1985).

Depression and loneliness affect family members of all ages but are particularly acute among teenagers, young adults, and the elderly. Where financial hardships, little hope for the future, powerlessness, and social isolation are at issue, they breed depression and loneliness. So, too, do geographic relocation and occupational mobility as factors that separate family members for indefinite or extended periods of time.

Problems of the aged include health and emotional problems, loss of family, loneliness, and needs for companionship and for transportation. Concerns about decreasing independence and loss of ability to care for themselves are major problems of the aged. Similarly, middle-aged children of the aged find themselves caught in the emotional dilemma of trying to be a parent to their children and to their elderly parents at the same time. Drains on financial and emotional resources can increase family vulnerability and tension.

Pregnant adolescents and associated concerns relate to keeping their babies, whether or not to marry, financial resources, medical care, foster care, continuing schooling, and many other matters that put family units at risk.

Alcohol and drug abuse have increased across age and sex groups. There is a marked increase in such use by adolescents and even younger children. Heavy drinking in families often is associated with unemployment. Drug abuse, including the misuse of prescription drugs, is a growing problem among the elderly, and there is a growing problem of cocaine and other drug use among young professionals and other young married couples.

Alcohol abuse and other types of substance abuse have also been found to be associated with family patterns that are thought to contribute to the maintenance of substance abuse (West, Hosie, & Zarski, 1987). In one of 35 families in which one member of the family was hospitalized for substance abuse, it was found that such families were highly interdependent and that they fear the separation and individuation of family members. This leads to maladaptive patterns of family interaction, including significant problems of boundary setting between spouses and children. Furthermore, the substance abuser, if a child, is likely to be "triangled" into the spouse's relationship, possibly forming a coalition with one parent against the other, or serving as the focus of spousal communication about unresolved intimacy or conflict problems (Minuchin, 1974). Frequently, the result is a hierarchy reversal in the family in which the substance-abusing child becomes more influential in determining family interactions and communication patterns than either one or both parents. Counselors working with such families need to assess family communication patterns, existing triangles, and potential hierarchy reversals, and help the family to restore appropriate role boundaries and to return the parents to an executive position in the family. To accomplish these goals, counselors need to engage in a systems-oriented approach to family counseling as well as in educational interventions designed to help family members consider the assumptions and possibilities underlying both the actual and the ideal family dynamics to which they are committed.

Parent-child communication problems continue to stress family units whether the mediating factor is parents' inadequate listening skills, financial pressures that limit the time and energy available to spend with children, confusion about disciplinary measures, or other parenting skills. Parent-child conflicts frequently become parent-parent conflicts and thereby permeate the family structure, creating environments of ongoing hostility and tension.

Although the respondents to the surveys conducted by Family Service America (1984) were of lower socioeconomic groups for the most part, most of the stresses identified characterize family units at all socioeconomic levels. Numerous problems plague various family units. For example, in the two-earner working class family that has "bought" into the American dream of material acquisition and the credit card culture, the loss of a job either the man or the woman holds is likely to plunge the family into financial disaster causing all types of family stresses. If it is the man who loses his job and his wife becomes the breadwinner, the shift in roles can be traumatic. The wife may gain a new sense of self-worth, but the husband loses his, causing a variety of tensions in the family. Some family tensions arise because the woman's career outdistances the man's in the dual-career family, or because of conflict about whose career is more important and under what criteria geographic moves should be made that would cause one spouse to follow the other. As noted previously, dual-career families frequently experience problems in time management, logistics regarding child care and children's medical emergencies, and housekeeping issues relative to which parent will deal with which role in maintaining the family structure.

Hodgson (1984), a family therapist who works with dual-career families, suggested using a number of therapeutic techniques to help such couples determine ways to reduce some of their problems. Some of her suggestions are paraphrased as follows:

1. Use a "caring days" form in the counseling session in which the counselor can ask the husband and wife to generate a list of 10 to 15 specific behaviors that the other could do to show caring. The form is then kept at home and each spouse logs the occurrence of caring behaviors on a daily basis.
2. Convene the whole family at least once in the counselor's office to explore ways to divide chores in an equitable manner and thereby alleviate division of labor conflicts.
3. Train the couple in communication skills, relationship enhancement, or problem solving to help them deal with the time crunch and the reduced conversation they experience.
4. Help the couple to negotiate the exercise of power in family decisions in ways that help them "to visualize the ways decisions are currently made, the ways that they would like them to be made, and the ways they agree to apportion decision-making authority in the future" (p. 50).
5. Expose the dual-career couples to other couples sharing the same types of stresses and conflicts through books, popular articles, and dual-career workshops that identify common problems and teach joint decision-making and communication skills.
6. Provide education about effective child-rearing practices or hold parenting workshops.

Although there are stresses and tensions in dual-career families, it would be inaccurate to assume that there are no strengths in such structures. Research studies (e.g., Knaub, 1986) indicate that both parents and children do rate their perceptions of the dual-career life style positively. They tend as well to perceive their families as high in family strengths, particularly with regard to concern, respect, and support. Nevertheless, there are primary problems of time constraints and needs for coping strategies in the areas of successful negotiation and conflict resolution.

Much of the conflicting evidence about the effects of dual-career families on the psychological or physical health of children is a function of methodological flaws in many of the studies as well as inconsistent study of the effects of dual-career families on different groups of children and youth. Lewis and Cooper (1983) criticized many studies for not taking into account family interactions or the circumstances surrounding both the family and the availability, use, and characteristics of day care. Bennett and Reardon (1985), in studying data about dual-career families and particularly about working mothers, suggested that the potential harm done by mothers working is not severe, and that negative effects, particularly for boys, may be reduced if several factors are present or accommodated. These factors include choosing day care that is stable, stimulating, and warm. Involvement of the father is increasingly considered important in child development, especially in dual-career families. According to Bennett and Reardon, specific actions that can be taken to enhance the experience of boys in dual-career families are to (a) encourage the active participation and support of the father, (b) try to make the mother's job as satisfying as possible and (c) be aware of the potential problems and offer special attention to boys in dual-career families.

In a major synthesis of the existing research on the effects of maternal employment on infants, preschoolers, and adolescents, the following conclusions were drawn by Herr and Cramer (1988, p. 388):

1. When the child is enrolled in high-quality day care, the intellectual effects are neither harmful nor helpful, except for children who grow up in a high-risk environment. For these children, quality day care actually seems to help to maintain or to raise IQ scores.
2. Maternal employment does not seem to alter the emotional bond between mother and child.
3. Maternal job satisfaction seems to be positively related to development in preschoolers.
4. There is no convincing proof of any negative effects of maternal employment on preschoolers. At the least, maternal employment seems to do no harm.
5. Maternal employment probably has a positive effect on a daughter's career involvement and commitment. When combined with such factors as educational and occupational status, sex-role ideology, and parental encouragement, maternal employment leads to a decrease in a daughter's sex-typing and to more assertive career planning.

6. Adolescent children of working mothers do not seem to experience any proven, consistently harmful effects.
7. Female adolescents may react somewhat differently to maternal employment than do male adolescents.

Latchkey children. As suggested earlier in this chapter, one of the major corollaries of the rise in dual-career and two-earner families has been the growing visibility of so-called "latchkey children." This term refers to children and youth, unsupervised by their parents, "who care for themselves before or after school, on weekends, and during holidays while their parents work" (Robinson, Rowland, & Coleman, 1986).

Because this phenomenon is relatively recent, research studies have not kept pace with the numbers of children and the circumstances involved. Indeed, the available research is mixed in its analysis of whether self-care by children is good or bad. For example, on the positive side, some research has shown that latchkey children are prone to become more independent, self-reliant, resourceful, and better informed about procedures for dealing with their own physical well-being than children who are supervised after school by adults or by older siblings (Long & Long, 1981; Stroman & Duff, 1982). On the negative side, some research suggests that latchkey children left in self-care frequently report nightmares and high fear levels (fear of noises and fear of the dark) (Long & Long, 1981). One longitudinal research study examined 1,000 former latchkey children and their parents. Most of these subjects were members of minority groups (Long & Long, 1983). These researchers found that one half of the adults who were former latchkey children were still afraid to be alone. Furthermore, it was found that many of these adults experienced residual feelings of loneliness, boredom, resentment toward parents, fears, social isolation, and a tendency to enter occupations oriented around things instead of people. The explanation for these findings, in contrast to other studies that found no high levels of fear among latchkey children (Galambos & Garbarino, 1983), seems to depend on where the children reside. For example, children who live in high-crime areas where violence, drug abuse, and related conditions predominate are likely to experience fear when they come home to an empty house and must supervise themselves. In contrast, children who live in rural, suburban, middle-class, or affluent neighborhoods considered to be safe are not likely to be fearful.

The one constant that seems to be evident in the research on latchkey children and their parents is the parents' ambivalence about such arrangements. Even when parents feel they have no choice but to leave the children under self-care because of the expense or lack of child care or transportation problems, more than 50% of the parents surveyed were concerned about leaving their children at home alone after school, many experienced embarrassment and guilt, and they tended to underreport that their children were latchkey children (Long & Long, 1983).

Counselors may work with either latchkey children or their parents. Or, they may work in behalf of latchkey children. For example, counselors may take the initiative to help their communities implement programs to assist latchkey children such as developing an afterschool telephone hot line for latchkey children, matching elderly care-givers with young latchkey children, encouraging local police and fire fighting agencies to provide programs for children on safety considerations in the home, promoting after-school activities and sports events conducted by community social services, and encouraging schools to run late buses for children whose parents work until late afternoon. Direct counseling services to latchkey children may involve addressing their feelings of self-confidence, security, or specific fears; it also may involve creating support groups for such children to help them consider their attitudes about self-care and to share the ways they handle such experiences. For parents, counselors can create opportunities to inform them of the various options and alternatives available for their children; form parent clusters whose schedules might permit rotation of child caregiving; and provide support groups and information for parents to help them deal with their apprehensions about leaving their children alone.

When one combines the problems of the dual-career family with those of the stepfamily or blended family, other tensions can enter the compound: those of residual guilt for a failed first marriage, divided loyalties for natural children and stepchildren, unresolved communication or identity issues of either parent, stepparents' overreactions to children's needs, anxieties about failing as a spouse or parent a second or third time, and other related issues. In the single-parent structure, depression, loneliness, anxiety, poverty, overinvestment by the parent in the children, enmeshment, and a lack of clarity about the role boundaries of parent and child are major problems. One might overlay any of these family structures with those of extramarital sex, multilateral adult structures, or same-sex coupling and find problems of jealousy, possessiveness, poor communication, sexual dysfunction, fear, incompatibility, and many other forms of stress, the roots of which may be in the macroenvironment. The actual playing out of the problem, however, occurs in the microenvironment, the intimate network of role relationships and interactions that makes up the specifics of the family, whatever its particular form.

The Microenvironment

Until recently, most of the research activity dealing with families was focused on the microenvironment—the activities, emotions, and interactions in the individual family. Such a perspective of how individual family units cope with stress continues to be a major and important issue.

Some past research has focused on the antecedents to family crises and postcrises adjustments (Hill, 1949); other research has been concerned with such elements of family stress as the importance of the decision-making process in the management of stress, the systematic assessment of family hardships, parental coping strategies and their effects on child launching, retirement, and widowhood. As research ensues about family adjustment to stress, considerable attention is being paid to the major forms of stressors on families, whether they be normative and predictable, or unusual, unexpected, and transitory. Lipman-Blumen (1975), for example, developed an elaborate scheme to examine the extent of stress in a family system. Other research directions have studied such factors affecting family adjustment to stressors as family members' personal resources (financial, health, educational, psychological), the family system's internal resources (family adaptability and cohesiveness, management of family resources, problem-solving ability), social support (kin, friends, neighbors, self-help groups, community agencies), and coping (McCubbin, et al. 1980), cohesion, and adaptability (Maynard & Olson, 1987).

Although each of these dimensions of family system reactions to stress is important, it is perhaps the family's ability to perceive accurately the stressors it faces and then to manage the various dimensions of family life simultaneously—to achieve balance in its coping behavior—that is most central to a microenvironment view of the family structure in action. Coping, in such a perspective, would include: "(1) maintaining satisfactory internal conditions for communication and family organization, (2) promoting member independence and self-esteem, (3) maintenance of family bonds of coherence and unity, (4) maintenance and development of social supports in transactions with the community, and (5) maintenance of some efforts to control the impact of the stressor and the amount of change in the family unit" (McCubbin et al., 1980, p. 135). The ability to understand how the family perceives and copes with stress, how to strengthen the relationship system, and how to empower the family to manage its resources effectively in any or all of the coping categories just identified becomes fundamental to counseling interventions.

Counseling Approaches to the Family

Although counseling of families is a relatively recent emphasis for mental health practitioners, it is nevertheless a rapidly growing area of interest and importance. Family counseling has been advocated in the schools, in rehabilitation settings, in employee assistance programs, in community agency settings, and in virtually every other context in which counselors are engaged. In its emphasis on the treatment of relationships within the core social institution, the family, family counseling has increasingly become the treatment of choice for a wide variety of problems such as child abuse, learning problems, juvenile delinquency, adolescent eating disorders, chemical dependency, and sexual dysfunction. Whether described as marital and family therapy, conjoint family therapy, or conjugal relations or family counseling, the techniques and the problems at issue are being explored by all types of mental health practitioners: counselors, psychologists, psychiatrists, and social workers. And, they are being applied to all types of relationships—gay and cohabiting couples, single-parent and reconstituted families, and intact nuclear or multigenerational families at all stages of relationships (e.g., premarital, divorce, reconstituting family structures) (Olson, Russell, & Sprenkle, 1980).

Within such a context of growth, the actual theoretical perspectives of family counseling are still relatively limited in their conceptualizations and in the specific focus of intervention. For the most part, existing approaches to family counseling have not yet become solid, but are still open and dynamic. Although the major unifying theme for family counseling is treating problems within a relationship context, models tend to emphasize many subelements or targets. Various classification schemes have been proposed to provide some typology of family therapy or counseling approaches. There are those, for example, that stress psychodynamic or systems approaches (Guerin, 1976), biopsychosocial or ecological approaches (Myerstein, 1981) and those that compare cultural and experiential approaches (Levine & Padilla, 1980; McGoldrick, Pearce, & Giordano, 1982). There are also a variety of approaches to integrating concepts of family, such as cohesion, adaptability, and communication, toward which therapy might be directed (Olson et al., 1979, 1980), and the resulting family types that emerge from the different combinations and magnitudes of these three elements. For example, Maynard and Olson (1987) described a circumplex model of family systems built around the concepts of cohesion and adaptability that permits the assessment, identification, and treatment of 16 specific types of marital and family systems and 3 more general types. Within such perspectives several major approaches to family counseling have evolved and are briefly summarized below.

Psychodynamic family counseling focuses on intrapsychic selves, unconscious dynamics, conflicts of family members, and how these interlock to create disturbances in family members (Getz, 1987). Ackerman (1958), Framo (1976), and Bowen (1978) are among the psychodynamically oriented therapists. The content they use to pursue insight and growth within the family consists of: the emotional life of the family constellation, the scapegoating of a symptomatic client as a function of unresolved family conflicts, the unconscious dynamics that remain unresolved from the parent's family of origin that are recreated and projected into the current family, and the needs for self-differentiation among family members who are enmeshed in intense interdependence within the family.

Structural family therapy focuses on how the subsystems that constitute families are connected and how the arrangements that govern family transactions are structured. Intervention focuses on promoting structural viability by establishing a clear generational hierarchy, clarifying and changing coalitions, and promoting semipermeable boundaries among subsystems. This approach does not explore and interpret the past but attempts to modify the present. Minuchin (1974) and his associates are the primary progenitors of this approach.

Strategic family therapy includes a blend of Minuchin's work with communication theory (Haley, 1976) and paradoxical relabeling (Selvini, Palazzoli, Boscolo, Cecchin, & Prata, 1980; Watzlawick & Weakland, 1977). It focuses upon the ways problems are labeled and the behaviors used to solve such problems in the family. Families are helped to reframe or relabel problems and they are provided directives composed of strategically planned behavioral tasks designed to change family behavior and to improve the functioning of the family organization.

Experiential family therapy is an existential orientation to having families experience their own irrationality and "craziness" (Whitaker,

1977). Changed behavior in the family occurs as individual members' self-esteem, communication patterns, and family rules are explored and altered (Satir, 1964).

Social learning approaches combine operant learning and social exchange theories, general systems theories, and attribution theory. Such an approach focuses on interaction patterns, problem solving, and other specific behaviors in family systems (Vincent, 1980).

Relationship enhancement is a psychoeducational model designed to teach couples or families specific problem-solving skills. The participants learn to express themselves in constructive ways to avoid arousing defensiveness and hostility in others and to interact with each other with understanding and acceptance. Participants learn nine sets of behavioral skills or modes of behavior: expressive, empathic, discussion/negotiation, problem/conflict resolution, self-change, helping others change, generalization, teaching/facilitative, and maintenance skills. In studies comparing the relationship enhancement approach to traditional discussion-oriented treatments, relationship enhancement was found to enhance communication, general relationships, and marital adjustment (Ross, Baker, & Guerney, 1985; Guerney, Vogelsong, & Coufal, 1983).

These approaches are obviously not mutually exclusive or exhaustive—nor does any one have a clear-cut advantage across different types of family problems. In their individual ways, each of these approaches attempts to treat the family as a system rather than treating a symptom the family experiences collectively or only one member manifests. Just as is true in other applications of counseling and therapy, approaches to family counseling are moving toward specifying which approach or mode of treatment is likely to be most effective for each type of family or group of clients experiencing specific sorts of problems. In addition, as in most other forms of counseling, family counseling is also generating preventive and enrichment programs designed to avoid major stresses and crises by promoting structured communication skill building and other forms of relationship enhancement. Such approaches can be used to help families of different structural types to anticipate and perceive stresses as expected and controllable.

A major question for the future is how and where counselors will receive the training they need to conceptualize and implement family counseling. Will such training be random or systematic? Will it be linked to other emphases in counselor education or stand independently?

It is obvious that such issues are of concern in counselor education programs. Hollis and Wantz (1983) indicated in a survey of counselor education programs and curricula that a major curricular trend in counselor education is the addition of courses in marriage and family counseling. Similarly Meadows and Hetrick (1982), in a national survey of counselor education programs, found that 55% of the departments reporting indicated that they were offering one or more courses in marriage and family counseling and intended to increase their development of this curriculum area. Several authors have examined issues of curriculum development, accreditation, supervision, and related topics as these relate to the implementation of training in marriage and family therapy within counselor education (Okun & Gladding, 1983).

Another major issue for counselors results from both the concerns of training and the concerns of practice. It has to do with how behavior is viewed in terms of its locus and its purpose. Traditionally, regardless of the psychodynamic model used, many counselors and psychologists viewed psychological difficulties as intrapsychic matters. The task was to alter the problem that was located within a client's head, or to modify internal states that were manifested in symptomatology. Although such premises continue to be viable for some psychological problems, family counseling shifts the focus from symptoms to strategies that people use to cope with their relationships with others. Such approaches seek to affirm that many psychological maladjustments are not biological or intrapsychic but social and interpersonal (Allen, 1975). In this perspective, symptoms are not viewed primarily as modes of coping with instinctual forces but as methods of dealing with the vagaries, rigors, and interpersonal confusions of daily living. The struggle for the counselor and the clients is to discover and act upon more effective ways to cope with social situations. This is a different view from that, for example, of a psychoanalytic persuasion, which sees family problems as the sum of the disturbances in the individuals involved. Rather, in the emerging, major family counseling perspectives, not one of the individuals involved is necessarily seen as a villain; instead it is assumed that the problems involved are found in the communication and interaction patterns of the system as a whole.

Families are basically interpersonal constellations in which the effects of interaction among the participants become the content of concern. Family counseling assumes that this content is better understood and dealt with in situ, in the family group, rather than by isolating each participant in one-on-one counseling and assuming that when these individuals are regrouped that the interpersonal dynamics will be improved. The notion of a family system suggests that there is a chemistry of relationships and interacting subsystems in which matters of communication, cohesion, adaptability, and resource management come together in unique ways. Individual actions in such a view do not simply spring forth out of some internal mechanism, but are, at base, responses to the actions of other family members. Thus, analyses of such dynamics and responses to them are much better effected if parents and children or whoever else makes up the particular family structure are engaged simultaneously in the process of treatment. The focus then becomes the present and the future rather than a reworking of the past; the identification and building of strengths within the family structure rather than the excising of some pathology; and the development of skills by which family members can more adequately cope with each other.

Finally, we come to a counseling implication as powerful as that of viewing families as systems of interaction that need to be seen holistically if intervention is to be effective. That is, "that family structures are not simply personal arrangements among family members. They are manifestations of the values of the cultural group to which the family belongs" (Aponte, 1982, p. 8). Therefore, if counselors are to effectively assess, treat, and communicate with a family they must be sensitive to their own and the family's cultural roots. Families of different ethnic backgrounds do not define the same phenomena as problems nor do they express their caring or pain in the same ways; they differ in what are acceptable solutions to problems and to whom they usually turn for help, and in the types of family patterns and expressive behaviors their cultural experiences have reinforced. Thus, in the midst of increasing attention to the counseling implications of cultural pluralism, therapies have been developed with little attention to the matters of cultural variability, the sustained residual of ethnic values and identifications on individual and family behavior, and the effects of common cultural history and traditions on communication and family rituals vis-à-vis dating, marriage, child-rearing, work, or retirement. "Ethnicity is a powerful influence in determining identity. . . . Just as individuation requires that we come to terms with our families of origin, coming to terms with our ethnicity is necessary to gain a perspective on the relativity of our belief systems" (McGoldrick, 1982, pp. 6–10). Indeed, family properties such as intermarriage among persons of different cultural traditions or ethnicity may require identification and redirection. In such roles as well as those between the family and the larger society, the counselor may need to be a "culture broker" (McGoldrick, p. 23), helping families to recognize their own ethnic values, to strengthen those that are adaptive, and to recognize conflicts that result from different perceptions and experiences of ethnicity. In addition counselors must realize that treatment approaches and counseling theories also have inherent cultural values that frequently are filtered through the counselor's own ethnic and value lenses. Ultimately, family counseling requires the counselor not to be an anthropologist or sociologist, but, rather, one who appreciates the variability in values, traditions, and patterns that become mediators of family systems and, indeed, of the effectiveness of counseling.

Other Counseling Problems Associated With Families

Not every problem that has relevance for the family or originates within a family structure necessarily requires family counseling or therapy. Some problems may need to be addressed primarily by an individual within the family and a counselor. For example, working or not working after childbirth may be one such concern. Using a subjective-expected utility model of decision making, Granrose (1985) suggested ways counselors can help women with such questions as whether or not to work after childbirth. In such circumstances, counselors may need to explore the relationship between the way clients frame the questions and the intentions they formulate. They also may need to help women examine the relative value of financial rewards, personal ambitions, and child welfare as key determinants of intentions and behavior. Exploring the relative strength of guilt and resentment of working or of staying at home is important as a context to identify emotional conflicts that may prevent adopting a rational plan. Thus, counselors need to help clients consider the decision and perceived consequences associated with their intentions to work or not work after childbirth and to prepare for the resulting eventualities.

Single Parent as Peer

Another concern in which counseling is focused primarily on one family member is the situation in a single-parent family when the parent becomes a peer and intergenerational boundaries and role expectations between the child and the parent are lost. In such cases, because most single-parent families are headed by women, the mother typically is the focus of counseling. In such instances, the counseling may address several emphases. The mother may need to be helped to reassume the maternal role and to be taught or reminded of the appropriate expectations for a child of a given age, so that the son or daughter can be given the sanction again to be a child. The mother may need help in working through feelings of guilt and apprehension about reinstituting discipline. She may need to explore the likelihood that her perceptions and emotions concerning her ex-spouse and the divorce may not be those of the child and therefore need to be differentiated from the child so that mother and child can behave in accordance with their separate identity. In addition, the mother will probably need some help with stress management, self-esteem, and the skills of independent living. Although the counselor's role in this situation is primarily to empower the mother to reassume her role, the counselor may want to refer the child to another counselor or work with the child independently of the mother. The focus of counseling with the child would probably include legitimizing the child's thoughts about the divorce, parents, parents' new friends, and a sense of identity, as well as feelings of anger, anxiety, and sadness that might be present (Glenwick & Mowery, 1986). In most instances, the single mother can profit from support networks to replace her marital relationship in order to avoid leaning too heavily on her children for emotional support (Hodgson, 1984).

Patterns of Time Use

It is likely that many single parents who do not have problems with their child-rearing roles or with intergenerational boundaries may have other problems for which counseling may be helpful. One of these is priority setting and time management. As might be expected, patterns of time use in single- versus two-parent families differ when parents are employed. As compared with unemployed single parents and married employed and nonemployed mothers, single employed mothers spend the least time on household chores and on recreation; they also spend the least time on personal care of all groups except employed mothers in intact family units. Obviously, for many single parents and, indeed, some employed mothers as well, such time allocations as identified above can induce guilt, frustrations, and other stresses for which counseling can be useful (Sanik & Mauldin, 1986).

Female Participation in the Work Force

The participation in the labor force of married women with children is not always for the same reason nor is it always seen as positive.

Avioli (1985) studied the labor force participation of married women with infants who elected to be employed immediately after childbirth as compared with those who remained out of the labor force for 3 years after giving birth. Four distinct patterns emerged characterizing the White employed wives, Black employed wives, White housewives, and Black housewives. Overall, White employed wives seemed to be working because of an interest in being in the labor force, seemed to be comfortable with their employment status, had substantial feelings of personal efficacy, and their husbands were supportive of their employment. In contrast, the Black employed wives seemed to be working because of financial need, had a history of being employed and planned to continue to work full-time, and were as likely to be employed with or without their husbands' approval.

In comparison to the White employed wives, White housewives tended to show little attachment to the labor force. They claimed to have substantial feelings of personal efficacy and, consistent with their employment status, reported that their husbands opposed their working.

The Black housewives tended to be the most stressed group of wives. Although they had high financial need and planned to work, they were constrained from entering the labor force by lack of work experience, high local unemployment, and the practical problems of having more children than did the other comparison groups. Unlike their White counterparts, Black housewives did not seem to derive a feeling of competence from their housekeeping and child-care activities, but rather a relatively low level of personal efficacy.

Within the limits of this research it is suggestive that working women with children and those who wish to work but cannot do so vary in the stresses, purposes for working, and feelings of personal efficacy they associate with labor force experiences. Thus, different female married populations have different needs for counseling and support. In some cases, the issues are feelings of self-worth and power; in others they are matters of labor force access, time management, and child-care; in some groups all of these factors may be present.

Beyond such perspectives, it seems useful to recognize that counselors need to help working mothers clarify and understand the implications of several other perspectives. For example, as Etaugh (1984) suggested, ''Many of the stresses they are experiencing are due not to their own shortcomings but to external pressures arising from family and employment systems. . . . Role conflicts and role overload experienced by working mothers are caused not by their inadequacies, but by the press of more demands than most people can handle effectively. The family counselor can help working mothers in setting priorities'' (p. 32).

Children of Divorce and Separation

Counselors in schools and in other settings increasingly are instituting individual and group counseling for children of divorce and separation. Frequently such counseling provides these children with opportunities to express and clarify their feelings of loss, anger, conflicting loyalties, anxiety about the future, and related matters. Although not all children experience significant trauma as a result of their parents' separation or divorce, many do. Wallerstein (1980) found that one third of the children in a research study were still distressed and unhappy 5 years after their parents' separation. Wallerstein (1984) found in another study that children who are 7 or 8 years of age when their parents divorce may harbor fantasies that the parents will reunite as long as 10 years after the separation.

Because children exposed to the divorce of their parents exhibit different levels of psychological vulnerability and distress, counselors can engage in multiple levels of intervention. One of these is primary prevention. In such roles, counselors can provide educational and group counseling activities for children and, indeed, separately for parents to examine divorce, the changes in role relationships that ensue, feelings of loss, guilt, or lessened self-esteem that accompany it, ways to maintain communications with a separated parent, coping skills, stress management, and related issues. In addition to an educational approach or primary prevention, counselors also can take more direct approaches to intervention, including making early identification of children of divorce who are at high risk for maladaptive response to their parents' separation; conducting group programs or individual counseling to directly address loneliness, fears of separation or abandonment, feelings of guilt, worry about custody decisions, loss of family or of a specific parent, parental dating, family violence, or posttraumatic syndrome in the case of children who have been "kidnapped" by one parent; and leading clinical groups that use play therapy, creative drama, or other techniques that allow for acting out of fantasies and feelings and promote problem solving (Robson, 1987).

Members of an Alcoholic Family

At certain points in the treatment of alcoholism, particularly in aftercare when the alcoholic is recovering and the family is being rebuilt, it is undoubtedly the treatment of preference to engage in family counseling. Prior to that time, however, it is likely that each member of the family needs individual counseling to help them understand the addictive process and how it has affected their lives. Because alcoholism breeds total family dysfunction, each of the family members, including the addicted person, is likely to have played a role in enabling the addiction or in adapting to the family dysfunction in ways that permit survival.

Current perspectives on the alcoholic family have come to view a variety of roles as essential within the family system where alcoholism is the primary problem. Among the roles are those of dependent (the addicted person), the enabler, the hero, the scapegoat, the lonely child, and the mascot. In a single-child family, that child may play all of the roles except that of dependent and perhaps enabler. In multiple-child families, however, it is likely that children at different places in the birth order will take on different roles. With each of these roles come problems of interpersonal relationships, anger, guilt, stress, low self-esteem, loneliness, and other mental health problems that need to be sorted out and explored on a one-on-one or possibly a peer group relationship. If such sorting out does not occur, it is very likely that the children of alcoholics will carry into adulthood the deficits in social skills, feelings of low self-worth, or other negative behaviors with which they lived and grew up in their family. They need to know that what they experienced was not under their control, to understand the process of addiction, and to examine and act upon the areas of arrested development they experienced as they played the family roles that became theirs because of birth order or other events.

Wegscheider (1981, p. 173) indicated that although the particular problems, stresses, and self-concepts of each of the alcoholic family members are different, there are primary care goals of similar importance to each family member. They include:

1. To let down the wall of defensiveness;
2. To let the pain emerge;
3. To begin to experience some positive feelings;
4. To accept the family illness and one's part in it; and
5. To make a personal commitment to an ongoing recovery program for the family and for themselves.

Battered Women

Although family therapy or family counseling may be the treatment of preference in the family where spousal abuse is occurring and the family is still together, individual counseling of battered women or group counseling with other battered women is likely to be the appropriate intervention when the woman has left the home. The magnitude of spouse abuse or the battering of women is difficult to determine precisely. At the beginning of this chapter it was indicated that probably up to 40% of families engage in family violence involving spouses. In addition, the literature indicates that the problem of abused or battered women is prevalent in all socioeconomic and occupational levels of society (Straus, Gelles, & Steinmetz, 1980; U.S. Commission on Civil Rights, 1978). Walker's research (1979) on battered women of diverse ages, races, religions, and educational and socioeconomic levels suggested that they share a number of common characteristics:

1. Low self-esteem;
2. A belief in all the myths characteristic of battering relationships (e.g., "I must have done something to deserve this," "This man needs me," "He will change," "He was drunk when he did it," "It is a man's right to strike his wife and children");
3. A belief in traditional values regarding the family, home, and sex-role stereotypes;
4. Acceptance of responsibility for the abuser's action;
5. Feelings of guilt and denial of terror and anger;
6. Passive behavior and inability to manipulate their environment to protect themselves;
7. Severe stress reactions with psychosomatic complaints;
8. Use of sex to establish intimacy; and
9. A belief that they are the only ones who can resolve the issue.

Other researchers (e.g., Bell, 1977) have suggested other characteristics that extend or overlap with Walker's research findings. They include insecurity and isolation, a conviction that the spouse or partner will reform, economic depression, doubts about getting along in a hostile world, and fear of the stigma of divorce.

Certainly, when battered women first leave the relationship they need crisis intervention and support. They need to be helped to cope with the transition to singleness, the implications of divorce, the care and protection of their children, and protection for themselves. Beyond this initial phase, however, battered women need to be helped to deal with their feelings of low self-worth, their passivity, and the need to move from a state of emotional, psychological, and economic dependence on the abuser toward a state of personal and psychological empowerment and economic independence. Such goals require a comprehensive counseling strategy that may include attention to divorce and singleness counseling, parenting education, reentry counseling, cognitive restructuring, and career development (Worell, 1980). Ibrahim and Herr (1987) offered a group model of life-career counseling especially designed for battered women. The model includes the following phases: *Inner preparation*—dealing with loss of the relationship; general fears of the world; fear of testing their potential; life skills in the world of work; intensive family involvement—dealing with the needs of children or other remaining family members and with changes in the family system. *Vocational experimentation*—preparing women to enter the world of work; dealing with occupational fantasies; using guided imagery and role play to try on new roles; examining difficulties they might face on the job; providing training in communication and problem-solving skills. *Vocational planning*—focusing on self-appraisal and the choices and options available, applying decision-making skills, and formulating realistic career plans. *Vocational implementation*—providing support during implementation of job choice and induction; dealing with new fears and anxieties; providing stress management skills. *Vocational analysis*—sharing of how implementation plans are going—what was successful and what was not. *Vocational resynthesis*—after 3 to 6 months reevaluating career goals and reassessing or reaffirming career directions. *Vocational development resource*—using the women who have completed the previous stages and are now engaged in work and are disengaged from their previous battering relationship as resource persons, role models, or group leaders for women just beginning the group counseling process.

The model Ibrahim and Herr proposed can be used not only in group contexts but as the content for individual counseling as well. In either case, the individual phases can be elongated or shortened depending on the needs of the women involved. In any case, the insights, activities, information, and support involved must continually focus on strengthening self-esteem, increasing assertiveness, and providing the skills by which the women can achieve economic independence.

Conclusions

Chapter 3 has provided an overview of how the changing American family represents the second major challenge for contemporary and future counselors. There seems little doubt that problems in the family carry residual effects in the communication patterns, feelings of self-esteem or their lack, role differentiation, and other facets of individual development that subsequently are manifested by behavior in the work place, school, or other social arenas.

The factors affecting family structures and the comprehensiveness of the forms they take are diverse. They come from economic sources, cultural traditions, and shifting perspectives on the roles and purposes of families in contemporary American society. As the society has become more specialized in the functions different social institutions play, many of the historical instrumental roles of the family to produce goods, perform services, and propagate and rear children as means of survival and interdependence of the family unit have been diluted and changed. Reasons for the existence of family units have changed from those of survival to those of personal and companionate social relationships. Because the latter occur for many reasons and can be met in many structural forms, family patterns have become more diverse, and the frustrations and stresses of family living have changed as well. Confusion about expectations for families and criteria for their success has created new tensions and discomforts for people within families and those contemplating creating a family.

Both the macroenvironment, the linkage between the family and the larger society, and the microenvironment, the patterns of intimacy, relationships, and communication within the family unit, are the sources of stressors with which members must cope. In some instances, such stressors are economic; in other instances, psychological. In some cases they lead to or are associated with substance abuse, child or spousal abuse, ineffective family relationships, problems with intimacy, family health, or divorce and reconstituted or blended families; in other cases, they suggest a lack of balance in family coping behavior or appropriate social support.

As the multiple stressors affecting families have become more apparent, so have the needs for the provision of counseling and therapy tailored to the unique characteristics of the relationships, coping mechanisms, cohesion, and adaptability of different family types. Such needs have stimulated several major approaches to counseling that emphasize differing theoretical or process dimensions related to family intervention. In addition to approaches that stress working with families as interacting systems, there also are problems that surface within families but require individual counseling, at least at certain developmental points. Depending on the specific circumstances, these might involve single parents having difficulties with intergenerational boundaries and role relationships with their children, children of divorce and separation, individual members of an alcoholic family, or battered women.

Finally, it seems clear that family counseling and therapy are not confined to a specific setting. The stresses and strains associated with family living are of concern to the school counselor, the counselor in the work place, or the counselor in a community agency, in independent practice, or within a religious institution. Family stressors and the ensuing problems will remain a challenge to counselors in all of these settings and across populations of children, youth, and adults.

References

Ackerman, N. (1958). The psychodynamics of family life. New York: Basic Books.

Ahrons, C.R. (1979). The binuclear family: Two households, one family. *Alternative Lifestyles, 2*, 499–515.

Allen, T.W. (1975). "For our next act . . .": An unsystematic prescript to marriage and family counseling; A counseling psychologist's view. *The Counseling Psychologist, 5*(3), 3–15.

Aponte, H. (1982). In M. McGoldrick, J.K. Pearce, & J. Giordano, (Eds.), *Ethnicity and family therapy* (pp. xiii–xiv). New York: Guilford Press.

Avioli, P.S. (1985). The labor-force participation of married mothers of infants. *Journal of Marriage and the Family, 47*, 739–745.

Barnett, E.R., Pittman, C.B., Ragan, C.K. & Salus, M.K. (1980). *Family violence: Intervention strategies.* Washington, DC: U.S. Department of Health and Human Services, Office of Human Development Services.

Bell, A.P., & Weinberg, M.S. (1978). *Homosexualities: A study of diversity among men and women.* New York: Simon & Schuster.

Bell, J.N. (1977). Rescuing the battered wife. *Human Behavior, 10*, 16–23.

Bennett, B., & Reardon, R. (1985). Dual-career couples and the psychological adjustment of offspring: A review. *School Counselor, 32*(4), 287–295.

Borgen, W.A., & Amundson, N.E. (1984). *The Experience of unemployment.* Toronto: Nelson Canada.

Bowen, M. (1978). *Family therapy in clinical practice.* New York: Aronson.

Brenner, M.H. (1973). *Mental health and the economy.* Cambridge: Harvard University Press.

Briere, J. (1984, April). *The effects of childhood sexual abuse on later psychological functioning: Defining a post-sexual-abuse syndrome.* Paper presented at the Third National Conference on Sexual Victimization of Children, Children's Hospital National Medical Center, Washington, DC.

Children's Defense Fund. (1982). *America's children and their families: Key facts.* Washington, DC: Author.

Constantine, L.L., & Constantine, J.M. (1973). Group marriage: A study of contemporary multilateral marriage. New York: Macmillan.

Cook, E.P. (1985). Sex roles and work roles: A balancing process. *Vocational Guidance Quarterly, 33*(3), 213–220.

Duberman, L. (1975). *The reconstituted family: A study of remarried couples and their children.* Chicago, IL: Nelson-Hall.

Education Commission of the States. (1985). Reconnecting youth: The next stage of reform. Denver, CO: Author.

Etaugh, C. (1984). Effects of maternal employment on children: Implications for the family therapist. In S.H. Cramer (Ed.), *Perspectives on work and the family* (Chapter 2). Rockville, MD: Aspen Systems.

Family Service America. (1984). *The state of families, 1984–85*. New York: Author.

Finkelhor, D. (1979). *Sexually victimized children*. New York: Macmillan.

Framo, J. (1976). Family of origin as a therapeutic resource for adults in marital and family therapy: You can and should go home again. *Family Process, 15*, 193–210.

Galambos, N.L., & Garbarino, J. (1983). Identifying the missing links in the study of latchkey children. *Children Today, 12*, 2–4, 40.

Garfield, R. (1980). The decision to remarry. *Journal of Divorce, 4*, 1–10.

Getz, H.G. (1987). Family counseling. In C.W. Humes (Ed.), *Contemporary counseling services, applications, issues* (Chapter 10). Muncie, IN: Acelerated Development.

Gilmartin, B.G. (1977). Swinging: Who gets involved and how? In R.W. Libby & R.N. Whithurst (Eds.), *Marriage and alternatives: Exploring intimate relationships* (pp. 161–185). Glenview, IL: Scott, Foresman.

Glazer-Malbin, N. (1978). Interpersonal relationships and changing perspectives in the family. In H.Z. Lopata (Ed.), *Family factbook* (1st ed.) (pp. 9–24). Chicago, IL: Marquis Academic Media.

Glenwick, D.S., & Mowery, J.D. (1986). When parent becomes peer: Loss of intergenerational boundaries in single parent families. *Family Relations, 35*(1), 57–62.

Glick, P.C. (1984). American household structure in transition. *Family Planning Perspectives, 16*(5), 205–211.

Goode, W.J. (1970). *World revolution and family patterns*. New York: The Free Press, pp. 7–10.

Granrose, C.S. (1985). Anticipating the decision to work following childbirth. *Vocational Guidance Quarterly, 33*(3), 221–230.

Guerin, P. (1976). *Family therapy: Theory and practice*. New York: Gardner Press.

Guerney, B.G., Jr., Vogelsong, E., & Coufal, J. (1983). Relationship enhancement versus a traditional treatment: Follow-up and booster effects. In D.H. Olson & B.C. Miller (Eds.), *Family studies yearbook, Vol. 1* (pp. 738–756). Beverly Hills, CA: Sage.

Guidubaldi, J., & Cleminshaw, H. (1985). Divorce, family health, and child adjustment. *Family Relations, 34*(1), 35–41.

Haley, J. (1976). *Problem-solving therapy*. San Francisco: Jossey-Bass.

Hayes, R.L., & Hayes, B.A. (1986). Remarriage families: Counseling parents, stepparents, and their children. *Counseling and Human Development, 18*(7), 1–8.

Hayghe, H. (1986). Rise in mothers' labor force participation includes those with young children. *Monthly Labor Review, 109*, 43–45.

Herr, E.L., & Best, J. (1984). The family as an influence on career development. In S.H. Cramer (Ed.), *Perspectives on work and the family* (Chapter 1). Rockville, MD: Aspen Systems.

Herr, E.L., & Cramer, S.H. (1988). *Career guidance and counseling through the life span: Systematic approaches*. Glenview, IL: Scott, Foresman.

Hetherington, E.M. (1979). Divorce: A child's perspective. *American Journal of Psychiatry, 34*, 851–858.

Hill, R. (1949). *Families under stress*. New York: Harper & Row.

Hodgson, M.L. (1984). Working mothers: Effects on the marriage and the mother. In S.H. Cramer (Ed.), *Perspectives on work and the family* (Chapter 3). Rockville, MD: Aspen Systems.

Hollis, J.W., & Wantz, R.A. (1983). *Counselor preparation 1983–85; Programs, personnel, trends*. (5th ed.). Muncie, IN: Accelerated Development.

Ibrahim, F., & Herr, E.L. (1987). Battered women: A developmental life-career counseling perspective. *Journal of Counseling and Development, 65*(5), 244–248.

Janoff-Bluman, R., & Frieze, I. (1983). A theoretical perspective for understanding reactions to victimization. *Journal of Social Issues, 39*, 1–17.

Johnson, W.R., & Skinner, J. (1986, June). Labor supply and marital separation. *American Economic Review*, pp. 455–469.

Josephson, G.S., & Fong-Beyette, M. (1987). Factors assisting female clients' disclosure of incest during counseling. *Journal of Counseling and Development, 65*(9), 475–478.

Keith, P.M., & Schaefer, R.B. (1985). Role behavior, relative deprivation and depressions among women in one and two job families. *Family Relations, 34*(2), 227–233.

Knaub, P.K. (1986). Growing up in a dual-career family: The children's perceptions. *Family Relations, 35*(3), 431–437.

Kukla, R.A., & Weingarten, H. (1979). The long-term effects of parental divorce in childhood on adult adjustment. *Journal of Social Issues, 35*, 50–78.

Levine, E.S., & Padilla, A.M. (1980). *Crossing cultures in therapy. Pluralistic counseling for the Hispanic*. Monterey, CA: Brooks/Cole.

Lewis, S., & Cooper, C.L. (1983). The stress of combining occupational roles and parental roles: A review of the literature. *Bulletin of the British Psychological Society, 36*, 341–345.

Liem, R., & Rayman, P. (1980). Health and social costs of unemployment. *American Psychologist, 37*(10), 1116–1123.

Lipman-Blumen, J. (1975). A crisis framework applied to macrosociological family changes. Marriage, divorce, and occupational trends associated with World War II. *Journal of Marriage and the Family, 27*, 889–902.

Long, T.J., & Long, L. (1981). *Latchkey children: The child's view of self-care*. Ann Arbor: University of Michigan. ERIC/CAPS. ERIC Documents. ED 211 229.

Long, T.J., & Long, L. (1983). *Latchkey children*. Ann Arbor: University of Michigan. ERIC/CAPS. ERIC Documents. ED 226 836.

Lopez, F.G. (1987). The impact of parental divorce on college student development. *Journal of Counseling and Development, 65*(9), 484–486.

Louis Harris and Associates, Inc. (1981). *Families at work: Strengths and strains*. General Mills American Family Report, 1980–81. Minneapolis, MN: General Mills.

Macklin, E.D. (1980). Nontraditional family forms: A decade of research. *Journal of Marriage and the Family, 42*(4), 175–192.

Maynard, P.E., & Olson, D.H. (1987). Circumplex model of family systems: A treatment tool in family counseling. *Journal of Counseling and Development, 65*(9), 502–504.

McCubbin, H.I., Joy, C.B., Cauble, A.E., Comeaw, J.K., Patterson, J.M., & Needle, R.M. (1980). Family stress and coping: A decade review. *Journal of Marriage and the Family, 42*(4), 124–141.

McGoldrick, M. (1982). Ethnicity and family therapy: An overview. In M. McGoldrick, J.K. Pearce, & J. Giordano (Eds.), *Ethnicity and family therapy* (pp. 3–30). New York: Guilford Press.

McGoldrick, M., Pearce, J.K., & Giordano, J. (Eds.). (1982). *Ethnicity and family therapy*. New York: Guilford Press.

Meadows, M.E., & Hetrick, H.H. (1982). Roles for counselor education departments in marriage and family counseling: Current status and projections. *Counselor Education and Supervision, 22*, 47–54.

Meyerstein, I. (1981). Family therapy training for paraprofessionals and community mental health centers. *Family Process, 20*(2), 477–493.

Minuchin, S. (1974). *Families and family therapy*. Cambridge, MA: Harvard University Press.

National Center for Health Statistics. (1986, July 18). *Monthly vital statistics report*; *Advance report of final natality statistics, 1984*. Hyattsville, MD: Public Health Service.

National Center for Health Statistics. (1986, September 25). *Monthly vital statistics report*; *Advance report of final divorce statistics, 1984*. Hyattsville, MD: Public Health Service.

National Center for Health Statistics. (1987, June 3). *Monthly vital statistics report*; *Advance report of final marriage statistics, 1984*. Hyattsville, MD: Public Health Service.

O'Neill, N., & O'Neill, G. (1972). *Open marriage: A new life style for couples*. New York: M. Evans.

Okun, B.F., & Gladding, S.T. (Eds.). (1983). *Issues in training marriage and family therapists*. Ann Arbor, MI: ERIC Counseling and Personnel Services Clearinghouse.

Olson, D.H., Russell, C.S., & Sprenkle, D.H. (1980). Marital and family therapy: A decade review. *Journal of Marriage and the Family, 42*(4), 239–259.

Olson, D.H., Sprenkle, D., & Russell, C. (1979). Circumplex model of marital and family systems: Cohesion and adaptability dimensions of family types and clinical applications. *Family Process, 22*, 69–83.

Petty, J.A. (1975). *An investigation of factors which differentiate between types of cohabitation*. Unpublished master's thesis. Indiana University, Bloomington.

Robinson, B.E., Rowland, B.H., & Coleman, M. (1986). Taking action for latchkey children and their families. *Family Relations, 35*(4), 473–478.

Robson, B.E. (1987). Changing family patterns: Developmental impacts on children. *Counseling and Human Development, 19*(6), 1–11.

Ross, E.R., Baker, S.B., & Guerney, B.G., Jr. (1985). Effectiveness of relationship enhancement therapy versus therapists' preferred therapy. *American Journal of Family Therapy, 13*(1), 11–21.

Sanik, M.M., & Mauldin, T. (1986). Single versus two parent families: A comparison of mother's time. *Family Relations, 35*(1), 53–56.

Satir, V. (1964). *Conjoint family therapy*. Palo Alto, CA: Science and Behavior Books.

Selvini, M., Palazzoli, M.S., Boscolo, L., Cecchin, G., & Prata, G. Hypothesizing—circularity–neutrality: Three guidelines for the conductor of the session. *Family Process, 19*, 3–12.

Sgroi, S. (1982). *Handbook of clinical intervention in child sexual abuse.* Lexington, MA: Lexington Books.

Shyne, A.W., & Schroeder, A.G. (1978). *National study of social services to children and their families.* Washington, DC: U.S. Department of Health, Education and Welfare, Children's Bureau.

Straus, M.A., Gelles, R.J., & Steinmetz, S.K. (1980). *Behind closed doors: Violence in the American family.* New York: Anchor Books.

Streib, G.F., & Beck, R.W. (1980). Older families: A decade review. *Journal of Marriage and the Family, 42*(4), 205–224.

Stroman, S.H., & Duff, E. (1982). The latchkey child: Whose responsibility? *Childhood Education, 59*, 76–79.

Studies target teen pregnancy. (1986, March). *Guidepost, 28*(14), 1, 16.

Sundal-Hansen, L.S. (1985). Work-family linkages: Neglected factors in career guidance across cultures. *Vocational Guidance Quarterly, 33*(3), 202–212.

Tedder, S.L., Scherman, A., & Sheridan, K.M. (1984). Impact of group support on adjustment to divorce by single, custodial fathers. *AMHCA Journal, 6*(4), 180–189.

Turkington, C. (1983). Lifetime of fear may be legacy of latchkey children. *APA Monitor, 14*, 19.

U.S. Bureau of the Census. (1981). *Statistical abstract of the United States.* Washington, DC: Superintendent of Documents. U.S. Government Printing Office.

U.S. Commission on Civil Rights. (1978). *Consultation on battered women: Issues of public policy.* Washington, DC: U.S. Government Printing Office.

Veeners, J.E. (1979). Voluntary childlessness: A review of issues and evidence. *Marriage and Family Reviews, 2*, 1–26.

Vincent, J.P. (1980). *Advances in family intervention: Assessment and theory (Vol. 1).* Greenwich, CT: JAI Press.

Visher, E.B., & Visher, J.S. (1982). Stepfamilies in the 1980's. In L. Messinger (Ed.), *Therapy with remarriage families* (pp. 105–119). Rockville, MD: Aspen Systems.

Wachowiak, D., & Bragg, H. (1980). Open marriage and marital adjustment. *Journal of Marriage and the Family, 42*, 57–62.

Walker, L.E. (1979). *The battered woman.* New York: Harper Colophon Books.

Wallerstein, J.S. (1980). The impact of divorce on children. *Psychiatric Clinics of North America, 3*, 455–468.

Wallerstein, J.S. (1984). Children of divorce: Preliminary report of a ten-year follow-up of young children. *American Journal of Orthopsychiatry, 54*, 444–458.

Wasserman, I.M. (1984). A longitudinal analysis of the linkage between suicide, unemployment, and marital dissolution. *Journal of Marriage and the Family, 46*(4), 853–859.

Watzlawick, P., & Weakland, J.H. (Eds.) (1977). *The interactional view.* New York: Norton.

Wegscheider, S. (1981). *Another chance; Hope and health for the alcoholic family.* Palo Alto, CA: Science and Behavior Books.

West, J.D., Hosie, T.W., & Zarski, J.J. (1987). Family dynamics and substance abuse: A preliminary study. *Journal of Counseling and Development, 65*(9), 487–494.

Whitaker, C.A. (1977). Process techniques of family therapy. *Interaction, 1,* 4–19.

Wilson, K.L., Zurcher, L.S., McAdam, D.C., & Curtis, R.L. (1975). Stepfathers and stepchildren: An exploratory analysis from two national surveys. *Journal of Marriage and the Family, 37,* 526–536.

Worell, J. (1980). New directions in counseling women. *Personnel and Guidance Journal, 58,* 477–484.

Zablocki, B. (1977). *Alienation and investment in the urban commune.* New York: Center for Policy Research.

CHAPTER 4

PLURALISM AND CULTURAL DIVERSITY IN THE AMERICAN POPULATION

In an attempt to define the cultural characteristics of the United States, one frequently uses terms like "land of opportunity," "melting pot," "heterogeneity," "equality," "democracy," and "individualism" as images, if not axioms accepted without qualification. These terms frequently have been incorporated into the national psyche as realities, not as ideals or even as sets of assumptions that sometimes may be at odds with other sets of assumptions within the cultural fabric of the nation. The egalitarian premise of the American creed that "all men are created equal" has been translated into the notion that "all people are pretty much alike" (Peabody, 1985, p. vii). Although these two premises do not necessarily follow, treating them as interchangeable permits one to avoid addressing the cultural differences that so obviously are a part of the demographics of the current and emerging American population. In addition, it is possible to rationalize that not acknowledging cultural differences restrains one from practicing stereotypical or discriminatory behavior toward people from different cultural backgrounds. The problem is, of course, that in practice discrimination and stereotyping continue despite official policies intended as egalitarian and democratic. It is for these reasons that Americans now benefit from civil rights legislation, affirmative action policies, and the protection from discrimination in employment, education, or housing because of age, sex, sexual preferences, or racial background.

Cultural diversity and pluralism in traditions and beliefs are not negative aspects of American culture; they represent who we, Americans, are. We are not a group of homogenized people from common stock. We are a land of immigrants who have brought with us to this nation, regardless of when we arrived and under what conditions— assumptions, traditions, world views, and cultural constructions. These carry their residual from the behavioral expectations, group interactions, values, and information-processing mechanisms of the cultural norms in the nations, societies, or tribes that are the ancestral legacies of individual Americans. Even the only nonimmigrant population in the United States, the Native American Indian, was not and is not monolithic in cultural background. The Indian tribes or "nations" that have been in place in this country since before the foreign settlements more than 4 centuries ago differed then as they do now in religious orientations, languages, sex roles, methods of economic and physical survival, and other behavioral norms (Benedict, 1934).

When one overlaps the cultural distinctiveness of Native American groups with the cultural diversity of past and continuing waves of immigrants to the nation from Europe, Africa, Latin America, Asia, and the Middle East, it becomes apparent that the implications of such pluralism must share a larger part of the national agenda in the planning for and the provision of social services, including counseling, in the future.

A major challenge in counseling stems from the fact that for most of its history in the United States, the assumptions and the techniques of counseling have treated cultural differences as unimportant or ignored them (Clark, 1987). Thus, counseling models have treated primarily intracultural phenomena, not intercultural phenomena. In essence, theories and practices have tended to take a universalistic, idiographic, or *etic* view (Sue, 1978) of human behavior rather than acknowledging the cultural distinctiveness of most people in the United States, a primarily *emic* or nomothetic view.

The danger in a predominantly *etic* view of counseling and of behavior is that not acknowledging cultural differences among people that would explain variations in verbal behavior, interpersonal interactions, the work ethic, individualism, or group identity makes it easy to resort to one approved model of behavior. This view assumes the role of counseling to be one of reinforcing this target model and associating any behavioral deviation with a "deficit model." The latter, then, suggests that perspectives or activities different from those in the universalistic, majority, or target model are inferior or abnormal. Such a point may be extended to locating the deficit, abnormality, or inferiority within the individual rather than within the model of normal behavior used, and to giving inadequate attention to how individual-environmental transactions are culturally mediated. Thus, individuals who may be acting quite appropriately within their cultural traditions or within the intergenerational, residual effects of such traditions, may be characterized as behaviorally aberrant if viewed from different cultural perspectives.

A further danger of an *etic* view of counseling is a belief that after an individual has been in a particular culture for several years, previous belief systems and culturally mediated behaviors will have been purged and the individual's behavior will then be guided by the norms of the adopted, current culture. However, cultural heritages are not extinguished easily. McGoldrick, Pearce, and Giordano (1982) in their modern classic, *Family Therapy and Ethnicity*, emphasized in persuasive terms the continuing, intergenerational effects that family background transmits or reinforces. One's orientation to the past, present, and future; how one views and interacts with strangers and people beyond the family boundaries; how one interprets one's obligations and responsibilities to others; how one views work or marriage or child-rearing; what one defines as a problem and an appropriate array of solutions; or how one copes with a cultural identity are all affected by the values of one's ethnic heritage. Such ethnic traditions and their original roots in other nations, cultures, or social structures persist for long periods of time in people's concepts of who they are and the behavioral norms to which they subscribe. These factors shape behavior and they lay a base for the interactions that are likely to occur in a counseling relationship whether it occurs one on one, in a group setting, or within a family therapy context.

The Interaction of Culture and Character

Different cultural traditions and histories give their members particular "world views" or "perceptual windows" on events. As Kluckhohn (1962) suggested a quarter of a century ago, every culture has a structure of expectancies. In essence, cultural differences are differences in the human experience; differences in general conceptions "of the human's place in the universe and of factors that cause human beings to act and interact in the way they do" (Horner & Vandersluis, 1981, p. 33). Culture is "the configuration of learned behavior and results of behavior whose components and elements are shared and transmitted by the members of a particular society'' (Linton, 1945, p. 32). As McDermott (1980a) suggested, ''Somewhere in between the general makeup of human nature and the specific makeup of each individual lie certain qualities that have been acquired and assimilated. They represent culture—the *values, beliefs,* and *ideologies* held by members of the various ethnic groups as fundamental and necessary for effective social function'' (p. 1–2). Cultures are similar to maps or to templates that provide rules of behavior and perceptual cues to their members. These guides shape what members are likely to attend and give meaning to, their views of right and wrong behavior, and their forms of self-perception and self-expression. ''Every culture attempts to create a universe of discourse for its members, a way in which people can interpret their experience and convey it to one another'' (Barnlund, 1975, p. 16).

Cultures attribute meaning to psychological and physical events and in so doing reduce ambiguity and increase predictability for their members. They provide structures or classification mechanisms for sorting and interpreting the constant profusion of signals and messages from the environment every individual experiences each day. Attributions of meaning allow one to respond selectively to environmental stimuli and to structure these stimuli and manage them in preparation for action. Culturally mediated interpretations and predispositions ultimately end up in an individual's cognition as assumptions and symbolic representations of a world that is, in the last analysis, unique to each individual, but in a less specific sense, unique to different cultures.

In a heterogeneous society such as that of the United States, many people are in constant interaction with and possibly in transition between at least two cultures. They must balance values and beliefs commonly shared in the dominant, national culture with those predominant in the subculture or ethnic group of their family of origin. In addition, in a constantly interacting society and one where immigrant populations are introduced constantly and social change occurs rapidly, two processes are always in motion: assimilation and accommodation. Assimilation is the dominant group's incorporation of the values of a new group so that the group fits into the existing social network. Accommodation occurs when a new individual or group adapts to the existing or dominant group values by changing in order to continue to live with the dominant group (McDermott, 1980a, p. 224). Societies differ in how hard or soft boundaries between cultural groups are and the degree to which these boundaries overlap or are sharply defined. In either case, members of a cultural subgroup tend to retain the core of their traditional cultural identity whether it emphasizes ''shame''

(Oriental) or "guilt" (European) as sanctions to promote the behavior expected in a specific cultural group.

According to a number of observers, culture and character are inextricably linked (Bellah, Madsen, Sullivan, Swidler, & Tipton, 1985). This, of course, is not a new perspective. Plato described it. So did Saint Augustine. Some 200 years ago Alexis de Tocqueville (1969) described the mores of the American people, which he occasionally called "habits of the heart," and talked about how the traits of the society—its religious traditions, emphasis on family life, local politics—resulted in a characteristic unique in Western society at the time. For him, that characteristic was individualism. He was the first to describe this trait. He believed that individualism explained how Americans made sense of their lives, how they thought about themselves and their society, and how their ideas related to their actions. It is in this sense that national social metaphors and rhetoric create behavioral expectations; attributions of the power of internal or external events; and expectations of the importance of the state, the group, or the individual as the focus of behavior.

Different cultures use different social sanctions to induce people to adhere to or embrace as their own the predominant beliefs that characterize their nation or group (Riesman, 1961). For example, the propensity of the United States has been to characterize itself as a nation in which individual achievement is unfettered by any cultural constraints and success is purely a function of how hard and how long one works. The belief that "every person can be president" or can rise from poverty to riches if he or she wants to enough and works hard enough gives little credence to the cultural obstacles to be overcome in such a quest. This is the stuff from which dreams come and achievement motivation is manufactured. Whether or not the statistical probabilities of being president, becoming rich, or, indeed, hitting the $10 million lottery are at all reasonable, such presumptions, emanating at the level of the macrosystem, identify individualism and purposeful action as the motive fuel of success. In the process, such a belief downplays the role of restraints in the environment that may impede progress and success. One result of such a context is that it causes some people to engage in self-blame if they fall short of an idealized goal.

Social goals or beliefs differ across countries and groups. Watts (1981), in comparing the evolution of career development in Britain and the United States, reinforced this point. He stated:

> It is intriguing that theories of career development in the U.S.A. have been so heavily dominated by psychologists

whereas in Britain the contributions of sociologists have been much more prominent. The dominant focus in the U.S.A. has been on the actions of individuals, while in Britain indigenous theoretical work has been more preoccupied with the constraints of social structures . . . . The failure of the American social structural evidence to have much influence on career development theory seems to be due basically to cultural and historical factors. From the beginning of its independent existence, the U.S.A. has been formally committed to the proposition that all men are created equal. . . . As a result there is belief that the individual controls his own destiny; that if he has appropriate abilities and if these can be appropriately developed, his fate lies in his own hands. (p. 3)

These perspectives remind us that decision making, the development of self-identity, and life chances do not occur in a vacuum. They occur within political, economic, and social conditions that influence the achievement images and belief systems on which individuals base their actions. They occur within different cultural constructs that reinforce certain types of behavior and try to extinguish others. They occur within different provisions of mechanisms to assist the individual to deal with questions of cultural identity, achievement, illness, and other areas.

Cultural constructions of achievement images and belief systems also vary across time within the same nation. An example of such shifts is particularly apparent in the meanings attributed to work. Maccoby and Terzi (1981) suggested that there have been four major work ethics throughout American history and that elements or residuals of each of these coexist today: the Protestant ethic, the craft ethic, the entrepreneurial ethic, and the career ethic. In addition, they contended that a fifth ethic, that of self-fulfillment, is rapidly emerging as a major motivation to work. The point of such observations is that "each work ethic implies a different social character, different satisfaction and dissatisfaction at work, and a different critique of society" (p. 165).

According to Maccoby and Terzi (1981), the Protestant ethic stimulates a drive to work for the glory of God and for personal salvation and does not tolerate unethical and undisciplined behavior. The craft ethic encourages an orientation to "savings and self-sufficiency, to independence and self-control, and to rewards on earth. The craftsman is most satisfied by work which he controls, with standards he sets" (p. 165). The entrepreneurial ethic promotes risk taking, boldness, the exploitation of opportunities and people, and a dislike of the bureaucracy, red tape, and regulations that stifle free enterprise and personal initiative. The career ethic represents other-directedness, a striving to get ahead and to become more attractive and valuable in the marketplace, and the survival of the fittest rather than seniority and loyalty as the prime requisite of promotion and reward. The emerging ethic of self-fulfillment represents a quest for challenge, growth, and work that is not so consuming that it denies a place for family, community, leisure, and other aspects of life. This profusion of work ethics affirms that both those who are in the process of choosing work and those who are engaged in work represent a pluralism of purpose and motivation.

Yankelovich (1981), too, contended that the United States is now in the throes of a transformation of work values and the work ethic. In his view, the work ethic that predominates in the society is so central to the American culture that if its meaning shifts, the character of the society will shift with it. Thus, Yankelovich uses the term "work ethic" as the term "social metaphor" has been used in this book—as a way people attribute meaning to work, how they internalize that meaning, and how central it becomes to their self-definitions. To illustrate his point Yankelovich compared the American life themes (metaphors) of the 1960s with those of the 1980s. For example, he suggested that four themes dominated the 1960s: "the good provider," "independence," "success," and "self-respect." They conveyed images of the man as the breadwinner, the value of standing on one's own two feet and avoiding dependence on others, the belief that hard work always pays off, and the conviction that a person's inherent worth is reflected in the act of working. The themes that dominate the 1980s include "reduced fear of economic insecurity," "economic division of labor between the sexes," "the psychology of entitlement," "the adversary culture challenges the cult of efficiency," and "the changing meaning of success." These themes are obviously different from those of the 1960s in their implications for individual behavior and for the meanings associated with individual actions. The themes of the 1980s imply that more people take economic security for granted and are willing to take some risks with it for the sake of enhancing the quality of life; that rigid sex roles are diminishing and women are working for purposes other than economic necessity; that a new agenda of social rights is growing whereby a person's wants and desires become a set of presumed rights; that more people are wondering whether too great a concern with efficiency and rationality robs life of excitement and pleasure; and that fewer people are ready to make sacrifices for economic success than was true in the past.

Such beliefs create behavioral expectations, define acceptable boundaries for psychological action, and provide, however subtly, criteria by which people from different cultural traditions judge themselves against a social norm or are judged by others. Such beliefs not only influence views of work but also affect the ways people express mental health symptoms, treat illnesses, raise children, or operate from an internal or external locus of control.

In this context it is important to consider the implications for counseling that result from the changing demographic composition of the American population. The emerging reality of pluralism in ethnicity and racial characteristics, regional value differences, and the diversity in life styles in different populations are all challenges to conventional counseling approaches. With this in mind, the importance of cross-cultural counseling, bilingualism, and notions of abnormality versus cultural distinctiveness will be considered.

Before turning to a consideration of counseling per se, and particularly models of cross-cultural counseling, it is useful to consider further how the demographics of the American population relate to cultural characteristics and then to consider the likely effects of cultural diversity.

The Emerging Cultural Demographics of the American Population

The United States is a nation of immigrants. Unlike in many other parts of the world, the White population has been in the majority and people of color have constituted the minority cultures. Obviously, that is not true in all parts of the nation. Some cities and states are populated primarily by persons of color and this is increasingly the case in other parts of the nation. Certain parts of the country house enclaves of ethnic populations who continue to speak the language they brought to this nation and to celebrate the traditions and rituals of major cultural importance to them.

The U.S. population is now composed of people from some 100 ethnic groups, about 50 of which have sizable populations. The first of the two most rapidly growing ethnic groups is Spanish-speaking Americans, who number more than 15 million people, or more than 6.5% of the American population. Included among the Hispanic or Latino populations are major concentrations of people from Mexico,

Puerto Rico, Cuba, Guatemala, San Salvador, Columbia, and other Central and South American countries. Today, the United States has the fourth largest Spanish-speaking population in the world. The Mexican population of Los Angeles is second only in size to Mexico City. The population of Miami is about two-thirds Cuban in origin (Naisbitt, 1984, p. 274). Given the unnumbered additional Spanish-speakers who are immigrant workers or who do not have official resident status in the United States but enter the country on a periodic basis to work in the agricultural and food service industries, the estimates of the number of Spanish-speaking people and the resulting implications for the social services, schools, and other social institutions are undoubtedly understated.

Both the rate of immigration to the United States and the fertility rate of Hispanic families (twice that of Whites; 60% higher than that of Blacks) have led demographers to estimate that the Hispanic population will exceed the Black population in numbers in about the first decade of the next century (Oxford Analytica, 1986, p. 37). Both populations are likely to number about 33 million at that time out of a total population of about 280 million. The Hispanic immigration to the United States, both through legal and illegal avenues, will contribute most of the U.S. population growth into the next century. Indeed, the level of Hispanic immigration exceeds that of the peak migration to this nation before the First World War. In general, most Hispanic immigrants are poor and ill educated by U.S. standards (Oxford Analytica, 1986, p. 38). Therefore, they tend to enter low-paying jobs that others in the work force shun. This situation perpetuates double employment ladders or possibility structures for Whites and Hispanics in many parts of the United States, particularly in California and other parts of the Southwest. As population growth continues among Hispanic Americans, so will their political power in many parts of the United States. The current tensions in states such as Florida that are trying formally to acknowledge that English is the official language will continue as Hispanic growth changes political patterns. Pressures to more effectively recognize language and cultural rights, improve employment opportunities, and change foreign policy relationships between the United States and the Latin American and Caribbean nations will influence these political patterns.

Several factors have combined to keep Hispanic immigrants separate from other population groups and have slowed their assimilation into the majority culture. These are: the Hispanic population's tendency to continue to use Spanish as the dominant language in the family and, frequently, in the work place; the continuing commitment to Hispanic culture and history within self-sufficient Spanish-speaking communities; the influence on individual and family behavior of Latin-American Catholicism; the historical importance of male dominance; and low levels of intermarriage (Oxford Analytica, 1986, pp. 39–40).

The second most rapidly growing ethnic group in the United States is Asian Americans. They compose about 3.5 million, or about 1.5%, of the U.S. population (Naisbitt, 1984, p. 275). Since 1975, however, about 700,000 refugees have come from Southeast Asia, primarily from Cambodia, Laos, and Vietnam. This large influx of refugees and immigrants is changing the demographics of Asian Americans and challenging findings previously reported on stable Asian-American populations (Sue & Sue, 1987). The Asian-American population is now composed of more than 29 distinct subgroups who differ in language, religion, and customs (Yoshioka, Tashima, Chew, & Murase, 1981). Unlike Hispanic immigrants who have tended to be absorbed into existing Spanish-speaking communities in the Southwest, South, Southeast, and Northeast, the refugees from Southeast Asia have been dispersed under various government programs to places where "unemployment, social isolation, family estrangement, a new language, racial tension, and other barriers to their leading a normal life are commonplace" (Owan, 1985, p. v). Sixty percent of Asian Americans are foreign born, yet the average Japanese American speaks English as his or her native language, whereas almost no Indochinese do (Hodgkinson, 1985).

Because of the traumatic events in Southeast Asia that precipitated refugee status in the United States, there is a high prevalence of chronic depression and chronic psychosocial maladjustment among the refugees. "It is associated with a variety of problems, including unemployment, illiteracy, cultural isolation, loss of religious practice and personal meaning in life, ignorance of American society, widowhood or singlehood, solo parenting, a generation gap, untreated major depression, and similar psychiatric and psychosocial ills" (Westermeyer, 1985, p. 87). These refugees, like other immigrants who have permanently left their homelands, are likely to experience the feelings of loss of a cultural identity, which have been found to be similar to those described by Kübler-Ross (1969) of people undergoing the bereavement and grief associated with the loss of a loved one (Sardi, 1982).

Southeast-Asian refugees are only a part of the growing Asian-American population. Asian Americans in the past have been divided among those of predominantly Chinese, Japanese, Phillipine, or Korean ancestry. Each of these Asian-American subgroups can be differentiated by language, religious background, family interaction patterns, and other characteristics that distinguish them from each other, Whites, and other minority groups, and there is considerable variance in these characteristics within each subgroup.

Along with the rapid rise of Hispanic and Asian-American populations, there are two more major growing minority groups in the United States. The third minority group that is growing in size but is not as large nor as visible as the Hispanic American or Asian American group is the Native American or American Indian population. Now numbering about 1.4 million people, or about 0.6% of the total American population (Oxford Analytica, 1986, p. 35), Native Americans are distributed among some 20 major tribal groups and are dispersed on reservations as well as within the majority culture of the Southeast, South, Southwest, North Central, and Northwestern parts of the nation. Native American populations, like other populations, vary in language, religious traditions, culture, and patterns of interpersonal interaction. Intermarriage with other minority populations or with Whites is limited, and the historical reality of the "Indian reservations" as separate enclaves has kept many Native Americans totally separated by language and geography from the majority culture or even other minority cultures. The resulting social isolation, rejection, and lack of opportunities have frequently been associated with unemployment, chemical dependency, suicide, and serious mental health problems. The answer to these problems is not necessarily assimilation into the dominant culture, which some Native Americans would not wish, but rather greater support from the government or the private sector to help create reservation economies by which Native Americans could find identity, opportunity, and purpose while respecting their cultural heritage.

The fourth and largest minority population is the Black-American or Afro-American population. According to the 1980 census, 26.5 million Blacks compose about 11.7% of the American population (up from 11.1% in 1970) (Oxford Analytica, p. 35). Like the other major minority groups, although Blacks are dispersed across the nation, they also are concentrated more heavily in some areas of the nation than in others. For example, "in the Northeast, for every 100 persons of Hispanic origin, there are 210 Blacks; in the Northcentral states, 590; in the South, 370. But in the West Hispanics outnumber Blacks by 50 percent" (Oxford Analytica, 1986, p. 35). It is projected that by the year 2000 the nation's Black population will total 35 million and be concentrated in five states: New York, California, Texas, Florida, and Georgia. Of major consequence to the identity of many Black Americans is their experience of a history of intense racial and ethnic prejudice and discrimination. They also have experienced unemployment, underemployment, single parenthood, physical health problems, and stress-related diseases in higher proportions than have most other populations in the United States. One third of Black Americans in the United States live below the poverty line.

As minority groups increase in number and in proportion to the total American population, the practical effect is a lessening of any historical propensity that encourages uniformity and an increasing credence to the notion that the concept of a ''melting pot'' must give way to a celebration of cultural diversity or at least a responsiveness to it. It is also becoming clear that a simplistic notion of majority and minority cultures no longer captures the reality of cultural interaction. The historic problems of Whites and Blacks in an either-or adversarial situation leading to discrimination and other problems become diffused and more complex. There are tensions among minority groups as well as between minority group members and Whites. As the number of non-English speaking minority groups grows, at least of groups where English is not the first language, bilingualism among Whites becomes prized and spurs many Whites to search for their own roots in a growing awareness that White society is itself culturally heterogeneous.

Regional Diversity

Counselors obviously have played and will play many roles in facilitating awareness of and effective responses to cultural differences among people. Those differences are likely to be more pronounced and of varying content from one part of the country to another. Specific counselor responses will be examined later, but it is useful to recognize that the growing differences from region to region of the United States are likely to have implications in their own right for the training and professional interventions of counselors. These differences may require individual counselors to specialize in the treatment of clients from specific ethnic groups; the cultural differences among minority groups will make it difficult for any given counselor to be sufficiently sensitive to and knowledgeable about the cultural characteristics of all groups. Indeed, the growing cultural diversity may require the rise of group practices of counselors who have expertise in dealing with different ethnic populations, or the collaboration of translators or interpreters in working with the counselor and client who do not share the same language or cultural history. It may ultimately require a renewed attention to the importance of indigenous paraprofessional counselors who can provide direct services to selected minority clients under the supervision of professional counselors. The continuing argument that only Blacks should counsel Blacks, homosexuals should counsel homosexuals, and women should counsel women will need to be tested comprehensively to either validate or reject it. But even if such a concept is found to be invalid for all minority or culturally different groups, training more bilingual and minority counselors should be a national priority for the foreseeable future.

Statistics depicting concentrations of different minority groups in different regions of the country are too general to be useful, but they do serve to reinforce the notion that counselors in different parts of the nation are likely to have more opportunity, if not the explicit need, to work with clients of specific cultural backgrounds. Although minority group members may be small in numbers compared to the majority group, they tend to be clustered in ways that magnify the importance of their numbers dramatically. Cluster groupings occur by city and by state. For example, "the cities of greatest Spanish influence in America are Los Angeles, New York, Miami, Chicago, and San Antonio; the states are California, with 4.5 million Spanish speakers, Texas, with 3 million, New Mexico, with 476,000, Arizona, with 441,000, and Colorado, with 340,000" (Naisbitt, 1984, p. 277). Certainly, the influence of Black Americans is dominant in such major cities as Washington, DC, Detroit, Atlanta, Philadelphia, and Chicago. By region, Black Americans vary from constituting 25% of the population in the South Atlantic states, including more than 33% of the population of the state of Mississippi and almost 70% of the population of the District of Columbia, to approximately 2% in Vermont and roughly 3% in Maine, Montana, Idaho, and the Dakotas. Native Americans, a much smaller population group overall, vary in concentration, for example, from less than .2 of 1% in Vermont to 6% of the population in Oklahoma, Arizona, and New Mexico. Asian Americans vary from constituting 5% of the population in California to .3 of 1% in Maine. Hispanic Americans vary from constituting approximately 30% of the population in New Mexico, 20% in California and Texas to .5 of 1% in North Dakota and .7 of 1% in Minnesota (U.S. Census Bureau, 1980).

If one assumes that the mix of cultures is different from one ethnic or religious group to another, then in general it is possible to hypothesize that there are regional variations in values, work ethics, religious beliefs, and other characteristics of greater or lesser importance to different population groups. Where greater heterogeneity of cultural groups exists or where major concentrations of certain ethnic populations are clustered, the "world view" or social metaphors on which people operate are likely to be different.

Garreau's fascinating book, *The Nine Nations of North America* (1981) suggests this reality. He has formulated a view that the North American continent and its offshore islands can be divided into nine different regions or "nations within a nation," not on the basis of political boundaries, but on the basis of variations in culture, history, problems, resources, opportunities, and people. Garreau, in drawing his map of these nine hypothetical nations, acknowledges that when one looks at the United States or North America in total it is almost impossible to understand the nine boundaries, but when one factors in conditions such as energy resources, unemployment, inflation, water policy, and the characteristics and traditions of the people who have migrated to and now occupy the different regions, one finds that events, issues, policies, and concerns are perceived and valued differently from one of the nine regions to another. Terms like self-sufficiency, pride, teamwork, achievement, freedom, self-reliance, or duty conjure up different meanings in the high plains of Montana and the streets of New York City or Miami.

In psychological terms, regional differences may be useful to help understand not only "where a person is from," but "where a person is coming from"! If one's identity is shaped by one's origins, regional differences help clarify why people born and raised in this vast nation understand and label events and processes differently and behave differently. Such an affirmation does not imply the absence of common values shared by Americans, but rather that whereas such shared values exist, it is also possible to hold separate values and "see or make interpretations" that are not the same for all Americans. Trying to understand the origins of such perceptual sets across ethnic, racial, and sex groups is at the heart of cross-cultural counseling. Indeed, the viability and the validity of cross-cultural psychology rest upon the belief that "members of various cultural groups have different experiences that lead to predictable and significant differences in behavior" (Brislin, Lonner, & Thorndike, 1973). Regional diversity, and the ensuing effects upon individual behavior, is a new and relatively untapped lens on such phenomena.

Garreau's view of the nine nations of North America is captured as follows:

> Consider, instead, the way North America really works. It is Nine Nations. Each has its capital and its distinctive web of power and influence. A few are allies, but many are adversaries. Several have readily acknowledged national poets, and many have characteristic dialects and mannerisms. Some are close to being raw frontiers; others have four centuries of history. Each has a peculiar economy; each commands a certain emotional allegiance from its citizens. These nations look different, feel different, and sound different from each

other, and few of their boundaries match the political lines drawn on current maps. Some are clearly divided topographically by mountains, deserts, and rivers. Others are separated by architecture, music, language, and ways of making a living. Each nation has its own list of desires. Each nation knows how it plans to get what it needs from whoever's got it. Most important, each nation has a distinct prism through which it views the world. (Garreau, 1981, p. 112)

The nine nations Garreau suggests include the following configurations of names and of places within them:

- *New England*. Bounded by New Haven, Conn., on the south and Burlington, Vt., and Albany, N.Y., on the west, it includes Boston, Mass., New Hampshire, and Maine as well as Nova Scotia, the Maritime Provinces of Canada, Prince Edward Island, Labrador, and Newfoundland.

- *The Foundry*. Bounded on the west by Milwaukee, Wis., Chicago, Ill., and Indianapolis, Ind.; in the south by Cincinnati, Ohio, and Washington, D.C.; in the north by Green Bay, Wis., and Sudbury and Ottawa, Canada; and on the east by Albany, N.Y., and New Haven and Bridgeport, Conn., it includes Pittsburgh, New York City, Columbus, Ohio, and Wheeling, W.Va.

- *Dixie*. Includes the area south of Indianapolis, Ind., Cincinnati, Ohio, and Washington, D.C.; east of St. Louis, Mo., and Fort Worth, Dallas, and Houston, Tex.; and north of Fort Myers, Fla. Included are New Orleans, La., Tampa, Fla., Atlanta, Ga., Charleston, W.Va., Louisville, Ky., and Raleigh, N.C.

- *The Islands*. Miami is the capital of this region, which includes southern Florida, Cuba, Puerto Rico, Jamaica, Haiti, the Dominican Republic, and all islands south to and including Venezuela and Columbia.

- *Mex America*. Bounded on the north by Sacramento, Calif.; on the west by Los Angeles; on the south by Austin and Houston, Tex.; and on the east by Houston, Tex., it includes Phoenix, Ariz., Albuquerque, N.Mex., Tijuana and Chihuahua, Mexico, and San Antonio, Tex.

- *Ecotopia*. This region is bounded on the south by San Francisco, Calif., and follows the Pacific Coast in a thin strip through Seattle, Wash., Vancouver, Br. Col., and Juneau, Alaska, and is bounded on the north by Anchorage, Alaska.

- *The Empty Quarter*. This region is bounded on the south by Las Vegas, Nev., on the east by Denver, Colo., and proceeds north through Salt Lake City, Utah, Boise, Idaho, and Spokane, Wash., to Fairbanks and Barrow, Alaska. It includes the vast plains in Canada in which Edmonton, Alberta, is located.

- *The Breadbasket*. This region is bounded on the south by Houston and Austin, Tex.; on the west by Denver, Colo.; on the north by Regina and Winnipeg, Canada; and on the east by Dallas and Fort Worth, Tex., Tulsa, Okla., St. Louis, Mo., Indianapolis, Ind., Chicago, Ill., and Sudbury, Canada.

- *Quebec*. This region is located entirely in Canada. It begins on the south at Ottawa and Sherbrooke and continues north and east until it is bounded by the Empty Quarter on the west and New England on the east.

Whether or not the reader feels comfortable with the names of each of these regions, they will probably stimulate images, sensations, and perspectives that will help clarify the differences they symbolize and the perceptual lenses or prisms through which their inhabitants view the world. The point is that each of these regions attracts different kinds of inhabitants, social arrangements, power, money, expertise, opportunities, and cultures. These become part of the psychology, the cognitions, and the values of the people who grow up and live in these locations.

Socioeconomic Diversity

Before discussing some of the specific meanings that cultural, if not regional, differences hold for people, it is useful to consider a different form of culture from that which rests with ethnicity, race, sex, or national ancestry—namely the cultural differences that emanate from economic circumstances and social class. Rich and poor people may both be White, but it is unlikely that the fact that they share ancestral roots in England or Scandinavia allows them to view the world or its opportunities in the same ways. Poor people are not rich people without money. Their values, risk taking, sense of self, sense of power, and focus on the past, present, and future are all conditioned by the environment in which they find themselves. Mitchell (1983), as a function of work at the Stanford Research Institute, described nine American life styles that characterize the American people.

The resulting typology was derived from national sampling in the United States and has been applied to the population of a number of other nations to examine the differences in the proportions of people in the life-style emphasis in each nation and the variance such differences create in elements of national character. The VALS typology is composed of four comprehensive groups that can be divided into nine life styles, each defined by its distinctive array of values, drives, beliefs, needs, dreams, and special points of view (Mitchell, 1983, p. 4). The four groups and nine life styles are described as the need-driven group—survivor life style, sustainer life style; the outer-directed group—belonger life style, emulator life style, achiever life style; inner-directed group—I-am-me life style, experiential life style, societally conscious life style; and combined outer- and inner-directed group—integrated life style.

In succinct terms, the need-driven groups are struggling to meet their basic needs. The survivor subgroup constitutes about 4% of the United States population. Its members are very poor, typically elderly, poorly educated, lacking in self-confidence, depressed, and essentially unable to take advantage of the work opportunities that might help them improve their position. The other need-driven group, the sustainers, are likely to be somewhat better off financially but still live on the edge of poverty and frequently engage in the underground economy rather than the secondary or primary labor markets. They tend to be angry, resentful, and rebellious. About one-fourth of this group are looking for work or work only part-time. Few of these people get much satisfaction from their work, primarily in machine, manual, and service occupations. People in this life-style category make up about 7% of the United States population. Although these people have not given up hope and seek financial security and economic improvement (many are hardworking and ambitious), they frequently have a difficult time finding opportunities because they are often immigrants without good English skills, minority persons with poor educational backgrounds, or single parents on welfare or with marginal incomes.

The outer-directed group include about two thirds of the American adult population. Belongers are the biggest group in this typology, about 35% of the population; emulators make up about 9%; and achievers, 22%. In a collective sense these are the people who dream the American dream, and many within their typology also live it. As the name of the typology implies, outer-directed people pay considerable attention to what others think, to what the media say is important, to the visible, tangible, and materialistic aspects of life. By life-style group, the research of Mitchell and his colleagues suggests that the belongers are likely to be highly patriotic, conventional, happy, aging, and quite traditional members of the middle class. They want to fit in, not to stand out. They follow the rules and cherish their family, church, and job. They need acceptance and are dependent and conformist to get it. They tend to live in small towns and rural areas, not large cities. The second life-style group in this typology, the emulators, tend to be younger than the belongers and much more intense in their striving to be like those who are richer and more successful than they are. They are hardworking, ambitious, and competitive. They are not likely to have completed college, although they may have attended college one or two years or graduated from technical school. Thus, they are not likely to achieve the highest levels of professional, technical, or administrative occupations for which they strive, although, of course, some do. Many, however, experience rejection and feel that the system has been unfair and that their primary ambitions have been frustrated. Frequently this results from a mismatch between their goals and their abilities or preparation. They, nevertheless, ask much of themselves and of the system, and they often take great responsibility to achieve success. The achievers, on the other hand, are the members of the outer-directed group who have made it. They are the people the emulators hope to be. They are typically gifted, hardworking, self-reliant, successful, and happy. They usually live a comfortable and affluent outer-directed life. They are generally middle-aged, self-assured, and prosperous leaders and builders of what is considered the American dream. Very few of these people are members of minority groups; for example, approximately 2% are Black. Many of the achievers have attended college and graduate school. They are often self-made successes, and are politically and socially conservative.

The inner-directed typology includes the I-am-me life style that characterizes about 5% of the adult population and the experiential group that constitutes about 7% of the population. As contrasted with the outer-directed group, the inner-directed group members are oriented to how they feel internally about different aspects of their life as compared to what other people or external systems suggest that they should feel. Thus, their attitudes toward their job, personal relationships, spiritual matters, and other daily satisfactions become preeminent to them. Many of these people are active in social movements. They are less driven by money and social status than are members of other groups. They tend to have excellent educations and frequently hold good jobs of a professional or technical nature. Inner-directed people are likely to have been raised in relatively prosperous, outer-directed families where they were relatively satisfied with material comforts and no longer feel driven to acquire them as a sole raison d'être.

Within the inner-directed typology, the I-am-me and the experiential life-style group members tend to differ in some ways. Although both are likely to be younger than the outer-directed group, the I-am-me group members tend to be in a turbulent stage of transition from outer-directed values and characteristics to those that dominate the inner-directed classification; there is considerable anxiety as they give up what have been secure and comfortable lives for more uncertain, contradictory situations. These are people in the throes of seeking out new life styles, new ways of life, new personal identities. They are, on balance, energetic and active participants in whatever they undertake. In some contrast to the I-am-me group are the slightly older inner-directed groups of experientials. For this latter group, action and interaction and direct, vivid experience with people, ideas, and events is their driving force. These people tend to be independent, self-reliant, excellently educated, and hold high-level technical and professional positions. They are concerned with quality-of-life issues, natural rather than artificial products, spirituality, and skepticism. They are participative, self-assured, interested in personal growth and learning, and socially sensitive. The last life style within the inner-directed typology is the societally conscious. This is the inner-directed group whose members have attained positions of influence and status and do not need to display them or be driven by economic motivations. They tend to be people of excellent education, liberal politics, and affluence who hold professional or technical jobs. A generally self-confident and independent group, they tend to believe that the economic and social systems of the country need an overhaul, and they try to make such changes by participating in the ''system'' and having their say. They are likely to be conservationists and ecologists who prefer simple living and frugality rather than ostentatiousness.

The final life-style typology is the combined outer- and inner-directed group, those who Mitchell's research suggests are the integrated types. These people, estimated to make up 2% of the population, combine outer-directed and inner-directed styles into an integrated outlook on life. They tend to adapt easily to existing norms and mores and have a fully developed sense of what is fitting and appropriate. They find ways to balance work and play, to combine close relationships with people with the motivation to accomplish. These people are likely to be middle-aged and above, very well educated, and working in very well-paid occupations in which they can either lead or follow when action is required.

The research of Mitchell and his colleagues indicates that groups with different life styles or values view life, work, and social interactions through lenses that vary with regard to their security-insecurity, self-concept, expectations of life, freedom of choices, and related phenomena. These ''windows on life'' are associated with different behaviors, motive systems, and expectations in all facets of life. People of different social classes or levels of affluence essentially "march to different drumbeats." The social stratum they occupy is likely to be directly related to the type and comprehensiveness of information they receive and the levels of reinforcement of certain types of behavior directed to them by the dominant culture or by people of other social classes.

Social class, like ethnic and racial characterization, functions as "a boundary mechanism operating to regulate family relationships, friendship networks, courting, recreational patterns, usage of language, expectations, and, of course, opportunities" (Johnson, 1981, p. 79). The breadth of the individual's culture or social class boundaries has much to do with the choices that can be considered, made, and implemented. As Moynihan (1964) pointed out, the circumstances in which poverty flourishes produce a distinctive milieu that conditions the social responses, educational attainment, vocational ambition, and general intellectual level of the overwhelming majority of those raised within it. As stated earlier, poor people are not simply rich people without money. Their life space, possibility structures, levels and types of reinforcement, models, information availability, and social resources all differ as a function of their social status (Herr & Cramer, 1988). Within this "culture of poverty," poverty itself becomes a great crippler of the career and personal development of many people (Lee, 1988).

Kleinman (1988), synthesizing a large volume of research on social relations, cultural meanings, and mental illness stated quite directly that "human misery of all kinds is greater among the poor, the oppressed, the helpless. . . . Most disorders—including a wide range of medical disorders—have their highest prevalence rate among the poor and disadvantaged. . . . In this sense, they can also be viewed as socially caused forms of human misery, which physicians euphemistically gloss over as life problems" (p. 61).

In many ways, the development of individuals is like the development of nations. Throughout the past 30 years, it has become conventional wisdom to classify nations as the most developed, developing, and the least developed. Such a scheme suggests a linear relationship between a nation's level of industrialism and the levels of affluence or life chances its people experience. Although it is a useful scheme for some sorts of classification, this notion obscures the view that within nations, one can identify individuals and groups of individuals who could be described as the most developed, developing, and the least developed. Such differences exist even in the most affluent countries of the world, such as the United States, where groups and individuals are more or less advantaged depending upon the resources they have available, their social support systems, knowledge and basic academic skills, command of the dominant language, and understanding of the cultural norms that govern the society. Where a given individual is located on such a continuum suggests how the person's behavior and "vision" of the world will be narrowed or broadened based upon the personal needs that are dominant. However much one wishes to pursue opportunities for affiliations or information, if one has to struggle to survive physically, it is these basic survival needs that govern one's behavior.

It was Maslow's (1954) early work in personality theory that helped counselors understand that one can view individual basic needs in a "hierarchy of prepotency." The prepotent needs are the more demanding of attention by the individual, more insistent than the other needs further up the hierarchy. Until the more primitive needs are relatively satisfied, the other needs are not likely to dominate or motivate behavior. As originally arranged by Maslow in the order of potency, the most demanding first, the basic needs are as follows:

1. The physiological needs;
2. The safety needs;
3. The need for belongingness and love;
4. The need for importance, respect, self-esteem, independence;
5. The need for information;
6. The need for understanding;
7. The need for beauty; and
8. The need for self-actualization.

In general terms, motivation of behavior directed to meeting the needs at the higher levels rests upon being able to take the lower and more basic survival needs for granted. It is difficult to be motivated by a need for beauty if one is starving. Nor is one likely to be principally motivated by a need for affiliation and good interpersonal conditions if one's basic security is constantly under threat. Thus, cross-cultural counseling has to be aware of ethnic and racial differences at one level but, certainly as well, the socioeconomic level and the assurance that one is able to meet one's basic needs or is, instead, preoccupied by a category of needs beyond which the individual seems unable to move. What one attends to in one's environment and the value attached to it is likely to be associated with culture and with affluence, with advantage and with disadvantage. Although these factors may be relative in their effect across groups in any population, a given individual may experience them as absolutes: "I am poverty-stricken," "I am hopeless," "I am unloved," "I am unable to find shelter or food," "I am alienated." Such perceptions are extremely powerful in organizing and stimulating one's behavior. In what has been described as the "culture of poverty," occupied by generations of welfare recipients as well as by many women with teenage pregnancies, people with a lack of power and hope, people of poor education and basic academic skills, and people exposed to racism and cultural prejudices are likely to experience these conditions as important barriers to growth and mobility. These people tend to be locked into a permanent underclass in which the limits on the level and range of opportunities are restricted. Factors such as poverty, poor education, and racism combine to affect negatively the self-concept, ambition, motivation, self-efficacy, and the energy or the perceived utility of engaging in long-range, future planning (Lee, 1988).

How one experiences one's basic needs, their prepotency, and their gratification also may be a function of one's cultural heritage. In the next section some elements of cultural diversity will be explored.

Perspectives on Cultural Diversity

To return to the basic issue of the existence of cultural diversity is to become more precise about the differences in such cultural diversity and the effects upon behavior that result. As Roe (1956) suggested, "Although behavior is almost always motivated, it is also always biologically, culturally, and situationally determined as well" (p. 25). Such cultural and situational determinants take many forms: universal, ecological, national, regional, local, and racio-ethnic (Vontress, 1986).

A major question is whether ethnic groups have separate and distinct cultures. On the basis of face validity as well as other more empirical data, it seems clear that Spanish-speaking and Asian Americans do have distinctive cultures. Increasing attention to perspectives on Afrocentrism as the cultural element important to Black Americans is providing perspective on how Black Americans are influenced by cultural attributes different from those of White Americans.

A concept helpful to understanding differences among ethnic and other culturally different groups is the notion of subjective culture. Jones and Thorne (1987) suggested that "subjective culture is a group's characteristic way of perceiving its social environment. People who live near one another, speak the same dialect, and engage in similar activities are likely to share the same subjective culture" (p. 490).

Obviously, there is within-group variability among people in a subjective culture based upon such factors as socioeconomic and educational level. It is also true that the intensity of interaction among subjective cultures is likely to transform them. In the process, some distinctive ethnic characteristics may persist whereas others may disappear. But, it is likely that ethnic cultural distinctiveness can be found to some degree within each cultural grouping or subjective culture. It may appear in individual self-concepts, a defensive use of ethnic identity, social alienation, feelings of powerlessness or lack of social control, or in commitment to an internal or external locus of control. And, such perspectives are likely to differ depending upon how recently an individual has arrived in the United States, the level of contact with the community of origin or immersion in a cultural enclave, the level of education, and other factors (Munoz, 1982).

Cultural effects apparently occur not only at the level of an ethnic community or subjective culture but in national terms as well. Peabody (1985) has recently summarized his research in a book describing national psychological characteristics. His research compares psychological characteristics among the English, Germans, French, Italians, Russians, Americans, Northern and Southern Europeans, Swiss, Swedes, Irish, Finns, Dutch, Southern and Eastern Europeans, Austrians, Greeks, Turks, Czechs, Hungarians, Spanish, and the Phillipines. He also summarized other major works that examine intercultural diversity across national groups. On balance, his work suggests that when national psychological characteristics are compared, there are partial differences rather than complete differences among groups. Some behavioral manifestations tend to overlap across nations whereas others are quite distinct. Another tenet of his study is that national characteristics are created by historical developments and therefore they can and do change over time. Some national psychological characteristics change rapidly under the onslaught of technology, for example, or occupation by foreign troops, whereas other national character changes are much more subtle and gradual.

If, then, there are national differences in psychological characteristics, what are they and how can they be described? In essence, what traditions and belief systems are immigrants to this nation likely to bring with them from their nations of origin? What cultural concepts are likely to endure across generations among families from selected national origins?

Peabody and his research colleagues in the several nations with which his study was concerned used scales composed of trait adjectives to differentiate national groups on the basis of such major behavioral sets as tight versus loose control over impulse expression and self-assertiveness versus unassertiveness. The varieties of trait adjectives composing the 14 scales used in his study assessed both descriptive and evaluative dimensions of national character. Pairs of adjectives such as thrifty-extravagant, inflexible-flexible, inhibited-spontaneous, cooperative-uncooperative, cautious-rash, opportunistic-idealistic, and peaceful-aggressive are exemplars of the substance that alternately went into factor loadings and studies of variance among native and out-of-country observers. Specific research results suggested that judgments, especially judgments by outgroups, tend to exaggerate the homogeneity within a group; outgroup judgments tend to be more polarized and ingroup judgments less polarized. Similarly, judgments may exaggerate the descriptive consistency between different characteristics. Outgroup judgments tend to show more descriptive consistency, and ingroup judgments less. Ingroup judgments may be based on conscious experience; outgroup judgments are more dependent on manifest behavior.

Perhaps the most striking result of the Peabody (1985) study is the finding that psychological characteristics of the national groups that were the targets of the investigation are distinguishable and consistent (p. 57). Space and purpose here do not permit an analysis of the specific psychological characterisics found in each of the national groups or their similarities or contrasts with those in other groups. Suffice it to say that the national groups tended to have comparative differences on the basis of: (1) social relationships, (2) social rules, (3) control of hostility, (4) impulse control, and (5) authority and hierarchical relations. Clearly, the variations in how each of these differences is reinforced and portrayed in a particular nation are internalized by many, if not most, of the individuals in that national group. Thus, modal behavior for one national group is likely to be different from that for other groups. Indeed, the rules for interaction or action in a situation are largely cultural with respect to private and public relationships, the formality of communications, and the intimacy or spontaneity by which such relationships are conducted (p. 31).

In a more limited but equally interesting comparison of American and Japanese cultures, Barnlund (1975) found, for example, that the proportion of the self that is shared with others, the public self, and that which is not shared with others, the private self, differs in these two countries. In the analyses by several instruments designed to probe the communication patterns of the Japanese and Americans, the cultural profiles that the Japanese attributed to themselves included such descriptions as "formal," "reserved," "cautious," "evasive," and "silent." Americans described themselves and were described as "frank," "self-assertive," "spontaneous," "informal," and "talkative." People in the two nations were found to differ in the topics discussed in ordinary conversation, the people with whom they were discussed, and the level of disclosure in face-to-face communication. "The Japanese rarely reported talking in more than general terms on any topic to any person. Americans, on the other hand, disclosed on all topics to all persons at deeper levels" (p. 143). The two national cultures also differ in what they view as essential for personal growth and development. Americans view the need for interpersonal interactions and deep verbal involvement as essential prerequisites to expanding maturity and developing a productive personality. The Japanese in Barnlund's study view silence as essential as speech in the cultivation of personality. "Meditation and contemplation are respected not because they imprison the mind, but because they free it. . . . Those who continually give out, who can always provide some statement, can have little energy left for taking in, for noticing or assimilating the world outside themselves" (p. 151).

Barnlund (1975) contended:

> Every society creates some entity or unit that serves as a psychological center of the universe for its members, the ultimate source of meaning and the locus for the interpretation of events. In some it is the individual. In others it is the work group. In still others it is the extended family (sometimes including even ancestors). It is this psychic unit that mediates all experience, that provides the incentive and frame for all behavior. . . . In the United States and in most Western Cultures, this psychological unit is the solitary human being. . . . To preserve this sense of personal uniqueness and personal identity, the individual must often stand apart or even stand against other members of his family, office, neighborhood or nation. . . . In Japan, the critical psychic unit may enclose not merely the person but all others who make up the nuclear group. It is this group that becomes the measure of all things; its identity must be asserted and defended above all. (pp. 153–154)

As will be discussed in the next section, the psychological entities, the social metaphors, that cultures create to define their uniqueness and to which their members are to give allegiance are also the sources of emotional disorder, stress, and pathology. In Japan, for example, people tend to be less clear and specific about their self-concepts or about their individual characteristics than are Americans. Japanese psychiatrists report that because of the intense subjugation of individuality to group identity, many of their patients experience a sense of "no-self," they feel that they have not "possessed their self," they do not appreciate the importance of their existence (Barnlund, 1975, p. 155). The human personality and the social structure are interlocking systems. Individual acts are framed within a cultural imperative.

Roots of Intercultural Diversity

Obviously, the historical influences on cultural diversity have diverse origins and timing. The Protestant ethic and the Calvinist traditions with regard to work and achievement have had similar influences for Americans and the English as compared with the lack of such influences on the Russians, French, or Italians. On the other hand, the latter two groups have been influenced by the Catholic and Latin traditions much more than have been the English, Americans, or Germans. The Russians and Germans have been imbued differently with supra-individual goals, communal feelings, and solidarity. This is true of many other groups. These characteristics can be conceived as relating to the contrasts between *Gemeinschaft* relationships and *Gesellschaft* relationships and the transitions between these relationship clusters as nations have evolved from primary, peasant, tribal, small community social orders to more complex, impersonal, secondary, socially differentiated interaction patterns (Parsons, 1951; Lipset, 1963). *Gemeinschaft* relationships are likely to be particularistic, ascriptive, and broad. In such a model, family and friends are treated differently from other people, standards of treatment of people are applied differently, people are related to and ascribed status in terms of their birth, not their actual performance, and relationships tend to be broad and communal. On the other hand, *Gesellschaft* relationships are more likely to be characterized by universalism in standards applied to people regardless of background, people are more likely to be treated in relation to achievement or performance rather than their ascribed status, and relationships are more likely to be limited than broad.

When one turns aways from European and Christian traditions to the East, to the Chinese and to the Japanese, one finds the major influences of Confucianism, Zen Buddhism, and the Code of Bushido. Here we find family fidelity, self-discipline, social bonding, and public and private virtues that are different in behavioral manifestation from those found in the national character of European nations.

From research across national psychological groupings, we find that national groupings are not only political units, but psychocultural shapers and reinforcers of behaviors culturally distinctive, at least in part, from those of other national groupings. Vaizey and Clarke (1976) suggested that nations create social metaphors as the bases for personality characteristics, child-rearing practices, education, and other social functions. Concepts such as the "socialist personality" used in a nation such as East Germany to define behavioral traits that youth and adults should try to emulate are not simply slogans—they are filters of information, sanctions of conduct, psychological boundaries, and seedbeds for value formulation. As Gestalt psychology and, more recently, the work of the cognitive therapists have demonstrated, human perception and judgment are determined by the organization and, indeed, the availability of information from the outside world. As Syngg and Combs (1949) stated many years ago, one behaves as one perceives. The fact is that one is taught what to perceive and how to behave, and these teachings are different across societies. "These differential schedules of reinforcement result in cultural differences in perceptual selectivity, information-processing strategies, cognitive structures, and habits" (Triandis, 1985, p. 22). According to Triandis (1972), cognitive structures may be best summarized by different elements of subjective culture such as categorizations of experience, associations among the categories, attitudes, beliefs, behavioral intentions (self-instructions about how to behave), norms, roles, and values.

Learning about self and about others is at the core of perceptual psychology and cultural differences (Linton, 1945; Christensen, 1985).

> From the perceptual viewpoint, learning is the discovery of personal meaning, and is an outgrowth of the kinds of differentiations the person makes in the process of development. Although the individual is selective in the personal meaning placed on his/her discoveries, the culture to which (s)he is exposed determines the perimeter of the perceptual field, within the societal context. Through socialization processes and interaction with significant others, the individual learns not only who and what (s)he is, but also acquires values, taboos, moral precepts, and beliefs about different ethnic, racial, and socioeconomic groups, which are prevalent in the particular culture. (Christensen, 1985, p. 66)

Therefore, how we behave toward people and things is a direct outgrowth of how we have learned to perceive them as a function of cultural models.

Other Perspectives on Cultural Diversity

In the sense of convergent and discriminant validity, it is useful to look for other types of confirmation that cultural diversity exists in terms that matter to cross-cultural counseling.

One form of evidence of cultural diversity lies with the way in which psychological disorders are viewed across national groups or cultures. Draguns (1985) reported that "while large-scale multicultural investigations have demonstrated that the same major disorders occur in a variety of very different cultures, . . . a wealth of research reports have documented the operations of cultural influences upon the manifestations, course, and outcome of psychological disorder" (p. 55). For example, the experience of personal guilt in depression is predominant in countries with a Judeo-Christian heritage but infrequent or atypical in settings with other religious traditions. In schizophrenia, ideational and paranoid symptomatology is characteristic of countries at a high level of economic development and high rates of literacy. Catatonic manifestations are prevalent in many traditional, rural, and nonindustrialized settings (p. 56). Similarly, among American ethnic groups many class-related and culturally and religiously based differences in psychiatric symptoms also have been observed (Dohrenwend & Dohrenwend, 1974). Thus, it is possible to argue that "the same basic patterns of psychopathology exist around the world (i.e., in similar forms) but that these psychopathological conditions are influenced by cultural values (i.e., to yield dissimilar content)" (Westermeyer, 1987).

Sue and Sue (1987) reported that Asian Americans seek treatment only when disorders are relatively severe and that those with milder disturbances do not turn to the mental health system. Part of the reason for such findings lies with the fact that there is much stigma or shame associated with emotional difficulties among Asian Americans and the assumption that mental illness, or the failure or weakness of an individual, is considered a disgrace to the family unit. In addition, Asian Americans are likely to feel that mental illness is associated with organic or somatic variables, and they tend to present somatic complaints when having psychiatric problems. Refugees from Southeast Asia display similar behaviors and tend to describe depression and psychological stress in somatic terms such as headaches, insomnia, general aches and pains, heart palpitations, fatigue, and dizziness (Nguyen, 1985).

In a major review of studies of depression in Asians, Marsella (1980) found that depression and how it is experienced vary as a function of sociocultural factors; some cultures do not "psychologize" depression and, therefore, do not show the psychological and experiential symptoms usually associated with the disorder in Western societies; and that assessment methods are culture-specific and need to be more attentive to somatic symptoms in non-Western countries. The prevalence of specific psychiatric disorders also has been found to vary by ethnicity, sex, and age. For example, Karno et al. (1987) reported on a comparative study of psychiatric disorders among Mexican Americans and non-Hispanic Whites in the Los Angeles area. They found that non-Hispanic Whites reported far more drug abuse or dependence and more major depressive episodes than did Mexican Americans. Mexican-American women infrequently abuse or become dependent on drugs or alcohol at any given age. Dysthymia, panic disorders, and phobias are somewhat more prevalent among Mexican-American women over 40 years of age compared with both non-Hispanic White women over 40 and Mexican-American women under 40 years of age. It was found that antisocial personality is predominantly a disorder of young men of both ethnic groups. Furthermore, when utilization of mental health services by Mexican Americans and non-Hispanic Whites was compared, it was found that Mexican Americans with mild mental health problems reported significantly fewer visits (in the order of one half as many). When mental health disorders are severe, however, there seems little difference in the use of mental health services by Mexican Americans or non-Hispanic Whites (Hough et al., 1987).

Kleinman (1980), a psychiatrist trained in anthropology, performed extensive cross-cultural studies on medicine and psychiatry, particularly in Taiwan. His work focuses on three major elements: illness experiences, practitioner-patient transactions, and the healing process. One of his major conclusions is that:

> . . . in the same sense in which we speak of religion or language or kinship as cultural systems, we can view medicine as a cultural system, a system of symbolic meanings anchored in particular arrangements of social institutions and patterns of interpersonal interactions. In every culture, illness, the responses to it, individuals experiencing it and treating it, and the social relationships relating to it are all systematically interconnected. . . . These include patterns of

belief about the causes of illness, norms governing choice and evaluation of treatment; socially legitimated statuses, roles, power relationships, interaction settings, and institutions. . . . Patients and healers are basic components of such systems and thus are embedded in specific configurations of cultural meanings and social relationships. They cannot be understood apart from this context. (pp. 24–25)

Furthermore, beliefs about sickness, the behaviors exhibited by sick people, their treatment expectations, and the ways in which family and practitioners respond to sick people are all aspects of "social reality" in a particular culture. In this sense clinical practice, the range of clinical phenomena in a particular culture, and conceptions of illness are cultural constructions, systems of symbolic reality, not entities with absolute, unequivocal reality across all people and cultures. These culturally mediated symbolic realities enable individuals to make sense of their inner experiences. They help shape personal identity in accordance with social and cultural norms. In this view, symbolic meanings influence basic psychological processes such as attention, state of consciousness, perception, cognition, affect, memory, and motivation (p. 42).

In a more recent work, Kleinman (1988) examined psychiatric diagnoses and treatment within the context of cultural and social differences worldwide. He reaffirmed that although some mental health problems have universal characteristics, others tend to be culture-specific. For example, anorexia nervosa, agoraphobia, and dysthymic disorders occur in some societies but not in others, and, if they do, patients experience different symptoms and precipitating events. In addition, bodily complaints, as is increasingly evident in the literature on stress, can be symptoms of personal, social, and even political distress—behavioral translations, if you will, of the transactions between the individual and social or life events. These perspectives argue that culturally different groups follow distinctive paths to counseling or other mental health assistance and that they arrive there at very different points in the course of their mental health disorders or problems in living, experience greatly divergent types of involvement with their family members, and respond to psychiatric or psychological treatment in different ways.

The work of Peabody (1985), Barnlund (1975), Kleinman (1980, 1988) and others leads to the conclusion that a major factor in intercultural differences is value sets. Much has been written in the counseling literature about how values influence, indeed, permeate, counseling and psychotherapy, theories of personality and pathology, the design of change methods, the goals of treatment, and the assessment of outcomes (Bergin, 1985, p. 99). Less has been said about the extension of this point to the receptivity to different approaches to counseling or to the provision of mental health services in different nations (Levinson & Haynes, 1984; Herr & Niles, 1988). Thus, although research in cross-cultural counseling attests to the importance of value differences between culturally distinct people and the effects these have for the counseling process in microlevel terms, such differences can also be addressed at the level of nations in macrolevel terms. The latter give us insights into differences in the provision of counseling across nations as well as to the transportability of counseling theory and practices across national boundaries.

As suggested previously, terms applied to national groupings— East and West, Communist-non-Communist, developed-underdeveloped—are not only geographical or political referents. They summarize the groupings of economic, psychological, and political characteristics that, however imperfectly, distinguish nations from each other on the bases of how their citizens are viewed, the idealized achievement motives or values to be espoused, and the social metaphors to be pursued. Because counseling and mental health services are promoters of values (London, 1964), national governments vary in their support for various expectations of such services. Depending upon where nations are in their own industrial or sociopolitical development, they may perceive counseling as a means to facilitate social or individual goals, to facilitate the development of human capital for achieving certain state goals, to enforce gatekeeping or social control, to maintain the status quo, or to promote self-actualization and personal growth (Watts & Herr, 1976).

In pluralistic societies such as the United States, there may be a mix of social and individual expectations for the outcomes of counseling services, particularly as they are provided to different population subgroups. Beyond that point, however, it is fair to state that the provision of counseling services is significantly affected by the characteristics of the society in which these services are found. In this sense, in every nation counseling, career guidance, psychotherapy, and other mental health services are sociopolitical processes that reflect the values individual nations hold about helping its citizens with various types of personal, career, or psychological problems. But, counseling provisions also vary because, in essence, every counseling approach is a form of environmental modification that carries political overtones through the assumptions and value sets inherent in it.

If the cultural characteristics of a nation and the value sets inherent in a particular counseling approach do not match, that counseling approach is not likely to have adherents and is not likely to be successful in that particular nation. As Reynolds (1980), among others, reported, Western psychotherapies have a particular way of looking at and processing human behavior; Eastern psychotherapies have a different way of defining and intervening in behavioral norms. One set of therapies is not necessarily a substitute for the other because cultural value sets and assumptions make some forms of counseling and psychotherapy ineffective or unacceptable in nations or cultures different from those in which such interventions were formulated. For example, psychoanalytic therapy has not acquired much clinical popularity in Japan despite its rather wide acceptance in Europe and lesser but substantial support in the United States. The explanation seems to lie with the fact that psychoanalytic theory prizes behaviors such as individuation, self-consciousness, and independence from parents as therapeutic outcomes. These are not the behavioral norms of Japan. Confucianism, the code of Bushido, Zen Buddhism, and related philosophical guides to Japanese behavior value family unity and respect, loyalty to others, subjugation of individualism to group identity, self-discipline, and gratitude to others.

A similar comparison of East and West in the acceptability of therapeutic models is found in the work of Yiu (1978) in Taiwan. Her research accents the view that Taiwanese-Chinese culture prizes interpersonal relations, group identification, and family bonds, but deemphasizes the individual expression of feelings. Such a frame of reference obviously conflicts with middle-class American tendencies toward self-disclosure. Speaking to the transportability of counseling theories, Saner-Yiu and Saner (1985) contended in their research that the value assumptions embedded in counseling approaches derived from an individualist culture (e.g., the U.S.A.) are in conflict with the value assumptions in a collectivist nation (e.g., Taiwan). Others addressing counseling in African and in Middle Eastern nations (Shanhirzadi, 1983) have indicated that many assumptions taken for granted in some cultures are simply not shared across cultures: "I consciousness, rights to private life and opinion, individual initiative and achievement, the forms and content of interpersonal relationship" (Okon, 1983).

Although much more deserves to be said about the subtleties or the overt differences that distinguish cultures, it is sufficient for the purposes of this chapter to contend that culture and social class are significant considerations for counselors (Vontress, cited in Jackson, 1987). Indeed, in cross-cultural counseling they are preeminent issues that must be acknowledged and responded to if the cultural differences between a counselor and a client are not to become barriers to effective communication and mutual understanding.

Cross-Cultural Counseling

The term cross-cultural, or multicultural, counseling has evolved to summarize those therapeutic techniques designed to be sensitive and responsive to cultural differences between counselors and clients. By definition, cross-cultural counseling involves "any counseling relationship in which two or more of the participants are culturally different" (Atkinson, Morten, & Sue, 1979, p. 7). A somewhat broader notion of cross-cultural counseling was provided by Pedersen (1978) who suggested, "If we consider the value perspectives of age, sex role, life-style, socio economic status and other special affiliations as cultural, then we may well conclude that all counseling is to some extent cross-cultural" (p. 480). Vontress (cited in Jackson, 1987) recently suggested that "cross-cultural counseling refers to counseling in which the counselor, and the client(s) are manifestly different due to socialization acquired in distinct cultural, subcultural, raciocultural or socioeconomic environments." As suggested throughout this chapter, the needs for more attention to cross-cultural counseling will intensify and expand as a major challenge to counselors in the future. In order to meet this goal, however, cross-cultural issues important in diagnosis, appraisal, and counseling must be identified and addressed.

In general, techniques in cross-cultural counseling are recent and more theoretical than empirical in their substance. There has been little research on how clients from different cultures present different profiles of concern or behavior in the counseling situation, although there is a growing descriptive and anecdotal literature about such matters. VanZijl (1985), for example, from extensive counseling with clients of different cultural backgrounds, suggested that the following barriers to communication may be present in the counseling relationship. They include, in paraphrased form, the following:

- *Transference*. A client of a minority background may react to a counselor of a majority background with resentment, distrust, and hostility because of negative experiences the client may have had with people from the majority culture in the past.

- *Countertransference*. The counselor may project onto the client negative feelings that he or she may have experienced with people of the client's cultural background. Or, a counselor may exhibit what Vontress (1976) described as the "Great White father" syndrome—a desire to both demonstrate power and authority as well as the image that the counselor is not like all the other majority group people the client may have previously known. Finally, the counselor may be overly sympathetic and indulgent to clients from other cultures and in the process act in a condescending or patronizing manner.

- *Resistance.* Because clients may expect counselors to tell them what to do, they may behave in a passive and nonverbal manner. Because of cultural constraints or a lack of trust of the majority counselor, culturally different clients may be reluctant to engage in self-disclosure.

- *Value orientation.* Culturally different value orientations may manifest themselves in many ways in the counseling relationship. The client may operate with a "present orientation" that deemphasizes planning for the future. A lack of time consciousness may devalue punctuality, meeting time schedules, or notions such as "time is money." Respect for age may cause an older client not to give attention to a youthful counselor, or a younger client to view an older counselor as a person of infallible judgment and wisdom.

- *Language.* A counselor's lack of fluency in or understanding of the cultural nuances important in the client's language may cause miscommunication and inaccuracy in messages given and received.

- *Nonverbal communication.* Cultures vary in meanings associated with space (physical closeness) and body language. What is normal and appropriate in one culture may evoke hostility or sexual feelings in people from another culture.

- *High levels of anxiety.* When a client from one culture tries to function in a very different one, he or she may experience a level of "culture shock" that causes anxiety and inhibits communication because the individual has lost familiar cues to reality.

- *Ignorance.* The counselor may suffer from a complete lack of knowledge of the client's culture and, therefore, make inferences about behavior that are inaccurate and constitute barriers to communication.

- *Expectations of the client.* Depending upon their cultural background, clients may expect the counselor to serve as a parental figure or they may expect to engage in a formal relationship with an authority figure who will give direct advice.

- *Cultural stereotyping.* The counselor may react to the client as a cultural stereotype, not as an individual. Assuming that all members of the same racial, ethnic, or cultural group share the same values, needs, goals, and abilities, the counselor operates not in terms of cultural sensitivity but in terms of cultural bias.

Ibrahim (1984) applied the work of Kluckhohn and Strodtbeck (1961) to an existential view of cross-cultural counseling. Basically Ibrahim contended that the skills needed for direct service to clients across cultures include two emphases: (1) an initial understanding of the client's world view and how it relates to the world views held by the client's specific cultural, ethnic, and racial group; and (2) the provision of skills important in intercultural communication including both verbal and nonverbal content of messages sent and received. These two emphases, then, apply to the existential categories among which cultures differ in their values orientations. They include:

- *The relation of people to nature (people-nature orientation).* In essence this orientation has to do with the terms of survival in the environment adopted by different cultures. Does this particular client come from a culture that believes in living in harmony with nature? Subjugating and controlling nature to meet the needs of people? Accepting the power of nature and how it controls people?

- *The temporal focus of human life (time orientation).* Is the client embued with a past, present, or future time orientation? Is life viewed as finite or eternal?

- *The modality of human activity (activity orientation).* Is the client's activity expressive-emotional, detached and meditative, or action-oriented? In which of these ways does the client seek personal meaning and through what specific mechanisms within this activity range?

- *The modality of human relationships (relational orientation).* How does the client view social relationships or social isolation? Does he or she view such relationships in terms of clearly drawn lines of authority, including rights according to rank and well-defined subordinate-superior relationships; collaterality, the person as independent and dependent at the same time; individualistic, autonomous?

- *The modality of human nature (good/bad/immutable).* The fundamental question here is how does the client feel about him- or herself and about other people? Are people viewed as basically evil, neutral, a combination of evil and good, or basically good?

Essentially, Ibrahim's intent is to help counselors recognize that there are different world views, culturally mediated, that influence feelings about oneself and others. These five categories provide counselors a paradigm by which to understand culturally different clients within the context of universal existential categories.

Another cross-cultural paradigm is based in perceptual psychology (Christensen, 1985). The fundamental notion is that to understand and effectively implement cross-cultural counseling requires attention to the perceptions and understandings of the counselor and of the client as well as of the counseling process in a social context. Overlaid against these three components of cross-cultural counseling are the perspectives from perceptual psychology. In this view, "the perceptual field is defined as the entire universe, including the self, as experienced by the individual at a given moment. This 'private map,' by which the individual lives, is his/her 'reality,' although experience as perceived may not correspond to any objective reality. All systems of the perceptual field are interrelated so that a change in one affects all other parts of the system" (Christensen, 1985, p. 65). In this view, both the counselor and the client have their own private maps of the self, or self-concept, and the values attached to it; relationships with significant others; a world view of their place in society that reflects past, present, and future orientations as well as their status with regard to being a part of a majority or minority culture; and, a universe view that provides for personal meaning, spirituality, and a sense of people's relationship to nature, time, space, a deity, or cosmic force. Counselor and client are also likely to have their own private map of what counseling is, how the counselor and client should relate to each other, and its purposes.

These several notions affecting the counselor-client-counseling relationship result from culturally mediated experiences that shape the content and the conscious awareness of the "private maps" interacting at any moment in cross-cultural counseling. The counselor sensitive to cross-cultural issues must consider the multiple frames of reference—the self, significant others, one's place in society, one's personal meaning, the meaning of counseling—that are likely to affect client behavior in the counseling relationship and the potential communication barriers that may be operating. In cross-cultural counseling as in other counseling conditions, a counselor-generated atmosphere of mutual trust and acceptance is vital if the client is to be enabled to share his or her feelings and perceptions of concerns. Beyond such a reality, however, many culturally different clients will perceive themselves to be and will, in fact, be members of oppressed minorities. In such cases counselors will have to be willing and have the capacity "to experience the pain, vulnerability, anger, frustration, helplessness and fear of the client" (Christensen, 1985, p. 78).

Beyond such general perspectives on cross-cultural counseling, there are more specific recommendations in the literature dealing with the nature and the emphases of therapeutic interventions for different cultural groups. Although no counselor can be a specialist in all of the culturally different groups that now reside in the United States, counselors should read as widely and gain as much experience as possible pertinent to the major ethnic, racial, religious, socioeconomic, or other culturally defined groups with whom they are most likely to work. A typology of the specific cultural characteristics of each of the culturally different groups in the United States that are relevant to cross-cultural counseling is beyond the scope of this chapter, but there are references to in-depth analyses of the mental health problems, behavioral characteristics, expectations of counseling and counseling techniques likely to be useful with different minority or ethnic populations. Among them are such references as the following:

Axelson, J.A. (1985). *Counseling and development in a multicultural society.* Belmont, CA: Brooks/Cole.

Dudley, G.R., & Rawlins, M.R. (1985). Psychotherapy with ethnic minorities. *Psychotherapy*, Special Issue, *22*(2).

Jones, E.E., & Korchin, S.J. (Eds.). (1982). *Minority mental health.* New York: Praeger.

Levine, E.S., & Padilla, A.M. (1980). *Crossing cultures in therapy; Pluralistic counseling for the Hispanic.* Monterey, CA: Brooks/Cole.

Marsella, A.J., & Pedersen, P.B. (Eds.). (1981). *Cross-cultural counseling and psychotherapy.* New York: Pergamon Press.

McDermott, J.F., Jr., Tseng, W.-S., & Maretzki, T.W., (Eds.). (1980). *People and cultures of Hawaii.* Honolulu: University of Hawaii Press.

McGoldrick, M., Pearce, J.K., & Giordano, J. (Eds.). (1982). *Ethnicity and family therapy.* New York: Guilford Press.

Owan, T.C. (Ed.). (1985). *Southeast Asian mental health: Treatment, prevention, services, training, and research.* Washington, DC: U.S. Department of Health and Human Services, National Institute of Mental Health.

Pedersen, P. (Ed.). (1985). *Handbook of cross-cultural counseling and therapy.* Westport, CT: Greenwood Press.

Pedersen, P. (1988). *A handbook for developing multicultural awareness.* Alexandria, VA: American Association for Counseling and Development.

Pedersen, P.P., Draguns, J.G., Lonner, W.J., & Trimble, J.E. (Eds). (1981). *Counseling across cultures* (Rev. expanded ed.). Honolulu: University of Hawaii Press.

Sue, D.W. (1981). *Counseling the culturally different.* New York: Wiley.

Triandis, H.C., & Draguns, J.G. (Eds.). (1980). *Psychopathology handbook of cross-cultural psychology.* Newton, MA: Allyn & Bacon.

The conceptual and research literature found in these references and in other sources indicates that groups that differ on the bases of sex, minority, or socioeconomic status are likely to experience problems or concerns that are relatively unique. Some of these have already been cited in previous sections of this chapter. There are many other examples. One concerns the prevalence of disorders among women that are not of major importance when providing psychotherapy to men. Hare-Mustin (1983) listed the following as of high prevalence in women but not adequately treated in the psychological or intervention literature: marital conflicts, hysteria, agoraphobia, reproductive problems, physical and sexual abuse, depression, and problems associated with eating. The point is that "if psychotherapy is to help female patients, therapists must become aware of sex differences where they do exist and refute assumptions about sex differences where they do not exist" (Hare-Mustin, p. 95). Obviously, in addition, counselors must avoid sex bias and sex stereotyping in diagnostic labeling and in providing treatment.

Speaking of the extensive literature on stress, Smith (1983) examined racial differences in relation to their function as stressor stimuli, external mediating forces, and internal mediating forces, the three factors typically defined as the sources of the general level of stress individuals experience. In turn, according to Dohrenwend and Dohrenwend (1979), stressor stimuli are events that cause stress by disrupting or threatening disruption of an individual's activities. External mediating forces are environmental factors—such as money, family, and level of social support—that act upon individuals; internal predictors of stress include personal values, life expectations, general feelings, and physical and psychological dispositions.

Within each of the three sets of factors, Smith (1983) analyzed the role of race in relationship to stress. For example, as a source of stressor stimuli, race becomes associated with out-group and in-group phenomena. Out-group status is associated with three forms of rejection: verbal rejection, discrimination, and physical attack. Minority status in a culture may also lead to social isolation, marginality, and status inconsistency or status ambivalence. There may be role conflicts between the majority culture assertions of superiority versus subordination for minority group members. Such role conflicts may be intensified by the proportion of racial minorities in particular locations. Where they are "tokens," racial minorities are likely to experience increased visibility and, indeed, their behavior may be viewed as symbolic of their racial group, thus casting them into a highly pressurized situation. Research data indicate that although racial differences alone do not account for the prevalence of mental illness, they certainly can be related to the incidence of depression, somatic complaints, alcoholism, and antisocial personality disorders.

With regard to race and external mediators of stress, Smith (1983) reported two classes of social stress: (1) social class membership, and (2) social support. In the first sense, there is an inverse relationship between social class and psychological symptomatology. Because racial minorities tend to be poorer than members of the dominant culture, there are also likely to be stresses in turning their educational achievement and credentials into appropriate earning power. This is true for Blacks, for Asian Americans, and for Hispanics. Another external mediator of stress is social support. Not having friends or family nearby and available in times of need can be particularly problematic for immigrants and for members of racial minority groups who are dispersed and separated from social or family networks.

With regard to internal mediators of stress, racial minorities also differ in their locus of control and vulnerability to stress. Locus of control can be defined as internal or external. Poor people, who are exposed to the continuous effects of racism and discrimination, are likely to experience high levels of stress, feelings that control of their lives comes from external sources, and learned helplessness. Obviously, such social and psychological assaults upon the individual will affect another internal mediator of stress, the self-concept, in negative ways. To the degree that minority group members internalize as self-hatred the racism and discrimination directed at them by the dominant group, their self-concept will be low and mentally unhealthy.

Against such a context, Smith (1983) suggested a cross-cultural counseling model that she identified as a Stress, Resistant, Delivery (SRD) model. This model posits that in counseling minorities the counselor should follow three basic steps: "(1) identify the source(s) of stress a client is facing; (2) analyze the mediating (both external and internal) factors of stress and the stress-resistant forces within an individual and within the culture from which an individual comes; (3) decide upon a method of delivering services to clients" (p. 573). Within these steps, Smith also suggested several counseling phases in which she engages. They include: finding the common reference point; educating the client about his or her symptoms and about what counseling entails; locating hope within the client; locating the injury to the self; reparenting in service of the ego; reworking the trauma; healing the wounds and getting on with self-improvement; and helping the client move to an ideal stage.

Guidelines for Cross-Cultural Counseling

Counselors who are engaged in cross-cultural counseling recognize that many points of reference need to be considered when working with culturally different clients. Some of the factors involved are racial or ethnic background; socioeconomic class; country of origin; bilingual/bicultural status; cultural expectations about counseling and mental distress; types of stress experienced; family status; social resources; and internal-external locus of control/internal-external locus of responsibility. Sue (1981) collapsed these and many other factors into four areas of most concern when counselors and clients are of different ethnic cultural traditions. They include: (1) barriers, (2) relationship factors, (3) cultural identity, and (4) the conditions for a culturally skilled counselor. Each of these areas will be briefly addressed.

Barriers. The four major classes of possible cultural conflicts or miscommunication according to Sue are: language, class-bound variables, culture-bound variables, and nonverbal communication styles. Counselors must be alert to the presence and to the implications of these as they affect goal setting and the creation of trust.

Relationship and rapport factors. Basically the counselor must be seen as credible by the client. This status depends upon the client's perceptions of counselor expertness and trustworthiness. These two outcomes also depend on the psychological mind-set the client brings to the relationship. What are the expectations the client holds for information and for how he or she will be treated with regard to the counselor as an authority? In addition, the more similar in background and experiences the counselor and client are the more likely credibility and rapport will be achieved. Furthermore, the psychological development of the client with regard to his or her security with a racial identity and his or her experiences of oppression will be a major factor in the substance and the effectiveness of the cross-cultural counseling that takes place.

Cultural identity. How counselor and client perceive and understand the client's views of and behavior regarding concepts of internality/externality of control will be important to what happens in the relationship. Perceptions of having control of life or being controlled by it operate as the frames of reference or windows through which events are interpreted and acted upon. Whether or not the client views him- or herself as having responsibility for what happens in life is likely to determine whether or not the client views planning, skill development, and training as making sense or not.

The culturally skilled counselor. According to Sue (1981), the culturally skilled counselor is one who is able to use differential approaches with different clients. A counselor sensitive to each client's language, values, class, and other culturally different characteristics will seek the most appropriate techniques available to meet the client's goals.

Henkin (1985) provided a set of suggestions primarily oriented to counseling with Japanese Americans. They tend to have broad generality, however, across culturally different populations. These guidelines in abridged form include the following:

1. Establish a clear-cut structure for the counseling process;
2. Explain the counseling process;
3. Allow the client to ask questions about the counselor and the counseling process;
4. Allow yourself as a counselor to ask culturally relevant questions;
5. Establish your own role clearly;
6. Be patient;
7. Refrain from making assessments as long as possible;
8. Ask your client about family and community relationships;
9. Provide assurances of confidentiality and honor them;
10. Find out about your client's prior counseling experience;
11. Restate your understandings of your client's statements frequently;
12. Bear in mind that some problems brought to a counselor do not indicate client pathology;
13. Be aware of the degree to which Japanese Americans may have internalized their cultural treatment; and
14. Work to counter your client's notions of personal fault, which may simply be internalizations of external issues. (Henkin, 1985, pp. 502–503)

The last three of the guidelines Henkin provided relate to what Draguns (1981) defined as the Autoplastic-Alloplastic dilemma in cross-cultural counseling. These two terms refer to the concept that, "In coping with the environment, all humans respond either autoplastically, by changing themselves to accommodate the external circumstances, or alloplastically, by imposing changes on the world at large" (p. 8). Put somewhat differently it is important in cross-cultural counseling, as indeed in all counseling, to distinguish problems within the individual from those in the environment. Although many counselors have been trained to look for sources of client problems inside the person, among minority clients the sources of the problem are frequently racial discrimination, social disadvantage, poverty, and other phenomena these clients may have internalized but for which they are not respon-

sible. The problem is that unless the counselor is culturally sensitive
to the effects of victimization, learned helplessness, and similar incorporation of what are primarily external deficits, the counselor is
likely to focus on what may be seen as an internal deficit when it is,
in fact, the result of social marginality, discrimination, and related
phenomena.

The notions of the Autoplastic-Alloplastic dilemma also are echoed
in the view of pluralistic counseling espoused by Levine and Padilla
(1980) for Hispanic clients. These perspectives, also, have wide generality to other cultural groups because the therapeutic approaches have
been found to be culturally adaptive. They include:

1. The therapist should ascertain whether a client's problems are
    due primarily to intrapsychic or to extrapsychic stress. If extra-
    psychic stress is predominant, therapy aimed, for example, at
    social action and the alleviation of discrimination and poverty
    may be appropriate. If intrapsychic conflict is most basic,
    introspective or behavioral therapy is the treatment of choice.
2. The therapist should expect less self-disclosure from Hispanics
    than from clients of other ethnic groups. It will be the client's
    responsibility to differentiate between personal privacy that is
    culturally sanctioned and psychological resistance.
3. The therapist should employ a different style of nonverbal
    communication with the Hispanic client. The therapist should
    attempt to greet the client as soon as he or she arrives, shake
    hands, and sometimes embrace the client. The therapist may
    sit closer to the Hispanic than to the Anglo or Black client.
4. Family counseling should be emphasized. Treatment modal-
    ities that facilitate action and interpretation of family inter-
    action, such as psychodrama and role processing, are vital
    tools. (Levine & Padilla, 1980, p. 256)

Draguns (1981) contended that cross-cultural counseling is not
"counseling as usual." Although relationship variables may be common across all sorts of counseling with all types of clients, the culturally
sensitive counselor must accommodate the cultural sensitivities and
uniqueness of the person sharing the counseling relationship. In a
general summation of advice to cross-cultural counselors, Draguns
suggested the following: "Be prepared to adapt your techniques (e.g.,
general activity level, mode of verbal intervention, content of remarks,
tone of voice) to the cultural background of the client; communicate
acceptance of and respect for the client in terms that are intelligible
and meaningful within his or her frame of reference; and be open to
the possibility of more direct intervention in the life of the client than

the traditional ethos of the counseling profession would dictate or permit'' (p. 11).

Within the broad context of cross-cultural counseling, at least two other areas are worthy of concern. One of these is testing, appraisal, or assessment. Because this chapter is not oriented to specific techniques per se, assessment will only be touched upon to note that it is an area that deserves much more attention than can be provided here.

Cross-Cultural Appraisal

Depending on the assessment tools used by a particular mental health worker—e.g., tests, clinical assessments, inventories, self-ratings—the basic assumption is that these appraisal techniques must be oriented toward:

> understanding how individuals construe their experiences, their predicaments, their lives. . . . Psychological problems cannot be studied, let alone treated, without a fundamental respect for the person and without a constant effort to grasp the experience of the person. . . . Behavioral approaches, especially the newer cognitive behavioral treatments, have increasingly emphasized the importance of the inner thought processes of the subject. Psychodynamically oriented practitioners have traditionally underscored the importance of personal interviews to provide background data that will contextualize and personalize the results of other, often more structured, tests and procedures. (Jones & Thorne, 1987, pp. 491–492)

The problem with culturally inappropriate or insensitive assessment techniques is that they may lead to misdiagnoses, inappropriate therapeutic plans, and treatment failures (Westermeyer, 1987). Easy solutions to such problems have not been forthcoming. Rather, assessment of culturally different clients should be considered very carefully in terms of what will be gained from the use of standardized instruments over what may be acquired from structured interviews or other indicators of performance or attitude.

If client assessment is to be undertaken, the counselor should be diligent in seeking instruments that have been validated for use with the client's cultural group.

Ethics in Multicultural Counseling

In large measure, the professional codes of ethics that define standards of behavior for counselors have not yet fully articulated how multicultural issues may affect ethical behavior. Ivey (1986) suggested that such conditions prevail because ethical codes, like counselors, are encapsulated or limited by views that result from Western culture and, therefore, are not sufficiently sensitive to culturally different clients. He suggested several steps to rectify such a situation. In paraphrased form, they include:

- The issue of multicultural awareness should be placed at the center of professional codes of ethics, and it should be a starting point for counseling practice.
- The issue of multicultural practice should be the core of publications and research journals.
- A long-term program of public and professional awareness should be initiated to make counselors aware of the implications of clients as cultural beings.
- Ethical codes and practice should be made more open for involvement with the public.

The underlying importance of ethical codes that are sensitive to multicultural or cross-cultural issues, as is true of using assessments that are culturally sensitive, is summarized in the observations of Pedersen and Marsella (1982): "A serious moral vacuum exists in the delivery of cross-cultural counseling and therapy sources because the values of a dominant culture have been imposed on the culturally different consumer. Cultural differences complicate the definition of guidelines even for the conscientious and well-intentioned counselor and therapist" (p. 498). They go on to stress that the problem with ethical guidelines is that they are based upon mental health assumptions and processes that were conceptualized or created in one cultural context and are used in a different context without validation. As has been shown throughout this chapter, cultural differences are important. People act in accordance with culturally mediated assumptions that are different from West to East, between ethnic groups, and among national societies.

Culturally Relevant Training

A major challenge to counseling in the near term is the creation of culturally relevant training programs. It is unlikely that culturally skilled counselors can exist in the numbers required without a dramatic increase in the number of culturally relevant counselor education programs across the United States. Copeland (1983) contended that counselors cannot be expected to understand and be able to work with culturally different clients unless they are exposed to at least four components: consciousness raising, cognitive understanding, affective components, and skills components. These might be delivered through separate courses, or through interdisciplinary, integrated, or area-of-concentration models. Vontress (Jackson, 1987) argued that because cross-cultural counseling is multidisciplinary, the effective counselor must be schooled in philosophy, psychology, anthropology, sociology, languages, and the life sciences. Sue, Akutsu, & Higashi (1985) suggested that three important elements for cultural competence include: knowledge of clients' culture and status, actual experience with these clients, and the ability to devise innovative strategies.

Ponterotto and Casas (1987) recently elicited nominations of the leading cross-cultural training programs in the United States. Nine such programs received 3 to 8 nominations from a panel of 20 professionals, who met a set of criteria suggesting that they were competent to identify such programs. The similarities in the 9 programs included having at least one faculty member sensitive and outspoken in behalf of multicultural issues, requiring at least one course in muticultural issues, attempting to infuse multicultural issues into all program curricula, and attempting to include racially diverse faculty members and students. Obviously, securing 9 nominations of multiculturally sensitive training programs out of the nearly 500 counselor education and counseling psychology training programs in the United States is simply an inadequate response to a major counseling issue and must be rectified immediately.

Among typical training proposals are systematic approaches to multicultural competency that have included the following elements:

- A triad model (Pedersen, 1981) that involves role-playing cross-cultural counseling with three persons. One student assumes the role of counselor, a second person plays a client from a different culture, and a third person tries to highlight cultural gaps, unique cultural values, and their effects on the cross-cultural interaction at issue. Such an approach tries to maximize the student counselor's sensitivity to the internal dialogue of the culturally different client. It also tries to maximize the counselor's skill in perceiving a problem from the client's perspective, recognizing resistance, reducing personal defensiveness, and recovering after making a culturally inappropriate remark or gesture.

- A multistage cross-cultural course (Parker, Valley, & Geary, 1986) that includes in sequence an assessment of the student's level of knowledge and increased sensitivity toward minority group members; exposure to multicultural experiences including touring an ethnic community or spending time in the home of an ethnic family; and making small-group presentations of multicultural issues.

Conclusions

Chapter 4 has examined the dimensions and directions of cultural diversity or pluralism in the United States. Clearly, the proportion of minority group members in the American population is growing in absolute numbers and in political, social, and economic influence in the nation. Rather than a nation of homogeneous traditions and beliefs, the United States is a mosaic of values, work ethics, "world views," communication patterns, and meaning systems. Although all Americans, regardless of their nation of origin or their particular ancestral roots, share a common commitment to freedom, justice, and equal opportunity, they also experience cultural differences in how they view individual achievement versus loyalty and subordination to a group, the use of time and space, religious commitments, and life values and goals.

In essence, it is the cultural differences between counselor and client, rather than the shared values, that stimulate the growing need for culturally sensitive counselors and cross-cultural techniques. Cross-cultural implications are pervasive for counselor understanding and communication with clients, the use of assessments, ethical behavior, and training. In either independent or collective terms, these elements of cultural differences will become increasingly major challenges to counselors in all settings throughout the United States.

References

Atkinson, D.W., Morten, G., & Sue, D.W. (1979). *Counseling American minorities*. Dubuque, IA: Wm. C. Brown.

Barnlund, D.G. (1975). *Public and private self in Japan and the United States*. Tokyo, Japan: Simul Press.

Bellah, R.N., Madsen, R., Sullivan, W., Swidler, A., & Tipton, S. (1985). *Habits of the heart; Individualism and commitment in American life*. New York: Harper & Row.

Benedict, R. (1934). *Patterns of culture*. New York: The New American Library.

Bergin, A.E. (1985). Proposed values in guiding and evaluating counseling and psychotherapy. *Counseling and Values, 29*, 99–115.

Brislin, R.W., Lonner, W.J., & Thorndike, R.M. (1973). *Cross-cultural research methods*. New York: Wiley.

Christensen, C.P. (1985). A perceptual approach to cross-cultural counseling. *Canadian Counsellor, 19*(2), 63–81.

Clark, L.A. (1987). Mutual relevance of mainstream and cross-cultural psychology. *Journal of Consulting and Clinical Psychology, 55*(4), 461–470.

Copeland, E.J. (1983). Cross-cultural counseling and psychotherapy: A historical perspective, implications for research and training. *Personnel and Guidance Journal, 62*, 10–13.

de Tocqueville, A. (1969). *Democracy in America*. Translated by George Lawrence. Edited by J.P. Mayer. New York: Doubleday, Anchor Books.

Dohrenwend, B.P., & Dohrenwend, B.S. (1974). Social and cultural influences on psychopathology. *Annual Review of Psychology, 25*, 419–452.

Dohrenwend, B.S., & Dohrenwend, B.P. (1979). Class and race as status-related sources of stress. In S. Levine & N. Scotch (Eds.), *Social stress*. Chicago: Aldine.

Draguns, J.G. (1981). Counseling across cultures: Common themes and distinct approaches. In P.P. Pedersen, J.G. Draguns, W.J. Lonner, & J.E. Trimble (Eds.), *Counseling across cultures* (Chapter 1). Honolulu: University of Hawaii Press.

Draguns, J.G. (1985). Psychological disorders across cultures. In P. Pedersen (Ed.), *Handbook of cross-cultural counseling and therapy* (pp. 55–62). Westport, CT: Greenwood Press.

Garreau, J. (1981). *The nine nations of North America*. New York: Avon Books.

Hare-Mustin, R.T. (1983). An appraisal of the relationship between women and psychotherapy: 80 years after the case of Dora. *American Psychologist, 38*, 593–601.

Henkin, W.A. (1985). Toward counseling the Japanese in America: A cross-cultural primer. *Journal of Counseling and Development, 63*, 500–503.

Herr, E.L., & Cramer, S.H. (1988). *Career guidance and counseling through the life span: Systematic approaches*. Glenview, IL: Scott, Foresman.

Hodgkinson, H.L. (1985). *All one system: Demographics of education—kindergarten through graduate school*. Washington, DC: Institute for Educational Leadership.

Horner, D., & Vandersluis, R. (Eds.). (1981). Cross-cultural counseling. In G. Olthen (Ed.), *Learning across cultures*. Washington, DC: National Association of Foreign Student Advisors.

Hough, R.L., Landsverk, J.A., Karno, M., Burnham, M.A., Timbers, D.M., Escobar, J.I., & Regier, D.A. (1987). Utilization of health and mental health services by Los Angeles Mexican Americans and non-Hispanic whites. *Arch General Psychiatry, 44*(8), 702–709.

Ibrahim, F. (1984). Cross-cultural counseling and psychotherapy: An existential-psychological approach. *International Journal for the Advancement of Counselling, 7*(3), 159–170.

Ivey, A.E. (1986). *Ethics and multicultural therapy: An unrealized dream.* Unpublished manuscript. University of Massachusetts, Amherst.

Jackson, M.L. (1987). Cross-cultural counseling at the crossroads: A dialogue with Clemmont E. Vontress. *Journal of Counseling and Development, 66*(1), 20–23.

Johnson, F.A. (1981). Ethnicity and interactional rules in counseling: Some basic considerations. In A.J. Marsella, & P.B. Pedersen (Eds.), *Cross-cultural counseling and psychotherapy* (pp. 63–84). New York: Pergamon Press.

Jones, E.E., & Thorne, A. (1987). Rediscovery of the subject: Intercultural approaches to clinical assessment. *Journal of Consulting and Clinical Psychology, 55*(4), 488–495.

Karno, M., Hough, R.L., Burnham, M.A., Escobar, J.I., Timbers, D.M., Santanna, F., & Boyd, J.H. (1987). Lifetime prevalence of specific psychiatric disorders among Mexican Americans and non-Hispanic whites in Los Angeles. *Arch General Psychiatry, 44*(8), 695–701.

Kluckhohn, C. (1962). *Culture and behavior.* New York: Free Press.

Kluckhohn, F.R., & Strodtbeck, F.L. (1961). *Variations in value orientations.* Evanston, IL: Row, Peterson.

Kleinman, A. (1980). *Patients and healers in the context of culture.* Berkeley, CA: University of California Press.

Kleinman, A. (1988). *Rethinking psychiatry: From cultural category to personal experiences.* New York: Free Press.

Kübler-Ross, E. (1969). *On death and dying.* New York: Macmillan.

Lee, C. (1988, January 15). *Cross-cultural counseling: Pitfalls and promise.* Paper presented at the NCDA 75th Anniversary Conference, Transformation in Work and Workers, Lake Buena Vista, FL.

Levine, E.J., & Padilla, A.M. (1980). *Crossing cultures in therapy: Pluralistic counseling for the Hispanic.* Belmont, CA: Brooks/Cole.

Levinson, R.W., & Haynes, K.S. (Eds.). (1984). *Accessing human services: International perspectives.* Beverly Hills, CA: Sage.

Linton, R. (1945). *The cultural background of personality.* New York: Appleton-Century.

Lipset, S.M. (1963). *First new nation.* New York: Basic Books.

London, P. (1964). *The modes and morals of psychotherapy.* New York: Holt, Rinehart & Winston.

Maccoby, M., & Terzi, K. (1981). What happened to the work ethic? In J. O'Toole, J.L. Scheiber, & L.C. Woods (Eds.), *Working, changes and choices* (pp. 162–171). New York: Human Sciences Press.

Marsella, H.A. (1980). Depressive experience and disorder across cultures. In H.C. Triandis & J.G. Draguns (Eds.), *Psychopathology handbook of cross-cultural psychology* (pp. 237–289). Newton, MA: Allyn & Bacon.

Maslow, A.H. (1954). *Motivation and personality.* New York: Harper.

McDermott, J.F., Jr. (1980a). Introduction. In J.F. McDermott, Jr., W.-S. Tseng, & T.W. Maretzki (Eds.), *People and cultures of Hawaii: A psychocultural profile.* Honolulu: University of Hawaii Press.

McDermott, J.F., Jr. (1980b). Toward an interethnic society. In J.F. McDermott, Jr., W.-S. Tseng, & T.W. Maretski (Eds.), *People and cultures of Hawaii: A psychocultural profile* (Chapter 12). Honolulu: University of Hawaii Press.

McGoldrick, M., Pearce, J.K., & Giordano, J. (Eds.) (1982). *Ethnicity and family therapy.* New York: Guilford Press.

Mitchell, A. (1983). *The nine American lifestyles: Who we are and where we are going.* New York: Warner Books.

Moynihan, D.P. (1964). Morality of work and immorality of opportunity. *Vocational Guidance Quarterly, 12*, 229–236.

Munoz, R.F. (1982). The Spanish-speaking consumer and the community mental health center. In E.E. Jones & S.J. Korchin (Eds.), *Minority mental health* (pp. 362–398). New York: Praeger.

Naisbitt, J. (1984). *Megatrends: Ten new directions transforming our lives.* New York: Warner Books.

Nguyen, S.D. (1985). Mental health services for refugees and immigrants in Canada. In T.C. Owan (Ed.), *Southeast Asians' mental health: Treatment, prevention, services, training, and research* (pp. 261–282). Washington, DC: U.S. Department of Health and Human Services, National Institute of Mental Health.

Owan, T.C. (Ed.). (1985). *Southeast Asians' mental health: Treatment, prevention, services, training, and research.* Washington, DC: U.S. Department of Health and Human Services, National Institute of Mental Health.

Oxford Analytica. (1986). *America in perspective: Major trends in the United States through the 1990s.* Boston: Houghton Mifflin.

Parker, W.M., Valley, M.M., & Geary, C.A. (1986). Acquiring counselor knowledge for counselors in training: Multifaceted approach. *Counselor Education and Supervision, 26*(1), 61–71.

Parsons, T. (1951). *The social system.* Glencoe, IL: Free Press.

Peabody, D. (1985). *National characteristics.* Cambridge, England: Cambridge University Press.

Pedersen, P.B. (1978). Four dimensions of cross-cultural skill in counselor training. *Personnel and Guidance Journal, 56*, 480–484.

Pedersen, P.B. (1981). Triad counseling. In R. Corsini (Ed.), *Innovative psychotherapies* (pp. 840–855). New York: Wiley.

Pedersen, P.B., & Marsella, A.J. (1982). The ethical crisis for cross-cultural counseling and therapy. *Professional Psychology, 13*(4), 492–500.

Ponterotto, J.G., & Casas, M.J. (1987). In search of multicultural competence within counselor education programs. *Journal of Counseling and Development, 65*(8), 430–434.

Reynolds, D.K. (1980). *The quiet therapies: Japanese pathways to personal growth.* Honolulu: University of Hawaii Press.

Riesman, D. (1961). *The lonely crowd,* New Haven, CT: Yale University Press.

Roe, A. (1956). *The psychology of occupations.* New York: Wiley.

Saner-Yiu, L., & Saner, R. (1985). Value dimensions in American counseling: A Taiwanese American comparison. *International Journal for the Advancement of Counselling, 8*, 137–146.

Sardi, Z. (1982). *The psychological aspects of immigration to Israel*. Paper presented to the International Round Table for the Advancement of Counselling, University of Lausanne, Switzerland.

Shanhirzadi, A. (1983). Counseling Iranians. *Personnel and Guidance Journal, 61*, 487–489.

Smith, E.M.J. (1983). Ethnic minorities: Life stress, social support, and mental health issues. *The Counseling Psychologist, 13*(4), 537–579.

Snygg, D., & Combs, A.W. (1949). *Individual behavior*. New York: Harper.

Sue, D., & Sue, S. (1987). Cultural factors in the clinical assessment of Asian Americans. *Journal of Consulting and Clinical Psychology, 55*(4), 479–487.

Sue, D.W. (1978). Eliminating cultural oppression in counseling: Toward a general theory. *Journal of Counseling Psychology, 25*, 419–428.

Sue, D.W. (1981). *Counseling the culturally different*. New York: Wiley.

Sue, S., Akutsu, P.D., & Higashi, C. (1985). Training issues in conducting therapy with ethnic-minority-group clients. In P. Pedersen, *Handbook of cross-cultural counseling and therapy* (pp. 275–280). Westport, CT: Greenwood Press.

Triandis, H.C. (1972). *The analysis of subjective culture*. New York: Wiley.

Triandis, H.C. (1985). Some major dimensions of cultural variation in client populations. In P. Pedersen (Ed.), *Handbook of cross-cultural counseling and therapy* (pp. 21–28). Westport, CT: Greenwood Press.

U.S. Census Bureau. (1980). *1980 Census*. Washington, DC: Author.

Vaizey, J., & Clarke, C.F.O. (1976). *Education: The state of the debate in America, Britain, and Canada*. London, England: Duckworth.

VanZijl, J.C. (1985). *Multi-cultural counseling: Mission impossible*. Paper presented at the International Round Table for the Advancement of Counselling, Lund, Sweden.

Vontress, C.E. (1976). Racial and ethnic barriers in counselling. In P. Pedersen et al. (Eds.), *Counseling cross cultures*. Honolulu: University of Hawaii Press.

Vontress, C.E. (1986). Social and cultural foundations. In M.D. Lewis, R.L. Hayes, & J.A. Lewis (Eds.), *An introduction to the counseling profession* (pp. 215–250). Itasca, IL: Peacock.

Watts, A.G. (1981). Introduction. In A.G. Watts, D.E. Super, & J.M. Kidd (Eds.), *Career development in Britain* (pp. 1–8). Cambridge, England: Hobson's Press.

Watts, A.G., & Herr, E.L. (1976). Career education in Britain and the U.S.A.: Contrasts and common problems. *British Journal of Guidance and Counseling, 4*, 129–142.

Westermeyer, J. (1985). Mental health & Southeast Asian refugees: Observations over two decades from Laos and the United States. In T.C. Owan (Ed.), *Southeast Asians' mental health: Treatment, prevention, services, training, and research* (Chapter 3). Washington, DC: U.S. Department of Health and Human Services, National Institute of Mental Health.

Westermeyer, J. (1987). Cultural factors in clinical assessment. *Journal of Consulting and Clinical Psychology, 55*(4), 471–478.

Yankelovich, D. (1981). *The meaning of work.* In J. O'Toole, J.L. Scheiber, & L.C. Wood (Eds.), *Working: Changes and choices* (pp. 33–34). New York: Human Sciences Press.

Yiu, L. (1978). *Degree of assimilation and its effect on the preference of counseling style and on self-disclosure among Chinese Americans in Hawaii.* Unpublished doctoral dissertation. Indiana University, Bloomington.

Yoshioka, R.B., Tashima, N., Chew, M., & Murase, K. (1981). *Mental health services for Pacific/Asian Americans.* San Francisco: Pacific Asian Mental Health Research Project.

CHAPTER 5

SPECIAL POPULATIONS AT RISK

The fourth major challenge for counselors now and in the future is the changing definition of who among the diverse populations of the United States is "at risk." Who is at risk of being physically ill or abused, experiencing mental disorders, taking on antisocial behavior, being economically disadvantaged, or experiencing other forms of negative psychological, social, physical, or economic life events? As suggested in previous chapters, these factors are not mutually exclusive. People who experience unusual amounts of stress from losing a job or being constantly thwarted in their efforts to become part of the social mainstream are likely to manifest physical symptoms and stress-related disease, mental disorders, chemical dependency, family difficulties and, possibly, abusive behavior. These behaviors are typically interactive and indicate that most of the problems of psychological vulnerability people experience are really multidimensional in their influence. They trigger ripple effects that flow through the interpersonal systems of which they are a part. For example, when a family member becomes an alcoholic, or mentally ill, or unemployed, such a condition affects a wide array of people with whom that family member comes in contact. In the vocabulary of alcoholism, the spouse or child of an alcoholic or substance abuser may become codependent, or they may become scapegoats or objects of abuse, or in some other way caught up in the network of problems, dysfunction, or negativism that may evolve from or surround the primary person at risk.

There are several ways to consider the notion of people being "at risk." One is to consider which groups in the population are most at risk of suffering personal vulnerability to mental disorders and related factors. Another is to consider how the definitions of "special populations at risk" are changing and on what basis additional groups are being identified as being "at risk." A third way is to identify "risk factors," the environmental, social, or personal characteristics that put people at risk. In epidemiological terms, "a risk factor is a condition which increases the likelihood of a person developing a particular disorder" (Lobel & Hirschfield, 1984, p. 28). A fourth way is to consider counseling approaches that may be targeted to groups or individuals at risk as well as other strategies beyond counseling that counselors may orchestrate or advocate. This chapter will combine each of these dimensions of individuals or groups "at risk" in the analyses that follow.

Special Groups at Risk

Although it is ultimately an individual who is at risk, membership in so-called special groups tends to be seen as increasing the likelihood that one will be exposed to the number or severity of factors that lead to behavioral disorders, problematic behavior, or a particular disadvantage. Frequently federal and state legislation serves to identify specific populations who are to receive or be eligible for some set of services designed to ameliorate their being at risk, vulnerable, or of special status. Depending upon the legislation at issue and its purposes, special populations at risk may be described as the physically handicapped, the socially and emotionally disabled, the mentally retarded, the economically or emotionally disadvantaged, single parents, prisoners or ex-offenders, dislocated workers, individuals of gay or lesbian orientation, members of specific minority, racial, or ethnic groups, Vietnam veterans, the aging, and the elderly. Within these groups at risk there may be other subgroups of people at even greater risk because they are suicidal, functionally illiterate, poverty-stricken, exhibit type A behavior, and so forth. When legislation identifies and targets certain groups to receive special services and resources, it is typically because members of such groups are seen as potential or actual problems to themselves or to others. Also, as understanding of the interaction of external events and of individual behavior has enlarged, it has become apparent to lawmakers and to mental health professionals that certain groups have heightened vulnerability to stress, crises, and personal turmoil at certain life transition points.

In essence, the notion of a "special population" is a way of suggesting that individuals in that population are more at risk or more vulnerable to psychological, interpersonal, and economic difficulties than people outside that population. Definitions of special populations change as legislative purposes change and knowledge about psychological definitions expands. Thus, the definition of persons at risk is dynamic and not absolute. Many people move into and out of at-risk populations as their environmental conditions, resource and support systems, or age changes. For example, a White male worker who has had a stable job and good health may not ever have been included in an at-risk population until he suddenly loses his job at age 50 because the major employer in his hometown closes the plant where he has worked since he was 18 years of age. Suddenly, he enters an at-risk population whose vulnerability to a drop in self-esteem, stress-related disease, chemical dependency, and economic disadvantage becomes real. Or, consider the woman who—after graduating from high school immediately marries, raises a family, and concentrates on being a homemaker—suddenly becomes a widow at 48 years of age. In an instant her psychological and financial status changes, as does her sense of personal identity, her interpersonal network, and her need to enter the labor market without the experience or the skills immediately available for occupational entry. She has immediately entered an at-risk population where dealing with grief and bereavement, loneliness, financial insecurity, identity confusion, and a lack of functional skills places her at risk of mental disorder, a psychological crisis, or a variety of economic problems.

Definitions of At-Risk Groups

Perry indicated in 1982 that, "In the past ten years, the delivery of relevant services to special populations has been a focus of mounting concern within the helping professions, in national legislation, and in the heightened awareness of these populations themselves" (p. 50). A basic premise of this chapter is that the concerns Perry identified will continue through the remainder of this century and probably beyond.

Perry indicated that one can define the concept of "special populations" in several ways. In a restricted sense special populations can be defined as the most underserved members of our nation. That is to say, these people are special because they experience limited access to counseling and other mental health services, and the services they do receive frequently are not relevant, in social or cultural terms, to what they need.

In a broader sense, however, populations can be defined as "special" from either a social or historical perspective or from a life span or developmental perspective. According to Perry (1982) the first category comprises all those special populations for whom:

> . . . historically and at present, cultural stereotypes, the legal system, processes of socialization, and corrosive social stigma operate to provide a negative social-psychological ecology: women, racial and cultural minorities, the elderly, the handicapped, learning-disabled or gifted children, and other groups such as the mentally ill, the incarcerated, and persons of alternative sexual orientation. The second major category consists of persons who are at significant points of transition and stress in their lives. Thus these changing 'developmental' special populations are cross-sections of the population at times of family planning, pre- and post-natal care, early childhood support and day care systems, school entry screening, school-employment transitions, illness and death in the family, separation and divorce, career transitions, periods of unemployment and retirement. (p. 52)

The definitions of special populations cited above suggest the following:

- The risk factors by which special populations are defined differ. Some special populations are special because they have been exposed to historical, social, legal, and educational inequities that have placed them at risk of not gaining access to the educational, social, and economic institutions that would allow them to acquire the personal competencies, self-confidence, and mentoring available to other groups. Therefore, their life chances and possibility structures have been restricted or constrained because of the stereotyping and bias they have experienced because of their disabilities, race, sex, sexual orientation, ethnicity, age, or other group membership characteristics. Other populations are special because at certain developmental or transition points they have experienced psychological or physical trauma, crises, or other conditions that have caused them to be unusually prone to extraordinary stress, abuse, or other emotional and behavioral disorders.

- Because the risk factors affecting special populations are variable, the counseling and other services available must be tailored to the different categories of risk. In some instances, the treatment of preference is primary prevention; in other instances, intense, individual psychotherapy is the preferred intervention. Sometimes the role of the counselor is a consultative one; sometimes direct services are required. Depending upon the etiology and maintenance of the risk factors involved, self-help groups, deliberate psychological education, or support networks may be the most appropriate treatments.

- Some people are at risk because of historical, social, legal, and educational inequities as well as developmental or transition problems. In other words, they are in both categories of risk, not only one or the other.

Perspectives on Risk Factors

As antecedents to risk, there are factors that predispose people to vulnerability or being "at risk." Sometimes clusters of factors are involved; sometimes there may be one factor (e.g., a physical handicap, racial background) that becomes encumbered with layers of prejudice and bias and ultimately internalized by the individual as part of his or her self-concept.

In terms of physical health risk factors, it has become common knowledge that widely practiced personal habits such as smoking, alcohol abuse, dietary excesses, sedentary life style, and coronary-prone behavior patterns contribute in substantial ways to disease incidence (Rosen & Solomon, 1985). Risk factors in psychological health are probably more complex and varied. Depending on the risk group, they involve such social variables as education, marital status, religious participation, social integration, employment status, and stress. Mechanic's (1985) research suggests the presence of such risk factors as the following in the use of psychiatric services: low psychological well-being, self-description of unhappiness, degree of worry about specific life problems, and low self-esteem. He found these factors related to three aspects: (1) body sensations, symptoms, or feelings different from those ordinarily experienced; (2) social stress; and (3) cognitive appraisals of what a person is feeling (Mechanic, p. 13).

In a broader context, Evans (1985) applied a social learning model to explanations of adolescent smoking behavior. It suggests that both the social environment and "personality" determinants contribute to the complex of psychological predispositions related to smoking. Perhaps more important for our purposes is to suggest examples of where risk factors can appear or what can shape them along the process that finally is manifested not only in an outcome such as smoking but also in mental disorders, chemical dependency, and other phenomena.

Specifically, Evans, in his model of adolescent smoking behavior, indicated the presence of such factors as:

- General social environment, including smoking-related behavior, and expressed attitudes of peers, siblings, parents, respected adults, and media figures;
- Interpersonal or "personality factors" such as low self-esteem, dependency or powerlessness, and frequent rewards for imitative behavior; and
- Psychological predispositions including smoking-related attitudes, beliefs, values, expectations, and learned behaviors.

These three factors in turn lead to a negative or positive attitude regarding smoking and, ultimately, to behavior—refraining from or engaging in smoking.

Such a paradigm indicates that negative and positive factors can appear in individuals' general social environment, in their personality or intrapersonal structure, and in their psychological predispositions. As negative factors appear in such of one's life space, one becomes increasingly "at risk" to engage in or to be excluded from certain behaviors or opportunities. Models of such paradigms also suggest where the points of intervention on risk factors should be— the mass media, family, public policy, the individual's self-concept or sense of self-worth, individual beliefs, values, or learned behavior. Depending on the problem at issue, any or all of these points of intervention may need to be considered.

Another broad view of risk factors relates to the prevention or the treatment of alcohol abuse. Nathan (1985) concluded that:

> Influences on drinking, including alcohol drinking, include genetic and prenatal factors, interpersonal and environmental factors, psychological, psychiatric, and behavioral factors, and sociocultural and ethnic factors. These influences on drinking, in turn, can operate at societal, institutional, community, family, peer group, and individual levels; influences on drinking, moreover, derive from social norms, social controls, access and availability of beverage alcohol in the society in question, the drinker's personal disposition and behavior patterns, etc. (p. 37)

Other terms for risk factors may be etiologic factors, predisposing factors, or psychosocial stressors. Each of these terms is used, for example, in the *Diagnostic and Statistical Manual of Mental Disorders, Third Edition*, popularly known as DSM-III or in its revised version, DSM-IIIR. DSM-III identifies, classifies, and suggests treatment for the broad range of mental disorders that are accepted as separate entities by the American Psychiatric Association. These include disorders that are organic, substance induced, or affective, psychosocial, anxiety, or adjustment based in their origin or manifestation. Part of the structure of the DSM-III is assistance to clinicians in organizing their diagnoses around a multi-axial system of five types of information. Within such evaluations, the DSM-III provides descriptions of factors that are associated with or precede the onset of each mental disorder classified and a taxonomy by which to assess the severity of the mental disorder or the events leading to it.

One example of how our discussion of risk factors or people "at risk" overlaps with the classification of psychosocial factors can be seen in Figure 3, which depicts an abridged rating of the severity of psychosocial stressors (American Psychiatric Association, 1980, p. 27). The range of severity ranges from 1, indicating no apparent psychosocial stressor, to 7, which indicates the presence of a catastrophic psychosocial stressor.

The examples in Figure 3 are not exhaustive of the types of psychosocial stressors that might be present in the etiology (the assignment of a cause) or the onset of a disorder. Rather, according to the American Psychiatric Association, a range of psychosocial factors may trigger problems or predispose individuals to being at risk, as shown in Figure 4.

Psychosocial stress factors typically are seen as interacting with predisposing factors (characteristics of an individual that can be identified before the development of a disorder that place him or her at higher risk for developing the disorder) in defining the conditions of being at risk or of vulnerability as it is used in this chapter. In a sense, predisposing factors frequently serve as thresholds for vulnerability, which, when exceeded, are manifested as a disorder depending upon the presence and severity of specific psychosocial stressors. The potency of psychosocial stressors depends on when these stressors appear in the individual life cycle and the meaning those stressors hold for a given individual. Obviously, given the same stressor, people respond differently. Aspects of the individual who experiences a psychosocial stressor vary and affect how the event is emotionally and cognitively processed.

The intent of this chapter is not to engage in an in-depth analysis of the research on "at risk" factors but rather to sensitize the reader to the notion of special populations at risk, the complexity of the issues, and the changing perspectives on populations of increasing concern to counselors because of their particular vulnerability and the need for responses to that vulnerability.

FIGURE 3
Severity Rating of Psychosocial Stressors

Code	Term	Adult Examples	Child or Adolescent Examples
2	Minimal	Minor violation of the law; small bank loan	Vacation with family
3	Mild	Argument with neighbor; change in work hours	Change in schoolteacher; new school year
4	Moderate	New career; death of close friend; pregnancy	Chronic parental fighting; change to new school; illness of close relative; birth of sibling
5	Severe	Serious illness in self or family; major financial loss; marital separation; birth of child	Death of peer; divorce of parents; arrest; hospitalization; persistent and harsh parental discipline
6	Extreme	Death of close relative; divorce	Death of parent or sibling; repeated physical or sexual abuse
7	Catastrophic	Concentration camp experience; devastating natural disaster	Multiple family deaths

From "Severity of Psychosocial Stressors" (p. 27) in *Diagnostic and Statistical Manual of Mental Disorders, Third Edition*, by the American Psychiatric Association, 1980, Washington, DC: Author. Adapted by permission.

FIGURE 4
Types of Psychosocial Stressors to be Considered

Conjugal (marital and nonmarital): e.g., engagement, marriage, discord, separation, death of spouse.

Parenting: e.g., becoming a parent, friction with child, illness of child.

Other interpersonal: problems with one's friends, neighbors, associates, or nonconjugal family members, e.g., illness of best friend, discordant relationship with boss.

Occupational: includes work, school, homemaker, e.g., unemployment, retirement, school problems.

Living circumstances: e.g., change in residence, threat to personal safety, immigration.

Financial: e.g., inadequate finances, change in financial status.

Legal: e.g., arrested, jailed, lawsuit or trial.

Developmental: phases of the life cycle, e.g., puberty, transition to adult status, menopause, "becoming 50."

Physical illness or injury: e.g., illness, accident, surgery, abortion.

Other psychosocial stressors: e.g., natural or manmade disaster, persecution, unwanted pregnancy, out-of-wedlock birth, rape.

Family factors (children and adolescents): In addition to the above, for children and adolescents the following stressors may be considered: cold or distant relationship between parents; overtly hostile relationship between parents; physical or mental disturbance in family members; cold or distant parental behavior toward child; overtly hostile parental behavior toward child; parental intrusiveness; inconsistent parental control; insufficient parental control; insufficient social or cognitive stimulation; anomalous family situation, e.g., single parent, foster family; institutional rearing; loss of nuclear family members.

From *Diagnostic and Statistical Manual of Mental Disorders, Third Edition* (p. 28) by the American Psychiatric Association, 1980, Washington, DC: Author. Adapted by permission.

Although it is not possible to deal at length with all of the populations potentially at risk, the following sections will address some of the major concerns related to populations at different age levels: children, youth, and adults. Such concerns represent problem areas that counselors in different settings are likely to encounter.

Children and Adolescents At Risk

Preschool Children

Researchers and behavioral scientists have been concerned for many years about identifying preschool children who, because of genetic predisposition or intense environmental stresses, run unusually strong risks of developing mental problems in adulthood. Rolf (1985), among other investigators supported by the National Institute of Mental Health (Quoted in Isenstein & Krasner, 1978), theorized that very young children do show symptoms of behavior disorders, which, if identified, could be treated with early intervention techniques designed to prevent these early behavioral disorders from developing into adult psychopathology. To these ends, Rolf and others have been developing "a high risk profile" that is useful in the early identification and selection of children for individualized treatment. Out of this research has come the consensus that the most vulnerable children are:

- Those with deviant parents, especially parents with psychotic and criminal histories;
- Those with chronic aggressive behavior disorders;
- Those who have suffered very severe social, cultural, economic, and nutritional deprivations; and
- Those who have physical, temperamental, or intellectual handicaps. (pp. 2–3)

Once preschool children who fall into these categories are identified, the further consensus is that individualized interventions should be designed that are preventive of future behavioral disorders. From a preventive standpoint, the intent of intervention is to help these children build up their resistance to environmental stressors, give them better methods of coping, and increase the flexibility of their behavioral repertoires. In order to achieve such outcomes a variety of interventions are of possible use. They include, in broad terms, special day-care or preschool curricula, consultation, referral, direct child contact, parent and family contact, and advocacy and follow-through. With respect to day-care or preschool curricula, social, intellectual, and physical competencies can be developed through graded series of play and work activities, practice of socially acceptable behavior, skits, visits to community sites (e.g., fire stations, police stations, churches, stores) that reinforce the value of socially acceptable behaviors, games, sports, dancing and rhythm exercises, cooperative activities with other children, formal instruction designed to stimulate creativity, verbal comprehension, critical thinking, and sensory discrimination.

Often, if not always, intervention with high-risk children requires intervention with high-risk parents that may take the form of parenting education, counseling and support in child-rearing, instruction in nutrition and management of resources, and therapy directed at the parents' own psychiatric, alcohol-related, or other problems.

Frequently high-risk children experience multiple problems. That is, they may simultaneously require speech and language therapy, socialization with other children, play therapy, behavioral modification, and other direct intervention.

Childhood Depression

High-risk children may also experience clinical depression. Clinical depression is a term that covers a large range of affective disorders that vary in their causes and in their intensity, severity, and duration. Typically, clinical depression is associated with a depressed mood, the "blues," feelings of rejection or isolation, and a loss of interest in usual activities. Symptoms also may include appetite, weight, or sleep disturbances, hyperactivity or lethargy, anxiety, crying, slowed thinking, suicidal tendencies, and feelings of guilt, worthlessness, and hopelessness. Although the symptoms of depression in adolescents are similar to those in adults, clinical depression may occur even in infants, and it certainly occurs as well in prepuberal children. In infancy, a depressive condition called the "nonorganic failure to thrive syndrome" has been identified in which babies with the condition are found to be unresponsive to external stimuli such as eye contact, tend to cry weakly, refuse food, sleep excessively, and seem apathetic (Lobel & Hirschfield, 1984). The immediate cause of such a syndrome seems to be inadequate care in the environment. Thus, as suggested above, such babies may have parents who are themselves at risk, troubled, unable to cope and, as a result, they put their children at risk of depression and other mental disorders.

In prepuberal and adolescent clinical depression, a variety of factors are likely to be implicated. It is possible that in some instances childhood depression may be a function of genetic predisposition and be associated with children of parents with a major problem of diagnosed depression. It is also true that viral disease, some malignancies or other illnesses, and some medications can cause depression. All of these can be considered risk factors for some children. The more common predisposing factors to depression in children are, like those for adults, stressful events: loss of a parent or sibling, illness, divorce, a move to a new community or a new home, teasing from peers, lack of friends, a bad experience with a teacher, or ineptness in sports when they are an important part of an environment. Usually in young children, psychotherapy or medication are not the treatments of choice unless the depression is severe. Rather, what is usually indicated is the need to change the child's environment in order to increase his or her self-esteem, promote friendships, provide more attention, or resolve school difficulties (Lobel & Hirschfield, 1984). As children become adolescents, episodes of clinical depression may, in fact, warrant medication, psychotherapy, or other adult treatments. The point here is that some portion of the population of children, perhaps as much as 10% to 12% (Lobel & Hirschfield) can experience levels of stress, clinical depression, or psychopathology that put them at high risk for subsequent problems in adolescence and adulthood.

Elementary School Children at Risk

High-risk preschool children are frequently unidentified or untreated. They enter elementary school and subsequent educational levels carrying the seeds of vulnerability that are likely to blossom into academic underachievement, suicide, dropping out of school, antisocial behavior, or other manifestations. These behaviors are not exclusive to preschool children at high risk; other children are at risk as well. We have alluded to some of the issues that put children at risk in chapters 3 and 4 as we spoke of the changing family as well as cultural diversity. Within those contexts, Hodgkinson (1985), in his review of current demographic trends, indicated that over the next 10 years, educators and counselors are likely to work with increased numbers of children with the following characteristics:

- Premature at birth;
- Born to a teenage mother;
- Born to parents who were not married;
- Come from single-parent households;
- Come from "blended families" that result from remarriage of one original parent;
- Come from poor households;
- Are minorities;
- Have not participated in Head Start or similar preschool programs; and
- Have working parents and could be described as latchkey children.

Although not every child with these risk factors is necessarily vulnerable to mental disorders or academic underachievement, research is not in their favor. More and more studies suggest that children with one or more of these characteristics are likely to perform poorly in school.

Students at Risk

"Students at risk" include elementary and secondary school students who, on the one hand, run the risk of not acquiring the knowledge, skills, and attitudes needed to become successful adults and, on the other hand, behave in ways that put them at risk for not graduating from high school. The negative behaviors at issue include "not engaging in classroom and school activities, using drugs and alcohol, committing disruptive and delinquent acts, becoming pregnant, dropping out, or attempting suicide" (Pennsylvania Department of Education, 1987, p. 1). A final use of the term "students at risk" relates to children whose family background and home and community conditions, such as poverty or low parental education, are associated with low achievement and the lack of success in school. Undoubtedly, within these definitions of students at risk are a number of children whose profiles in preschool would have been defined as high risk. The pool of such children gets larger as environmental stresses accumulate.

Students at risk are of major concern to parents and teachers. For example, teachers surveyed in a major study of schooling in 38 school districts around the nation (Goodlad, 1983) ranked highest the problems of lack of student interest, lack of parent interest, and student misbehavior.

Drug Use

Data from national surveys about drug and alcohol use among students reflect another facet of students at risk. A random sample of 2,400 high school seniors by the National Institute on Drug Abuse (1985) revealed that the steady decline from 1980 to 1984 in illicit drug use, including marijuana, among high school seniors seems to have halted, with high school seniors reporting an increased use of cocaine from 4.9% in 1983 to 6.7% in 1985. Seventeen percent of the seniors who responded to the National Institute on Drug Abuse survey indicated that they had tried cocaine. The same survey suggested that the monthly use of alcohol had declined from 72% in 1980 to 66% in 1985. Even so, however, 5% of the seniors reported that they drink alcohol daily, and 37% reported that they had had five or more drinks in a row at least once in the prior 2 weeks.

In 1984, the Pennsylvania Department of Education surveyed 10,683 high school students from 10 school districts in the state with the following selected results: students who reported spending more time on academic activities also reported using less drugs and alcohol; students who reported being heavy users of cigarettes, beer, marijuana, stimulants, depressants, and cocaine also reported dissatisfaction with school and their teachers, lower grade point averages, and less self-confidence (Pennsylvania Department of Education, 1987).

Delinquent Behavior

Students at risk are also likely to be involved with delinquent acts. Data from the Federal Bureau of Investigation (1983) indicate that on the average 14.2% of 14- to 17-year-olds are arrested annually and that figure tends to fluctuate very little from year to year. Indeed, the data indicate that children under 18 years of age accounted for approximately 16.8% of all arrests and 30.5% of all "serious crime" arrests. In a study of delinquent behavior in two birth cohorts, one of 10,000 boys born in 1945, and a second of 13,160 boys and 14,000 girls born in 1958, Tracey, Wolfgang, and Figlio (1985) found that one third of each of these cohorts had had at least one episode with the police before they were 18 years of age. They found that within these youth cohorts there were between 7% and 8% who could be considered chronic offenders, and that many of these youth had begun to commit delinquent acts when they were 7 to 9 years of age. On balance, this research found that youth involved with police were two and one half times more likely to be male than female, from unstable homes, with fewer years of schooling, and with records of lower scholastic achievement. In another study of youth who engage in delinquent behavior, Gottfredson, Gottfredson, and Cook (1983) found that such youth tend to have weak attachments to parents; feel alienated from any social order and do not respect rules of law as having validity; dislike school, are frequently truant, and expend little effort on school work; associate with delinquent peers; and experience low self-esteem or a delinquent self-concept.

Some children and adolescents will exhibit violent behavior. For example, between 1971 and 1980, arrests of juveniles for violent offenses increased by 38%, from 62,302 to 86,220 arrests nationally. However, violent offenders constitute a small percentage (4% in 1980) of juveniles arrested (U.S. Federal Bureau of Investigation, 1981).

One study suggests that in stable communities fewer than 2% of juveniles will ever be arrested for a violent offense (Hamparian, Schuster, Dinitz, & Conrad, 1978). Thus, juvenile offenders who commit violent offenses constitute a small number of all juvenile offenders and a very small percentage of all juveniles. Many but not all of these children will have been previously identified as juvenile delinquents. In any case, violent behavior can occur in school, in the family, in the work place, or in other community settings. Just as is true of other forms of behavior, "violent behavior occurs within a social context that includes both antecedents and consequences" (Roth, 1985, p. xiii). Thus, certain risk factors predispose youth and adults to violent behavior.

Violent individuals manifest both a "psychology" and a "social psychology" that must be understood and addressed if behavioral change is to be facilitated. Violence, like most human behavior, is multifactored; rarely is there a single cause for a person's violent behavior. Psychological, situational, medical, and other factors may be implicated in any particular instance of violent behavior. Monnhan and Klasson (1982) proposed that violent behavior often emerges because of an interaction between stressful life events, a person's cognitions and affects, and a person's behavioral coping responses. In sum, "violence does not occur in a vacuum but in response to psychological, social, and environmental stress" (Lion, 1985, p. 41). A first step for the counselor and other mental health workers is determining what the stress is and whether it can recur.

A wide range of categories of risk factors is associated with the presence of violent behavior in children and adolescents. The following are among those adapted from reviews of diagnostic and treatment issues concerning violent juveniles reported by Lewis (1985) and by Lion (1985):

- Social, familial, medical, cognitive, and psychiatric factors often combine to contribute to a particular act of violence.

- Although most violent juveniles come from family conditions of social deprivation, it is apparently not the social deprivation per se that triggers violence; it is important to be mindful that most people raised in social deprivation do not behave violently.

- Within conditions of family social deprivation, risk factors for juvenile violent behavior are the presence of past physical abuse; a psychotic parent; severe central nervous system injury from beatings, blows to the head, being thrown down steps; or psychotic and organic symptomatology.

- Delinquents tend to come from chaotic family situations of family discord that may lead to broken homes and to parents' failure to supervise and discipline their children properly. In addition, in contrast to nondelinquents, delinquent juveniles are much more likely to have parents who have been psychiatrically hospitalized as manic-depressive or schizophrenic. Antisocial children are frequently found to have fathers who themselves have learning or behavior problems. Thus, at one level it is apparent that many violent juvenile offenders suffer psychopathology that has genetic, inherited, or physiological underpinnings.

- Whether or not they themselves are psychopathological, a large proportion of children and adolescents, perhaps 75%, have experienced physical abuse at the hands of their parents or parent surrogates. Violence tends to beget violence as children imitate behaviors they have experienced. They may displace their rage at being brutally mistreated by their parents to other children or adults with whom they come in contact. They may be inordinately suspicious of others. Physical abuse frequently leads to brain damage, neurological deficits, psychomotor seizures, minimal brain dysfunction, and other injuries to the central nervous system that reduce the child's ability to control aggressive impulses or that are manifested in epileptic seizures or a variety of learning and behavioral problems associated with brain damage. Severe physical injury can lead to psychotic behavior, hyperactivity, or episodic violence.

- Children who have been severely abused may develop paranoid tendencies, excessive wariness and suspicion, thinking disorders, or perceptual problems that lead to misinterpretation and miscommunication about events that result in violent reactions.

- An adolescent or an adult who was treated cruelly as a child can grow up with a lack of interpersonal warmth, become aloof to the suffering of others, be indifferent to hurting others, and be prone to excessive discipline of children or pets. These people learn coping styles and adaptations to violence they may use with others, including their own offspring, later in life.

- Violent adolescents and adults are typically characterized by low self-esteem resulting from parental deprivation or alcoholism. Low self-esteem in antisocial adolescents or adults frequently is combined with little tolerance for introspection and considerable projection to external causes and people for their problems. They convert any criticism into externally directed rage, lashing out at others in physical and verbal outbursts.

- A host of toxic factors has been associated with violent behavior. Abuse of hallucinogens, LSD or PCP, amphetamines, barbiturates, and inhalants such as glue fumes has been associated with aggression and homicidal behavior. Alcohol remains the most frequent toxic substance linked to violence.

As suggested by the multiple risk factors associated with violent behavior, assessment of the specific etiology or stresses associated with the violent behavior a particular individual displays is critical. Following such assessment, however, treatment will probably need to be multidimensional. Medication may be necessary to control aggressive impulses. If so, the medication will need to be highly individualized. Anticonvulsants, antipsychotics, or antidepressants may be indicated in particular cases. Educational interventions in response to learning disabilities or other learning problems will be important for many violent youth. Psychotherapy and group counseling frequently will be used for most delinquent and violent youth. And, of major importance, either through therapeutic interventions or in other ways (e.g., Big Brother/Big Sister programs), most violent, seriously delinquent adolescents need at least one adult relationship that is steady, stable, caring, and understanding. They need someone who cares about their successes and is dismayed about their setbacks. Without such an empathic, emotionally supportive relationship it is unlikely that violent, delinquent adolescents will be motivated or able to change their behaviors. Even where multiple forms of treatment and support are available, it is likely that many of the risk factors identified as associated with violent behavior will be chronic and incurable; at best, they will be able to be controlled and the incidence of violent behavior significantly reduced. Some of these youngsters will never be able to return to their original family or to function within the normal school environment. Instead, they will require a residential setting, a group home, or other structured and perhaps secure environment where their self-control and increasingly independent behavior can be monitored and supported.

Teenage Parents

Another category of students at risk are those who become pregnant as adolescents. There are now more than one million teenage pregnancies annually, with 94% of the mothers who do not have abortions keeping their babies (Saed, 1979), and about 50% of these mothers becoming pregnant again in 3 years. Teenage mothers tend to give birth to children who themselves become teenage parents. Because teenage mothers themselves frequently come from families in poverty, their babies suffer low weight, poor nutrition, and, in some instances, drug addiction at birth. The rate of live births among teenage mothers is lower than among older mothers. The rate of teenage pregnancies is related to the amount of adolescent premarital intercourse which is, in turn, related to a large number of risk factors: peer pressure, sexually active friends, living in an urban setting, poverty, low success in school, low educational expectations, use of drugs and alcohol, low self-esteem, feelings of alienation, and engaging in disruptive acts (Chilman, 1980).

Huey (1987) suggested that the invisible or forgotten half of the teen pregnancy phenomenon is the unwed fathers. His review of the research literature indicates that these young men are just as confused, afraid, and anxious as the young women they impregnate and that they often face a lifetime of frustration. Unlike the frequent stereotypes of unwed fathers, most teenage fathers do care about what happens to their children and they need opportunities to explore their concerns and feelings. Huey described a group counseling session for unwed fathers in which they were helped to focus on their three Rs: Rights, Responsibilities, and Resources. Using both outside experts and intense group discussions, the unwed fathers explored their own feelings, including their guilt and frustration, their responsibility for the pregnancy, contraceptive use and planned parenthood, their legal and emotional rights and responsibilities, present and future options, problem solving and decision making, and available resources and their use. Huey found that just as teenage mothers need assistance and support, so do unwed fathers; becoming a father during adolescence has serious consequences for individual development, and teenage fathers are not psychologically prepared for their new role. Indeed, without help they are at risk of dropping out of school, not furthering their education, and becoming an economic drain on society.

Child Abuse

Another large "at risk" population is composed of children who have experienced abuse by their parents. According to Cooney (1988), it is possible to divide child abuse into three categories that are not necessarily mutually exclusive: emotional abuse, physical abuse, and sexual abuse. Each of these forms of abuse may be present in the life of a single child. Each also puts the child at risk for other immediate problems such as violent or antisocial behavior, dropping out of school, mental disorders, stress-related disease, or, in the case of sexual abuse, possible teenage pregnancy. The child who was abused is also at greater risk of becoming an abuser of his or her own children.

Child abuse has many specific manifestations and is a complex phenomenon. As Cooney effectively described, each form of child abuse tends to be associated with developmental problems for the abused children that vary with the intensity, severity, and duration of such abuse. To differentiate the three major forms of abuse, Cooney (1988) suggested the following:

> *Emotional abuse* implies a pattern of continual attacks on a child's self-esteem, self-confidence, sense of belonging, or safety. The child who is emotionally abused may be the recipient of constant criticism, threats, or embarrassment. He or she may be a scapegoat, treated as an unwelcome intruder in the family. (p. 3)

> *Physical abuse* is the nonaccidental injury of a child by a parent or caregiver. (p. 5)

> *Sexual abuse* is not limited to sexual intercourse; sexual abuse encompasses a range of sexual activity including genital exposure, fondling, forced touching, inappropriate kissing, oral sex, and intercourse. Typically, sexual abuse occurs over a period of years with gradual escalation of sexual demands. If intercourse occurs, it is likely to begin in puberty or prepuberty. (p. 7)

The extent of child abuse is difficult to know precisely. Waterman and Lusk (1986) recently reported that one out of four girls and one out of four or five boys will be sexually abused before reaching age 18. Data from the work of other observers (Finkelhor, 1979; Russell, 1982) suggest that 9% to 16% of all girls experience incest before age 18. Incest in this context is seen as a form of child sexual abuse that includes any type of sexual activity between a child and a parent, stepparent, sibling, extended family member, or surrogate parent figure (Sgroi, 1982). Alter-Reid et al. (1986) reported that the children at highest risk for incest are those with stepfathers. A stepfather is six times more likely to abuse a daughter sexually than a biological father.

In an important review of the research literature on incest, Josephson and Fong-Beyette (1987) indicated that the experience of incest is linked to subsequent psychological problems including the inability to trust, low self-esteem, self-hatred, passivity, sexual identity conflicts, impairment of sexual functioning, feelings of isolation, guilt, shame, and somatic complaints. They reported the presence of a pattern of behavior, which Briere (1984) described as a post-sexual-abuse syndrome, that is common to incest victims and includes dissociation, anxiety, isolation, sleep disturbances, anger, sexual dysfunction, substance addiction, and self-destructiveness. Many of these problems continue on into adulthood, by which time many women have repressed the link between the difficulties they are experiencing and the incest or sexual abuse that occurred earlier. At a different level, it has been reported that a high percentage of adult prostitutes have disclosed being victims of childhood sexual abuse (Kempe & Kempe, 1984). Shapiro (1987) described a high relationship between incest, self-blame, and self-mutilation. Many victims of incest abuse drugs and engage in suicide attempts.

Cooney (1988) suggested that "the effects of sexual abuse vary depending on the duration of the abuse, the age of onset, and the closeness of the relationship of the victim to the abuser" (p. 7). Thus, at different developmental ages, one may observe different behavioral indicators in children who experience sexual abuse. Prior to age 6, for example, some children may seem very withdrawn whereas others may indicate sexual knowledge, make sexual overtures to others, or display behavior that seems too advanced for their years. These children may also commonly exhibit depression and anxiety, stomachaches, headaches, encopresis, enuresis, and sleep disturbances. Older sexually abused children, ages 6 to 12, may seem to be distracted or daydreaming, they may feel different from their classmates and thus be loners or seek older children as friends, they may dress in a seductive manner beyond that expected of their age, or experience anxiety, depression, and low self-esteem. In adolescence, sexually abused children may run away from home, become abusers of drugs and alcohol, attempt suicide, or act out in a sexually promiscuous manner.

Physical abuse of children may occur independently of sexual abuse, or both may occur together. The number of children who are injured or die from physical abuse by their parents or caregivers is hard to estimate. Frequently injuries occur to the brain or central nervous system of young children who have been violently shaken, struck, or thrown against a wall or hard object. O'Brien (1980) estimated that 7 to 15 children die each day in the United States from such injuries. Physically abused children not only experience bruises, burns, broken bones, and internal injuries but they also suffer emotional effects that ultimately translate into behavioral indicators. Preschool age abused children may appear shy and withdrawn, tense and fearful, overcompliant, lacking in spontaneity—or hostile and aggressive, cruel to other children, and destructive of their belongings. Abused children at ages 6 to 12 may become bullies, exhibit learning problems, or be so anxious as to experience impaired speech and motor performance. They also may be overly withdrawn around adults of the same sex or adults who resemble their abusers. Many physically abused children tend to internalize these experiences as meaning that they are bad children who deserve the punishment they receive. Frequently the result is a low sense of self-worth, self-esteem, or efficacy that is reflected in poor social relationships or poor academic achievement. The negative self-image and self-blame incorporated by many physically abused parents tends to be strongly internalized by the adolescent. Such children may still be trying desperately to please the parents who have found them so unsatisfactory, they may stay away from home to avoid parental abuse, or they may run away from home.

Emotional abuse pervades the presence of either physical or sexual abuse, but it can also occur independently. Psychological assaults on a child's esteem or self-confidence probably occur in most families on a spontaneous and nonreoccurring basis. Parents feel guilty and try to make amends to the child for the behavior. Emotional abuse, however, tends to be a constant pattern indicating that the child is unworthy, inferior to a sibling or to another child, or unacceptable. Depending upon the severity of the abuse, the developmental age at onset, and the duration, the behavioral effect may be a lack of opportunity to develop self-confidence or self-worth. Such children may find it difficult to relate to other children or to adults, may become agitated or withdrawn, or may manifest shyness or poor socialization skills. In severe cases of emotional abuse, preschool and older children may manifest severe emotional and affective disorders and need to be placed in special education programs or other therapeutic environments (Cooney, 1988). As emotionally abused children age, they may treat other children as they have been treated at home, as scapegoats or with threats. They may find it difficult to accept positive feedback or to allow others, children or adults, to befriend them. By adolescence, many such children will have been labeled troublemakers or potential dropouts because of poor achievement, low motivation, or hostility to those in authority. Or, they may simply fade into the masses and become essentially invisible, drifting along without recognition or personal attachment to the school or anyone in the school.

The implications of the different forms of child abuse for counselors in schools and in community agencies are diverse. In virtually all states, counselors are required to report suspected or actual abuse to state and local agencies concerned with child protection and welfare. The precise reporting requirements differ from state to state, but reporting has legal precedence over the counselor's obligations to maintain confidentiality for either the child victim or the abuser. The counselor also has a role in the prevention of child abuse through a variety of possible activities. Cooney (1988, p. 10) suggested the following: "parent education for teen and adult parents, parenting classes for children and adolescents, self-esteem workshops and groups for parents and children, assertiveness training, and training in problem solving." Counselors can also serve as advocates for community after-school programs, emergency child-care centers, and hot lines for parents who are afraid they will abuse their children or who feel so stressed that they feel they are out of control and may take it out on their children.

Counselors also have important therapeutic roles. They may provide parental retraining individually or in groups to help parents find alternative ways of communicating with their children other than through abusive behavior. They may implement such parenting programs as Systematic Training for Effective Parenting (STEP) or Parent Effectiveness Training (PET). Counselors may refer abusive parents to such groups as Parents Anonymous. Many abusive parents who were abused themselves are simply imitating how they were disciplined. They learned a style of parenting that needs to be unlearned and replaced with more positive parenting. Many of these parents need to learn techniques of anger management, and most need help with their own feelings of self-esteem and self-worth. Many parents need help to cope with their unresolved feelings about their own parents' expectations of them. They frequently need help with stress management, family conflicts, or work problems to avoid such stress from spilling over on their children. For abused children themselves, counselors can develop after-school and in-school programs designed to build their self-esteem, to buffer them from parental abuse, and to increase their positive interpersonal and communication skills. In addition, both individual and group counseling are vital to reduce child and adolescent self-blame and guilt for the abuse suffered. Counselors frequently need to engage classroom teachers and other adults in creating environments that are positively reinforcing for abused children and provide encounters with adults who are caring and supportive of the children. Counselors may also engage in family counseling to try to rebuild the family-child bond as a way of protecting the child from further sexual, physical, or emotional abuse. In cases of incest, Josephson and Fong-Bayette (1987) recommended that:

> . . . counselors acknowledge and validate the significance
> of the incest. Incest experiences should not be minimized
> even when they were unsuccessful attempts or occurred one

time or infrequently. Incest should be identified as an important trauma that is related to clients' current life difficulties. Perceiving incest clients as survivors who developed complicated coping skills that were actually adaptive to their early environment can help these clients see themselves as survivors rather than as sick or helpless victims. (p. 478)

Children of Alcoholics

Although often not thought about as child abuse per se, parents' alcoholism may lead to childrens' low self-esteem and other psychological problems, including vulnerability to alcoholism in later life. In chapter 3, problems of children of alcoholics were discussed within the context of dysfunctional families. That discussion will not be repeated here.

Suffice it to say briefly in this chapter that children of alcoholics are "at risk." As has been cited throughout this chapter, the characteristics of the family of origin can provide a positive or negative environment for child development. In their negative sense, they can create problems that predispose children to be at risk for a variety of problems. Growing up in an alcoholic family also puts one in an "at risk" environment. As we found in our discussions of violent behavior, alcoholism in the family can lead to physical abuse of children that can, in turn, lead children to behave violently toward others. Alcoholism in parents also is associated with alienation, suicide, and other phenomena.

Children of alcoholics must cope with a unique set of difficulties (Lewis, 1987). The alcoholic dependence of one or more family members creates a disequilibrium in the family that tends to be reflected in a set of roles that are fashioned by a child's relationship to the alcoholic family member. Where one parent is the abuser, the other parent is likely to try to care for the alcoholic parent, and in so doing be diminished in his or her capacity to provide for the children. The consistency of parenting may be undependable or episodic. Children may find it difficult to find personal support in the family and may seek it in peers or elsewhere beyond the family.

As suggested in the growing literature on children of alcoholics, some children blame themselves for their parents' problems. Some may try to take over the parenting responsibilities for maintaining the family or rearing their siblings. These children may become overresponsible, reliable, and controlled. They may lose touch with their own childhood needs. Other children may become the scapegoats or the focus of parental abuse. Others may try to distance themselves from their parents' behavior.

Counseling children of alcoholics needs to deal with where children who have adopted different coping styles are in their development. For children who are not receiving support and affection within the family or feel isolated within that context, counseling may need to help them reach out to others. For children who are afraid to acknowledge their feelings, counseling needs to provide them the opportunity to express these feelings and to deal with them. Children who think their life is unique and unusual may need to be involved in a support group of other children of alcoholics or referred to Al-Anon or other such organizations. Some children of alcoholics need to understand the mechanisms of substance abuse and what addiction does to their parents as a way of reducing their feelings of personal responsibility for their parents' behavior. These children need support to build self-worth and self-esteem.

The effects of being a child of an alcoholic are multidimensional and enduring. Counselors need to be alert to the signs of being at risk in children and adolescents and sensitive to the individual and group counseling responses that can respond to such conditions.

The School Dropout

Certainly a major outcome of the various risk factors children and youth experience is dropping out of school. It is perhaps the most well documented but the most intractable of statistics. Again, just as teenage mothers tend to spawn teenage parents themselves, school dropouts put their own life chances and those of their children at increased risk of economic and educational disadvantage and related mental health problems.

Depending on how the statistics are calculated and on what cohort group they are based, roughly 25% of all those who start school do not graduate, and approximately 19% of those who get to the ninth grade do not continue to graduation. In a major analysis of the longitudinal data available in the High School and Beyond national data set, Ekstrom, Goertz, Pollack, and Rock (1986) found that a variety of risk or predisposing factors differentiated those who dropped out of school from those who stayed in school. Some of the differences included the following: dropouts were disproportionately from low socioeconomic families and from racial or ethnic minority groups; they tended to come from homes with weak educational support systems (e.g., few books and other study aids, mothers with lower levels of formal education and lower levels of educational expectations for their children, parents less likely to be interested in or monitor the child's in-school and out-of-school activities); dropouts as sophomores reported less interest in school, attended classes less regularly, were less likely to feel popular with other students, were less likely to participate in extracurricular activities, were less likely to have plans to go to college, were more likely to report spending time outside of school "driving around" and going on dates, and reported working more hours per week. Twenty-three percent of the girls who dropped out of school between their sophomore and senior years cited pregnancy as the reason. Like other groups at risk, school dropouts are the products of multiple risk factors.

Suicide

The ultimate expression of being at risk is attempting or committing suicide. The U.S. suicide rate continues to accelerate. Suicide is now the third leading cause of death among youth and young adults, 15 to 24 years of age, following accidents and homicides, which in some instances may have, in fact, been suicides. In 1980, 142 children under 15 took their own life, and almost 1,800 between the ages of 15 and 19 did so (National Center for Health Statistics, 1983). Among adolescents, the suicide rate has risen dramatically from 4.0 per 100,000 in 1957 to 12.2 per 100,000 in 1975 (Hart & Heidel, 1979). Suicide and adolescent depression are linked, and some 15% of adolescents who suffer major episodes of depression are likely to commit suicide. Put another way, it is estimated that 50% to 80% of youth who commit suicide each year have some type of depressive disorder (Tugend, 1986).

A recent review of the factors involved in adolescent suicide (Pennsylvania Department of Education, 1986) indicates that the following are involved:

- External stress (e.g., school achievement, fear of nuclear war, community violence);
- Physical and psychological changes (e.g., stress associated with dating, sexuality, drugs, and alcohol);
- Breakdown of the family unit (e.g., increasing divorces, working parents, mobility, and decreasing role models and support networks);
- Responsibilities and privileges (e.g., increased responsibility and privileges with too little adult guidance); and

- Inaccurate perception of death (e.g., the inaccurate portrayal of death in the movies, television, and music).

A variety of checklists and sets of risk indicators have been developed to create profiles of the person likely to attempt suicide. They include in summary form such emphases as the following:

Sex: Men commit suicide more often than women, although more women than men attempt suicide.

Age: In general, as age increases, suicide risk increases. However, the suicide rate for men tends to level off after age 35 but does not level off for women until after age 70.

Race: Whites have a greater suicide risk than do non-Whites, except in the case of young male Blacks, for whom the rate is about twice that as for young male Whites.

Socioeconomic status: The lower the socioeconomic status the higher the suicide rate is likely to be, although suicides occur at all socioeconomic levels.

Marital status: Single persons are twice as likely as married persons to commit suicide; the suicide rate for widowed and divorced persons is four to five times higher than that for married persons.

Previous suicide attempts: The risk of suicide increases with a history of previous suicide attempts and as suicidal ideation continues to endure over a long period of time. The lethality of suicide attempts also is related to whether other family members or close friends have attempted or committed suicide. Young people tend to imitate in close proximity the suicides of others in a community or school. Such suicidal impulses following a successful suicide by one person are seen by some observers as a form of contagion (Phillips, 1985).

Character and life style of the individual: Alcoholism, drug abuse, psychotic behavior involving bizarre or highly lethal suicidal ideation, living alone, and refusing help are important risk indicators. So is the effect of significant losses—death of a loved one, divorce, separation, broken relationship, loss of a job, money, status, or self-esteem.

Symptoms: Depression, anxiety, panic, helplessness, hopelessness, despair, and sleep disruption are all symptoms of major concern in suicidal ideation. Sleep disruption can be a particularly important indicator because it is likely to increase depression, and it may be a function of hallucinating—perhaps from drug dependency, overuse of stimulants, or depressants.

Factors to consider when evaluating emergency risk: Does the person have a definite plan by which to commit suicide? Is the method available? Is the method reversible (e.g., planning to jump from high places or use of a gun is typically irreversible; taking pills is usually less lethal because there is a chance for reversibility)? Has a time been set for the attempt? Has the person given away possessions or finalized certain social or business affairs?

One can conceive the counselor's role with suicidal clients in terms of several points of involvement. One is prevention; a second is intervention, usually of a crisis nature; a third is postvention, working with attempters or survivors (Fujimura, Weis, & Cochran, 1985). Each of these stages has its own concepts and techniques. In prevention, for example, it is necessary to be able to recognize the person's pleas for help before a suicide attempt is made. This involves understanding the risk factors, symptoms, and other behavioral clues for identifying persons at risk. This may require, in the case of schools particularly, instituting and monitoring a referral system of teachers, peers, and parents who have been educated to be sensitive to the signs of potential suicide victims and to refer those at risk. Prevention may also involve a suicide education program, as part of a counseling outreach scheme, to help students understand the feelings and factors involved, the resources for help that are available, and the support systems that can be devoted to suicide prevention. Either the counselor or others in the referral system need to be sensitive to the patterns of verbal and non-verbal communication that frequently give clues to suicidal ideation and, if not confronted, may suggest a rejecting or uncaring attitude to the suicidal individual. At the level of individual counseling, prevention encompasses helping the youth or adult client deal with the predisposing or risk factors and the psychological and situational stresses that could lead to a suicide attempt. Within this context, the counselor's role may be to help the client discover options other than suicide to cope with his or her perceived problems.

Intervention is likely to involve interrupting a suicide attempt that is about to occur or is occurring, or dealing with the immediate result of an unsuccessful attempt. Typically this requires crisis intervention techniques designed to assist the individual to regain a sense of control over his or her life. Intervention may require a multidimensional approach to deal with all of the symptoms that are operating at the moment (e.g., depression, panic, drug overload, physical injury). It may be necessary to cooperate with parents or others to place the person into psychiatric hospitalization, or to use other referral sources (e.g., a crisis intervention team) to deal with the immediate self-destructive ideation or behavior. The counselor who works with a young person exhibiting suicidal symptoms but who has not made an attempt may engage this client in a suicide contract by which the person makes a signed, concrete commitment not to attempt suicide prior to contacting the counselor or another referral source (e.g., a crisis or suicide intervention center). A contract is a tangible expression of caring by the counselor and a commitment to be available and render assistance as needed. A contract also buys time in which to help the client come to terms with the predisposing factors that place him or her at risk, consider options other than suicide to cope with the stresses that have led to the contemplation of suicide, and find access to other resource and support systems that may be of assistance.

The third stage of counselor activity suggested by Fujimura, Weis, and Cochran (1985) is that of postvention. Counselor behavior in this stage may vary according to need. For example, postvention may involve the aftercare, monitoring, and in-depth counseling of a person who has attempted suicide but not completed the act. Postvention also may be directed to the parents, spouse, classmates, or other survivors of a person who has successfully committed suicide. Because of the possibilities of a copycat, imitative, or contagious effect among adolescents when one of their classmates commits suicide, school and community counselors frequently are required to work with immediate classmates, teachers, and the larger school community in the aftermath of a death. Alexander and Harman (1988) described how they were involved in a middle school following the suicide of a 13-year-old student. In this instance, the counselor, working from a Gestalt therapy perspective, focused on helping the student's classmates to say their good-byes to their deceased classmate, to express their feelings of personal isolation, hopelessness, and despair as well as their feelings of anger, betrayal, resentment, guilt, grief, confusion, sadness, and emptiness with specific regard to the student who committed suicide. The students were encouraged to speak to the empty seat of the dead student as a way of saying good-bye, letting go of him, and experiencing the collective responses to the death in the present rather than letting the death gain romanticized attraction. Students in each of the classes the dead student had been enrolled in were encouraged to address his empty seat by telling the dead student what they would have liked him to know and how they would have wished to help him if they had known of his suicidal intentions. Students who did not wish to engage in such an overt display were encouraged to write their good-

byes to the student or to look at his seat and imagine saying their good-
byes to him and telling him what they would have liked him to know.
In art class, the students were encouraged to depict their feelings in
some artistic representation.

Following these classroom interventions, the counselor encouraged students to engage in either individual, dyadic, or small group
counseling. As a result of the expressed needs of several students, a
long-term group with weekly sessions continued for the remainder of
the school year. This group provided a supportive and caring environment for students who felt guilty because they had not anticipated
and prevented their classmate's suicide or who felt highly vulnerable
to engaging in such behavior themselves.

Another approach to dealing with loss and group survivorship
after a suicide was described by Zinner (1987). In this case, the student
who had committed suicide had been a member of a nine-student sixth-
grade class in a small private school. The counselor was a consultant
brought into the school the day after the suicide and prior to the funeral.
The assumption in this circumstance was that "the early actions of
professionals or of group leaders themselves can bring the appearance
of strength and reassurance to a situation that is unanticipated and
overwhelming" (p. 499). It can provide the surviving classmates and
teachers permission to vent a wide range of feelings and to engage in
a group ritual of coping with the suicide loss. In this school, the
counselor engaged members of the suicide victim's class in reviewing
the life of the deceased and the death. In the first step, the children
could review shared anecdotes about the deceased, lessen tensions,
and include the professional as one of their group. In the second
emphasis, the children were helped to understand the details of the
death so that secrets and rumors would not divide the classmates. While
dealing with these matters, students were encouraged to speak of their
anger at the suicide or their guilt or extreme emotional reaction to the
death. Students also were helped to anticipate what would occur at the
funeral and to attend it as a part of their leave-taking. They were
encouraged to engage in some symbolic act that expressed their response to the victim. In this case, they bought a toy cat, decorated
with the school colors to be placed in the casket, to reflect the suicide
victim's love for animals and as part of their leave-taking of the victim.
The children planted an azalea bush at the parents' home as a remembrance of the child who died, and the sixth-grade graduation
ceremony included a remembrance of the boy. Finally, the consultant
helped the principal and faculty to engage in an "academic autopsy,"
a term used by death educators to describe the evaluation of actions
taken subsequent to a particular death or crisis. The key questions in

such an activity include: "What could have been done to prevent the death? What actions taken after the death seem appropriate and meaningful in hindsight? What actions might be modified or added in the future should there be another crisis?" (Zinner, 1987, p. 301). Such questions lead a school to develop a response plan tailored to the characteristics and needs of a particular setting.

School Programs for Children at Risk

Although suicide is the most dramatic of the problems of students at risk, in this chapter a range of other problems has been identified that requires focused and systematic schoolwide intervention. Teen pregnancy and parenting, alienated youth, underachievement, violence, truancy, and drug abuse all require efforts directed at identifying students at risk, isolating and intervening in the predisposing factors, and mounting sustained follow-up activity. Most of these programs are multidimensional and require teams of professionals to provide the services required. The Pennsylvania Department of Education (1987) identified some exemplary programs in the state targeted to different groups of students at risk. A few examples follow.

Exemplary Programs for Students at Risk

Truancy Intervention Program. The Philadelphia Public Schools have implemented a Counseling or Referral Assistance (CORA) Truancy Intervention Program (TIP) designed to assist students with high absentee rates to establish a positive direction in their life. The program is based on an intervention counseling model in which guided group discussions are a primary strategy. Students attend six weekly small group sessions (day or evening). Families are invited to participate, and, when they do, students and parents participate in several sessions together. The group sessions in the program include the following areas for discussion: self-esteem, communication with family and at school, decision making, peer pressure and drug and alcohol use, career exploration, problem solving, and values. In addition, counselors conduct assessments designed to reveal specific student needs that may be academic, physical, or psychological. Students are then assisted to find appropriate support services targeted to their specific needs: reading, speech and language, drug and alcohol abuse, teen pregnancy, and psychological counseling. Each student in the program explores alternative strategies for improving school attendance and develops an attendance plan of action.

Program for Alienated Youth. The goal of this counseling program for disruptive or withdrawn youth in the Montoursville, Pennsylvania, schools is to improve students' self-concepts and perceptions of school, and to strengthen students' commitment to the conventional social goals and activities schooling represents. The improvement of student achievement is an intermediate objective that is expected to result from an improved self-concept and improved social bonding. This program serves approximately 20 students at any one time, primarily through individual counseling, tutoring, and crisis intervention. One counselor is responsible for this program and employs such strategies as the following:

- Tutoring and coaching on classroom assignments and occasional peer tutoring;
- Counseling based on reality therapy and Adlerian psychology;
- Instruction in social skills and problem solving;
- Value clarification exercises;
- After-school tutoring;
- Lunchtime basketball practice and other after-school sports activities, on an occasional basis;
- Systematic Training for Effective Parenting (STEP) course for parents; and
- Parent conferences.

The students in this program are also supported by regular school counselors, to whom they are assigned for scheduling and testing, and by community resources as needed.

Adolescent Parenting Program (GAPP). Any pregnant student or student parent in the Gettysburg Area schools may participate in the program. The program is districtwide, implemented by a team composed of the director of pupil services, director of counseling, school social worker, home economics teacher, school nurse, school counselors, and school psychologist. When a student enters the program, the GAPP team prepares an Individual Graduation Plan (IGP). The plan is designed to meet the specific needs and goals of the student, but contains formal life skills coursework in addition to basic skills subjects. The program contains seven parts:

- Formal coursework in human development, basic and advanced culinary skills, and infant and toddler laboratories are provided.
- Infant and toddler laboratories provide day care for the children of the adolescent parents and provide opportunities for mothers to learn child care and development. The children are taught

gross and fine motor skills, language development, socialization, and cognitive development. Mothers are taught to interact effectively with their children and care for their needs.

- A full-time social worker provides support and individual and group counseling to students; liaison with the community and referral services, including medical treatments for mother and child; and attendance monitoring.

- Career counseling, both individual and group, is provided to help students plan for work or further schooling after graduation.

- Personal counseling is provided by any member of the team to assist students in dealing with problems they may experience with the father of their child, their family, their self-concept, and other related matters.

- Health care services are provided to monitor and coordinate the medical needs of individual students.

- Transportation to the program is provided for mothers and children.

The fathers of the students' children and their families can participate in any part or all of the program. In addition to the ongoing academic program of the school that leads to graduation and the seven-part adolescent parenting program, other support services involved are the housing, welfare, and health departments; drug and alcohol abuse, family planning, Joint Training Partnership Act, and child services.

Student Assistance Program (SAP). The major goal of this program in the Quakertown (Pennsylvania) High School is to create a system of early identification, intervention, referral, and aftercare for students who exhibit all forms of at-risk behaviors. These behaviors include suicide, alcohol and drug abuse, defiance or belligerence, truancy, pregnancy, and eating disorders of anorexia and bulimia. In addition, the system is designed to identify youth who may suffer from all forms of abuse and neglect, or from malnutrition. The Student Assistance Program is an intervention system that trains school personnel to identify and refer "high-risk" students who seem likely to benefit from the community's health and mental health treatment system. High-risk students are identified and referred by staff personnel who complete an extensive Behavior Assessment Form. This form is a 105-item checklist and includes an inventory of behaviors that may be checked for individual students under each of the following categories: academic performance, school attendance, disruptive behavior, atypical behavior, physical symptoms, illicit activities, extracurricular activities, home problems, and additional crisis indicators (e.g., suicide, threats, victim of rape or abuse, etc.).

Once a student has been referred with a completed Behavior Assessment Form, the first order of intervention is a Student Assistance Case Management Group. This team, which consists of school counselors, administrators, nurses, a psychologist, and representatives from the core team, receives the Behavior Assessment Form and provides a first-level assessment of the student's needs. If a support person assigned by this team cannot help a student resolve a problem, the student is then referred to the Student Assistance Care Team. The latter includes a district central office administrator, counselor, nurse, SAP coordinator, and teacher. This group establishes and maintains school-based crisis intervention policies and procedures regarding early identification and treatment referrals. This group also coordinates parent involvement in the range of interventions possible with outside agencies: community drug and alcohol agencies, health and mental health resources, the YMCA, and hospital adolescent programs.

Under the assumption that early intervention in the lives of children and families will lead to the prevention of child and adolescent high-risk, self-destructive behaviors, the Student Assistance Program emphasizes major training efforts involving the following:

- Staff training (to foster skill development in crisis identification, appropriate intervention/prevention, and referral processes to out-of-school treatment) includes in-service training for all faculty, large group Problem-Solving Theatre Performance, and on-site consultation for individuals and small groups.
- Student training includes small groups for peer referral, large group Problem Solving Theatre Performance, and classroom programs.
- Parents' training includes all-day workshops and local cable television instructional programs on crisis identification and problem solving.

Many other examples could be cited of risk categories affecting children and youth and how counselors might intervene in them. The examples provided, however, suffice to illustrate the growing concern about and the content of programs designed to help children and youth at risk, which will be a part of the major challenges for counselors well into the foreseeable future. It seems clear that any programmatic design for counselor training or for skill application needs to include concepts and strategies to enable counselors to be sensitive and responsive to at-risk factors or behaviors.

Because many of the seeds of personal feelings of vulnerability are first planted in childhood and adolescence, notions of children at risk in these age groups overlap with adults at risk. The remainder of this chapter will concentrate on the latter.

Adults at Risk

Many of the problems that put adults at risk begin in childhood and adolescence barring successful intervention. Children who have been abused or who are chronically violent or chemically dependent continue to exhibit such behavior in adulthood. Adults who were abused or brutalized as children tend to imitate this behavior in their own parenting and in their approach to others.

Beyond the outcomes of violence in childhood, other forms of being "at risk" in the early years of youth and adolescence also continue into adulthood. For example, teenage and unmarried mothers have difficulty staying competitive with their cohorts in education or at work. Because of the additional time and resources required in child-rearing and because of the discrimination they may face in their own family and in the larger community, teenage parents are more likely to settle for less education and training than they might have planned. Similarly, they have more difficulty gaining access to and maintaining a place in the work force than people who are not encumbered by the problems engendered by early pregnancy, single parenting, and the environment that surrounds such circumstances. At best, their potential employment and occupational status falls behind that of others, and the possibilities of financial insecurity, unemployment or underemployment, and stress-related problems tend to accompany them throughout adulthood. Obviously, such conditions are likely to be reflected in the nutritional, psychological, and educational environment in which their children are reared. Adolescents and young adults who are chemically dependent are likely to give birth to children who are themselves addicted. Adolescents who have poor early labor market experiences are likely to continue to have jagged work histories in adulthood.

Without extending this litany of the continuity of risk status from one stage of life to the next, from adolescence to young adulthood and beyond, it might be noted that adults also face other issues that put them at risk. One of these is minority status in the society. As was suggested in chapter 4 and at the beginning of this chapter, being a member of a racial minority potentially sets one apart in the society and places one at risk of encountering discrimination, racism, and other barriers to the fullest realization of one's potential or to equal access to jobs and education. A similar situation exists for the disabled and, in some cases, older citizens, who may experience other forms of discrimination. Sexual preference may lead to additional bias and discrimination. Such group characteristics as ethnicity, race, disability, age, and sexual preference represent factors that may be defined as putting those so characterized "at risk." Not all members of a particular group necessarily share the same amount of vulnerability. Many other factors may compound the degree of being at risk. For example, poor education, functional illiteracy, chemical abuse, single parenthood, and ex-offender status may add to or exacerbate the difficulties that any group already at some risk may experience.

Beyond drawing attention to the special circumstances of adults who face discrimination because of some form of group identification that tends to amplify their risk factors, the past decade or more has shed increasing light on the nature of transitions as times of heightened vulnerability. Transitions caused by job loss, separation and divorce, retirement, or the loss of a loved one are only some of the many points in life when people who had not formerly been "at risk" suddenly become so. Indeed, transitions may, in fact, be crises for some, times when the aggregate of stress factors in their lives has grown beyond their psychological resources to cope.

In essence, the factors that cause adults to be at risk can be chronic, sudden and time-limited, or both. Chronic factors that place adults in jeopardy of psychological, physical, financial, or educational difficulties include deficits in academic skills, membership in a racial minority group, physical disability, poverty, mental illness, age, homosexuality, and chemical dependencies. Acute, sudden, or time-limited transitions that put people at risk include the death of a spouse or loved one, sexual difficulties, pregnancy, incarceration, financial problems, major personal injury or illness, involuntary unemployment, returning to or leaving schooling, or retirement. In a sense, these factors suggest that being at risk may be a dynamic condition that may affect any person at some point in his or her life, or it may be a chronic or "fixed effect."

The remainder of the chapter will discuss some of the categories of being at risk into which adults may fall. This analysis is certainly not exhaustive of all possibilities nor of all possible combinations of risk factors, but it will identify some of the major groups about which counselors must be aware.

Chronic Risk Factors

Poverty and Homelessness

Among the major factors that make people vulnerable to stress, anxiety, and a host of other difficulties is poverty. Poverty may be more generally described as the lowest level of the socioeconomic spectrum, or it may be described as a condition in which people must survive on an annual income of less than $11,203 for a family of four. However poverty is described, it is a condition that places people at extreme risk of early death, malnutrition, educational deficits, inadequate employability skills, chemical dependency, and psychological and physiological disorders.

As poignantly portrayed in the theater and in literature, and as discussed in chapter 4 of this book, poverty has its own culture. In its extreme and chronic phases it extinguishes ambition and breeds hopelessness, powerlessness, and dependency; it cripples or stifles social mobility, educational achievement, and skill development. Poverty affects the individual's self-concept, self-esteem, and feelings of self-efficacy. It perpetuates itself and robs people of opportunity.

Poverty sometimes occurs on a crossgenerational basis; it becomes chronic within certain families. People who are poverty stricken may still be employed. In other words, they may work in unskilled jobs, in stoop labor, or in jobs that pay meager wages with no additional benefits. The economic existence of the poor is so insecure that if they lose a day's or a week's work because of illness they may be pushed into such dire circumstances that they cannot afford food or housing. Some of the most poverty stricken in the society are the elderly who live on very small fixed incomes from social security or pensions. Many of the poverty stricken are from racial minority groups, are chronically unemployed, or are able to find employment only periodically and temporarily, or have skills that permit them only menial and poorly paid work. Many of the latter have families but not homes.

These families are not drifters. More than one-fifth of our homeless are employed. Very often they are working parents—one or both of whom hold jobs. But their combined earnings never total a month's rent and a matching security

deposit with enough left to buy food. As a result, they are
rent-poor, forced to live in overpriced, often substandard
lodgings and left with little for life's necessities as they
struggle to keep their families united. Some must scatter to
survive—with the children living perhaps in various dwell-
ings or the fathers barred from the premises of residences
provided through public assistance to mothers and children
only. (Whitemore, 1988, p. 5)

The National Coalition for the Homeless estimates that the nation's homeless include some 3 million people, nearly 500,000 of
whom are children (Whitemore, 1988). Some of these people live in
temporary, government-subsidized housing, some in shelters, some
with relatives, and some on the streets. The environment for child-
rearing and for nurturing self-respect and hope is not present in such
circumstances. Thus, children in such families typically do not do well
in school, experience significantly more depression than do more rooted
and affluent children, and develop serious deficits in social skills.

At the beginning of the Kennedy presidency, Michael Harrington
(1962) wrote a book entitled *The Other America*. That book, which
has now become a classic, described the plight of the poor in the early
1960s and portrayed their lives of despair and misery. This book played
a major role in stimulating President Lyndon B. Johnson's "War on
Poverty," which in turn spawned an outpouring of federal legislation
designed to provide financial aid and training to the poor as a way of
breaking the poverty cycle. Obviously, as we look at the plight of the
poor three decades later, the problems of poverty still exist but they
are changing in some ways. For example, the stereotype of the poor
as composed principally of unemployed inner-city minority people or
mothers on welfare trying to care for large numbers of children born
out of wedlock does not include those who have become labeled the
"hidden poor." These are the poor who are working and have families.
Most of these people, whose annual cash income for a family of four
is below $11,203—the official poverty line, are White, with one or
more members working. These poor tend to be divided evenly between
the central cities, suburbs, and rural areas.

The welfare poor, the underclass with which most stereotypical
views of poverty seem to be associated, have essentially stabilized in
size but the number of working poor, the so-called hidden poor, has
grown rapidly. The estimate is that there are now 9 million poor adults
who work, most of whom are in the prime working age of 22 to 64.
"In 1986, two million Americans worked full time throughout the
entire year and were still poor—an increase of more than 50 percent

since 1978'' (Whitman, Thornton, Shapiro, Witkin, & Hawkins, 1988, p. 20). Part of the problem these families face is that the existing welfare and tax systems do not reward the impoverished for working. For example, a mother on welfare typically qualifies for medicaid, child-care subsidies, food stamps, and public housing. A mother who is poor but works typically does not qualify for or use such social services. As a result, in many states, a mother with two children is actually better off financially on a combination of welfare and food stamps than is a mother who works full-time at a minimum wage job.

In a series of interviews with the working poor, Whitman et al. (1988) found that most have no health insurance and constantly worry about the effect an illness or accident may have on them or their dependents. Also common among the working poor is the absence of a sense of ease or leisure. Having to wear second-hand clothes and drive rattletrap cars contributes to a feeling of living on the margin at all times. Many of the working poor are also the ''new poor''—those who have been machine operators, farmers, and others and have lost their jobs because of plant closings or economic downturns. Some of the working poor are migrant workers; others are illegal aliens whose survival in this nation depends on their taking low-paying jobs, frequently on a part-time basis, for which health insurance and other benefits are unavailable.

The effects of poverty rest somewhat differently on the welfare poor, the working poor, and the new poor. Such effects are also somewhat different in rural areas where there is a greater sense of community support and shared conditions and generally lower prices than in urban areas. Wherever poverty exists, however, it breeds frustration and stress. These, in turn, cause family fights, drinking and depression, feelings of being hemmed-in and not in control of one's destiny, limited prospects for youngsters, functional illiteracy, high rates of teen pregnancies, intellectual stunting, and narrow horizons.

Minority Group Membership

As discussed in chapter 4, the reality of pluralism in the United States stems from the large numbers of people who belong to different minority groups. If one talks in absolute numbers, in some major cities and in other geographical locations people classified as minority group members—Blacks, Hispanics, Asians, and Native Americans—are really in the majority. Across the nation in general, however, people classified as minority group members have not gained the power, fiscal resources, or access to educational and occupational opportunities to permit them to compete equally with those in the majority culture. Thus, considering minority group membership as a risk factor does not imply that minority group members are inferior or inadequate compared to majority group members. Risk, in this case, refers to the likelihood that purely because of status as members of a minority group, people are less likely to be able to meet their full potential, to be equitably served in education and by social services, or to have the same opportunities and incentives for achievement that majority group members experience.

According to Perry (1982), "Blacks, Hispanics, Asian Americans and Native Americans have long been foremost among the underserved, with higher incidences of unemployment, mental and physical illness, and mortality in adults and youth" (p. 54). These conditions stem from discrimination, language and cultural discrepancies, poor nutrition, inadequate education, and other factors that place minority group members at risk for unemployment and underemployment, feelings of powerlessness, and loss of hope. To illustrate only one aspect of the effects of minority group membership on employment and unemployment, one can compare unemployment among different population groups. For example, in 1983, the national unemployment rate was 8.8%. That rate in 1988 has dropped to slightly less than 5.3%, although the profile of who is affected by unemployment still remains similar. The 1983 rates of unemployment for various subgroups in the population were as follows (Herr & Long, 1983, p. 25):

1983 Unemployment Rates by Subgroup	
Adult men	8.2%
Adult women	7.4%
Whites	7.7%
Blacks	18.1%
Hispanics	12.3%
White teenagers	18.5%
Black teenagers	48.3%

A cursory look at such data suggests that Blacks and Hispanics in general and Black teenagers in particular have significant employment problems. But, these findings are no surprise; they have been reflected in the employment picture for the better part of 30 years. Indeed, some observers fear that racial differences in employment and unemployment are growing, not receding. Mare and Winship (1980) reported that racial differences have grown in the proportion of the youth population that is employed and unemployed. For example, the

Black-White unemployment rates for 18- to 24-year-olds showed a difference of 5.8 percentage points in 1954. In 1960 that difference grew to 8.7 percentage points. It was 12.0 in 1970 and 14.5 in 1980. The risk factor of minority membership relative to unemployment is also evident in data that show that after periods of recession, Blacks do not recover employment prospects as successfully as do Whites (Newman, 1979), and they tend to experience high levels of under-employment (O'Toole, 1973).

Within any minority or majority group, there are subpopulations likely to be at particular risk because of a combination of negative social and psychological factors, economic insecurity, and other reasons. Given some of the information on populations most susceptible to unemployment and underemployment, it is no surprise that many authors are concerned about Black men as a group at particular risk (e.g., Parham & McDavis, 1987). Some of the reasons for such characterization include high rates of unemployment, poor education, inadequate health care facilities, discriminatory judicial processes, lack of adequate legal representation, racist police practices, incarceration (42% of the inmate population in the United States is Black) (Staples, 1982), and front-line military combat duty in Vietnam, Grenada, the Persian Gulf, and other conflicts (Butler, 1980).

However, there are other risk factors for Black men as well. Parham and McDavis (1987), in their review of the existing literature, suggested the following. Black men as a group have a shorter average life expectancy, 64 years, than any other group. Black youths have a 50% higher probability of dying before age 20 than White children, and from different causes. The two largest causes of death among White youths are accidents and cardiovascular disease; among Black youths, the primary causes are homicide, drug abuse, suicide, and accidents. Black men now have a higher rate of cancer, especially lung cancer, than does any other group in the United States primarily because Black men smoke more cigarettes than do men in any other age or sex group in America. Black men also have been found to have a more serious problem with alcohol abuse than is true of White men, White women, or Black women. The consequences of alcohol abuse ripple negatively throughout the personal and social lives of Black men and are related to the high rates of homicides, arrests, accidents, assaults, and physical illnesses (Harper, 1981). Davis (1981), among others, reported that the suicide rate for Black people, and particularly young Black men, has been increasing steadily since the 1960s. Although the average suicide rate for Blacks is still below the national average, the increase in these rates is dramatic, and if it continues at the present levels, will soon exceed the national average.

The profile presented here of the experience of many Black men is one characterized by intense stress, tension, hostility, internalized anxiety, frustration, and resentment. The causes of these are discrimination, the pressures of functioning in educational systems or business and corporate structures dominated by Whites, and the perceived need to compromise their Blackness to incorporate behaviors and values acceptable to the majority culture. Clearly, in such circumstances, many Black men pay a high emotional and physical price as they try to cope with achieving a personal identity, a family life, educational success, and economic security and advancement.

Parham and McDavis (1987) suggested a wide range of recommendations by which counselors in schools, colleges and universities, mental health agencies, and other settings can provide both indirect and direct services to Black men. Among these recommendations, in paraphrased form, are the following:

- Seminars on parenting for Black parents to help them attend more systematically to the developmental issues and problems of their male children;

- Counseling groups to help Black men develop more positive self-concepts and to identify with available role models;

- Career counseling to help Black men gain more confidence in their abilities and skills and to help them understand and prepare for career opportunities;

- Outreach counseling services, in cooperation with Black churches and community organizations, directed to developing value systems and support groups to strengthen Afrocentricism, principles of collective survival, and ways to help young Black men resist actions such as suicide, homicide, and drug abuse;

- Formal programs to help young Black men build strong family lives, develop leadership skills, or communicate effectively their academic expectations to teachers and others; and

- Support systems, stress management programs, and other services for upwardly mobile Black men to help them deal with the pressures of their jobs and their identity crises.

Besides Black men, many other minority groups also experience frustrations and stress that deserve more attention from counselors in the future than has been true in the past. Native Americans, for example, are among the most underserved of all minority groups despite extensive evidence that their levels of stress, substance abuse, suicide, and feelings of hopelessness are of epidemic proportions in some tribes and reservations. As suggested in chapter 2, Latinos or Hispanics are a rapidly growing and heterogeneous minority group. Composed of people whose heritage is Mexican, Cuban, Puerto Rican, Central American, South American, or Spanish, Hispanic men and women are concentrated more in the lower-paid and lesser-skilled occupations than is the total work force. Thus, like large proportions of people in all minority groups, many Hispanics suffer from poverty, restricted educational opportunity, and limited occupational mobility. Many Hispanics speak limited English, are restricted in their ability to function within the dominant culture, may be exploited by employers, and experience anxiety from having left their native land and customs.

Other groups at risk are immigrant populations. Depending on why and how they came to the United States, they may have severe health problems, language difficulties, educational and occupational deficits, and lack of information. Initial adjustment problems stem from considerable feelings of loss from leaving loved ones behind or mourning the loss of a cultural self and identity in their homelands. Indeed, many immigrants undergo significant loss of social status.

Chapter 4 discussed counseling skills necessary to deal with culturally diverse populations. Suffice it to say here that counselors working with minority populations should, above all, possess the generic counseling knowledge, skills, understandings, abilities, and behaviors thought to be appropriate to any helping relationship. They must be conscious of how their own attitudes and values impinge on counseling specific ethnic and racial groups. They must be aware of the cultural traditions and contexts from which their clients come but not assume a stereotypical perspective that these clients are bound by such backgrounds. Counselors must work to separate their clients' socioeconomic deficits from problems based on race or ethnicity. Counselors must help minority clients find ways to cope with discrimination without internalizing its effects as valid for them. Finally, counselors must be prepared to help minority clients analyze life-style and career options and to take action based upon goal-setting and problem-solving strategies.

Women

Women also constitute a minority group subject to risk factors. As reported in other chapters as well as here, women tend to be more at risk of unemployment and underemployment than are men, they are more likely to be single parents than are men, they experience different forms of mental disorder (e.g., depression) than do men, they are prone to violence and abuse (e.g., sexual assault and rape) in ways different from men, they are more likely to be in poverty than men, and they experience psychological pressures or identity issues that differ from those of men.

As noted in chapter 2, women are entering the labor force in rapidly growing numbers. Many women do so deliberately and positively as part of a dual-career family. Other women, however, after having completed a child-rearing stage of their life, are reentering the work world after a long period of time or are entering it for the first time. Many women enter the work force out of economic necessity. They are either single parents who have no choice but to work to support themselves and their children, or they are married women who must become part of a two-earner family in order to maintain the economic integrity of the family. Many women enter the labor force because they feel that this society does not condone their desire to be a homemaker, and they want to resolve their identity confusion and ambiguity about their self-concept and a work role. Many of the women in any of the above groups may feel considerable insecurity, stress, or a variety of emotions and uncertainties that put them "at risk" of psychological distress—this argues for counseling intervention.

Mogul (1979) described from a psychiatric perspective some of the tensions with which the women reentering the work force must contend. Although primarily directed to the older woman entering the work force after a substantial period at home, many of the same insecurities are internalized by other working women. Mogul contended:

> Women resuming outside work after an interval . . . have to struggle simultaneously with the realities of the work world, friction at home, and their own inner conflicts. The more a woman's sense of herself was grounded in her identity as a wife and mother, the greater the readjustment in her sense of self when she re-enters the occupational world. The sense of femaleness, attractiveness, and lovability is often related to being dependent, and less competent than men, so that doubts about important parts of the self are stirred up as other parts are developed. To be aggressive and actively self-promoting—necessities in the school or work world— are characteristics to which (an older) generation of middle-aged women did not aspire in their youth. Since women primarily grew up to be those who nurture and give to others and are sensitive and vulnerable to real or imagined disap-

proval from people who are important to them, the sense of guilt and failure is almost unavoidable as they begin to do for themselves.

In order to change her lifestyle during her middle years without either too much guilt and inhibition or too much angry repudiation of her former life, a woman has the psychological task of testing and making room for new identities and new self-perceptions without entirely discarding old ones that had offered grounds for previous self-regard. It is helpful to have social and family support for these changes and also to have derived solid gratifications from the previous role. (p. 1140)

When considering the psychological factors related to women's entry into, adjustment to, and mobility within the work force, other barriers also need to be addressed and considered. Lenz and Shavitz (1977) suggested that social and psychological barriers such as the following also affect occupational reentry women: job discrimination, lack of marketable skills, guilt feelings, and a low opinion of their abilities. In studying the effect of the Carl Perkins Act on the provision of vocational education and vocational guidance for special populations in several geographical entities, Herr (1987) found that in programs for single parents and displaced homemakers, the major issue that women faced was not securing training but rather gaining a sense of self-efficacy, the confidence that they could actually do what was expected of them in the work place. This finding is consistent with that of Welborn and Moore (1986) in their work with displaced homemakers. They reported:

Often the displaced homemaker is in the position of not only actively needing and seeking employment, but also of being required to cope with a number of other issues, such as feeling out of control, feeling isolated from those segments of society in which she must now operate, feeling little sense of personal power, feeling a void where she once felt intimacy, and feeling a keen sense of disorientation as the emphasis on family is necessarily reduced as she prepares to go to work. (p. 104)

Whether or not women are described as reentry women, displaced homemakers, or by some other label, Gilligan (1982), Hotelling and Forest (1985) and others considered the possibilities that the two sexes experience dependence-independence and relationships differently. In the case of women, certain overreactions may occur that have implications for counseling in general. Hotelling and Forest described the condition as follows:

> From Gilligan's perspective, a woman's development is restricted because she fails to realize that she must incorporate both self-care and care of others into her identity. Many women may view this as an overwhelming task. Two responses, both of which are maladaptive, are the super woman phenomenon (an attempt to uphold extremely high standards both at work and home) and the male model (which requires one to excel at work only). The consequences of the first model are emotional and physical strain and overload; often the woman feels not only exhausted and confused but guilty if she does not perform all tasks perfectly. The second model, which defines self through separation, may result in a woman progressing in her career but ignoring her need for connection with others. The expectation to maintain autonomy and independence in a vacuum of human intimacy at work can be painful, confusing, and lonely to a woman who has learned that connection with others is essential. (p. 184)

Counseling of women in relation to work and career will take many forms depending on the education, motivation, and experience of specific women. For reentry women in general, Herr and Cramer (1988, pp. 365–366) suggested such goals as the following, reported here in abridged form:

1. Reinforce positive feelings about self-worth and ability to make a contribution in the work force outside the home.
2. Provide any information that may be lacking about basic career decision making: personal assets and limitations, values and attitudes, the world of work, resources, and so on.
3. Assist in exploring changes in life style that may be occasioned by first-time entry or reentry into the labor force.
4. Help clients understand the implications of full-time versus part-time work.
5. Prepare women to deal with possible discrimination, both overt and covert.
6. Provide specialized experiences, if necessary, in such areas as consciousness raising and assertiveness training.
7. Explore entry-level jobs with extant education versus possible jobs with additional education or training.

8. Provide a referral system for placement assistance and teach job-seeking skills.
9. Provide follow-up and continuing support.

In addition to following these recommendations, counselors assisting women to deal with career-related issues probably will need to engage in other possible functions as well: networking, peer counseling, support groups, financial and personal counseling to deal with such issues as divorce or other major life changes, time management, and stress management.

Although being a woman constitutes a risk factor in relation to work and career, women are certainly at risk in other areas as well. One of these is rape and sexual abuse. Abel, Becker, and Skinner (1980) estimated that 1 out of 30 women will be a victim of rape. FBI statistics (U.S. Federal Bureau of Investigation, 1984), that pertain to the rape of women, indicate that there was a 54% increase in the number of reported cases of forcible rape from 1973 to 1983. In 1984, rape was found to be increasing at a higher rate than any other form of violent crime. In contrast, bearing in mind that data are very difficult to obtain, indecent assault or rape of men constitutes about a tenth or less of that of women. Force or violence is associated with 85% of adult rapes (Brownmiller, 1975).

Counseling and medical treatment for victims of rape and sexual assaults need to be combined. Initial counseling of the victim or the family, depending on the age of the victim, needs to be designed to combat the negative effects of the experience. Appropriate emphases include:

- Reassure the victim of present safety;
- Affirm that the victim has regained control of the situation;
- Emphasize rapist or sexual abuser responsibility for the crime;
- Help the victim conceptualize the experience through verbalization;
- Encourage and support expression of feelings;
- Acknowledge the traumatic nature of the experience;
- Provide information regarding possible immediate and long-term effects (rape trauma syndrome); and
- Use such counseling techniques as teaching victims to deal with adverse symptoms through relaxation sequences, thought stoppage, covert modeling, and other techniques. (Sproles, 1985, pp. 15–16)

According to the National Center for Prevention and Control of Rape of the U.S. Department of Health and Human Services (Sproles,

1985), the major effects of rape on the adult are brought about through the following characteristics of the incident, resulting in a loss of control and heightened victim vulnerability:

- Inability to defend against the suddenness of the attack;
- Intentional cruelty;
- The feeling of being trapped and unable to fight back; and
- Physical trauma.

These effects lead to a rape trauma syndrome that can be divided into an acute (initial phase) and a long-term (reorganizational) phase. According to Burgess and Holmstrom (1974), the acute phase can last from a few days to several weeks. The typical symptoms are a wide range of emotional responses emanating from shock and disbelief. These responses can be demonstrated in an expressive way through anger, fear, and anxiety or in a controlled way through hiding one's feelings and seeming composed or subdued. After the initial phase, a reorganization phase may last for months or even years. In this phase a variety of complications may occur unless initial counseling or psychiatric therapy is available and effective. Such complications include a limitation of activities and general life style, inability to feel safe, and aversion to all sexual activity. In addition to experiencing chronic depression, the victim may develop fears and phobias specific to the rape and then generalize the fears to symbols of the rape: fear of being alone, fear of men, fear of sex, and so forth. Counselors involved in the initial phase or in the reorganization phase need to develop not only treatment plans with the victim but also follow-up checks to assess the needs for referral or reinitiation of counseling. In many parts of the nation, rape crises centers have been implemented to provide such services as crisis intervention, counseling, advocacy and accompaniment, community education and prevention, and self-defense training (Harvey, 1985).

A final area we will identify here as a risk factor for women is depression. In general, clinical depression is twice as common in women than in men (Lobel & Hirschfield, 1984). The predisposing factors are not clear. Clinical depression can be associated with another psychiatric disorder such as schizophrenia, or with alcoholism; it can be related to a physical illness such as a viral disease or endocrine disorder; or depression can occur without any intermediary disturbances. The reasons for the comparatively large amount of depression in women as compared with men may be genetic, sociocultural, hormonal, a function of diagnostic practice, or the fact that women are more likely than men to seek help.

Clinical depression usually is characterized by a set of symptoms that persist longer than 2 weeks and are manifested by a depressed mood or a loss of interest in usual activities. Symptoms may include appetite, weight, and sleep disturbances; hyperactivity or lethargy; anxiety; crying; slowed thinking; suicidal tendencies; and feelings of guilt, worthlessness, and hopelessness.

Clinical depression, as defined by the American Psychiatric Association in the *Diagnostic and Statistical Manual of Mental Disorders, Third Edition*, (DSM-III) (1980), includes a range of categories known as major depressive disorder (single episode, recurrent), bipolar disorder (mixed, manic, depressed), dysthymic disorder (depressive neurosis), and cyclothymic disorder (chronic mood disorder). The disorders differ in their intensity, severity, and duration. About 11% of the resident inpatients in state and county hospitals suffer from a severe depression (Morrissey, Witkin, Manderscheid, & Bethel, 1986).

About 10 to 14 million people in the United States suffer from a diagnosable depression. Only about one half of these seek treatment. Treatment ordinarily includes a variety of antidepressant drugs and lithium, a combination of drugs and psychotherapy, or electroconvulsive treatment. When psychotherapy or counseling is used in combination with medication, or alone if the depression is mild or moderate, cognitive, behavioral, interpersonal, or short-term therapies may be used. In some cases, group, marital, and family therapies are useful. Cognitive/behavioral therapies that focus on the depressed person's negative or distorted thinking patterns are increasingly used in clinical depression. They will be discussed more fully in the next chapter, but the basic assumption of such approaches is that negative thought patterns lead to depressed feelings and behaviors. Thus, the way to change the feelings is to change the thoughts.

The Disabled

The disabled are another major population "at risk" of psychological and economic vulnerability. "With the onset of a potentially disabling condition, an individual experiences both economic and psychic losses as he or she faces restricted choices. The individual may suffer pain, incur increased medical costs, lose income, and face societal prejudice" (Berkowitz & Hill, 1986, p. 1). The disabled are victims of social stigma, just as other populations suffer the effects of sexism, ageism, and racism.

The terminology of disability is a bit confused. Some authors use the terms *disabled*, *handicapped*, and *persons with a disability* interchangeably (Campbell, 1985). Other authors approach the issue differently. Berkowitz and Hill (1986) defined disability thus:

> . . . the loss of the ability to perform socially accepted or prescribed tasks and roles due to a medically definable *condition*. . . . In some relatively few cases, the condition leaves a person with some residual *impairments*, that is, some physiological, anatomical, or mental loss or abnormality that persists after the condition has stabilized. . . . In some cases, (again, relatively few) these residual impairments cause a person to have *functional limitations*. . . . As a consequence of these functional limitations (physical or emotional), some persons may perform their expected roles only with extreme difficulty; hence we classify them as being *disabled*. (pp. 4–5)

Using the term *handicapped* rather than *disabled* at the federal level, the Rehabilitation Act of 1973 defines "handicapped" as "any person who (1) has a physical or mental impairment which substantially limits one or more major life activities, (2) has a record of such an impairment, or (3) is regarded as having such an impairment."

Dunham and Dunham (1978) took another perspective on disability, one that is closest to the views in this book. They considered the disabled person to be structurally, physiologically, and psychologically different from a normal person because of an accident, disease, or developmental problem. A person who is handicapped, they maintained, feels less adequate than others, either in general or in a specific situation. Absent such a view of self, a disability may not be a handicap.

Disability, then, may take one of several forms: *physical* (such as amputations, birth defects, cancer, heart problems, burns, deafness, blindness, multiple sclerosis, muscular distrophy, orthopedic deformities, spinal injury), *intellectual* (mental retardation, learning disability, brain damage, speech and language disorders), *emotional* (mental illness, substance abuse, alcoholism, obesity and other eating disorders) or *sociocultural* (limited English, victim of racial or ethnic bias, inadequate social understanding or skills). In an important sense, each of these categories represents a set of risk factors that can cause a disability to become a handicap, limiting the person's economic, social, and psychological well-being.

Given the differences in definition of the disabled, it is difficult to be precise about the numbers of people involved. One method of identifying the magnitude of those with disabilities is to determine the number of people with a work disability. Quoting Campbell (1985):

According to the Census Bureau, there were 147.3 million non-institutionalized persons 16 to 24 years of age in March of 1982. Of this working-age population, 13.1 million reported a work disability. There were 6.67 million disabled males, 41.5 of whom participated in the labor force. Unemployment of disabled males was 16.9 percent in contrast to 10.2 percent for the non-disabled. The disabled female population was 6.4 million with a labor participation rate of 23.7 percent and unemployment of 18.3 percent. Non-disabled females had an unemployment rate of 8.8 percent. . . . Disabled females in central cities are one of the most disadvantaged groups throughout the nation. Their earnings approximate only 42.1 percent of the mean earnings of disabled males. (pp. 15–16)

Campbell suggested that external influences affect the employment opportunities for the disabled even when they are qualified by knowledge, skill, and motivation. These include environmental access, job conditions, personnel management practices, management attitudes and behaviors, employer relations practices, affirmative action efforts, law enforcement, and protection of rights. Embedded in such environmental influences are the effects of employment myths and stereotypes, the degree to which employers have attempted to modify their work places to accommodate the needs of disabled workers to function effectively, and apprehensions about the productivity of disabled workers.

Clearly, the unemployment rates of the disabled are much higher than those reported above. Many disabled people cannot or do not seek work, thus they are not counted when unemployment rates are calculated. Indeed, if one counts the difference between disabled men who actually participate in the labor force (41.5%) and those who do not (58.5%) and then calculates the 16.9% unemployment rate on the first figure, the unemployment rate or, perhaps more precisely, the number of disabled men of working age who do not work is close to 65% or more. Disabled people are considerably less likely to be employed full-time (8% for partially disabled men, 31% for partially disabled women), compared to the nondisabled population (86% for men, 49% for women). In 1977, median family income of the severely disabled was approximately half that of the income of the nondisabled (Daniels, 1985).

The problem of being disabled is not only that of not working. It is also a function of self-perception. What labels are used? What stereotypes from the able-bodied population are internalized as valid about the inferiority, incompetence, or worthlessness of the disabled?

The disabled, then, are themselves a minority who are at serious economic and psychological risk.

Given the wide variation in types of disability and the levels of their severity—mild, moderate, profound—it is not possible to describe here a major approach to working with the disabled. Many of the disabled will need a counseling emphasis on ego-building and strengthening of self-esteem. Some will need assertiveness training. Many will need advocacy, financial support, retraining, job skills, and placement within supportive, therapeutic milieus. Others will need ongoing medical services and support while they learn to use prostheses and other medically induced adaptations. Some disabled persons and their spouses or children will need family counseling, marital or couples counseling, and help in reassessing their sexual needs and how to deal with them. Others will need to develop crucial life skills for successful living within whatever functional limitations they now face—personal/social, routine survival, or occupational skills. Because a disability may, in fact, restrict or totally alter a life or career trajectory, individuals may need help to examine where in their developmental progress the disability has intruded, and then to find alternative ways to reach their goals within their available resources. They will need to redefine capacity and potential, not only loss and limitations.

The Aging

An expression that is frequently used to describe the United States is the "graying of America." The United States is no longer a nation in which children and youth are the largest population groups. Currently one in five Americans is over 55; by 2010, one in every four will be over 55 (Morrison, 1984). More than 30 million people in the United States are now over age 60, and most of them are active and functioning well. But, in many instances, myths and stereotypes captured by the term "ageism" have restricted the productivity, potential contributions to society, and the feelings of well-being and acceptance for many older people.

Thus, chronological age can be considered a risk factor for many, whether or not any other risk factors are present in their lives (e.g., disability, minority group membership, etc.). Both because of the growing number of people who are at or beyond conventionally defined retirement ages or are elderly, and because of the growing understanding of the effects of ageism and other risk factors for these populations, counselors and psychologists are recognizing the need to provide counseling and related services and, indeed, to develop new therapeutic tactics to work with this population.

Like other population groups, the aging also have "distressing emotional problems they seem unable to solve by themselves—problems like depression, intense fears, anxiety, persistent anger, frustration, unrelieved loneliness. And others have occasional problems which are too much for them, especially grief and depression caused by the death of a loved one" (Sargent, 1980, p. 1).

Even under the best of circumstances, many of the aging and retired learn that they must come to terms with perceptions they and the larger society have come to believe or manifest toward aged persons: that one is now "on the shelf" and less important than when one was fully engaged in the work force or child-rearing; that because one is not working and productive, one is parasitic and generally disapproved of; that living on a fixed income places one in a vulnerable position in case inflation runs rampant in the future; that one has entered the last stage of life and has to consider how much time one has left; and that chronic illness and aging tend to go together and are likely to restrict one's freedom and independence in the near future.

Because of the need to cope with the social stigma of ageism and the phenomena associated with aging just described, older people probably have more psychological problems than any other age group, with the possible exception of adolescents (Sargent, 1980). Although this statement is difficult to prove conclusively, there is relevant evidence to support it. For example, even in an era of deinstitutionalization of state and county mental hospitals, large numbers in the resident populations of these institutions are older citizens. In 1980, for example, 54% of resident patients in mental health hospitals were 45 years old or older. In three states—New York, Virginia, and Pennsylvania—more than 40% of the resident patients were age 65 or older. Although not broken down into admissions by age category, the majority of the annual admissions fell into three categories of mental disorders: schizophrenia (37%), alcoholism (24%), and depression (11%) (Morrissey, Witkin, Manderscheid, & Bethel, 1986).

Several observers have contended that a conservative estimate of those in the older age population who need mental health services is about 15% (Sargent, 1980). Those who argue that this figure is overly conservative do so because a large number of the older population who have physical illnesses or impairments that are complicated by emotional reactions amenable to therapeutic intervention do not obtain mental health services (Butler & Lewis, 1977). Shanas and Maddox (1976) estimated that of those aged 65 or over who are living in the community, 5% are severely impaired in their psychological functioning, and a further 20% are moderately impaired. A final indicator of the needs for counseling and psychological assistance among the older population is the estimate that 25% of suicides in the United States are committed by people, particularly White men, over age 65, a figure that is higher than that for any other age group.

Older people do not avail themselves of mental health services for many reasons. Some do not trust "head doctors," and others feel that one should handle one's own problems. Some feel that they do not deserve help or feel guilty or too worthless to receive help. Some do not know whom to turn to for help or feel they cannot afford it, even if it is covered by medicare or other insurance.

As a result of such resistance to the use of counseling and mental health services, an array of "nontraditional therapies" has arisen in senior citizen and community mental health centers around the nation. These include such emphases as assertiveness training for the aging; widows groups and emeritus classes; adult day-care centers; creative aging workshops; peer counseling programs; behavioral approaches to therapy with the elderly; counseling and reassuring the dying, in or outside of hospices; and, programs to facilitate the transition to nursing homes (Sargent, 1980).

Certainly, within the aging population, older workers and those considering retirement are major constituencies for counseling. As suggested in chapter 2, the demographics of the work force are changing. The baby boom is over and the number of adolescents and young adults entering the work force is rapidly decreasing. Rather than finding ways to encourage older workers to retire and make room in the work force for younger people, it is likely in the future that the emphasis will shift to finding ways to retain older workers and help them to remain productive. This will require redesigning jobs, educating employers or management about coping with the needs of or the myths about older workers, designing programs to retrain older workers or to find new placements for dislocated workers, and providing opportunities for older workers to engage in part-time as well as full-time work. Kieffer (1980) suggested some methods to assist older workers now on the job. Most of these are counseling-related processes. He advocated more effective performance evaluation programs; identification of alternative jobs or work arrangements in the same or related organizations; alternative job placements; development and improvement of counseling services for furthering a career or for retirement; improvement or adaptation of systems for training, development, and promotion; updating of advisory services on pensions and fringe benefits; review of terminating procedures; and mental health counseling.

A final group we will mention here as important within the aging population are people contemplating retirement. Older people approach retirement with various feelings: apprehension, threat, eagerness, psychological malaise, surprise, anxiety, depression, or deliberation. Among the factors that seem to be involved in a positive transition to retirement are adequate income, voluntary rather than involuntary retirement, good health, specific plans, staying active, and a history of an orderly rather than a disorderly career (Herr & Cramer, 1988). Ultimately retirement is very much an individual matter that can be facilitated by counseling and by preretirement programs in industry.

Counseling for retirement can include many strategies. Dillard (1982) suggested teaching specific retirement life styles. Herr and Cramer (1988) advocated that counseling for preretirement and retirement should include assistance in planning for and obtaining information about health, finances, housing, and other concerns related to daily living; clarification of affective reactions to retirement; and appropriate referrals to community agencies designed to deal with particular aspects of the aging. Corporations offer preretirement programs for their older workers that vary across a continuum of narrow to broad content. Across such a continuum, the topics usually covered, starting with the narrow and expanding to the broadest or most comprehensive, include social security and medicare; financial benefits and options; physical and mental health; leisure; legal aspects; employment; housing; community resources; options for employment after retirement; interpersonal relations; and life planning.

Transition Points as Risk Factors

The preceding sections of this chapter have dealt with the effects of various chronic or ascribed "at risk" factors in populations served by counselors. This is certainly not a complete inventory of the factors that put people at risk. Other at-risk characteristics that have been only lightly mentioned are alcoholism and substance abuse, eating disorders, sexual orientation and preference, and violence in the family. Each of these areas deserves a fuller treatment than is possible here.

The other major perspective on risk factors that will occupy our attention in the remainder of this chapter is the growing literature that addresses the vulnerability of persons at key transition points in life.

Several terms tend to interact when one thinks of transition points as inducing risk. They include *transition, crisis, life events, stress, developmental,* and *situational*. First, it is useful to note that there are clear relationships between life events and physical and mental health. Such a concept is central in analyses of stress. In other words, stress is associated with life events or the accumulation of life events, and when stress rises to unhealthy levels or the body runs out of resources or is completely fatigued, physical or mental disease is likely to result. Life events are essentially points of transition that may occur as a part of normal and predictable developmental tasks, or they may be crises precipitated by unexpected and traumatic events. Sometimes transitions turn into crises.

As research on individual growth through the life span has unfolded over the past two decades, it has become apparent that each phase of life has its own developmental tasks that individuals need to master if continuous growth is to ensue without their progress being arrested or fixated at a particular developmental level. Throughout life earlier themes or processes may be revisited as one moves through the transition from one stable period of life to another. Thus, in terms of biological and cultural timing, many life events and transitions can be predicted and anticipated. Some examples of major transitions and life events from adolescence forward are listed in Figure 5.

Obviously, not all of these transitions or life events will occur to one person. But, particularly if their likelihood is unanticipated, such transitions or life events can become crises when they are embedded in considerable turmoil, or when a particular developmental stage is disrupted or made particularly difficult. Such a circumstance can occur when transitions are thwarted by a lack of skills, knowledge, ability to take risks, physical resources, or social resources (Danish & D'Augelli, 1980).

A crisis can also unfold because transitions or life events have occurred too fast and with too much intensity for the individual to cope. This is what Slaikeu (1984) called "demand overload" and what led Holmes and Rahe (1967) to define as a life crisis the accumulation of life events totaling more than 350 Life Change Units a year as measured by their Social Readjustment Scale. As noted in the scale, life events are weighted in terms of their severity of stress. Experiencing an accumulation of 350 or more life change units in a year is likely to result in a life crisis. For example, on the scale, the death of a spouse would be rated as 100 points and divorce, 73 points. At the other end of the scale, a vacation would be rated as 13 points and minor violations of the law, 11 points. The rapid accumulation of these life changes increases stress and pushes many beyond their resources or ability to cope, thus precipitating a crisis.

Slaikeu (1984) reported that a transition or life event can precipitate a crisis if the timing of it is inconsistent with society's expectations. Not being settled in a career or being married at a particular age, being forced to retire too early, having children late in life, or becoming a grandmother at too young an age can precipitate a crisis because these situations call for changes in self-concept, identity, and

FIGURE 5
Major Transitions and Life Events

Graduation from high school	Adjusting to changes in children
Going to college	becoming young adults
Finding a first major job	Divorce of a child
Adjusting to a job	Dealing with responsibilities
Breaking up with a girl friend or	regarding aging parents
boyfriend	Death or prolonged illness of
Breaking engagement to marry	parents
Selecting and learning to live with a	Setback in career
mate/partner	Financial concerns
Developing parenting skills	Dissatisfaction with goals achieved
Purchase of home	Promotion
Conflict between career goals and	Marital problems
family goals	Death of a friend
Adjusting to physiological changes	Health problems
of middle age	Empty nest
Change in physical living	Preparing for retirement
arrangements	Death of a spouse
Conflict with grown children	Awareness of loneliness
Illness or disability	Difficulty in adjustment to
	retirement

From *Crisis Intervention: A Handbook for Practice and Research* (Table 3.1, pp. 42–44), by K.A. Slaikeu, 1984, Boston: Allyn & Bacon. Adapted by permission.

use of time that the individual may be unprepared to make or finds unusually difficult to accommodate.

Beyond what might be called normal or predictable transitions or life events, one's development can be upset by situational life crises. These can strike virtually anyone at any time and usually are defined by such criteria as sudden onset, unexpectedness, emergency quality, potential effect on entire communities, danger, and opportunity. The categories of situational crises ordinarily considered are physical illness and injury, unexpected/untimely death, being a crime victim or offender, natural and man-made disasters, war and related acts, and situational crises of modern life (e.g., psychedelic drug experiences, economic setbacks, migration/relocation) (Slaikeu, 1984).

Such situational life crises are so intense that they challenge the individual or family's ability to cope and to adjust. They may make life goals unreachable or even threaten life itself. They may precipitate a state of disorganization characterized by inability to cope and potential for long-lasting damage.

The concern about situational life crises in which violence and other forms of intense trauma are involved have spawned such relatively new terms as *post-traumatic stress disorder* and, as a response, *post-traumatic therapy*. Post-traumatic stress is most typically associated with reactions that occur to victims of violent crimes, including sexual abuse; hostages; Vietnam combat veterans; prisoners of war; survivors of the Holocaust and their dependents; and refugee survivors of torture and violence. Post-traumatic therapy is a clinical approach that focuses on recent events, the coping skills and strengths of the victim, the realistic options available, and the misconceptions or self-defeating thoughts that interfere with rapid emotional healing (Ochberg, 1988). The assessment procedure a counselor uses in crisis intervention needs to be sensitive to the possibility of post-traumatic stress disorder in the client. For example, it is common for the trauma of combat experiences or violent crime to be repressed and to lie dormant for years until reactivated by some other life crisis such as divorce or unemployment. Because of the possible residual feelings of guilt, shame, and low self-esteem and the clients' projections of danger and distrust on their children or spouses, post-traumatic therapy frequently needs to include the victims' immediate family and social group (Slaikeu, 1984). In addition, in the case of Vietnam combat veterans experiencing delayed forms of post-traumatic stress, group counseling with other veterans who have shared and understand the trauma they have mutually experienced may be an important therapeutic modality.

The post-traumatic stress syndrome can take a number of behavioral forms. Extended emotional vulnerability is one. Substance abuse is another. Interpersonal problems, unresolved grief and feelings of defeat, explosive violent behavior, social ostracism and isolation, as well as exceptionally vivid and persistent reexperiencing (flashbacks) of psychological trauma are all likely to be present and must be dealt with as manifestations of the underlying, unresolved stress (Rosenheck, 1985).

As suggested above, people who experience either developmental or situational crises are not pathological or mentally ill. They are people who typically have exceeded their levels of emotional resources or support systems to cope with a particular event or transition. Frequently, they are people who have reached levels of stress that finally produce exhaustion or other maladaptive responses. Using a stress paradigm proposed by Tubesing (1981), it is possible to suggest that all people are exposed to stressors of different types: overwork and fatigue, fear and hate, exposure and injury, hurry and tension, and expectations and pressures. When these stressors occur with too much intensity or in too great a quantity, the body protects itself or tries to maintain stability and balance by initiating the general adaptation syndrome that includes an alarm reaction, resistance or adjustment, and then exhaustion (Selye, 1976). Each initiation of the general adaptation syndrome uses up a portion of the body's adaptive energy, which is limited and cannot always be restored through rest. Continual fighting by the body against stressors can ultimately lead to such exhaustion that it begins to break the body down. As it does so, symptoms of distress may appear in the form of cardiovascular, emotional, gastrointestinal, arthritic, or other diseases. Thus, the linkage between life events, stress, and physical or mental health is clear.

Because of the pervasiveness of stress and burnout and their predisposition to put people at risk, counselors are increasingly engaged in stress management and other interventions. One view is that such intervention should be holistic (Sparks, 1981). In this perspective, the appropriate treatment of stress includes attention to physical health, nutrition and exercise, relaxation techniques (e.g., meditation, progressive relaxation), biofeedback, yoga, listening to certain types of music, massage, controlled breathing, rational-emotive therapy, cognitive restructuring, psychological education, social support, and action goal setting.

Slaikeu (1984) suggested other coping strategies that counselors might use in either developmental or situational crises. They include in vivo and systematic desensitization, group sharing or writing of experiences and feelings, coping imagery, calming imagery, assertiveness training, behavior rehearsal, thought stopping, rational emotive therapy, deep muscle relaxation, Gestalt empty chair technique, and outside readings.

Clearly, counselors need to be aware that people in transition are people for whom change is likely to cause stress. Stress in turn needs to be viewed holistically and as the focus of counselor proactivity and outreach as stress prevention and management are implemented. In dealing with the issues surrounding developmental transitions and situational crises, counselors must be prepared to take their own medicine, monitor their own stress, and provide opportunities for personal relaxation and support.

Conclusions

As previous chapters have suggested and chapter 5 has amplified, advanced technology, changing family structures, and pluralism and cultural diversity combine with other individual and group factors to put children, youth, and adults "at risk" of becoming physically ill or abused, experiencing mental disorders, taking on antisocial behavior, being economically disadvantaged, or experiencing other forms of negative psychological, social, physical, or economic life events. Risk factors can be classified in many ways: as social, psychological, economic, or political; in terms of alcohol or substance abuse and their attendant codependencies; or in terms of such group characteristics as age, disability, sex, or minority group membership.

Related to the broad categories of risk factors described above are notions about special populations. Two general classifications of special populations were described in this chapter. The first used social/historical criteria; the other life span/developmental criteria. The first category is composed of people who, because of social stigma and bias, cultural stereotypes, or legal or institutional barriers have been denied full access to opportunities or services in the society. The second category of special populations is composed of people who are at significant points of transition in their lives and are attempting to cope with the stress, uncertainty, and indecision that may accompany such status. Many of the risk factors that place people in special populations or categories are dynamic, not fixed. People who have never been considered "at risk" may be thrown into that category at certain points in their lives and, on the other hand, people who have been at risk on a long-term basis may, because of changes in social or political circumstances, no longer be considered to be at risk. What is apparent in either case, however, is that although people may evidence certain personal predisposing factors that make them more vulnerable to stress and other external factors, being at risk is largely triggered by outside events. With rare exceptions, people at risk are not psychopathological. Rather they lack adequate psychological resources or support systems to cope effectively with the risk factors (social/historical/bias/transition/stress) with which they are confronted.

Chapter 5 has described a range of counselor responses that have been found to be effective or that have been recommended as appropriate for different types of "at-risk" problems. These responses range from primary prevention to intense clinical intervention, from advocacy and environmental redesign to psychoeducational models of skill development. Chapter 6 will elaborate on the assumptions and use of many of these counseling techniques and describe others that are useful with people at risk and others not so classified.

References

Abel, G.G., Becker, J.V., & Skinner, L.J. (1980). Aggressive behavior and sex. *Psychiatric Clinics of North America, 3*, 133.

Alexander, J.A., & Harman, R.L. (1988). One counselor's intervention in the aftermath of a middle school student's suicide: A case study. *Journal of Counseling and Development, 66*(6), 283–285.

Alter-Reid, K., et al. (1986). Sexual abuse of children: A review of the clinical findings. *Clinical Psychology Review, 6,* 249–266.

American Psychiatric Association. (1980). *Diagnostic and statistical manual of mental disorders, third edition.* Washington, DC: Author.

Berkowitz, M., & Hill, M.A. (1986). *Disability and the labor market: An overview.* Chapter 1. Ithaca, NY: Cornell University, ILR Press.

Briere, J. (1984, April). *The effects of childhood sexual abuse on later psychological functioning: Defining a post-sexual-abuse syndrome.* Paper presented at the Third National Conference on Sexual Victimization of Children, Children's Hospital National Medical Center, Washington, DC.

Brownmiller, S. (1975). *Against our will: Men, women, and rape.* New York: Simon & Schuster.

Burgess, A.W., & Holmstrom, L.L. (1974). Rape/trauma syndrome. *American Journal of Psychiatry, 131,* 981–985.

Butler, J. (1980). *Inequality in the military: The Black experience.* Saratoga, CA: Century Twenty-One.

Butler, R.N., & Lewis, M.I. (1977). *Aging and mental health: Positive psychosocial approaches* (2nd ed.). St. Louis, MO: Mosby.

Campbell, J.R. (1985). Approaching affirmative action as human resource development. In H. McCarthy (Ed.), *Complete guide to employing persons with disabilities* (pp. 14–30). Alberton, NY: Human Resources Center, National Center on Employment of the Handicapped.

Chilman, C.S. (1980). *Adolescent sexuality in a changing American society: Social and psychological perspectives.* Washington, DC: U.S. Department of Health, Education and Welfare.

Cooney, J. (1988). Child abuse: A developmental perspective. *Counseling and Human Development, 20*(5), 1–10.

Daniels, S. (1985). Attitudinal influences on affirmative action interpretation. In H. McCarthy (Ed.), *Complete guide to employing persons with disabilities* (pp. 31–46). Alberton, NY: Human Resources Center, National Center on Employment of the Handicapped.

Danish, S.J., & D'Augelli, A.R. (1980). Promoting competence and enhancing development through life development intervention. In L.A. Bond & J.C. Rosen (Eds.), *Competence and coping during adulthood.* Hanover, NH: University Press of New England.

Davis, R. (1981). A demographic analysis of suicide. In L.E. Gary (Ed.), *Black men* (pp. 179–196). Beverly Hills, CA: Sage.

Dillard, J.M. (1982). Life satisfaction of nearly retired workers. *Journal of Employment Counseling, 19*(3), 131–134.

Dunham, J.R., & Dunham, C.S. (1978). Psychosocial aspects of disability. In R.M. Goldenson (Ed.), *Disability and rehabilitation handbook.* New York: McGraw-Hill.

Ekstrom, R.B., Goertz, M.E., Pollack, J.M., & Rock, D.A. (1986). Who drops out of high school and why? Findings from a national study. *Teachers College Record*, *87*(3), 356–373.

Evans, R.I. (1985). Psychologists in health promotion research: General concerns and adolescent smoking prevention. In J.C. Rosen & L.J. Solomon (Eds.), *Prevention in health psychology* (pp. 18–33). Hanover, NH: University Press of New England.

Finkelhor, D. (1979). *Sexually victimized children*. New York: Macmillan.

Fujimura, L.W., Weis, D.M., & Cochran, J.R. (1985). Suicide: Dynamics and implications for counseling. *Journal of Counseling and Development*, *63*(10), 612–615.

Gilligan, C. (1982). *In a different voice*. Cambridge, MA: Harvard University Press.

Goodlad, J.I. (1983). *A place called school: Prospects for the future*. New York: McGraw-Hill.

Gottfredson, G.D., Gottfredson, D.C., & Cook, M.S. (1983). *The school action effectiveness study: Second interim report, Part 1*. Baltimore, MD: Johns Hopkins University Center for Social Organization of Schools.

Hamparian, D., Schuster, R., Dinitz, S., & Conrad, J. (1978). *The violent few: A study of dangerous juvenile offenders*. Lexington, MA: Lexington Books.

Harper, F.D. (1981). Alcohol use and abuse. In L.E. Gary (Ed.), *Black men* (pp. 169–178). Beverly Hills, CA: Sage.

Harrington, M. (1962). *The other America: Poverty in the United States*. New York: Macmillan.

Hart, N., & Heidel, G. (1979). The suicidal adolescent. *American Journal of Nursing*, *79*, 80–84.

Harvey, M.R. (1985). *Exemplary rape crisis programs, A cross-site analysis and case studies*. Rockville, MD: U.S. Department of Health and Human Services, National Center for the Prevention and Control of Rape.

Herr, E.L. (1987). *A case study of the impact of the Carl D. Perkins Act in Philadelphia*. Washington, DC: U.S. Department of Education.

Herr, E.L., & Cramer, S.H. (1988). *Career guidance and counseling through the life-span: Systematic approaches*. Boston, MA: Scott, Foresman/Little, Brown Division.

Herr, E.L., & Long, T.E. (1983). *Counseling youth for employability: Unleashing the potential*. Ann Arbor, MI: The University of Michigan, ERIC/CAPS.

Hodgkinson, H.C. (1985). *All one system: Demographics of education, kindergarten through graduate school*. Washington, DC: The Institute for Educational Leadership.

Holmes, T.H., & Rahe, R.H. (1967). The social readjustment rating scale. *Journal of Psychosomatic Research*, *11*, 213–218.

Hotelling, K., & Forest, L. (1985). Gilligan's theory of sex-role development: A perspective for counseling. *Journal of Counseling and Development*, *64*, 183–186.

Huey, W.C. (1987). Counseling teenage fathers: The maximizing a life experience (MALE) group. *The School Counselor*, *35*(1), 40–47.

Isenstein, V.R., & Krasner, W. (1978). *Children at risk*. Rockville, MD: Mental Health Studies and Reports Branch, National Institute of Mental Health.

Josephson, G.S., & Fong-Beyette, M.L. (1987). Factors assisting female clients' disclosure of incest during counseling. *Journal of Counseling and Development, 65*(9), 475–478.

Kempe, R., & Kempe, C.H. (1984). *The common secret: Sexual abuse of children and adolescents*. New York: W.H. Freeman.

Kieffer, J.A. (1980). Counselors and the older worker: An overview. *Journal of Employment Counseling, 17*(1), 8–16.

Lenz, E., & Shavitz, M.H. (1977). *So you want to go back to school*. San Francisco, CA: McGraw-Hill.

Lewis, D.O. (1985). Special diagnostic and treatment issues concerning violent juveniles. In L. Roth (Ed.), *Clinical treatment of the violent person* (pp. 145–163). Rockville, MD: U.S. Department of Health and Human Services, National Institute of Mental Health.

Lewis, J. (1987). Children of alcoholics. *Counseling and Human Development, 19*(9), 1–9.

Lion, J.R. (1985). Clinical assessment of violent patients. In L. Roth (Ed.), *Clinical treatment of the violent person* (pp. 1–12). Rockville, MD: U.S. Department of Health and Human Services, National Institute of Mental Health.

Lobel, B., & Hirschfield, R.M.A. (1984). *Depression: What we know*. Rockville, MD: National Institute of Mental Health.

Mare, R.D., & Winship, C. (1980). *Changes in the relative labor force status of black and white youths: A review of the literature*. Madison, WI: University of Wisconsin, Institute for Research on Poverty. (ERIC No. ED 191937).

Mechanic, D. (1985). Health and behavior: Perspectives on risk prevention. In J.C. Rosen & L.J. Solomon (Eds.), *Prevention in health psychology* (Chapter 1). Hanover, NH: The University Press of New England.

Mogul, K.M. (1979). Women in midlife: Decisions, rewards, conflicts related to work and careers. *American Journal of Psychiatry, 136*(9), 1139–1143.

Monnhan, J., & Klasson, D. (1982). Situational approaches to understanding and predicting individual violent behavior. In M.E. Wolfgang & N.A. Weiner (Eds.), *Criminal violence* (pp. 292–319). Beverly Hills, CA: Sage.

Morrison, M.H. (1984). The aging of the U.S. population: Human resources implications. *Aging and Work, 71*(1), 79–83.

Morrissey, J.P., Witkin, M.J., Manderscheid, R.W., & Bethel, H.E. (1986). *Trends by state in the capacity and volume in inpatient services, state and county mental hospitals, United States, 1976–1980*. Rockville, MD: U.S. Department of Health and Human Services, National Institute of Mental Health.

Nathan, P.E. (1985). Prevention of alcoholism: A history of failure. In J.C. Rosen & L.J. Solomon (Eds.), *Prevention in health psychology* (Chapter 3). Hanover, NH: The University Press of New England.

National Center for Health Statistics, Division of Vital Statistics. (1983). *Mortality statistics*. Washington, DC: Author.

National Institute on Drug Abuse. (1985). *The 1984–85 Pennsylvania report*. Bethesda, MD: Author.

Newman, M.J. (1979). The labor market experience of black youth, 1954–78. In U.S. Department of Labor, Bureau of Labor Statistics, *Young workers and their families: A special section*. (Special Labor Force Report No. 233). Washington, DC: U.S. Government Printing Office.

O'Brien, S. (1980). Child abuse: A crying shame. Provo, UT: Brigham Young University.

Ochberg, F.M. (Ed.). (1988). *Post-traumatic therapy and victims of violence*. New York: Brunner/Mazel.

O'Toole, J. (1973). *Work in America*. Cambridge, MA: MIT Press.

Parham, T.A., & McDavis, R.J. (1987). Black men, an endangered species: Who's really pulling the trigger? *Journal of Counseling and Development, 66*(1), 24–27.

Pennsylvania Department of Education. (1986). *Adolescent suicide*. Harrisburg, PA: Author.

Pennsylvania Department of Education. (1987). *Achieving success with more students: Addressing the problem of students at risk*. Harrisburg, PA: Author.

Perry, L. (1982). Special populations: The demands of diversity. In E.L. Herr & N.M. Pinson (Eds.), *Foundations for policy in guidance and counseling* (Chapter 5). Falls Church, VA: The American Personnel and Guidance Association Press.

Phillips, D. (1985). The Western effect: Suicide and other forms of violence are contagious. *The Sciences, 25*, 32–39.

Rosen, J.C., & Solomon, L.J. (Eds.). (1985). *Prevention in health psychology*. Hanover, NH: The University Press of New England.

Rosenheck, R. (1985). Malignant post-Vietnam stress syndrome. *American Journal of Orthopsychiatry, 55*, 166–176.

Roth, L.H. (Ed.). (1985). *Clinical treatment of the violent person*. Rockville, MD: U.S. Department of Health and Human Services, National Institute of Mental Health.

Russell, D.E.H. (1982). *Rape in marriage*. New York: Macmillan.

Saed, W.W. (1979). Counseling the adolescent parent. *School Counselor, 26*, 346–349.

Sargent, S.S. (Ed.). (1980). *Nontraditional therapy and counseling with the aging*. New York: Springer.

Selye, H. (1976). *The stress of life*. New York: McGraw-Hill.

Sgroi, S. (1982). *Handbook of clinical intervention in child sexual abuse*. Lexington, MA: Lexington Books.

Shanas, E., & Maddox, G.L. (1976). Aging and health resources—Study of physical and mental health status of the elderly. In R.H. Binstock & E. Shanas (Eds.), *Handbook of aging and the social sciences*. New York: Van Nostrand.

Shapiro, S. (1987). Self-mutilation and self-blame in incest victims. *American Journal of Psychotherapy, 16*, 46–53.

Slaikeu, K.A. (1984). *Crisis intervention: A handbook for practice and research*. Boston: Allyn & Bacon.

Sparks, D. (1981). *Helping clients manage stress: A practical approach.* Ann Arbor, MI: The University of Michigan, ERIC/CAPS.

Sproles, E.T., III. (1985). *The evaluation and management of rape and sexual abuse: A physician's guide.* Rockville, MD: U.S. Department of Health and Human Services, National Center for Prevention and Control of Rape.

Staples, R. (1982). *Black masculinity.* San Francisco: Black Scholar Press.

Tracey, P.E., Wolfgang, M.E., & Figlio, R.M. (1985). *Delinquency in two birth cohorts: Executive summary.* Washington, DC: U.S. Department of Justice.

Tubesing, D.A. (1981). *Stress skills: A structured strategy for helping people handle stress more effectively.* Duluth, MN: Whole Person Press.

Tugend, A. (1986, June 18). Suicide's "unanswerable logic." *Education Week*, pp. 15–17.

U.S. Federal Bureau of Investigation. (1981). *Uniform crime reports for the United States.* Washington, DC: Superintendent of Documents, U.S. Government Printing Office.

U.S. Federal Bureau of Investigation. (1983). *Crime in the United States.* Washington, DC: Author.

U.S. Federal Bureau of Investigation. (1984). *Crime in the United States.* 1983 uniform crime reports for the United States Department of Justice. Washington, DC: Author.

Waterman, J., & Lusk, R. (1986). Scope of the problem. In K. MacFarlane, J. Waterman, S. Conerly, L. Damon, M. Durfee, & S. Long (Eds.), *Sexual abuse of young children* (pp. 3–12). New York: Guilford Press.

Welborn, A., & Moore, S.S. (1985). Counseling displaced homemakers. In D. Jones & S.S. Moore (Eds.), *Counseling adults: Life cycle perspectives* (pp. 103–107). Lawrence, KS: University of Kansas.

Whitemore, H. (1988, January 10). We can't pay the rent. *Parade Magazine*, pp. 4–6.

Whitman, D., Thornton, J., Shapiro, J.P., Witkin, G., & Hawkins, S.L. (1988, January 11). America's hidden poor. *U.S. News and World Report*, pp. 18–24.

Zinner, E.S. (1987). Responding to suicide in schools: A case study in loss intervention and group survivorship. *Journal of Counseling and Development*, 65(9), 499–501.

CHAPTER 6

CHANGING CONCEPTS, PROCESSES, AND PRACTICES OF COUNSELING

The preceding chapters have examined several major environmental and ecological processes likely to shape the types of problems that clients will bring to counselors in the foreseeable future. Economic and occupational changes, shifting family structures, cultural diversity, and risk factors make people captive to the attitudes and knowledge associated with their place in externally defined social, political, cultural, or economic environments. The influence of these environments is ingrained in individual self-concepts, in feelings of self-efficacy, in behavior.

Against such a context, counseling and related therapeutic activities can be viewed as mechanisms that free people from the captivity of negative attitudes, obsessions, irrational beliefs, information deficits, and low self-esteem. In such a view, counseling and related interventions represent both release and purpose: opportunities to shed the shackles of self-imposed or environmentally imposed limits on self-worth, dignity, or ambition as well as processes by which to translate renewed feelings of confidence and competence into plans of action, risk taking, and growth.

There have been many analyses of the role of the counselor in contemporary society. In one recent analysis, (Bellah, Madsen, Sullivan, Swidler, & Tipton, 1985), for example, the counselor is seen as a secular priest, one who has replaced the clergy and the church, and who assists people to pursue an elusive personal meaning as well as support. In other instances the counselor is portrayed as a kind of psychic mechanic who diagnoses and repairs trouble spots in individual behavioral systems. In still other perspectives, the counselor is viewed as a broker of information and as a confronter of self-imposed and inaccurate attributions about self and others. This focus is intended to help free people from restricting attitudes and belief systems and therefore connotes counselor proactivity, outreach, facilitating transactions between the individual and his or her environment; and helping the client learn new skills, acquire more accurate self-understanding, and feel less socially isolated. In this view the counselor is a sort of switching mechanism between the individual and the environment, an enabler of personal initiative and control, a maximizer of opportunity.

Any metaphor that can be conceived to describe the counselor's role in society rests upon and shapes conceptual models of counseling, the appropriateness of specific interventions and ethics, and the application of such processes within a possible range of populations and settings. In this chapter we will discuss several aspects of the changing place of counseling in contemporary societies around the world. In particular, the following major emphases will be discussed: comprehensiveness of settings and populations; changing conceptual paradigms for practice; the use of technology in counseling; the ethics of counseling; and emerging trends in interventions.

Comprehensiveness of Settings and Populations

As one considers the changes in counseling over the past half century, it becomes evident that counseling is seen as important not only for a small percentage of any population; rather counseling is now considered to be useful for virtually all people at some time or at several times during their lifetime. The target populations for counseling are not only the severely emotionally distressed on the one hand, or those choosing or adjusting to work on the other hand. The need for counseling across populations is not a discrete or absolute need, it is rather a continuum.

Characteristics of a Mental Health Continuum

Frequently, mental illness and mental health are treated as though they were discrete and dichotomous entities, as homogeneous opposites. In casual terms we frequently talk as though one is either ill or well, sick or healthy, normal or abnormal, distressed or not distressed. Such appellations frequently are seen as absolute and fixed characteristics and not as dynamic and changing systems of behavior. Unlike the linear, causal, categorical thinking of Western psychology, Eastern psychology tends to see variations in "mental health" or "normality" as a dynamic part of individuality. Thus, in this perspective, people are not typically mentally ill or mentally well. They are continually both as they react to one life event or another and as they move through the transitions from one life stage to another.

Glasser (1970) put such views of human behavior in perspective in his observations:

> Most people, even those with effective egos, have many different types of ego defects. We are all at times a little neurotic, a little psychotic, and have elements of character disorder and depression. Few of us escape some manifestation of psychosomatic disease at one time or another. . . . We have these ego defects transiently as our ego is constantly adjusting to variations of internal and external stresses. (p. 58)

Thus, one might suggest that any given individual across the course of life might profit from counseling help at times of crises, major life transitions, or periods of unusual stress or frustration. These are occasions when decisions must be made, conflicts resolved, or problems solved, when depression needs to be conquered, feelings of self-worth need to be strengthened, or skills need to be acquired to deal more effectively with anger, anxiety, job access, and other behaviors. If one extrapolates the needs of entire populations for counseling from the counseling needs of one individual, a continuum of counseling needs begins to emerge. At one end of the continuum are people or populations who truly qualify as mentally ill, people who have organically based mental diseases, substance-induced disorders, or other organic brain syndromes. These are people whose etiology or causative factors for the mental "illness" are relatively clear and well understood. They typically require medical intervention or medication to stabilize their behavior. In such instances, counseling or psychotherapy is helpful as supportive treatment after the organic pathology is treated and the person's cognitions are sufficiently intact to address behavioral management and decision making verbally. The mental disorders at this point on the continuum are those described in the American Psychiatric Association's *Diagnostic and Statistical Manual of Mental Disorders, Third Edition*, or the DSM-III (1980), under the classification of organic mental disorders. Within such a context organic factors or etiological agents are defined as a "primary disease of the brain. It may also be a substance or toxic agent that is either currently disturbing brain function or has left some long-lasting effect. Withdrawal of a substance on which an individual has become physiologically dependent is another cause of organic mental disorder" (p. 102).

With the categories of organic mental disorders or organic brain syndromes, the DSM-III includes such diseases as Alzheimer's and Pick's diseases, brain tumors, Huntington's chorea, and substance-induced disorders (e.g., intoxication, delirium, delusion, hallucinoses, or affective disorders caused by alcohol, barbiturates, opium, cocaine, amphetamines, PCP, hallucinogens, cannabis, etc.). Organic brain syndromes include delirium, dementia, amnesia, intoxication, and withdrawal. Increasingly, the etiology of schizophrenic disorders is considered to have organic dimensions.

The categories just described can appropriately be defined as mental illness or mental disease. They are primarily organic in nature and their etiology or risk factors are reasonably clear. They are not likely to be "cured" by counseling or psychotherapy alone; they typically require medication or other medical intervention.

Once one moves to other points on a mental illness-mental health continuum, the role of counseling as a primary therapeutic modality becomes clearer. If organic factors are not the primary risk factors or predisposing elements, then the etiology, or causes, of the behavior is primarily responses to psychological or social factors, faulty learning, inaccurate labeling of events, chronic neglect or abuse, inappropriate internalization of feedback from pathological social environments, insufficient socialization, or inadequate skill development. The resulting categories of mental health problems include antisocial behavior, academic problems, occupational problems, indecision, marital problems, parent-child difficulties, feelings of victimization, feelings of bereavement and loss, anxiety, inappropriate anger, interpersonal maladjustment, and related phenomena. These "problems of living" (Szasz, 1961) are not mental diseases nor mental illnesses per se. They do not emanate from pathology. They stem from other factors: inadequate information, unassertiveness, too much stress, fatigue, intense emotional crisis, lack of self-confidence, deficient social or interpersonal skills, incorrect perceptions of events, and other similar explanations. Often these psychological or social traumas are self-limiting; they are likely to improve over time even though, without counseling interventions, they will probably recur in some form whenever the precipitating social or psychological conditions elicit them. These are the domains in which counselors have their primary function.

At the other end of the mental health continuum from organic mental illness and problems in living are a variety of issues concerned with the quality of life. In this area we find emerging concerns about health psychology, behavioral medicine, and behavioral health. Those whose primary concerns are neither mental illness nor problems in living might ask, "How can I promote wellness and improve my physical and psychological quality of life?" Here one finds techniques like relationship enhancement; stress inoculation or reduction, systematic relaxation; couples or family counseling; constructive use of leisure; analyses of healthy life styles and their reinforcement through exercise and positive emotional behavior; and prevention of health risk behaviors such as obesity, smoking, and type A behavior (Rosen & Solomon, 1985). Enhancing the attitudes, knowledge, and skills central to achieving wellness and promoting quality of life are also within the professional repertoire of counselors and will probably be of increasing importance in the future.

Comprehensive Counseling Responses on a Mental Health Continuum

Although the continuum from mental illness to problems of living and on to enhancement of wellness just described can be fleshed out in far more specific ways, the point of major concern here is that the application of counseling has become increasingly comprehensive in application to populations and settings. As suggested earlier, counseling is not only for the severely troubled adult, or for the youth choosing courses, a form of vocational preparation, or a first job while in high school. Counseling has broad utility in schools, community agencies, universities, work places, and independent practice. It has utility for children, youth, and adults. People who are dealing with major life events, dislocated and underemployed workers, new immigrants and the culturally different, disintegrating and blended families, single parents, the terminally ill and their families, the aging and senior citizens, those contemplating retirement, those considering reentering the work force, those who have been abused or are codependents, those attempting to cope with major changes and life transitions, and those concerned with life enhancement and reduction of risk factors are the major but not the only populations for whom counselors will be increasingly important agents of support, change, education, growth, and development in the future. As the involvement of counselors with such broad population groups across the life span becomes more visible, counselors and counseling are likely to be increasingly seen by policymakers as being of central importance to achieving national goals of productivity, purposefulness, health, and happiness.

Accepting a continuum of perspectives on mental health may also ultimately resolve some of the controversies among the various mental health professionals about who should provide services to clients and under what conditions. Controversies among the helping professions frequently arise from different conceptual systems (Herr & Cramer, 1987). Different mental health occupations have tended to use different theoretical or explanatory systems to interpret human behavior and act upon it. Such phenomena have invariably given rise to interprofessional conflicts about which system is the most correct, the most scientifically or empirically valid, or the most comprehensive. Some ensuing controveries have focused on the overlap in techniques used (e.g., psychotherapy) rather than on the differences in meaning or definition attributed to such terms.

A major aspect of such controversy has to do with definitions of mental illness or mental health or both. Embedded in such controversies are concerns about biological versus psychological interpretations of behavior. Questions are raised about whether mental illness exists as an entity and about the etiology of its various manifestations. The further models of mental disorders depart from biological or disease entities, the more difficult it is to sustain some of the hierarchical models of the helping professions in which psychiatrists and clinical psychologists are viewed as being at the zenith in training, prestige, and skills and other groups of mental health professionals arrange themselves in a descending order of autonomy, competence, and training. Increasingly, a paradigm emerges in which a range of mental health occupations clamor for parity in providing mental health services to people experiencing mental illness (as defined primarily in terms of organic and chemical imbalances that require medication in conjunction with other therapeutic regimes), problems in living (those who need to acquire skills and learning pertinent to various life transitions), and needs for life enhancement (as defined in terms of holistic health and wellness). Thus, such mental health professionals, although overlapping to some degree in the intervention processes used (e.g., psychotherapy) and even in populations served, will be seen to differ significantly in their purposes and in their contributions to treatment, education, or prevention on a continuum from mental health "wellness" to mental illness, the latter defined in quite precise and circumscribed terms of an organic nature (Herr & Cramer, 1987), and across a large proportion of the population whose needs for counseling, its duration, and its intensity vary widely.

Changing Paradigms for Practice

As the application of counseling becomes increasingly comprehensive in the settings where it is available and in the populations served, there are also shifting views of how counseling should be conceptualized and practiced. If one were to attempt to summarize such paradigm shifts, they might be described by such traits as cognitive, brief, planned, interdisciplinary, eclectic, educative, preventive, and technological. In the following sections we will examine some of these concepts.

The Cognitive Sciences in Counseling

Perhaps the major advance in counseling and psychology during the recent past has been the concern of researchers and practitioners about cognitive phenomena: what the person is thinking as well as what he or she is feeling and doing.

Tyler (1983) suggested that cognitive theories of behavior are replacing the dominance of such theories as associationism and behaviorism. In her view, cognitive theories can be sharply distinguished from the latter theories because:

> First of all, they assume an active process of some sort, occurring in sequential phases, rather than the automatic linking of contiguous ideas or stimuli. Second, they postulate mental structures of some sort that impose form on input and control output. Third, they merge lines of research that have traditionally been separate, perception, memory, learning of skills, problem solving, and various others, incorporating the findings of experiments in these separate fields in their more inclusive formulations . . . the distinction between cognition and motivation is becoming blurred. Finally, many theorists are emphasizing the interdisciplinary aspects of the new cognitive science. (pp. 77–78)

The research underlying cognitive science takes many forms. Posner and Shulman (1979) suggested four major topics: (1) Representation—How the mind represents either concrete or abstract concepts; (2) Laws or rules of thought—How do people process information? Do they follow rules of logic or psychology? (3) Products of the thought processes that emerge during problem solving—How do people make decisions? What are the elements of differences in decision-making styles? How do choice outcomes differ? (4) Individual differences in cognitive abilities—What differences in cognitive processes account for the differences revealed by intelligence tests and other assessments of cognitions?

The importance of cognitive science to counseling lies with the growing attention to how individuals process information within the framework of how they construct reality. All people develop symbolic maps or representations of what they perceive to be reality and, indeed, their personal identity or place within this reality. These representations are systems of meaning, attitudes, or belief systems by which one interprets and acts upon events and the perceptual cues or information that attends them. In such a view, what is meant by phenomenological or perceptual fields is the construction an individual gives to his or her experiences. Such constructions evolve over time and assimilate the mirroring of meaning that comes from parents, peers, and others.

Beck (1985) contended that a major commonality among systems of psychotherapy "is the mechanism by which the specific therapy produces therapeutic results. There is considerable evidence accumulating that each of the effective therapies has an impact on cognitive processes. When measures of these cognitive processes show a shift from negative to positive, they are accompanied by a general improvement in depression and anxiety" (p. 333). Thus, a cognitive approach assumes that the individual's primary problem has to do with his or her construction of reality—faulty assumptions, irrational beliefs, or misconceptions. The task of the counselor is to help the individual modify the inaccurate or maladaptive cognitive set he or she holds about self, others, and life events.

As Beck suggested, most theories of psychotherapy are devoted to influencing the cognitive structures that trigger or sustain behavior. In this sense, it is difficult to find a clear beginning for cognitive behavioral approaches to counseling.

Beck and Rush (1988) indicated that in historical terms, cognitive therapy shows the confluence of three main sources of theoretical underpinnings: (1) the phenomenological approach to psychology, (2) structural theory and depth psychology, and (3) cognitive psychology:

> The phenomenological approach to psychology emphasizes the view of the self and the personal world as central to the determination of behavior. This concept was originally formulated in Greek stoic philosophy and in most recent times was evident in the writings of Adler (1936), Alexander (1950), Horney (1950) and Sullivan (1953). The structural theory

and depth psychology of Kant and Freud, particularly Freud's concept of the hierarchical structuring of cognition into primary and secondary processes, was the second major influence. The third sphere of influence stems from developments in contemporary cognitive psychology. George Kelly (1955) is generally recognized as being the first to describe the personality in terms of personal constructs and to define the role of beliefs in behavior change. The cognitive theories of emotion of Magda Arnold (1960) and Richard Lazarus (1984), which assigned primary importance to cognition in emotional and behavioral change, also contributed to the theoretical structure of cognitive therapy. (p. 533)

Various researchers claim that psychoanalysis, the individual psychology of Alfred Adler, Frankl's logotherapy, Freud, Karen Horney, Sullivan's interpersonal psychiatry, and Skinner, among other theorists of this century, were the first methods or initiators of a cognitive approach to therapy (Hoffman, 1984; Mahoney & Freeman, 1985). It is likely that each of these methods or practitioners did help to shape conceptions of how individuals formulate perceptions of reality and how these are ultimately misconstrued or require modification if the person is to develop a changed personal identity and restructure the attitude toward reality through which the world can be seen and dealt with in a different manner (Guidano & Lotti, 1985).

In describing the commonalities in the processes used by cognitive therapists, Hoffman (1984) contended that:

cognitive approaches . . . are included under directive therapy. The directive therapist endeavors to structure the situation as strongly as possible. His (her) function consists mainly in directly influencing the client's symptoms in order to effect necessary changes.

In this sense, the manner of proceeding used by cognitive therapists is very similar to that employed by behavioral therapists. Both conduct a series of diagnostic interviews to obtain a detailed description of the client's current difficulties. Subsequently, a synthesis of the problems is made, formulated in the therapist's respective theoretical language, which provides the client with an explanation for the emergence of his difficulties. The therapist, in order to eliminate the target symptoms, gives precise instructions about the procedures during the sessions and for the time between. On the basis of the therapist's personal and professional authority, the patient commits himself to adherence to these instructions.

In this sense, cognitive therapy, like behavior therapy, is to be understood as a technology which builds upon the findings of basic research concerning the part played by cognitive factors in the regulation of behavior, both in general and in the origin and maintenance of specific disorders, and which develops strategies of intervention whose effectiveness must be established through follow-up investigations. (p. 7)

The most typical contemporary attributions of the beginning of cognitive behavioral therapy tend to be the work of Ellis and the work of Beck. Ellis's work began in the 1950s (Ellis, 1958, 1962) and evolved from notions of rational psychotherapy into the system known as Rational-Emotive-Therapy (RET). Beck's work began in the 1960s as cognitive therapy.

In Ellis's view of RET, the main concern is people's emotional disturbances, how they largely create their own normal or healthy (positive and negative) feelings, and how they can change them if they wish to work at doing so (Ellis, 1985). The theoretical perspectives on the latter are defined by the ABCs. A stands for Activating events or experiences, Activities "or Agents that people disturb themselves about" (Ellis, 1985, p. 313). B stands for rational or realistic beliefs or irrational beliefs about the activating events that then lead to C, appropriate consequences, or IC, inappropriate consequences. More recently, Ds and Es have been added to the theory. D means Disputing irrational beliefs—detecting them, discriminating them from rational beliefs, and debating them. E stands for effective rational beliefs to replace irrational beliefs, effective appropriate emotion, and effective functional behaviors to replace disturbed emotions and dysfunctional behaviors.

"According to RET theory, people have almost innumerable beliefs (Bs)—or cognitions, thoughts, or ideas—about their activating events (As) and these Bs importantly and directly tend to exert strong influences on their cognitive, emotional, and behavioral consequences (Cs)" (Ellis, 1985, p. 315). On the other hand, irrational beliefs (IBs) are those cognitions, ideas, and philosophies that sabotage and block individuals' fulfilling their basic or most important goals. These can be learned from parents, teachers, and others.

From the beginning of his approach, Ellis emphasized confronting and eliminating irrational beliefs and providing an educational approach to client needs (e.g., teaching clients self-help skills to apply in solving their own problems).

Ellis made many important contributions to the conceptualization of cognitive therapy, including the specification of basic irrational ideas many people accept as valid assumptions and to which their behavior is oriented to preserving or manifesting. According to Ellis (1962), such major irrational ideas include those listed below.

1. You must—yes, must—have sincere love and approval almost all the time from all the people you find significant.
2. You must prove yourself thoroughly competent, adequate, and achieving, or you must at least have real competence or talent at something important.
3. You have to view life as awful, terrible, horrible, or catastrophic when things do not go the way you would like them to go.
4. People who harm you or commit misdeeds rate as generally bad, wicked, or villainous and you should severely blame, damn, and punish them for their sins.
5. If something seems dangerous or fearsome, you must become terribly occupied with and upset about it and make yourself anxious about it.
6. People and things should turn out better than they do, and you have to view it as awful and horrible if you do not quickly find good solutions to life's hassles.
7. Emotional misery comes from external pressures, and you have little ability to control your feelings or rid yourself of depression and hostility.
8. You will find it easier to avoid facing many of life's difficulties and responsibilities than to undertake more rewarding forms of self-discipline.
9. Your past remains all-important, and because something once strongly influenced your life, it has to keep determining your feelings and behavior today.
10. You can achieve happiness by inertia and inaction or by passively and uncommittedly "enjoying yourself."
11. You have to view things as awful, terrible, horrible, and catastrophic when you are seriously frustrated, treated unfairly, or rejected.
12. You must have a high degree of order or certainty to feel comfortable, or you need some supernatural power on which to rely.
13. You can give yourself a global rating as a human, and your general worth and self-acceptance depend upon the goodness of your performance and the degree to which people approve of you.

Other therapists have integrated the work of Ellis within other conceptions of cognitive science. An excellent example is the work of

Krumboltz (1983). As a major theorist in his own right, Krumboltz has been instrumental in advancing and refining a social learning theory of career selection (Krumboltz, Mitchell, & Gelatt, 1975; Mitchell & Krumboltz, 1984). Social learning theory, as an outgrowth of the general social learning theory of behavior as proposed by Bandura, Adams, and Meyer (1977), assumes

> . . . that the individual personalities and behavioral repertoires that persons possess arise primarily from their unique learning experiences rather than from innate developmental or psychic processes. These learning experiences consist of contact with and cognitive analysis of positively and negatively reinforcing events . . . . Social learning theory recognizes that humans are intelligent, problem-solving individuals who strive at all times to understand the reinforcement that surrounds them and who in turn control their environment to suit their own purposes and needs. (Mitchell & Krumboltz, pp. 235–236)

Krumboltz and his associates described the categories of influences on career selection and the types of outcomes that would be predicted by social learning theory. First, the four categories of influences include the following:

1. Genetic endowment and special abilities (such as race, sex, physical appearance and characteristics, intelligence, musical ability, artistic ability, muscular coordination).
2. Environmental conditions and events (such as number and nature of job and training opportunities, social policies, physical events, family characteristics, community and neighborhood emphases).
3. Learning experiences. There are two major types of such experiences. *Instrumental Learning Experiences* (ILEs) are those in which antecedents, overt and covert behavioral responses, and consequences are present. Career planning skills and those of other educational and occupational performance tend to be learned through Instrumental Learning Experiences. *Associative Learning Experiences* (ALEs) are those in which the learner pairs a previously neutral situation with some emotionally positive or negative reaction—examples are observational learning and classical conditioning.
4. Task approach skills include such processes as problem-solving skills, work habits, mental set, emotional responses, and cognitive approaches.

The combined influences of genetic endowment and special abilities, environmental conditions and events, and instrumental and associative learning experiences lead to several types of outcomes. They include:

1. Self-observation generalizations (SOGs) that are composed of overt or covert statements evaluating one's actual or vicarious performance in relation to some set of learned standards;
2. Task approach skills (TASs) that include cognitive and performance abilities and emotional predispositions for coping with the environment, interpreting it in relation to self-observation generalizations, and making covert or overt predictions about future events. Task approach skills of relevance to career planning, for example, might include such skills as value clarifying, goal setting, alternative generation, information seeking, estimating, planning, and related processes; and
3. Actions that include behaviors that reflect overt steps in a career progression, including such possibilities as applying for a specific job or training opportunity, changing a college major, and so forth.

Krumboltz links and explains individual-environmental transactions through the medium of learning, and particularly learning that is socially mediated by families, peers, or community representatives. It is within the context of social learning through modeling, reinforcement systems, information availability, and content that Krumboltz's theoretical views intersect with those of Ellis. Krumboltz (1983), for example, suggested that each person conceives a system of private rules that guide his or her decision making. These private rules are affected by the social learning influences previously described, and particularly by the self-observation generalizations and task approach skills that result. Within such outcomes, self-observation generalizations and perceptions of environmental conditions can be affected by irrational beliefs as they are described by Ellis. In Krumboltz's view, the irrational beliefs that can affect career decision making, and by extrapolation other problem solving, are those involving faulty generalizations, self-comparison with a single standard, exaggerated estimates of the emotional effect of an outcome, false causal relationships, ignorance of relevant facts, undue weight given to unlikely events, and self-deception.

Krumboltz contends that the content, character, and preservation of private rules of decision making and the irrational beliefs that sometimes infuse such rule-making systems relate to the reality that decision making is painful and can be associated with different types of stress:

threats to self-esteem, surprise, deadlines, and absence of time. When such stresses are present, they are likely to lead to or be accompanied by impaired attention, increased cognitive rigidity, narrowed perspectives, and displaced blame.

The counseling techniques that Krumboltz proposes in his various books as effective in dealing with irrational beliefs, stresses, and inaccurate self-observation generalizations range across a wide array of options. Of importance is examining assumptions and presuppositions that underlie the expressed beliefs; looking for inconsistencies between words and behavior; testing simplistic answers for inadequacies; confronting attempts to maintain an illogical consistency; identifying barriers to stated goals; challenging the validity of key beliefs; building a feeling of trust and cooperation; thought listing; in vivo self-monitoring; imagery; career decision-making simulations; reconstruction of prior events; use of psychometric instruments; cognitive restructuring techniques to alter dysfunctional or inaccurate beliefs and generalizations; use of positive reinforcement and appropriate role models; use of films depicting problem-solving strategies; teaching belief-testing and self-monitoring processes; analyzing task approach skills and teaching those in deficit; using computerized guidance systems to provide and reinforce problem-solving tasks and skills (Krumboltz, 1983; Mitchell & Krumboltz, 1984).

Beck, like Ellis, is considered by many to be one of the original founders of cognitive approaches to therapy. In Beck's view, a phenomenon like depression can be understood by integrating biochemical, psychological, behavioral, psychoanalytic, and cognitive perspectives. But from a cognitive perspective, Beck would contend that depression arises from a cognitive blockage that interferes with the reception or integration of positive data (Beck, 1985). According to Beck, studies have shown that clinically depressed patients have impaired recall of favorable feedback, pleasant events, self-referent positive adjectives, or pleasant schemes in stories. They may selectively block out positive aspects of experience and attach much higher probabilities to mishaps occurring than do "normal" people. In cognitive therapy, Beck's approach would emphasize providing a series of selected positive experiences and instructing a patient to write down experiences relevant to pleasure and mastery and to repeat them during the therapy sessions. In cognitive therapy, it is assumed that negative cognitive reactions occur in automatic and maladaptive ways. Thus, this automatic thought sequence must be interrupted through coaching, reality testing, disproving the irrational conception, providing a series of selected positive experiences, and interjecting a more realistic perspective into the client's thinking.

Beck (1985) also interpreted depression in terms of a "cognitive future triad," the activation of three major cognitive patterns that induce the patient to see him- or herself and the future in an idiographic, negative manner:

> [The] first component of the cognitive triad concerns the patient's negative view of himself. He sees himself as deficient, inadequate, or unworthy, and he tends to attribute his unpleasant experiences to his physical, mental, or moral defects. . . . he regards himself as lacking in those attributes that he considers essential for the attainment of happiness or contentment. . . . The second component of the triad is the patient's distorted interpretation of experience. He consistently construes experience in a negative way. He interprets his interactions with the environment as representing defeat, deprivation, or loss. . . . The third component of the triad consists of viewing the future in a negative way. The depressed patient anticipates that his current troubles will continue indefinitely. As he looks ahead, he sees a life of unremitting hardship, deprivation, and frustration. (pp. 156–157)

Beck's model assumes that the concepts that predispose people to depression originate early in life and derive from personal experiences, identification with significant others, and perceptions of the attitudes of others toward them. Within Beck's view cognitive therapy is technically eclectic and uses the entire range of current psychotherapeutic strategies from role playing to marriage counseling and relaxation training. Other techniques include induced fantasy, labeling and relabeling, redefining goals, anxiety management training, reattribution, confrontation, homework, and graded positive experiences. The point at issue, however, is that each technique is chosen as a means of expanding the depressed person's perceived range of options and altering negative views of self, the world, and the future (Beck & Greenberg, 1984).

Burns (1980), a colleague and student of Beck's, translated much of Beck's work into a book directed to the lay public for self-monitoring and self-help. In it, many of Beck's premises are accented. A major concept that underlies this view of cognitive therapy is that whether one talks about anger, anxiety, depression, or other emotions, the individual creates these emotions by the meanings given to specific events. Thus, the emotions that result in any situation are a function of one's thoughts or cognitions. Feelings or emotions result from the cognitions, labels, and meanings assigned to the event, not the other way around. Thus, cognitive therapy is focused on helping individuals change the way they interpret or look at events to make them feel better and act more purposefully and productively.

To put Beck's approach in its simplest form, Burns (1980) presented Beck's thesis as follows:

> (1) When you are depressed or anxious, you are *thinking* in an illogical, negative manner, and you inadvertently act in a self-defeating way. (2) With a little effort you can train yourself to straighten your twisted thought patterns. (3) As your painful symptoms are eliminated you will become productive and happy again, and you will respect yourself. (4) These aims can usually be accomplished in a relatively brief period of time, using straightforward methods. (pp. 3–4)

The therapeutic regimen in cognitive therapy rests on helping clients understand the foundation of their moods, anxieties, or depression and the direct linkage between their thoughts and their feelings; and teaching them how to interpret the automatic thoughts they tend to accept about themselves and their beliefs about how others feel about them. A second dimension is helping clients to understand and label the 10 areas of cognitive distortions that underlie their automatic thoughts and negative feelings. These 10 distortions are similar to but not the same as the irrational beliefs identified by Ellis. The distortions proposed by Burns are listed in Figure 6. Once clients identify and understand these distortions, they are provided homework as well as techniques by which to interrupt and rebut negative feelings. Depending upon clients' needs, the counselor or therapist will help them to build self-esteem and eliminate feelings of worthlessness. In doing so, it is often necessary to help the client overcome the all-or-nothing perspective and overgeneralization of a problem and reduce it to a more manageable size and perspective. Doing so frequently involves the therapist and client in defining the real problem, breaking it down into its specific parts, and then applying appropriate solutions.

Other Cognitive Behavioral Approaches

Although it contains basic components of cognitive therapy, the work of Ellis and Beck does not capture the whole of the emerging cognitive behavioral treatments of anxiety, depression, anger, divorce, work adjustment, panic disorders, suicidal ideation, or similar mental health problems. Five other approaches include systematic desensiti-

FIGURE 6
Definitions of Cognitive Distortions

1. All-or-Nothing Thinking: You see things in black-and-white categories. If your performance falls short of perfect, you see yourself as a
   total failure.
2. Overgeneralization: You see a single negative event as a never-ending
   pattern of defeat.
3. Mental Filter: You pick out a single negative detail and dwell on it
   exclusively so that your vision of all reality becomes darkened, like
   the drop of ink that discolors the entire beaker of water.
4. Disqualifying the Positive: You reject positive experiences by insisting
   they "don't count" for some reason or other. In this way you can
   maintain a négative belief that is contradicted by your everyday experiences.
5. Jumping to Conclusions: You make a negative interpretation even
   though there are no definite facts that convincingly support your conclusion.
   a. Mind Reading: You arbitrarily conclude that someone is reacting
      negatively to you, and you don't bother to check this out.
   b. The Fortune Teller Error: You anticipate that things will turn out
      badly, and you feel convinced that your prediction is an already-
      established fact.
6. Magnification (Catastrophizing) or Minimization: You exaggerate the
   importance of things (such as your goof-up or someone else's achievement), or you inappropriately shrink things until they appear tiny (your
   own desirable qualities or the other fellow's imperfections). This is
   also called the "binocular trick."
7. Emotional Reasoning: You assume that your negative emotions neces-
   sariy reflect the way things really are: "I feel therefore it must be
   true."
8. Should Statements: You try to motivate yourself with shoulds and
   shouldn'ts, as if you had to be whipped and punished before you
   could be expected to do anything. "Musts" and "oughts" are also
   offenders. The emotional consequence is guilt. When you direct
   should statements toward others, you feel anger, frustration, and resentment.
9. Labeling and Mislabeling: This is an extreme form of overgeneralization. Instead of describing your error, you attach a negative label to
   yourself—"I'm a loser." When someone else's behavior rubs you the
   wrong way, you attach a negative label to him: "He's a goddam
   louse." Mislabeling involves describing an event with language that is
   highly colored and emotionally loaded.
10. Personalization: You see yourself as the cause of some negative exter-
    nal event which in fact you were not primarily responsible for.

From "You Feel the Way You Think" (Table 3–1, pp. 40–41) in *Feeling Good: The New Mood Therapy* by D.D. Burns, 1980, New York: Signet. Reprinted by permission.

zation (Wolpe, 1973); anxiety management training (Suinn, 1976); systematic rational restructuring (Goldfried, Decenteco, & Weinberg, 1974); stress inoculation training (Meichenbaum, 1985); and anger management (Novaco, 1976). Deffenbacher (1988) analyzed the basic premises of the first four of these approaches. In abridged form they can be discussed as follows using as a constant their treatment of anxiety.

Systematic desensitization (Wolpe, 1973) incorporates the principle of reciprocal inhibition by arranging learning conditions in such a way as to pair a response that reduces (reciprocally inhibits) anxiety (usually relaxation) with an anxiety arousing stimulus. Using a hierarchy of the low to high anxiety-arousing stimuli for the particular individual, the client is taught progressive relaxation techniques to counteract each level of anxiety until he or she is able to be exposed to the anxiety-producing stimulus either in imagination or in reality and still maintain a relaxed or comfortable approach to it. The types of anxieties that might be at issue here are test anxiety, math anxiety, or communication or social skill anxieties.

Anxiety management training (Suinn, 1976) also uses relaxation and anxiety imagery but in a different format than in systematic desensitization. Anxiety management training helps the client to become aware of his or her internal cognitive, emotional, and physiological cues of anxiety arousal and to use these to initiate relaxation coping skills. The focus of this technique then is to train clients in progressive relaxation techniques on the one hand, and, on the other hand, how to recognize and respond to internal anxiety cues.

Systematic rational restructuring (Goldfried, Decenteco, & Weinberg, 1974) would not necessarily use relaxation techniques but rather would focus on the effects of cognitive processes, particularly irrational beliefs, in the creation of and continuation of anxiety relative to a particular type of performance such as speech anxiety. In this process clients learn about their dysfunctional cognitive beliefs and they obtain help in applying methods of countering such cognitions and thereby reducing anxiety. Frequently clients try to counter irrational beliefs while anxiety-producing stimuli are visualized in some form of an anxiety hierarchy. The cognitive skills acquired are transferred to the anxiety situations encountered in the daily life of the client through homework.

Stress inoculation training (Meichenbaum, 1985) is an active process involving both cognitive and relaxation coping skills. In this approach the client is also taught relaxation coping skills in relation to an anxiety-producing hierarchy in the area about which he or she is concerned such as math, test, or speech anxiety. Beyond the relaxation coping skill training, however, the client is taught cognitive coping skills related to restructuring of dysfunctional or irrational cognitions, task-oriented self-instruction, and self-reward and self-efficacy responses. The client rehearses the cognitive coping skills in role plays, simulations, or imagery of circumstances in which the client will have to perform. Reinforcement and transfer of the skills to daily living is accomplished through homework assignments.

The applications of cognitive-behavioral therapy are not confined to individual counseling or therapy. Sank and Shaffer (1984) described the use of cognitive behavior therapy in groups. This program also includes a psychoeducational model by which the group participants are trained in coping skills. Although such models will be discussed more fully later in this chapter, suffice it to say here that the categories or modules of skills used in this group program include relaxation, cognitive restructuring, assertion training, and problem solving. These four coping skills modules are seen as being pertinent, in selective terms, to group members or others experiencing depression, angry outbursts, job stress, headaches, and related problems.

Within the group process, other techniques have been used with the coping skills training. One of these is bibliotherapy, the reading of selected books that translate coping skills into self-monitoring and easily understandable formats.

Psychoeducational Models and Prevention

Another major trend in the present and the foreseeable future is psychoeducational models and prevention. Although psychoeducational models and prevention of mental health problems are not precisely the same, they frequently overlap in form and substance if not always in purpose.

Psychoeducational models are frequently linked to cognitive-behavioral or behavioral therapies, but that relationship is not absolute. Psychoeducational models tend to combine educational procedures such as planned or structured curricula, didactic teaching, and specific content, exercises, and homework with a range of psychological techniques such as simulations, role playing, behavioral rehearsal, modeling, feedback, and reinforcement. Basically psychoeducational models teach clients coping skills pertinent to dealing with current and future problems. Counselors in educational institutions, community agencies, business and industry, and independent practice are likely to use psychoeducational models either for treatment or for prevention of problems. Programs as diverse as career education, deliberate psychological education, stress management, decision-making training, anxiety or anger management, job-search strategies, parent effectiveness training, assertive training, social skills development, and communication skills each incorporates psychoeducational models and skills. In some instances they do so to provide clients skills that their problems in living affirm they need if they are to effectively correct some skill deficit implicated in their behavioral difficulties. For example, clients who have problems with anger may simply not have a behavioral repertoire from which to select behaviors likely to be more socially acceptable or interpersonally sound. Therefore they are likely to use physical violence or intense verbal aggression that leads to education, job, or social maladjustment. The solution to this problem may be coping skills training by which clients can better understand what precipitates their anger, how they can exert more self-control in dealing with anger-producing situations, and learn communications, positive assertiveness, or other skills that allow them to express anger in a constructive fashion. In contrast, coping skills training or psychoeducational models may be used to prepare students or clients to anticipate certain types of problems and help them acquire needed skills when they face such problems, thereby reducing the surprise, novelty, or other stress-inducing emotions when a problem of a particular type occurs.

Some researchers advocate structured learning approaches to teaching prosocial skills. For example, Goldstein, Sprafkin, Gershaw, and Klein (1980) argued that the research on adolescents indicates that three categories of behavior problems can account for most adolescent behavior disorders. These three categories are aggression, withdrawal, and immaturity. From a psychoeducational view, however, the important point is that each of these sets of problems can be related to some set of skill deficits. More conceptually, "Each type may be described in terms of both the presence of a repertoire of dysfunctional and often antisocial behavior and of the absence of a repertoire of prosocial or developmentally appropriate behaviors" (Goldstein, Sprafkin, Gershaw, & Klein, p. 5). Thus, one approach is to diagnose the dysfunctional behaviors and try to remove them; another is to teach the desirable, functional skills under the assumption that the absence of such prosocial skills leads to dysfunctional behaviors, and that the presence of desirable skills will allow the individual to be more discriminating and able to choose from a range of skills appropriate to a certain type of occasion.

In describing the developmental tasks adolescents must face, Goldstein et al. (1980) suggested that love, sex, peer relationships, and school-related tasks are likely to require social skills, skills for dealing with feelings, skills for dealing with stress, planning skills, and related skill clusters. Each of these skill categories can be taught in a systematic, structured fashion. In addition, each of these skill categories is likely to be composed of a number of subskills that need to be acquired. For example, beginning social skills taught to a withdrawn or immature adolescent might include listening, starting a conversation, engaging in a conversation, asking a question, saying thank you, introducing him- or herself, introducing other people, and giving a compliment.

Psychoeducational models include different emphases but they typically involve teaching of skills, homework and practice, the use of audiovisual materials, simulations, or similar approaches. "Thus, in the typical psychoeducational training session, skill-deficient trainees are shown examples of competent skill behavior, given opportunities to rehearse what they have seen, provided with systematic feedback regarding the adequacy of their performance, and encouraged in a variety of ways to use their new skills in their real-life environment" (Goldstein et al., 1980, p. 13). In the model proposed by Goldstein, Shafkin, Gershaw, and Klein (1980):

Structured Learning consists of (1) modeling, (2) role playing, (3) performance feedback, and (4) transfer of training. The trainee is shown numerous specific and detailed examples (either live or on audiotape, videotape, film, or filmstrip) of a person (the model) performing the skill behaviors we wish the trainee to learn (i.e., modeling). The trainee is given considerable opportunity and encouragement to rehearse or practice the behaviors that have been modeled (i.e., role playing) and provided with positive feedback, approval, or praise as the role playing of the behaviors becomes more and more similar to the behavior of the model (i.e., performance feedback). Finally, the trainee is exposed to procedures which are designed to increase the likelihood that the newly learned behaviors will in fact actually be applied in a stable manner in class, at home, at work, or elsewhere (i.e., transfer of training). (p. 15)

The application of psychoeducational elements as just suggested appear in different emphases in such approaches as microtraining and micro-counseling, deliberate psychological education, and similar programs.

Prevention, Personal Competence, and Behavioral Promotion

Psychoeducational models can be used for remediation of skill deficits already apparent in the dysfunctional behavior of adolescents and adults or for the prevention of behavioral disorders likely to ensue in the absence of appropriate social, planning, and other skills. Such intervention strategies rest upon conceptualizations of mental dys-functions as other than organic, as behavioral and learned or, at least, as frequently preventable. Albee (1982), a major spokesman for a preventive rather than remedial approach to problems in living, sug-gested:

> If your purpose is to reduce the incidence of the different conditions or life styles we refer to as mental disorders . . . there are several strategies for accomplishing our purpose: the first of these is to prevent, to minimize, or to reduce the amounts of the organic factors that sometimes do play a role in causation (e.g., lead poisoning, brain damage from au-tomobile accidents). . . . A second strategy . . . involves the reduction of stress . . . (p. 1046). Another area . . . involves increasing the competence of young people to deal with life's problems, particularly with the problems of social interactions, and the development of a wide range of coping skills. . . . Increases in support systems and self-esteem have been shown to reduce psychopathology (p. 1045). . . . Those who argue against the concept of mental illness do not deny the existence of behavior that can be called abnormal or pathological. They simply hold that abnormal behavior can be learned through perfectly normal processes—and what can be learned can be unlearned or prevented. (p. 1050)

Albee (1980) also argued that a competence model must replace the defect or illness model of mental disturbance. A competence model contends that individuals, youth or adults, have adaptive potential and competencies that can be enhanced by mental health professionals by strengthening individual coping skils, self-esteem, and social support systems.

From such a view, most of the problems that people bring to counselors are not pathological or organic. Rather they are matters of personal competence and the degree to which people have knowledge or skills that permit them to cope with or master the various developmental tasks, transitions, or crises they face across the life span. Personal competence can be seen in many ways. Gladwin (1967) suggested that competence includes the ability to utilize various alternatives in reaching a goal, an understanding of social systems of which one is a member, the ability to use one's resources, and effective reality testing. *Personal competence* can also be seen as a series of skills an individual either possesses or can learn through training. The acquisition of certain skills may generalize to facilitate the development of competence in other aspects of one's life (Danish, Galambos, & Laquatra, 1983). Some observers term these skills "life development skills" and their content includes *cognitive* and *physical* skills; *interpersonal skills* such as initiating, developing, and maintaining relationships (e.g., self-disclosing, communicating feelings accurately and unambiguously, being supportive, and being able to resolve conflicts and relationship problems constructively); and *intrapersonal* skills (e.g., developing self-control, managing tension and relaxation, setting goals, taking risks, etc.) (Danish et al.).

A preventive approach to counseling, whether group or individual, presupposes that the elements of personal competence, the skills needed to handle problems in living, and the behaviors on which relationship enhancement, marital harmony, or positive interpersonal relationships rest can be known and understood.

Such a notion implies that the knowledge, attitudes, and skills central to "life coping skills" or to "personal competence" can be identified, used as the content of preventive structured learning or psychoeducational approaches or as targets of other therapeutic interventions, and thereby learned, changed, or strengthened. These assumptions are implicit in psychoeducational models of the increasingly common counseling language of assertiveness training, anger management, stress inoculation, obesity or smoking control, decision-making training, or other forms of planned psychosocial development.

The next, and rapidly emerging, application of such conceptualizations is not simply the prevention of behavioral or mental health problems but, indeed, the promotion of mental or physical health. In somewhat simplistic terms, one can argue that primary prevention includes processes and activities intended to reduce the incidence of a disorder or the likelihood of its occurrence in a population at risk. Thus, teaching parents who were abused as children effective parenting strategies and other skills that strengthen personal competence may reduce or eliminate the likelihood of these parents abusing their own children, children who under ordinary circumstances would be "at risk" of receiving such abuse. The intent then would be to prevent or reduce the incidence of such abuse. By contrast, mental health promotion includes psychoeducational activities or other skill-development processes designed to increase people's sense of competence, coherence, and control so that they can live effective and satisfying lives in a state of social well-being (Perlmutter, 1982). In such a focus, the intent of the counseling or skill development processes used is not to prevent problems but to enhance the quality of life. The latter approaches are found in such rapidly expanding domains as behavioral medicine, health psychology, and behavioral health. The latter term particularly has come to mean approaches used by counselors and psychologists to help currently healthy people to maintain health and prevent illness and dysfunction (Goldstein & Krasner, 1987). It has application in physical health (e.g., diet and stress management) as well as in work adjustment or what might be termed occupational health.

Whether in terms of prevention or enhancement, the approaches included apply the findings of psychology to prevent certain behaviors from occurring by either developing, strengthening, or enhancing other behaviors. But behavioral health has come as well to refer to the use of counseling interventions in areas in which the problems brought to the counselor have physiological and stress-related components. One such growing relationship is that of career counseling and behavioral health.

Career Counseling and Behavioral Health

For most of its history, career counseling has not been seen as directly related to the reduction of emotional distress or to other aspects of mental health. Indeed, some observers have argued that career counseling and psychotherapy are separate processes. In such perspectives, career counseling has not been seen as a therapeutic modality but traditionally portrayed as more oriented to economic health, to the choice of an occupation, and to the development of prevocational skills and the preparation for work than to the reduction of stress and other factors that put many at risk of work pathologies or physical and mental illness. Such a view is slowly changing in the face of growing evidence that career counseling is critical to reconnecting unemployed and underemployed youth and adults to a sense of purposefulness and self-efficacy, and in so doing to a diminution of the stress-related side effects of hopelessness and despair.

The past decade has seen a broadening of perspectives on career behavior including those that center around the effects of work that does not enhance self-esteem, inappropriate person-job fit, and the multiple personal problems associated with unemployment and underemployment. In each case, research has demonstrated that a variety of life difficulties and mental health problems ensue when work life is unsatisfactory. Distress about work and, particularly, unemployment is associated with a range of personal and social problems. Levine (1979) reported that although there are individual differences in coping with unemployment, the virtually predictable emotional and cognitive consequences include boredom, identity diffusion, lowered self-esteem, guilt and shame, anxiety and fear, anger, and depression. These are not benign emotional reactions.

Dawis (1984), speaking to the literature on job satisfaction or dissatisfaction, contended that:

> . . . from a behavioral standpoint, job satisfaction is a response (a verbal operant) that has behavioral consequences. On the positive side are tenure, longevity, physical health, mental health, and productivity; on the negative side, turnover, absenteeism, accidents, and mental health problems. . . . The turnover literature documents a negative relationship between job satisfaction and turnover. . . . Quitting the job is the means by which the individual avoids the aversive condition that is job dissatisfaction. . . . The absenteeism literature has likewise documented a negative relationship between job satisfaction and absenteeism; like turnover, absenteeism is a form of avoidance adjustment. . . . Negative but low correlations have been reported between job satisfaction and accidents. (p. 289)

Dawis also reported that job dissatisfaction is related to mental and physical health problems including psychosomatic illnesses, depression, anxiety, worry, tension, impaired interpersonal relationships, coronary heart disease, alcoholism, drug abuse, and suicide.

Many existing research studies link work and mental health. In a major study of mental health in America and the contrasts in patterns of seeking help from 1957 to 1976, Veroff, Kulka, and Douvan (1981) reported that about 10% of their respondents in 1957 and in 1976 either used help or could have used help with job problems or vocational choice (p. 190). Undoubtedly, this number is understated because several other problem areas reported probably also included job-related problems (such as situational problems involving other people, non-psychological situational problems, "nothing specific—a lot of little things," and marriage). The researchers also found that younger workers are more distressed in their work, more aware of their own shortcomings, and more sensitive to difficulties, and that they seek greater gratification from their work life. Older people are more often locked into a job to which they already have adapted and hence tend to make the best of what they have. Such findings indicate that some groups are more likely to experience psychological distress associated with work than others.

Borgen and Amundson (1984), in a major study of the experiences of unemployed people from a variety of educational, cultural, and work backgrounds in Canada, extended the findings of Levine. Borgen and Amundson contend that the experience of unemployment depicts an emotional "roller coaster" that is comparable in its effect and stages to those found by Kübler-Ross (1969) as describing the grief process associated with the loss of a loved one: denial, anger, bargaining, depression, and acceptance. In regard to Maslow's model of prepotent needs, which suggests that as needs at the bottom of a hierarchy are satisfied, other needs emerge, Borgen and Amundson suggest that unemployment brings with it a needs shift, involving tumbling down the hierarchy from need levels attained under previous employment to more primitive need levels that are dominant under unemployment. According to Maslow (1954), the categories of needs that emerge as lower levels of needs are routinely met or taken for granted begin with the most basic, the physiological needs, and proceed next to the safety needs (security, stability), to the love and belonging needs (relatedness), to the esteem needs (prestige, self-worth, recognition), and, finally, to the self-actualization needs (creative self-expression). Although people rarely attain the highest level of self-actualization in their work, it can be assumed that most people successfully employed will be able to attain needs beyond the most primitive physiological necessities and to meet needs for safety, love, belonging, and esteem. The research of Borgen and Amundson suggests, using Maslow's model of prepotent needs, that whatever needs are attained in employment shift downward significantly under unemployment. The psychological reactions are not only those of loss as defined by the Kübler-Ross paradigm but also feelings of victimization similar to those experienced by victims of rape, incest, disease, and crime. Such feelings include shock, confusion, helplessness, anxiety, fear, and depression (Janoff-Bluman & Frieze, 1983).

Borgen and Amundson's research also shows that unemployment is experienced differently by different groups of men and women who did or did not anticipate job loss, and by immigrant populations. The factors that vary among these groups and mediate the emotional reactions to unemployment include: attachment to the job, social status, individual personality variables, financial situation, social support system, and future expectations.

In applying Borgen and Amundson's model to the situation of a long-established plant closing, Hurst and Shepherd (1986) found similar emotional stages among workers anticipating job loss prior to plant closings. In such instances, the emotional roller coaster is likely to be prolonged as older workers remain while younger workers are laid off to pare down the work force. The research of Lopez (1983), as well as that of Borgen and Amundson (1984) shows that groups varied in their reaction to job loss. Hurst and Shepherd found in their sample that those employees most likely to experience prolonged depression are the few who are handicapped by physical, skill, and age barriers, and those with very low self-esteem. But even workers who do not experience clinical depression, as Lopez also found, tend to experience "feelings of loss, sadness, resentment, and anger because of the end of the company, close collegial relationships, and a way of life for most employees" (Hurst & Shepherd, p. 404).

Borgen and Amundson's research (1984) highlights what other theorists and researchers have also observed in relation to the interaction of mental health and the state of the economy, unemployment, or related phenomena. One is that such interactions are likely to include multiple variables, not simply unidimensional relationships. Different people experience economic downturns and unemployment differently, and mental health outcomes can be precipitated by factors in the environment (sociogenic) as well as factors within individuals (eugenic) (Berg & Hughes, 1979). Thus, there are questions of social causation, social selection, precipitating factors, and individual predispositions that relate to how work and mental health are related. Brenner (1979) attempted to clarify the differences among some of these concepts. For example, physical or mental health are not unitary concepts. Some people react to stress in physical terms (e.g., cardiovascular disease, cirrhosis, hypertension, chemical dependency, early death); others in behavioral terms (e.g., aggressiveness, violence, spouse abuse, child abuse); others in psychological terms (e.g., depression, anxiety). Thus, precipitating factors in the environment (e.g., a plant closing, losing a job) can cause different reactions among people (e.g., physical, behavioral, psychological) depending on individual predisposing factors to stress.

The links between unemployment and other individual or social costs are complex. Liem and Rayman (1980), among others, reviewed studies of the social and private costs of unemployment. They indicate, "Prolonged unemployment is commonly a serious threat to health and the broad quality of life. These costs, furthermore, are borne not only by individual workers, but also by their families and communities" (p. 1116). They go on to indicate, "There is good evidence that losing one's job can increase health risks, exacerbate chronic and latent disorders, alter usual patterns of health-seeking behavior, and exact numerous other social and interpersonal costs" (p. 1116).

Among the specific problems found in the research literature to be associated with unemployment and economic decline are first admissions to psychiatric hospitals, a rise in infant mortality rates, increased deaths from cardiovascular and alcohol-related diseases, a sharp increase in suicide rates, greater demand for mental health services due to increased psychological impairment (Brenner, 1973, 1974); threats to the structural interdependence between the family and the work place (Kantor, 1977); stress in the children of unemployed parents—such as moodiness at home, new problems in school, strained relationships with peers (Liem & Rayman, 1980); digestive problems, irritability, and retarded physical and mental development (Riegle, 1982); child and spouse abuse, and juvenile delinquency (Riegle). The "ripple effect" of unemployment touches not only the individual who is unemployed but all parts of the system of which he or she is a part. Each person involved commonly manifests a wide range of physical, emotional, and social stresses and strains. In chapter 2 a more detailed discussion of unemployment and its effects was presented.

Much more could be said about these matters, but suffice it to say here that the stress reactions and stress-related physical and psychological diseases that accompany problems of work adjustment, work choice, and the exit from work bring career counseling directly into the realm of the emerging movement in behavioral health and, more broadly, behavioral medicine. Flowing from earlier work in psychosomatic medicine and studies on alcohol in the work place, behavioral medicine is a broad interdisciplinary study of scientific inquiry, education, and practice concerned with health and illness or related dysfunctions (e.g., essential hypertension, cholesterolemia, stress disorders, addictive smoking, obesity, etc.). The term *behavioral health* is usually considered a subspecialty within behavioral medicine, which is specifically concerned with the maintenance of health and the prevention of illness and dysfunction in currently healthy persons (Matarazzo, 1980). Behavioral health conceptualizes health-related activity in overt behavioral terms in much the same way as is true of perspectives on the developmental tasks underlying career behavior and the transitional elements of performance, understanding of the affective context in which work is played out, being able to work with others, and being able to implement self-discipline, loyalty, and career mobility. Many of the techniques in behavioral health are also those used in career counseling—behavior therapy, cognitive restructuring, psychosocial skills training, family counseling, stress inoculation, and stress management.

Career counseling approaches in or out of business and industry can provide dislocated workers, unhappy workers, maladjusted workers, and underemployed workers information, support, encouragement, or skill-building approaches that can facilitate hope and reduce feelings of being a social isolate and unworthy. Skill building approaches can deal directly with such matters as anger management, assertiveness, planning, interpersonal competencies, and openness to constructive supervision. These approaches educate people regarding choice and emphasize personnel development, not only personnel management. Their availability and implementation are not just matters of occupational choice and adjustment, rather they also help people to create reality and make meaning for themselves within the context of work and career. The latter are directly related to behavioral health.

In conclusion, personal adjustment and work adjustment exist in a symbiotic relationship. The work place becomes an environment in which both positive and negative, healthy and unhealthy, good and bad outcomes are stimulated, and an environment in which the conflicts, thwarted aspirations, and emotional baggage from one's life outside the work place that are brought into it filter and shape one's life as a worker. Undoubtedly there will be more conceptualization of career counseling, career assisting, and career intervention in the future as a complex blend of development and remediation, of education and skill facilitation, and of therapeutic modalities as increasingly concerned not only with the economic life of the individual but in more multidimensional and holistic terms.

As theory and research on career behavior have matured, they have acknowledged both the complexity of influences upon and the psychological characteristics of career choice and adjustment throughout the life span. In so doing, credence has been given to career counseling as a therapeutic modality that goes beyond dispensing and discussing information. Crites (1981) suggested that as insights from client-centered and psychodynamic approaches are applied to career counseling, choice problems are viewed as essentially personality problems. Therefore, the assumptions that guide the provision of career counseling need to be considered in relation to personal adjustment counseling or psychotherapy.

Brown (1985) pushed the interaction of career counseling and personal counseling even further than did Crites. Brown, who defined career counseling "as the process of helping an individual select, prepare for, enter, and function effectively in an occupation'' (p. 197), viewed career counseling ''as a viable intervention with clients that have rather severe emotional problems.'' In particular, Brown distinguished between clients who have intrapsychic (cognitive or emotional) problems and those who work in a nonsupportive, stress-producing environment that may cause symptoms that seem to be intrapsychic, mental health disorders rather than functions of poor personal-work environment fit. Obviously, how the counselor makes such distinctions will determine whether the therapeutic approach focuses upon intrapsychic changes, as in personal counseling and psychotherapy, or on altering the work environment, choosing another work environment through career counseling, or assisting the individual to manage the stress induced by such an environment. Such a view obviously extends both the range of problems likely to be addressed by career counseling and the settings in which career counseling should be offered. Viewing career counseling in such ways provides almost an inevitable connection to behavioral health.

Mental Health Counseling and Behavioral Medicine

Although it may seem somewhat radical to some readers to connect career counseling and behavioral health, it is less difficult to connect mental health counseling and behavioral medicine. As observed by Nicholas (1988), ''today's 10 major causes of death, in rank order, beginning with the highest, are heart disease, malignant neoplasms, stroke, accidents (other than from motor vehicle accidents), influenza and pneumonia, motor vehicle accidents, diabetes, cirrhosis of the liver, arteriosclerosis, and suicide'' (p. 69). at least 7 of these 10 causes of death are directly related to life style, personal behavior, and personal choices. Thus, mental health counselors, as practitioners concerned with behavioral change, have major roles to play in the prevention and remediation of behaviors that put one's health at risk and in promoting those behaviors that promote health and wellness.

Nicholas suggested that from the beginnings of the professional identity of mental health counseling, practitioners have been committed to the promotion of well-being. Citing the interdisciplinary background of behavioral medicine, Nicholas advocated the work in medical sociology of Antonovsky (1979) who proposed the term salutogenesis— the origins of health—as the counterpoint to pathogenesis—the origins of sickness, thereby prompting mental health counselors to primarily concern themselves with the question of what keeps people healthy rather than the question of what makes people sick.

Within the above context, then, Nicholas (1988) suggested that there is a conceptual convergence between behavioral medicine and mental health counseling in their joint emphases on "(a) a conceptual shift away from pathogenesis toward salutogenesis; (b) the assumption of personal responsibility for one's health; (c) an integrative, holistic view of health and the recipients of health care; and (d) prevention as one of the full-range of health care services" (p. 73).

Finally, it is useful to note that the model proposed by Nicholas illustrates a continuum of intervention as suggested earlier in this chapter. He contends that on the end of the continuum concerned with tertiary prevention or the modification of risk factors associated with premature death, or the results of near death experiences, there is an array of chronic illnesses that is likely to precipitate mental health issues as well as behavioral issues to which counselors can respond. The areas in which such tertiary prevention is appropriate include stroke, heart disease, cancer, diabetes mellitus, epilepsy, spinal cord injuries, asthma, bronchitis, emphysema, chronic pain, as well as treatment compliance and social support. At the other end of the continuum is the role of the counselor in providing primary prevention and promoting optimal health. In this context, the counselor may be in a support role to a physician or work alone to create the coping skills and insights associated with preventing risk factors implicated in disease. Thus, counselors may provide individual or group approaches designed to help people implement weight management, smoking cessation, aerobic exercise, stress management, appropriate alcohol use, social support, or adherence to a regimen leading to optimal health.

Systematic Eclecticism

Cognitive psychology, psychoeducational models, and the use of such approaches for both prevention and treatment have spawned a further emerging trend in counseling, that of differential treatment or systematic eclecticism. Fundamentally, such a model of counseling assumes that specific treatments or counseling approaches are effective for some purposes and not for others, and that clients come to counselors for many different reasons. Rather than assuming that the same treatment or approach is useful for all people, the counselor tailors the counseling response to the unique needs of an individual client. In this view counselors would ideally be trained in a repertoire of treatments— individual, group, psychoeducation, self-monitored, etc.—that would be based on scientific analyses of their effectiveness under certain conditions and for specific purposes. As the counselor and the client define the goals of the counseling relationship and clarify the reasons the client has come for counseling, one assumption of systematic eclecticism is that the counselor can implement the most powerful or relevant approach.

Systematic eclecticism does not suggest that the counselor should flail about for treatments in a random way. Rather, it suggests that it is possible to think of counseling approaches and client outcomes as a matrix of possible interactions. Some counseling approaches or treatments will be more effective for certain purposes and not for others. The scientific problem, given the complexity of factors that brings people to counseling, is how precise the matching of treatment and outcome might be. A further problem is the likelihood that counselors can be trained equally well to implement a large range of treatments or interventions. Traditionally counselors have been trained in counseling approaches that are essentially theory-bound: psychodynamic, client-centered, behavioral, cognitive-behavioral. Systematic eclecticism, however, suggests that each of these theory-bound approaches has utility for certain purposes to achieve certain client outcomes. But, systematic eclecticism also suggests that no one theory-bound approach has all the answers to all the client needs that are brought to counselors. Therefore, counselors should be trained across theoretical domains to learn about the most effective contributions of each in order to apply such approaches systematically and scientifically.

Systematic eclecticism as a structure for conceiving counseling interventions rests upon another notion as well. It is, in essence, that most clients who come to counselors do not have one problem, they have several. People may need help, for example, with behavior, emotions, nutrition, and problem solving, not only one of these, if they are to overcome their problems in living. This view of the multiple dimensions of client problems is the basis for such models of counseling as that of multimodal therapy (Lazarus, 1981).

The assumptions of systematic eclecticism, differential treatment, or multimodal therapy are giving rise to other terms as well. For example, the tendency for counselors to use whatever approach is technically useful and practical regardless of theoretical orientation has been labeled "pragmatic technical eclecticism" (Keat, 1979), eclectic psychotherapy (Norcross, 1986), and adaptive counseling and therapy—an integrative eclectic model (Howard, Nancy, & Myers, 1986). The momentum that eclectic approaches to counseling now have is suggested by the research of Smith (1982). This study reported that about two thirds of the counselors queried indicated that the primary movement or trend was toward some form of eclectic approach. Although the terms used varied (i.e., *multimodal*, 19%; *creative synthesis*, 17%; *emerging eclecticism*, 17%; *technical eclecticism*, 9%), the hybridization or combining of previously discrete approaches to counseling seems to be advancing rapidly.

Brief Therapy

As new configurations of counseling are advocated and a continuum of treatment, prevention, and mental health promotion is advanced and refined by theorists and researchers, an underlying concern in the field is the problem of scarce resources and their effective use.

Sometimes the argument about scarce resources takes the form of deploring the large counselor-student ratios in school counseling across the nation. Or, sometimes the argument centers around the imbalance or shortcomings in federal expenditures for different types of mental health services. As an illustration, Grossman (1981) estimated that 96% of federal expenditures for all forms of health care are for treatment and only 4% for efforts in prevention. Yet, other data suggest that 50% of all deaths can be attributed to an unhealthy life style in which 7 of the 10 leading causes of death are behaviorally determined and could be reduced by the appropriate application of counseling techniques for prevention and for the promotion of wellness.

Sometimes the resource argument relates to the needs in the population for mental health services and the lack of availability of mental health practitioners to serve such needs. Estimates are that 15% (Kiesler, 1980) to 35% (Dohrenwend et al., 1980) of the population is in need of mental health services in any given year. Using the conservative estimate of 15% of the population means that approximately 33 million people need some form of mental health service. Kiesler's analyses (1980) of mental health service availability suggested that if all the available licensed and certified psychiatrists and psychologists were to provide psychotherapy on a full-time basis, offering it 3 times a week to each client, they could provide such a service to only 2% of those needing it. When one adds to this estimate the growing number of clinical mental health, nationally certified, and professional counselors being licensed to practice in many states, the pool of mental health providers is larger than estimated by Kiesler. Nevertheless, using the assumptions on which his estimates are based, it may well be that the pool of mental health resources available can at best meet only 5% to 10% of the needs for such services.

An important question in relation to Kiesler's estimates is whether it is necessary to provide psychotherapy 3 times a week to meet the mental health needs of those who have a need of such services. One approach might be to demystify mental illness and mental health into the behavioral deficits or competencies on which they rest and then to identify the range of mental health responses available to treat or prevent mental health problems on the one hand and to promote mental health on the other. In addition, however, there is a stimulus to search for brief therapies that may address mental health problems with more precision and efficiency than has often been achieved in the past.

Some evidence suggests that brief therapy can be helpful to many clients (Cummings, 1977) and that targeted brief therapy (Cummings, 1986) will be increasingly required to meet the needs for mental health services. Of particular interest here are the findings of Cummings and Follette (1976) with regard to the cost-effectiveness of psychotherapy as a way to reduce the utilization of medical services. They found, for example, that one psychotherapy session only, with no repeat visits, can reduce medical utilization by 60% over the following 5 years, and that a 75% reduction in medical utilization over a 5-year period can be achieved for patients initially receiving 2 to 8 psychotherapy visits (brief therapy). In an 8-year follow-up study of patients involved in psychotherapy within a health plan, results reinforced earlier findings that reduction in medical utilization occurred as a "consequence of resolving the emotional distress that is being reflected in the symptoms and in the doctors' visits" (Cumming & Follette, p. 716).

Cummings (1977), in other studies designed to summarize the cost-effectiveness of psychotherapy in reducing the need for medical services and, particularly, the utility of brief therapy, found several interesting results. One was that rather than increasing the intensity or frequency of psychological services for the most interminable or difficult clients, the commonly accepted remedy has become to see these clients at spaced intervals of every 2 or 3 months as a way of maximizing both cost- and therapeutic effectiveness. Beyond these findings, however, Cummings (1977) reported that

> . . . when active, dynamic, brief therapy is provided early and by psychotherapists who are enthusiastic and proactive regarding such intervention, it is the treatment of choice for about 85% of the patients seeking psychotherapy . . . by providing such brief therapy, it makes economically feasible the provision of long-term psychotherapy to the approximately 10% of the patients who require it for their treatment to be therapeutically effective . . . therapeutically cost-ef-

fective programs can be developed for groups with such problems in living as alcoholism, drug abuse, drug addiction, chronic psychosis, problems of the elderly, and severe character disorders. (p. 717)

Various authors have described brief therapy in different ways and as appropriate for different settings. For example, Fuhriman, Paul, and Burlingame (1986) discussed "eclectric time-limited therapy" in a university counseling center. They indicated that the model they developed was conceived for pragmatic rather than theoretical reasons. Their initial concern was the stress that results for potential clients, staff members, and referral agencies from incessant, growing client waiting lists for services. The eclectic brief therapy model they conceived included several elements that other brief therapy models seem to hold in common: (1) time limitation on amount of therapy provided, (2) specific, restricted, and focused goals, (3) expectation-sharing between therapist and client about the time limitations and the goals to be achieved, (4) more directive therapeutic intervention, and (5) selection of appropriate clients. They overlaid these five elements on the developmental model of the helping process outlined by Egan (1985). Table 7 illustrates how the 10 sessions of the eclectic time-limited model are allocated across the stages of the Egan model. In essence, this model begins with an intake session, a concluding session, and eight sessions in between.

A particularly important part of implementing brief therapy or time-limited approaches is identifying clients who can profit from this focused and brief approach. In the counseling center described by Fuhriman et al. (1986), clients who are severely depressed and require medication, who experience anger as the main affect, who are borderline or actual psychotics, or who suffer from an organic mental disorder are excluded from this approach. Those who are excluded are referred to other treatment modalities or time-unlimited approaches. Thus, the intake session is vital to ensuring that the time-limited therapy is likely to be effective.

The treatment process is outlined in Table 7. Beyond the descriptions provided there, it is useful to note that the standard format includes one 50-minute session per week. The client problems seen as amenable to time-limited therapy include mild to severe anxiety; ambulatory disorders; concerns of identity, independence, and career choice; problems resulting from absent or disruptive relationships; and lack of success in educational pursuits. Within this array of problems, there are a variety of individual treatment possibilities, ranging across client-centered, psychodynamic, behavioral, and cognitive-behavioral meth-

TABLE 7

Brief Psychotherapy Program: Therapeutic Stages

Intake	Stage I	Stage II	Stage III	Stage IV
1st Session	*2nd Session*	*3rd Session*	*5th Session*	*8th Session*
Exploration and assessment	Role description, rapport building, and problem specification	Enhanced self-understanding and anticipated action	Active coping	Pretermination
		4th Session	*6th Session*	*9th Session*
		Action planning	Active coping	Termination
			7th Session	*10th Session*
			Active coping	Follow-up

From ''Eclectic Time-Limited Therapy,'' (Table 4) by A. Fuhriman, S.C. Paul, and G.M. Burlingame, in J.C. Norcross (Ed.), *Handbook of Eclectic Psychotherapy* (pp. 226–259), 1986, New York: Brunner/Mazel. Reprinted by permission.

odologies. It is possible within the parameters of a time-limited approach to use group approaches, including marriage therapy, rather than brief individual therapy.

Eclectic time-limited therapy as portrayed in this model allows counselors to work from their own theoretical orientations while observing the overall goals prescribed for the delivery of services (e.g., 10 sessions, a problem-solving and focused approach, etc.). From this vantagepoint, eclectic time-limited therapy is different from other approaches to brief therapy that are both more theoretical in their orientation and more prone to focus on specific psychological issues such as "separation and individuation, dynamic conflict between present and past and unconscious and conscious, decisional conflict, and dysfunctional and maladaptive behaviors" (Janis, 1982; Malan, 1976; Mann, 1973; Fuhriman, Paul, & Burlingame, 1986, p. 229).

Time-Limited Therapies and Crisis Intervention

It is also important to acknowledge that briefer therapies are the treatments of choice in crisis intervention. When people experience major traumatic episodes, natural disasters, drug overdoses, and other similar phenomena, brief therapy can serve to reduce the likelihood of more pervasive or chronic problems. Small (1971), for example, reported that brief psychotherapy has prevented or decreased the need for rehospitalization of schizophrenic patients, decreased the acting out of suicide threats, restricted and minimized the effects of a full-fledged mental disorder, and served as a procedure for saving life in severe depression. Crisis intervention using brief and focused therapy and counseling in such situations can result in a decrease in pain, a shortening of the period of disturbance, and a greater awareness of other possibilities and resources in one's life by which purpose and control can be restored.

There are many different models of crisis intervention; some are psychodynamic in origin, others are behavioral or insight-oriented. Crisis intervention continues beyond the immediate traumatic episode that precipitates or attends the actual crisis. Although estimates of time involved vary, crisis intervention as a form of brief therapy usually takes anywhere from 1 to 6 weeks as the client regains equilibrium and control of the coping skills important in dealing with the factors that triggered the crisis (e.g., marital breakup, intense emotional experience, loss of a loved one, abrupt unemployment, acute illness, drug overdose).

In crisis work, counselors are typically more active, directive, and goal-oriented than in noncrisis situations. "Since time is short, therapists become active participants in assessing the difficulty, pinpointing immediate needs, and mobilizing helping resources. In some situations, crisis counselors give advice and initiate referrals to help a person 'make it through the night' " (Slaikeu, 1984, p. 79). Although various authors recommend different process models, the salient steps, according to Slaikeu, in crisis intervention include the following: *Make psychological contact* (e.g., invite client to talk, listen for facts and feelings, summarize and reflect facts and feelings, make empathic statements, communicate concern, encourage catharsis, physically touch or hold, bring calm control to an intense situation); *explore dimensions of the problem* (e.g., inquire about needs, the precipitating event, lethality, the status of present inner and social resources, the immediate future, impending decisions); *examine possible solutions* (e.g., ask what client has done thus far, explore what client can do now, brainstorm possible actions together, help the client to redefine the problem and possible solutions); *assist in taking concrete active steps* (e.g., give advice, refer, mobilize other resources, act on the person's behalf, control the situation to ensure that the person is safe); *follow up* (establish a procedure to follow up and maintain contact with the client to assess progress and to reinforce the use and availability of resources) (p. 87).

Crisis intervention or brief therapy is sometimes called "psychological first aid". Within this context, Slaikeu has proposed three subgoals: providing support, reducing lethality, and providing linkage to helping resources. Earlier, Pasewark and Albers (1972) suggested that crisis intervention involves three main areas: (1) establishing or facilitating communication with the person in crisis and with others who are significant (e.g., family members) or who can be of immediate help (e.g., suicide prevention teams, medical personnel); (2) assisting the individual or family in perceiving the situation correctly and concretely with respect to the meaning of the events at issue and their possible outcomes; (3) assisting the individual or the family to manage feelings and emotions openly and comprehensively.

Obviously, there is much overlap betwen crisis intervention and brief or time-limited therapy. Counselors in many different settings will find such techniques important in their direct service delivery to clients, in their provision of consultation and inservice to other potential caregivers in the community (e.g., clergy, teachers, policymakers, attorneys, hospital emergency room personnel, managers or supervisors in the work place) and in their supervision of peer-counseling mechanisms (e.g., telephone hot lines, etc.).

Program Planning of Counseling and Related Services

Implicit, if not explicit, in systematic eclecticism and in psychoeducational approaches to counseling described here is the concept of planned approaches to intervening in client behaviors either on a preventive or a remedial basis. In other words, rather than waiting until a client with a demonstrated problem arrives in the counselors's office, planned approaches allow the counselor to reach out and to be proactive in relation to the likely needs of potential clients. Such approaches are particularly useful in the prevention of certain types of problems or in the promotion of health and wellness. Examples are programs in stress management or reduction, developing problem-solving skills, managing anxiety more consciously and with more control, assuming personal responsibility, gaining an internal locus of control, and increasing feelings of power or reducing feelings of powerlessness. These programs involve planned application of the skills of interpersonal communication, anger management, assertiveness, decision making, values clarification, and relaxation. They represent developmental content designed to equip clients with the attitudes, knowledge, and skills by which they can anticipate, plan, and act on a variety of personal, psychological tasks.

Planned approaches in counseling can be designed specifically to modify risk factors, as described in chapter 5, that predispose certain individuals or groups to develop psychopathology or problems of living. The content of such programs might include promoting social competence and coping in children and adults, facilitating infant development, and providing systematic parent training to reduce instances of child abuse and to create environments that foster healthy growth and development. These approaches involve a body of content that is psychological in nature, is designed to address some set of life skills, and embodies varous techniques of learning (e.g., identifying the target behavior, modeling appropriate strategies, giving homework, providing practice and feedback).

Planned approaches not only reflect important content but are useful in describing the likely results of counseling, group work, or other therapeutic approaches. Rather than arguing that if a school, or community agency, or independent practitioner offers a specific, defined set of services, the effect on clients will probably be positive, planned approaches identify the outcomes or results to be achieved. The intervention strategies can vary in relation to the intended outcomes, but a counseling program can be evaluated and held accountable for the results it achieves and the difference it makes, not whether or not certain functions are in place. Planned approaches in any setting endeavor to specify clearly the ends sought and the specific methods by which such ends will be realized.

The impetus toward planned programs in counseling has been particularly evident in schools, colleges and universities, and career counseling programs in business and industry. For example, in school counseling for at least the past decade there has been a press to make school counseling programs more specific in the results they intend to achieve and in the ways they hope to achieve them. In a major report on school counseling in the United States about 10 years ago (Herr, 1979), major emphasis was given to the then emerging trend to apply "systems thinking" to guidance and counseling programs in the school and to create planned programs. Examples of the outcomes to be expected from such systematic problems were identified as the following:

1. Statements of program goals and behavioral expectations for students that lay a base for a clearer national definition of how guidance and counseling integrate with larger educational goals;
2. Clarity about expected outcomes from guidance and counseling with their contributions distinguished from those of other aspects of education;
3. Clear rationale for the provision of guidance and counseling at elementary, middle and junior, and senior high school levels as part of an articulated program from kindergarten through grade 12;
4. The basis for identifying the counselor competencies necessary to achieving each of the outcomes assigned to programs of guidance and counseling and, as such, a knowledge base for designing both preservice and inservice preparation for school counselors;
5. A conceptual framework for considering not only guidance and counseling as processes but also as curriculum; and
6. A conceptual structure for aligning the goals of guidance and counseling with those of education and for delineating the guidance responsibilities of teachers, parents, community representatives, administrators, and school counselors (p. 117–118).

More recently, the need for such planned approaches to counseling programs in schools was reaffirmed by the Commission on Precollege Guidance and Counseling of the College Board (1986) when it recommended the following as priorities for schools:

1. Establish a broad-based process in each local school district for determining the particular guidance and counseling needs of the students within each school and for planning how best to meet these needs.
2. Develop a program under the leadership of each school principal that emphasizes the importance of the guidance counselor as a monitor and promoter of student potential, as well as coordinator of the school's guidance plan.
3. Mount programs to inform and involve parents and other members of the family influential in the choices, plans, decisions, and learning activities of the student.
4. Provide a program of guidance and counseling during the early and middle years of schooling, especially for students who traditionally have not been well served by the schools. (pp. 5–6)

Although statements about planned programs of counseling in colleges and universities are less apparent than is true of schools, such programs, particularly in career development and placement, have clearly become more planned and systematic. In university centers concerned with career development, planning, and placement, placement of students into majors or jobs is no longer seen as an event but rather as a process in which various types of information, skills, and attitudes need to be developed. Thus, many career guidance activities are sequenced throughout the college experience to bring the college student to a point of maturity and decision making that can culminate in effective placement. In such situations, universities are seen as interacting systems of academic departments, experiential opportunities, and career specialists that can by systematic planning be brought to bear on student career development through career advising, career counseling, and career planning; through courses, workshops, and seminars that offer structured group experiences in career planning, job-access skills, decision making, and related topics; through group counseling, individual counseling, placement programs, peer counseling, and computer-assisted career guidance.

Business and industry have also become increasingly conscious of planning the provision of programs of human resource development, employee assistance programs, career development, and other areas of importance to counselors. The intent in these efforts is to assist workers to become more productive, reduce job dissatisfaction, combat substance abuse, and plan their career mobility and informal or formal education. Because of the costs involved as well as the potential long-term value to workers and to employers, such employee counseling and development programs need to be comprehensively planned in their design and implementation. Gutteridge (1986) reinforced such a point using the language of industry when he stated that "human resource management is comprised of four distinct yet interrelated job systems: organizational design, human resource (manpower) planning, career development and control and evaluation" (p. 53).

Leibowitz, Farren, and Kaye (1986) argued that comprehensive, systematic career development programs have become essential to maximize employee productivity and meet the human resource needs of organizations. To that end, they developed a change and planning model to install career development systems in industry that includes 12 principles or tasks classified into four categories. They include Needs: Defining the present system; Vision: Determining new directions and possibilities; Action plan: Deciding on practical first steps; Results: Maintaining the change. These stages roughly parallel those proposed by Herr and Cramer (1988) as appropriately applied to the design of comprehensive programs of career development in schools, colleges and universities, work places, or agencies. They include:

1. Develop a program philosophy;
2. Specify program goals;
3. Select alternative program processes;
4. Describe evaluation procedures; and
5. Identify milestones (crucial events) that must occur for program implementation.

The basic set of assumptions on which rests the viability of planned programs, whether psychoeducation, prevention, career, or eclectic, include the following:

1. Individuals can be equipped with accurate and relevant information translated in terms of personal development level and state of readiness.
2. Individuals can be assisted to formulate hypotheses about themselves, the choice points that will be in their future, and the options available to them.
3. Individuals can be helped to develop appropriate ways of testing these hypotheses against old and new experiences.
4. Individuals can be helped to come to terms with the personal, educational, and occupational relevance of what they already know or will learn about themselves in the future.
5. Individuals can be helped to see themselves "in process" and to acquire the knowledge and skills that will allow them to exploit this process in positive, constructive ways.

6. Individuals acquire feelings of personal competence or power from self-understanding and the ability to choose effectively.

Still within the rubric of planning is the development of programs of Life Skills Training (Gazda & Pistole, 1986). Although it might just as easily be described under the section on psychoeducational models previously discussed in this chapter, skills training represents a systematic and planned program for sharing psychological knowledge and expertise. The focus of the program, according to Gazda and Pistole, is on "the kind of behavior-based psychological learning needed to help people cope with predictable developmental tasks" (Adkins, 1985, p. 46, quoted in Gazda & Pistole, 1986) that occur throughout the life span. In particular, the Life Skills Training Model draws from a developmental taxonomy of generic life skills based upon seven areas of human development: psychosocial, physical-sexual, cognitive, moral, vocational, ego, and affective. In turn, the Life Skills Training program is composed of developmental families of life skills including such areas as interpersonal communication/human relations; problem solving/decision making; physical fitness/health maintenance; and identity development/purpose in life.

After identifying, together with the client, the gaps in knowledge or the skills deficits to be addressed in either individual or group counseling, a 5-step training model is implemented. The steps include in a flexible sequence: (1) didactic instruction; (2) leader modeling of skills or the use of videotaped models of skills being demonstrated; (3) demonstration using simulations to allow the clients to practice the skills in a controlled environment using role play or paper-and-pencil responses; (4) the use of skills in personally relevant interactions with others in real situations; and, (5) transfer of training to enable spontaneous use of the life skills in dealing with problems on a day-to-day basis.

As suggested in each of the examples cited in this section, counseling and related processes, particularly those related expressly to psychoeducational and deliberate skill development, whatever the setting, are not random events, but planned and systematic events. Much more of such program development is likely to be seen in the future.

Computers and Counseling Technology

As the previous sections of this chapter have suggested, counselors are inexorably becoming applied behavioral scientists and program planners. They are also becoming technologists. For the past two decades or more, a variety of technologies have been developed to extend or reinforce the counselor's potential to effect behavioral change in clients. Depending upon the specific point in time at issue, new counseling technologies have included the application of gaming, audio-video processes, simulations, films, assessment centers, problem-solving kits, self-directed inventories and programmed resource material, and, perhaps most comprehensively, computer-person interactive systems designed to facilitate client behavior rehearsal and exploration, information retrieval, assessment, planning, the simulation of the likely outcomes of action, and treatment.

Implicit in the above observations is the notion that advanced technology as described in chapter 2 does not have implications only for effecting the lives of clients. It also continues to promise new tools, new conceptual models, and new ethical dilemmas for counselors. Of particular concern in this regard is the effect of computers in counseling.

Computers in Counseling

Whether mainframe, mini, or micro, computers have been to many counseling, guidance, and mental programs what electricity has been to the light bulb, a source of energy that gives form and substance to many types of intervention impossible without such energy. Many metaphors have implicitly or explicitly been applied to explain the effects, potential and actual, of computers and related technology on individual personal and career development, mental health, decision making, or information retrieval and analysis. In some instances, the computer has been cast as a mind multiplier, as a way of compounding an individual's vision about possible futures in which she or he can engage, or as the pathway to such futures and the risks or investments associated with different behaviors. In other instances, the computer has been conceptualized as a prosthesis, a replacement for a specific individual's disabilities or limitations that enhances mobility, communication, or problem solving, thereby expanding an individual's development. Beyond these roles, computers have been conceived of as forecasters of possibilities, organizers of time, schedulers, and information retrieval devices. They have been used for assessment and diagnoses, for psychophysiological measurement and biofeedback, for behavior observation and assessment, for statistical and visual analyses of data, for motivation of children, for administrative support of counseling programs—billing, financial management, budget preparation, maintaining data bases, word processing—for telecommunications

(Romanczyk, 1986), for consultation on emotional crises (Hedlund, Vieweg, & Cho, 1987), and for intervention with psychiatric patients (Matthews, DeSanti, Callahan, Koblenz-Sulcor, & Werden, 1987).

Within such possibilities, computers have been found useful in extending the capability of counselors in managing client or student development information; monitoring medication usage by psychiatric patients; record keeping; assessment or test scoring; helping people develop a predictive system about opportunities available to them, creating a personal profile of their strengths, and developing job seeking skills; and guiding individual decision making. In social terms, the information and the images that computers can provide have the potential to neutralize the differences or deficits in experiences that characterize the life opportunities of different people as these are related to socioeconomic background, race, sex, or disabling condition; to alter decision-making patterns; and even to alter human identity (Mruk, 1987).

Perhaps more importantly, computer-based technology potentially empowers individuals to have an internal rather than an external locus of control. It says, however indirectly, "You can choose, you have options, you can make connections between the present and the future." In this sense, computers not only provide information as the fuel for decision making but they say, in figurative terms, to the chooser, "You can control how you will participate in education, training, work, or life." Thus, computers not only help to educate people for choice but they also represent a tool by which one is enabled to choose uniquely, as an independent person who is encouraged to impose a planning structure upon possible behavioral scenarios rather than let behavior fluctuate randomly at the whim of external forces.

As such, computers have inexorably redefined the content, the time spectrum, and the characteristics of the intervention strategies appropriate to influencing the personal and career development of different groups of people. Although many of the uses of computers in personal and career development are still promises, not actualities, they have required that counselors increasingly become technologists. As technologists counselors have been stimulated to think as applied behavioral scientists and as program planners, as professionals who can use computers as part of an integrated set of elements that extend the capabilities of counselors, not replace them; as specialists who recognize that the personal and career development of individuals and groups is multidimensional and requires differential treatments. Although many of the questions to be confronted in the incorporation of advanced technology in the work place or in counseling are theoretical and abstract in nature, the computer, and its effect on the profession of counseling, is no longer an abstraction. It is a tool, a form of technology, that fits not in an absolute sense but in a relative way into some conception of program, some formulation of goals, some pattern of methodology. It is a powerful tool capable of overwhelming and overshadowing the very elements it is designed to promote; to an unprecedented extent, the medium is a very important component of the message that has implications for ethical issues, professional standards, counselor preparation, and professional development (Herr & Best, 1984). Viewed in somewhat different terms, the use of computers and other forms of technology has made it important for individual counselors and the profession to come to terms with at least the following: recognizing the meaning of technology in personal or career development; identifying the counselor's role in technology; encouraging appropriate preparation of counselors in the use of technology in personal and career development; and, paying attention to the ethical issues and problems generated by technology (Herr, 1985).

The Meaning of Technology in Personal and Career Development

As discussed in chapter 2, technology is applied science. The technologies affecting personal and career development flow from theoretical conceptions of behavior, empirical validation of such conceptions, assumptions about interventions in such behavior, and finally empirical verification of the effects of such interventions. Technology is not hardware, or, indeed, software. "The objective of technological discoveries as well as of their applications, is information. . . . High technology is not a particular technique, but a form of production and organization that can affect all spheres of activity by transforming their operations in order to achieve greater productivity or better performance, through increased knowledge of the process itself" (Castells, 1985, p. 11).

Applied to personal, educational, and career development, computers and technology are valuable to the degree that the outcomes they facilitate are appropriate to the program planning or counseling outcomes to be achieved. An isolated computer sitting in a room removed from the mainstream of a counseling program is unlikely to affect significantly the development of students or clients unless the information it is capable of providing is relevant to the types of behavior change a counseling program intends to promote and is systematically integrated into a program of behavioral change. The presence of the computer must affect the organization and the process of career counseling, guidance, or psychotherapy if the applied scientific potential it represents is to influence systematically the resulting personal or career development of clients.

Therefore, counselors must be proficient in those approaches— e.g., differential treatment, multimodal approaches, systematic eclecticism—that reflect the need for and the structure of multiple intervention. Counselors must learn to view the use of computer-assisted approaches to individual development as part of a plan, as one of the treatments of preference, not the only, or even the preferred, approach for all counseling programs. In so doing, they must demysticize technology, understand its uses and abuses, and reduce the propensity to imbue technology of any kind with a spirit and life that it does not have.

Computer Applications

As suggested above, many computer applications are possible in counseling and in psychotherapy. Only three will be briefly discussed here in terms of their utility.

Computerized career guidance systems. Perhaps the most well known computer application, computer-assisted programs of career guidance have been in development and use for nearly 20 years. Over 30 major projects to apply computers to career guidance have occurred in the past 10 years, although the major systems in operation are confined to not more than 6 to 10. Those systems that do survive have become increasingly comprehensive in their coverage and in their incorporation of content that emanates from the work of major theorists. For example, the DISCOVER II Program offered by the American College Testing (ACT) program (Rayman & Harris-Bowlsbey, 1977) incorporates Super's developmental stages, Tiedeman and O'Hara's decision-making model, the data-people-things paradigm of the Dictionary of Occupational Titles, and the Holland personality-work environment typology. In the modular approach to the various elements of self-analysis inquiry into occupational and educational opportunities and decision-making processes, people can assess interests, aptitudes, and values; compare input to job requirements, occupations, and programs of study available; determine their location on a world of work map; and engage in various decision-making exercises and in other forms of inquiry. The SIGI system (The System of Interactive Guidance and Information) developed by the Educational Testing Service (Katz, 1980) focuses on the interaction of values and decisions. In this system people engage in a dialogue with the computer as they examine their values and identify and explore options, receive and interpret data, and practice decision making.

Several other major systems (e.g., GIS, CHOICES, CECIL) have similar purposes. Within the broad arena of computerized guidance systems there are at least eight in America that are primarily concerned with job matching (Botterbusch, 1983). The basic purpose of each of these systems is to match a client's vocational characteristics (or profile) with the requirements for specific jobs. One of the fundamental purposes of employment counseling and, more specifically, vocational evaluation, has been to help a person find a job that requires or relates to what he or she can do. The availability of computer technology has not changed the goal. It has, however, made the goal more attainable, included a larger pool of information to be considered in decision making, and synthesized the interaction of different forms of data with one another so that the likely consequences of choices can be more fully considered. Each of the computer systems discussed above has multiple purposes related to job matching. Although the systems do not cover each of the five purposes usually considered under the rubric of job-person match, they tend to accommodate several of these purposes: conducting job searches for placement, identifying skills from previous jobs that relate to present job conditions and requirements, and providing occupational information, support for decision making, and identification of education/training needed or available as related to various jobs.

A variety of studies have assessed the effectiveness or utility of computer-assisted career guidance systems compared to more traditional career counseling interventions or to other computer-assisted systems. Among the findings are that computers cannot replace professional counselors, but, when combined with counselor-delivered career counseling, the combined treatments produce stronger effects than either component alone (e.g., Garis, 1982; Glaize & Myrick, 1984).

Computerized personal counseling. The use of computers in personal counseling has been described as one of the most controversial issues in mental health (Sampson, 1983), partly because of the ethical issues involved and partly because of stereotypes about the amount of interpersonal respect, understanding, and love required in a counseling relationship (Weizenbaum, 1976). Nevertheless, a variety of approaches to the use of computers in personal counseling and psychotherapy are apparent and such applications are growing.

According to Wagman (1984), there are two general ways to develop a computer-assisted personal counseling system. One is to design the computer software to model the behavior of the counselor in responding to a client, and the other is to model the computer's intervention after a particular technique of counseling. Several systems have been developed to incorporate one or both models. One of the aspects of computer-assisted counseling programs is the provision of absolute privacy to an individual, who can seek information and assistance without revealing the problem or question to another human being. As these counseling systems become more sophisticated, ethical issues become more complex. For example, ELIZA, developed by Joseph Weizenbaum of MIT in 1966, mimics the patterned responses of a counseling session. Although the program operates on a superficial level, people are intrigued by its seemingly "human" responses and feel they have "discussed" their personal problems with the machine. Weizenbaum (1976), however, characterized as immoral attempts to use computer technology as a substitute for providing human empathy, respect, understanding, and love.

A related example of the computer as counselor is the PLATO Dilemma Counseling System (DCS), which teaches a generic method for solving life choice problems and counsels people regarding their current psychological dilemmas. The 5-step process includes: (a) formulating the original case problem as a psychological dilemma; (b) formulating the extrication route for each dilemma component; (c) formulating the creative inquiry for each extrication route; (d) generating solutions for each creative inquiry; and (e) ranking and evaluating solutions.

The components of this system contain 69 representative life choice problems and over 400 specific and general solutions that assist users in solving their psychological dilemmas (Wagman & Kerber, 1980). An important question in ELIZA, PLATO, and similar systems is on what basis, or according to what criteria, does the computer "flag" the counselor or transfer responsibility for the client back to the counselor? As recently developed systems become more interactive, the question of integrating what the machine does best with what the counselor does best in counseling requires serious consideration.

Sampson (1986) drew important distinctions between computer instruction in support of psychotherapy and computer-assisted psychotherapy. Computer-assisted instruction (CAI) in support of psychotherapy involves the use of computer technology to facilitate the human interaction between the psychotherapist and the client. Computer-assisted psychotherapy involves the direct and exclusive provision of psychotherapeutic services to the client by the computer. The latter, for technical reasons (e.g., the state of the use of natural language and artificial intelligence), is less advanced than the former. As Sampson suggested, computer-assisted support to all clients is not equally feasible. For example, such an approach is likely to be inappropriate

> . . . for individuals when emotional, cognitive and/or neurological factors severely limit the capacity to perceive, process, and respond to CAI. For example, individuals who are experiencing motivational difficulties related to a major depression, who have a poor reading ability related to intellectual capacity, or who have an impairment in short-term memory as a result of a closed head injury, are not likely to profit from CAI as an adjunct to psychotherapy. These individuals tend to need the high degree of structure available from conventional psychotherapy. (pp. 4–5)

Sampson goes on the discuss the conditions under which some clients may be able to use stand-alone, "self-help" CAI software to facilitate behavior change or when CAI is most useful in conjunction with counselor intervention in the provision of psychotherapy. In the latter sense, Sampson also discusses the ways in which CAI can be used as an adjunct to psychotherapy. Examples might include its use as an orientation to psychotherapy, as an assessment tool for standardized tests and immediate computer scoring, as a "second opinion" in diagnosing or classifying the etiology of the client's problem, as an aid to intervention by providing the client examples of cognitive distortions and ways to exercise alternative cognitions (about which the computer would provide feedback), or as a method to simulate or model desirable skills that the client might imitate and practice. Undoubtedly many other such applications will emerge in the future.

One precursor of the future is the use of a computer for consultation for emotional crises. Hedlund, Vieweg, and Cho (1987) described the use of a proposed computer-assisted evaluation and treatment program for senior enlisted medical corpsmen on nuclear submarines where physicians or psychiatrists are not available. The psychiatric component is intended to provide evaluation and treatment of emotional/behavioral emergencies for nonexperts or paraprofessionals (the medical corpsmen). The system functions as follows.

When a crew member is referred for some type of emotional or behavioral problem, the corpsman uses a highly structured paper-and-pencil interview guide, the Groton Interview Schedule (GIS), to obtain specific information about the problem involved. Whatever information is obtained, including the corpsman's physical examination results, any available collateral information, and any other observations, is entered into a microcomputer. The corpsman is then able to obtain a computer-generated "Patient Summary" that provides a probable diagnosis, along with a listing of all related symptoms. From this Patient Summary, specific changes or corrections may be made to the data already entered, and the corpsman may obtain treatment suggestions. After initial emergency treatment, the corpsman may modify the patient's database directly through the Patient Summary or by completing GIS data collection, which may have been impossible initially, for additional (or more complete) diagnostic and treatment suggestions. Four references/glossaries (Emergency Treatment Principles, a Diagnosis and Treatment Glossary, a Medications Glossary, and a Glossary of Psychiatric Terms) are available to the corpsman interactively and in hard copy at any time during the assessment-treatment procedures. The diagnostic concepts follow those of the *Diagnostic and Statistical Manual of Mental Disorders, Third Edition* (DSM-III) (American Psychiatric Association, 1980). Treatment suggestions for each psychiatric diagnostic category were adduced from standard texts and expert opinion. A single psychotropic medication for each major problem area (e.g., anxiety, depression, psychotic symptoms) would be stocked on the submarines for use by corpsmen as suggested by the diagnostic and evaluation computer system.

Computerized psychological testing. Already alluded to previously is the use of computers for test administration and scoring. Such processes may occur in immediate conjunction to the process of counseling or psychotherapy or simply as an administrative procedure in support of but distant from the actual counseling with a client. Nevertheless, computer-based test interpretations are becoming increasingly important in counseling and in psychology. Such applications include computerized adaptive testing that tailors the difficulty of a test to the test taker's ability level. This approach depends upon having a large bank of test items to measure a particular psychological trait that would be precalibrated to assess people with different levels of ability or other characteristics (Weiss & Vale, 1987). There are also computer-based test interpretations that rest on systems of knowledge that can be applied to patterns of test scores, thereby providing narratives, profiles, classifications, diagnoses, and suggestions for treatment; project hypotheses about the client to be pursued in counseling; and second opinions that can aid the client and the counselor in psychological decision making. These are so-called expert systems. Obviously, computer-based test interpretation systems can score tests rapidly, accurately, and in large volume and, where required, engage in data reduction important for research purposes and for the creation of new tests or test forms.

In broad terms computer-based test interpretation refers to the automation of a set of prespecified rules for use in analyzing, interpreting, and assigning certain qualities to a response or response pattern (e.g., test score, profile pattern) (Harris, 1987). Implicit in this observation, however, are concerns that the quality of the data used in developing software becomes paramount to successful computer applications, as do the training and expertise of test users. These, in turn, affect the accuracy of interpretative output, speed of interpretation, and validity of explanations or classifications (Eyde, 1987).

Identifying Counselor Role in Technology

A major current and future challenge for the profession is to apply the possible uses of technology in personal or career development to alter existing counselor roles or to highlight the need for new counselor roles. Achieving such changes in counselor roles will frequently begin by using strategies designed to eliminate dichotomous thinking among some counselors: to wit, you either have a computer or you have a counselor. The inherent notion that computers will replace counselors is not borne out in existing research studies (Garis, 1982; Herr & Cramer, 1988). Instead, investigations suggest that the availability of computers alters certain counselor roles (e.g., retrieval of relevant information, maintaining current information) and intensifies other roles (e.g., personal counseling). It does not eliminate such roles.

Beyond helping eliminate dichotomous or simplistic either/or thinking about computers and other technology in personal and career development, counselors need to understand why technology has begun to pervade counseling programs and the conditions that underlie such adaptations. Technological adaptation does not occur simply because technological innovation exists. Technological breakthroughs only prepare for the possibility of the adaptation of new technology. The actual adaptation of technology occurs when there is a change in the economic or psychological structure that requires it. As related to the application of technology in counseling, such observations indicate that the assimilation of technology into career guidance or counseling programs does not occur simply because computer-assisted guidance systems exist. It occurs because someone makes a decision that the technology available will change current conditions more effectively than will other possible solutions.

A number of empirical advantages to the use of a computer within a counseling program, however, could undergird the decision to include new technology. These advantages include positive client response, cost-effectiveness, increased staff efficiency, reduction in time required for administration and scoring, and facilitation of test administration to individuals with visual, auditory, and physical disabilities (Sampson, 1984). In addition, as Wagman (1984) stated, "computers always deliver the same, efficient service, are never late, sick, limited to an eight-hour day, upset by family or work problems or subject to the problems of countertransference" (p. 172). Thus, if the economic conditions in a particular program do not, for example, favor lowering the counselor-student ratio from 400 to 1 to 250 to 1, or the cost of maintaining a career resource center of hard-bound print material seems to be excessive compared to its positive effect of career development, adopting a computer-assisted career guidance system may be the economic solution of choice. When such a choice is made, however, it in turn must alter how counselors will interact with clients and the technology. Ultimately, questions do exist about the elements composing a computer program, the presenting problems of typical client populations, how computers can be used in such areas, and what the answers to these questions mean for counselor knowledge and performance. Perhaps equally important to the questions of skill and knowledge in relation to computer technology are questions of balance in the counselor's identity as a professional, as an applied behavioral scientist, as an ethical being, and as a technologist. How these roles interact, the skills and knowledge they require, and the ways they affect one's self-concept as a professional "helper" are issues of considerable importance, perhaps central importance, to the future counseling metaphors that will describe counselors and their roles.

Encouraging Professional Development of Counselors in Technology

It seems clear that in the future counselor educators will need to make counselor training models reflect the concept that the effect of computers and, indeed, other technologies on the role of counselors can be addressed in at least three ways: computer as content or subject matter, computer as process, and computer as method (Herr & Best, 1984).

Computer as content or subject matter. Within such an emphasis, counselors need to be educated to understand the effects of computers and other forms of advanced technology on the changing occupational structure, the organization and distribution of work, and the demographics of the labor force. They also need to understand the effects of the resulting changes on the choice possibilities for youth and adults and on the mental health and stress-related adjustments of workers to technology. Such content needs to include the changing psychology of work, nonwork, and leisure; the traumas associated with unemployment and underemployment; the implications for education and training of the emerging technological occupations; and the social implications of the computerization of America and its effects upon family structures and values, opportunities for the disabled, and the quality of life. The thrust of an emphasis on the computer as content or subject matter in counselor preparation assumes that preparing counselors to facilitate the decision making of different populations occurs with an understanding of the effect of computers on job access, skills, and opportunities and on the social and psychological contexts likely to ensue (e.g., Mruk, 1987; Jackson, 1987).

An examination of the social implications of the computerization of America should include the following issues: (a) the widening gulf between the haves and the have-nots as a result of the economic restrictions on computer accessibility; (b) the anxiety associated with the sweeping changes in the work place and the uncertainties about the future; (c) the vastly different computerized environment of the young and its effect on the relationship between generations; (d) the ability of the handicapped to gain greater participation in society through the use of computerized prosthetic devices, and (e) the possible advent of the "electronic cottage" (Toffler, 1980) and its effects on family and community. These are but a few examples. If counselors perceive learning as the essence of the counseling process and themselves as agents of change, then considering issues such as these needs to be an integral part of the content of counselor education or counseling psychology training programs.

Computer as process. One of the terms used frequently in education is "the need for computer literacy." As applied to counselor training, does such a term mean to know how to turn on and use the computer, to program it, to create software for it, to think conceptually with it, to understand its potential? Each of these is a possible meaning of computer literacy, but it is not clear that counselors need all of these. Which counselors need which forms of computer literacy and for what purpose? Answers to these questions are still to be found, although some perspectives are emerging. For example, Gaushell (1984) defined computer literacy for counselors as the ability to: (1) have a working knowledge of computer terminology, (2) be able to read and write simple programs, (3) understand the type of problems that are and are not open to computer solution, (4) know some of the history of computing, and, (5) understand some of the moral and human issues of using computers. Johnson and Sampson (1985) advocated that counselors have competencies in knowing how to manage and implement computer-assisted guidance, how to counsel effectively with a computer, how to select software and hardware, and how to integrate results in a group counseling setting. Undoubtedly, other perspectives about computer literacy for counselors need to be considered and training programs designed to be responsive to such conceptualizations.

Computer as method. In one sense, this is the most instrumental of the three emphases by which the counselor needs to be introduced to the computer as an agent of change in counseling programs. Here the question is how can the counselor use the computer as a tool, as an extension of the counselor's repertoire of techniques applied to assessment, instruction, data management, career or personal development, exploration, and research? What are the available models by which the computer can be used as an adjunct to other techniques, or as the primary tool to facilitate certain types of client information gathering and evaluation? How can the counselor in training or in practice be helped to merge knowledge of ''computer as process'' and ''computer as method'' into a system of functional intervention that can realistically target the contextual learnings inherent in computer as content or subject?

Computer as method involves learning to regard this form of technology as an extension of the counselor's repertoire of tools or techniques for use in assessment, instruction, data management, counseling, and research. The counselor's theoretical orientation, work setting, population to be served, and expected client or program outcomes contribute to the selection of appropriate methods. Sampson (1983), for example, described an integrated approach using the computer in scheduling, intake, and developing client information systems; in initial assessment aided by computer-assisted testing and interviewing; in interventions that might include computer-assisted career guidance, instruction, and counseling; and in a computer-assisted termination interview. Within such a comprehensive context, counselor education programs clearly need to provide prospective practitioners with experience in the use of computers as an adjunct to a variety of counseling functions. In this sense, the computer must be seen as a tool, as an instrument, as another way of accomplishing counseling goals, not as a replacement for the other tools counselors might use: tests, games, work samples, films, and books. To achieve such a goal requires the merger of ''computer as process'' and ''computer as method.''

Ultimately there is a need to consider the elements composing a counseling program, the presenting problems of typical client populations, and how computers can be used in each of these areas. Sampson and Pyle (1983) suggested that relevant topics include: "(a) the rationale for using computer applications; (b) common operational procedures; (c) common counselor intervention strategies; (d) strategies for implementing computer applications into existing services (including staff training); and (e) related ethical issues" (p. 286).

The facts listed above together with the competencies required of counselors in areas affected by computers and in areas not so affected form a matrix necessary for the professional development of counselors and their accountability.

Promoting Ethical Standards

The forms of technology, including computer-assisted career guidance or counseling systems that currently are available to influence client development, are not benign. They carry with them the potential to harm or to help individuals. As such, they become the focus of ethical dilemmas and the impetus for revised ethical standards.

Although both the American Association for Counseling and Development and the American Psychological Association provide documents entitled *Ethical Standards* and *Ethical Principles of Psychologists* respectively, both continue to integrate into these guidelines responses to the peculiar issues associated with computerized systems in counseling.

Ethical standards promulgated by professional associations are statements of principle; they are essentially moral codes of professional standards of practice. Many of their existing elements, although not specific, do pertain to technological applications to personal and career development. For example, the counselor's responsibility to maintain the confidentiality of client information is an overarching ethical principle regardless of the theoretical approach or the particular technology used in counselor-client interaction:

> . . . it is primarily in this domain that questions concerning the ethical use of computer technology arise. Computerized information systems complicate the issues involved and point to the need for clarification of how confidential material will be managed in view of the potential abuses and distortions peculiar to this technology. As computerized systems become more efficient, the tendency to store and retain increasing amounts of data, relevant or not, useful or not, remains

unchecked because the technology reduces the external constraints imposed by time, expense, and space required for
paper record keeping. (Herr & Best, 1984, p. 192)

Violations of ethical principles in the maintenance of confidential
client information can be exacerbated by information being retained
after its original purpose is exhausted, by permitting the use of information that may be biased or unfair because it is used for a different
purpose than that for which it was originally collected, or by imparting
an inappropriate scientific legitimacy to assessment information generated by computers. Undoubtedly there are many other ethical dilemmas associated with computer technology as a counseling form. Such
possibilities need to be examined systematically and their consequences
reflected in ethical guidelines that are sufficiently comprehensive to
embrace the application of computer technology to all aspects of the
counselor's role: diagnosis, testing, records maintenance, career exploration, and decision making. Obviously, such ethical dilemmas and
the guidelines that bound professional practice relevant to such dilemmas must be fully communicated to counselors in the field and those
in training. It is the responsibility of the profession to confront these
issues and to continually define an ethical code that provides a framework for the appropriate and effective incorporation of computer technology in counseling.

Conclusions

As much of the content of this book affirms, the roles of the
counselor and of counseling are changing in contemporary society and
are likely to change in the foreseeable future. Counseling has become
an important method of dealing with mental or emotional disorder,
decision making, stress management, the prevention of problems in
living, as well as the promotion or enhancement of wellness and the
quality of life. Counseling, then, is increasingly important across the
population spectrum of children, youth, and adults as well as in diverse
settings: educational institutions, work places, community agencies,
and independent practice.

If counseling is important to such a wide range of people and
settings, it must also serve diverse purposes. As such, counseling
cannot be seen as a singular process but rather as a set of techniques
and approaches that is dynamic in its substance and in its capability
to be tailored to the specific needs of populations and settings. Chapter
6 has identified some of the changes in counseling that are becoming

standard elements of a counselor's professional repertoire and that enlarge the counselor's ability to differentiate treatments to match client needs. Inherent in such a notion is the likely reality that many clients will need multiple treatments, some of which counselors can provide and some that may come from other referral sources. For example, some clients will need cognitive behavioral therapy provided in a one-on-one format, computer-assisted career guidance, training in nutrition or budget management, a redesigned job environment, and assistance with subsidized housing or transportation. The counselor alone will not be able to deliver each of these responses, but will probably provide some of these in a differential treatment design or serve as a broker of referral sources to address some of the multidimensional needs of the client.

Although the range of possible counseling interventions in client behavior is likely to be larger than any given counselor can use effectively, several trends are changing how counseling is being conceptualized and delivered. These trends deserve to be considered fully by every counselor. Paradigm shifts arise from a fuller understanding of human behavior and from refinements in the application of technology to counseling.

Among the trends in counseling described in chapter 6 most likely to be pervasive in their effect on counseling are those that derive from applying advances in the cognitive sciences—insights into how people process information, connect thinking to feeling and doing, and link cognition to motivation—to methods of intervening in client behavior. The seminal work discussed in this chapter of such authors as Ellis in rational emotive therapy, Beck in cognitive therapy, Krumboltz in social learning and in describing the private rules of decision making, Burns in cognitive distortions, Wolpe in systematic desensitization, Meichenbaum in stress inoculation training, Novaco in anger management, and Suinn in anxiety management represents the ingredients of modified views and approaches to psychotherapy and counseling. These emphases on the cognitive structures that trigger or sustain behavior provide the substance for counseling approaches that, as compared to many earlier approaches, include more active participation between counselor and client in designing appropriate treatments, greater focus on client cognitions and how they might be changed, and the transfer of skills learned in counseling to daily living through homework and other exercises.

Beyond the rapid and pervasive effects of cognitive behavioral approaches to individual and group counseling, but not necessarily independent of such perspectives, is the rise in the use of psychoeducational models for purposes of treatment, prevention, and promotion. These approaches combine educative and psychological methods to help people develop skills relevant to more effective coping or to management of different forms of behavior.

Other rapidly emerging trends in counseling include the linkages between career counseling and behavioral health, as well as between mental health counseling and behavioral medicine. These connections, the format and content of such trends as psychoeducational models, and the increasing demands for mental health services in excess of available capacity, among many other factors, have combined to stimulate growing attention to the systematic planning of counseling programs; to brief or time-limited therapy; to new views of eclecticism, multimodal therapy, or differential treatment; and to the use of computers in counseling and psychotherapy. As such changes emerge, they subtly and profoundly alter the professional identity of counselors, expand the range of situations in which counselors must be sensitive to ethical dilemmas, and create new content to be assimilated into counselor training.

The challenges to counselors, theorists, and researchers to find new and increasingly efficient ways to provide counseling have not ended. Chapter 7 identifies additional recurring, emerging, and future challenges that promise to continue to affirm the needs and importance of counseling and to shape the ways by which such processes are defined, organized, and provided.

References

Albee, G.W. (1980). A competency model must replace the defect model. In L.A. Bond & J.C. Rosen (Eds.), *Primary prevention of psychotherapy, Vol 4: Competency and coping during adulthood* (pp. 75–104). Hanover, NH: University Press of New England.

Albee, G.W. (1982). Preventing psychopathology and promoting human potential. *American Psychologist, 37*, 1043–1050.

American Psychiatric Association. (1980). *Diagnostic and statistical manual of mental disorders, third edition*. Washington, DC: Author.

Antonovsky, A. (1979). *Health, stress, and coping*. San Francisco: Jossey-Bass.

Bandura, A., Adams, N.E., & Meyer, J. (1977). Cognitive processes mediating behavior change. *Journal of Personality and Social Psychology, 35*, 125–139.

Beck, A. (1985). Cognitive therapy, behavior therapy, psychoanalysis, and pharmacotherapy: A cognitive continuum. In M.J. Mahoney & A. Freeman (Eds.), *Cognition and psychotherapy* (Chapter 14). New York: Plenum Press.

Beck, A., & Greenberg, R. (1984). Cognitive therapy in the treatment of depression. In N. Hoffman (Ed.), *Foundations of cognitive therapy: Theoretical methods and practical applications* (pp. 155–176). New York: Plenum Press.

Beck, A., & Rush, A.J. (1988). Cognitive therapy. Foreword to Section V, Volume 7. In A.J. Frances & R.E. Hales (Eds.), *Review of psychiatry* (pp. 533–537). Washington, DC: American Psychiatric Press.

Bellah, R.N., Madsen, R., Sullivan, W.M., Swidler, A., & Tipton, S.M. (1985). *Habits of the heart: Individualism and commitment in American life.* New York: Harper & Row.

Berg, I., & Hughes, M. (1979). Economic circumstances and the entangling web of pathologies: An esquisse. In L.A. Ferman & J. Gordus (Eds.), *Mental health and the economy* (Chapter 2). Kalamazoo, MI: W.E. Upjohn Institute for Employment Research.

Borgen, W., & Amundsen, N. (1984). *The experience of unemployment; Implications for counseling the unemployed.* Scarborough, Ontario: Nelson Canada.

Botterbusch, K.F. (1983). *A comparison of computerized job matching systems.* Menomonie, WI: Materials Development Center, Stout Rehabilitation Institute, University of Wisconsin-Stout.

Brenner, M.H. (1973). *Mental health and the economy.* Cambridge: Harvard University Press.

Brenner, M.H. (1979). Health and the national economy: Commentary and general principles. In L.A. Ferman & J.P. Gordus (Eds.), *Mental health and the economy* (Chapter 3). Kalamazoo, MI: W.E. Upjohn Institute for Employment Research.

Brown, D. (1985). Career counseling: Before, after, or instead of personal counseling? *Vocational Guidance Quarterly, 33*(3), 197–201.

Burns, D.D. (1980). *Feeling good: The new mood therapy.* New York: Signet.

Castells, M. (1985). High technology, economic restructuring and the urban-region process in the United States. In M. Castells (Ed.), *High technology, space, and society* (Chapter 1). Beverly Hills, CA: Sage.

Commission on Pre-College Guidance and Counseling. The College Board. (1986). *Keeping the options open; Final report.* New York: Author.

Crites, J.O. (1981). *Career counseling: Models, methods, and materials.* New York: McGraw-Hill.

Cummings, N.A. (1977). The anatomy of psychotherapy under national health insurance. *American Psychologist, 32*(9), 711–718.

Cummings, N.A. (1986). The dismantling of our health system: Strategies for the survival of psychological practice. *American Psychologist, 41*(4), 426–431.

Cummings, N.A., & Follette, W.T. (1976). Brief psychotherapy and medical utilization: An eight-year follow-up. In H. Dorken and Associates (Eds.), *The professional psychologist today: New developments in law, health, insurance and health practice.* San Francisco: Jossey-Bass.

Danish, S.J., Galambos, N.L., & Laquatra, I. (1983). Life development intervention: Skill training for personal competence. In R.D. Felman, L.A. Jason, J. Mortisuqur, & S.S. Farber (Eds.), *Preventive psychology: Theory, research, and practice* (pp. 49–66). Elmsford, NY: Pergamon Press.

Dawis, R.V. (1984). Job satisfaction: Workers' aspirations, attitudes, and behaviors. In N.C. Gysbers (Ed.), *Designing career counseling to enhance education, work and leisure* (Chapter 10). San Francisco: Jossey-Bass.

Deffenbacher, J.L. (1988). Introduction: The practice of four cognitive-behavioral approaches to anxiety reduction. *The Counseling Psychologist, 16*(1), 3–8.

Dohrenwend, B.P., Dohrenwend, B.S., Gould, M.S., Link, B., Neugebar, R., & Wunsch-Hitzig, R. (1980). *Mental illness in the United States: Epidemiological estimates.* New York: Praeger.

Egan, G. (1985). *The skilled helper.* Monterey, CA: Brooks/Cole.

Ellis, A. (1958). Rational psychotherapy. *Journal of General Psychotherapy, 59*, 35–39.

Ellis, A. (1962). *Reason and emotion in psychotherapy.* Secaucus, NJ: Lyle Stuart and Citadel Press.

Ellis, A. (1985). Expanding the ABCs of Rational-Emotive Therapy. In M.J. Mahoney & A. Freeman (Eds.), Cognition and psychotherapy (Chapter 13). New York: Plenum Press.

Eyde, L.D. (1987). Computerized psychological testing: An introduction. *Applied Psychology: An International Review, 36*(3/4), 223–235.

Fuhriman, A., Paul, S.C., & Burlingame, G.M. (1986). Eclectic time-limited therapy. In J.C. Norcross (Ed.), *Handbook of eclectic psychotherapy* (pp. 226–259). New York: Brunner/Mazel.

Garis, J.W. (1982). *The integration of a computer-based system in a college counseling center: A comparison of the effects of DISCOVER and individual counseling upon career planning.* Unpublished doctoral dissertation. The Pennsylvania State University, University Park, PA.

Gaushell, W.H. (1984). Microcomputers, the school, and the counselor. *The School Counselor, 31*(3), 229–233.

Gazda, G.M., & Pistole, M.C. (1986). Life skills training: A model. *Counseling and Human Development, 19*(4), 1–7.

Gladwin, T. (1967). Social competence and clinical practice. *Journal for the Study of Interpersonal Processes, 30*, 30–38.

Glaize, D.L., & Myrick, R. (1984). Interpersonal groups or computers? A study of career maturity and career decidedness. *Vocational Guidance Quarterly, 32*, 168–176.

Glasser, W. (1970). *Mental health or mental illness, psychiatry for practical action.* New York: Harper & Row.

Goldfried, M.R., Decenteco, E.T., & Weinberg, L. (1974). Systematic rational restructuring as a self-control technique. *Behavior Therapy, 5*, 247–254.

Goldstein, A.P., & Krasner, L. (1987). *Modern applied psychology.* New York: Pergamon Press.

Goldstein, A.P., Sprafkin, R.P., Gershaw, N.J., & Klein, P. (1980). *Skill-streaming the adolescent: A structured learning approach to teaching prosocial skills.* Champaign, IL: Research Press.

Grossman, J. (1981). Inside the wellness movement. *Health, 13*, 10–15.

Guidano, V.F., & Liotti, G. (1985). A constructivistic foundation for cognitive therapy. In M.J. Mahoney & A. Freeman (Eds.), *Cognition and psychotherapy* (Chapter 4). New York: Plenum Press.

Gutteridge, T.G. (1986). Organizational career development systems: The state of the practice. In D.T. Hall & Associates (Eds.), *Career development in organizations* (Chapter 2). San Francisco: Jossey-Bass.

Harris, W.G. (1987). Computer-based test interpretations: Some development and application issues. *Applied Psychology: An International Review, 36*(3/4), 237–247.

Hedlund, J.L., Vieweg, B.W., & Cho, D.W. (1987). Computer consultation for emotional crises: An expert system for "non-experts." *Computers in Human Behavior, 3*(2), 109–128.

Herr, E.L. (1979). *Guidance and counseling in the schools: Perspectives on the past, present, and future*. Falls Church, VA: APGA Press.

Herr, E.L. (1985). The role of professional organizations in effecting the use of technology in career development. *Journal of Career Development, 12*(2), 176–186.

Herr, E.L., & Best, P.L. (1984). Computer technology and counseling: The role of the profession. *Journal of Counseling and Development, 63*, 192–195.

Herr, E.L., & Cramer, S.H. (1987). *Controversies in the mental health professions*. Muncie, IN: Accelerated Development.

Herr, E.L., & Cramer, S.H. (1988). *Career guidance and counseling through the life span: Systematic approaches*. Glenview, IL: Scott, Foresman.

Hoffman, N. (1984). Cognitive therapy. Introduction to the subject. In N. Hoffman (Ed.), *Foundations of cognitive therapy* (pp. 1–20). New York: Plenum Press.

Howard, G.S., Nancy, D.W., & Myers, P. (1986). Adaptive counseling and therapy: An integrative, elective model. *The Counseling Psychologist, 14*(3), 363–442.

Hurst, J.B., & Shepherd, J.W. (1986). The dynamics of plant closings: An extended emotional roller-coaster ride. *Journal of Counseling and Development, 64*, 401–405.

Jackson, L.A., Jr. (1987). Computers and the social psychology of work. *Computers in Human Behavior, 3*(3/4), 251–262.

Janis, L. (1982). *Counseling on personal decisions*. New Haven, CT: Yale University Press.

Janoff-Bluman, R., & Frieze, I. (1983). A theoretical perspective for understanding reactions to victimization. *Journal of Social Issues, 39*, 1–17.

Johnson, C.S., & Sampson, J.P., Jr. (1985). Training counselors to use computers. *Journal of Career Development, 12*(2), 118–128.

Kantor, R.M. (1977). *Work and family in the United States: A critical review and agenda for research and policy*. New York: Russel Sage.

Katz, M. (1980). SIGI: An interactive aid to career decision-making. *Journal of College Student Personnel, 21*(1), 34–40.

Keat, D.B. (1979). *Multimodal therapy with children*. Elmsford, NY: Pergamon.

Kiesler, C.A. (1980). Mental health policy as a field of inquiry for psychology. *American Psychologist, 35*, 1066–1080.

Krumboltz, J.D. (1983). *Private rules in career decision making*. Columbus, OH: The National Center for Research in Vocational Education.

Krumboltz, J.D., Mitchell, A., & Gelatt, H.B. (1975). Applications of social learning theory of career selection. *Focus on Guidance, 8*(3), 1–16.

Kübler-Ross, E. (1969). *On death and dying*. New York: Macmillan.

Lazarus, A.A. (1981). *The Practice of multi-model therapy*. New York: McGraw-Hill.

Leibowitz, Z., Farren, C., & Kaye, B.L. (1986). *Designing career development systems*. San Francisco: Jossey-Bass.

Levine, S.U. (1979). The psychological and social effects of youth unemployment. *Children Today, 8*(6), 6–9, 40.

Liem, R., & Rayman, P. (1980). Health and social costs of unemployment. *American Psychologist, 37*(10), 116–122.

Lopez, F.G. (1983). The victims of corporate failure: Some preliminary findings. *Personnel and Guidance Journal, 61*, 631–632.

Mahoney, M.J., & Freeman, A. (Eds.). (1985). *Cognition and psychotherapy*. New York: Plenum Press.

Malan, D. (1976). *The frontier of brief psychotherapy*. New York: Plenum Press.

Mann, J. (1973). *Time limited psychotherapy*. Cambridge, MA: Harvard University Press.

Maslow, A.H. (1954). *Motivation and personality*. New York: Harper & Row.

Matarazzo, J.M. (1980). Behavioral health and behavioral medicine: Frontiers for a new health psychology. *American Psychologist, 35*, 807–817.

Matthews, T.J., DeSanti, S.M., Callahan, D., Koblenz-Sulcor, C.J., & Werden, J.I. (1987). The microcomputer as an agent of intervention with psychiatric patients: Preliminary studies. *Computers in human behavior, 3*(1), 37–48.

Meichenbaum, D. (1985). *Stress inoculation training*. New York: Pergamon Press.

Mitchell, L.K., & Krumboltz, J.D. (1984). Research in human decision making: Implications for career decision making and counseling. In S. Brown & R. Lent (Eds.), *Handbook of counseling psychology* (pp. 238–280). New York: Wiley.

Mruk, C.J. (1987). The interface between computers and psychology: Toward a psychology of computerization. *Computers in Human Behavior, 3*(3/4), 167–180.

Nicholas, D.R. (1988). Behavioral medicine and mental health counseling. *Journal of Mental Health Counseling, 10*(2), 69–78.

Norcross, J.C. (Ed.). (1986). *The handbook of eclectic psychotherapy*. New York: Brunner/Mazel.

Novaco, R. (1976). Treatment of chronic anger through cognitive and relaxation controls. *Journal of Consulting and Clinical Psychology, 44*, 681.

Pasework, R.A., & Albers, D.A. (1972). Crisis intervention: Theory in search of a program. *Social Work, 17*, 70–77.

Perlmutter, F.D. (1982). New directions for mental health promotion. In F.D. Perlmutter (Ed.), *Mental health promotion and primary prevention* (Chapter 1). San Francisco: Jossey-Bass.

Posner, M.I., & Shulman, G.L. (1979). Cognitive science. In E. Hearst (Ed.), *The first century of experimental psychology*. Hillsdale, NJ: Erlbaum.

Rayman, J., & Harris-Bowlsbey, J. (1977). DISCOVER: A model for a systematic career guidance program. *Vocational Guidance Quarterly, 26*(1), 4–12.

Riegle, D.W., Jr. (1982). Psychological and social effects of unemployment. *American Psychologist, 37*(10), 113–115.

Romanczyk, R.B. (1986). *Clinical utilization of microcomputer technology*. New York: Pergamon Press.

Rosen, J.C., & Solomon, L.J. (Eds.), (1985). *Prevention in health psychology.* Hanover, NH: The University Press of New England.

Sank, L.I., & Shaffer, C.S. (1984). *A therapist's manual for cognitive behavior therapy in groups.* New York: Plenum Press.

Sampson, J.P. (1983). An integrated approach to computer applications in counseling psychology. *The Counseling Psychologist, 11*(4), 65–74.

Sampson, J.P. (1984). Maximizing the effectiveness of computer applications in counseling and human development: The role of research and implementation strategies. *Journal of Counseling and Development, 63*(3), 187–191.

Sampson, J.P. (1986, April 4–7). *The use of computer-assorted instruction in support of psychotherapy.* Paper presented at the annual conference of the British Psychological Society, University of Sheffield.

Sampson, J.P., Jr., & Pyle, K.R. (1983). Ethical issues involved with the use of computer-assisted counseling, testing, and guidance systems. *Personnel and Guidance Journal, 61,* 283–286.

Slaikeu, K.A. (1984). *Crisis intervention: A handbook for practice and research.* Boston: Allyn & Bacon.

Small, L. (1971). *The briefer psychotherapies.* New York: Brunner/Mazel.

Smith, D. (1982). Trends in counseling and psychotherapy. *American Psychologist, 37*(7), 802–809.

Suinn, R.M. (1976). *Manual: Anxiety Management Training (AMT).* Fort Collins, CO: Rocky Mountain Behavioral Sciences Institute.

Szasz, T. (1961). *The myth of mental illness: Foundations of a theory of personal conduct.* New York: Harper & Row.

Toffler, A. (1980). *The third wave.* New York: Morrow.

Tyler, L.E. (1983). *Thinking creatively: A new approach to psychology and individual lives.* San Francisco: Jossey-Bass.

Veroff, J., Kulka, R.A., & Douvan, E. (1981). *Mental health in America: Patterns of help-seeking from 1957 to 1976.* New York: Basic Books.

Wagman, M. (1984). Using computers in personal counseling. *Journal of Counseling and Development, 63*(3), 172–176.

Wagman, M., & Kerber, K.W. (1980). PLATO DCS, an interactive computer system for personal counseling: Further development and evaluation. *Journal of Counseling Psychology, 27,* 31–39.

Weiss, D.J., & Vale, C.D. (1987). Adaptive testing. *Applied Psychology: An International Review, 36*(3,4), 249–262.

Weizenbaum, J. (1976). *Computer power and human reason: From judgment to calculation.* San Francisco: Freeman.

Wolpe, J. (1973). *The practice of behavior therapy* (2nd ed.). New York: Pergamon Press.

CHAPTER 7

RECURRING AND EMERGING CHALLENGES IN COUNSELING

Previous chapters have identified four major challenges that will significantly shape the expectations for and the content of counseling during at least the next decade. These challenges—the economic climate and the effects of advanced technology, changing family structures, growing pluralism and cultural diversity, and expanded perspectives on populations at risk—are both dynamic and comprehensive in their effects upon individual behavior. As such the elements of these challenges encompass many of the factors that precipitate or underlie the majority of problems brought to counselors. In addition, other less encompassing but important challenges to counselors are also related to effects upon human behavior and counselor functions that tend to recur across time, are now emerging, or are only dimly perceived as future possibilities. Although these three sets of challenges may be more limited in the proportion of the population they affect than the four major categories of challenges discussed, they are also likely to have differential effects on counselors in schools, in colleges and universities, in community mental health centers or private practice, or in business and industry.

While attempting not to duplicate what has already been discussed in other parts of the book, the following sections of this chapter will consider some more specific challenges, their temporal characteristics, the populations and settings most affected, and the substance of the challenges or problems at issue. The focus here will be on recurring and emerging challenges. Chapter 8 will explore future challenges.

Recurring Challenges

Recurring challenges are those that tend to reappear under new guises as the national social, political, or economic environment of the country changes. There is no attempt to address all such challenges here, but several seem sufficiently encompassing to note.

A major recurring challenge is the continuing national debate about the role of school counselors in a changing society. Because this debate affects many potential readers of this book, it will be given attention first. A second recurring challenge is the broader issue of the professional identification of counselors as compared with other mental health professionals. Within this challenge are played out the notions of history, language system, power, and other variables that affect how counselors, particularly clinical mental health counselors, are likely to be able to function in the future. A third recurring challenge has to do with contemporary views of testing or assessment and the recurring issues that emanate from such concerns, particularly in relation to culturally different clients. These three recurring challenges will be discussed in turn.

The Role of School Counselors

As the national rhetoric about educational excellence has proceeded in the spate of reports spawned by the National Commission on Excellence report, *A Nation at Risk* (1983), one group of professionals whose role has been ignored, treated negatively, or debated as to new directions is that of school counselors. Individuals both in and out of the counseling profession question whether school counseling is now obsolete or irrelevant. Others speak of its imminent demise and disappearance. Still others address the need for a total restructuring of the school counselor's role around a results-based rather than a process-based model. Those who question the role of school counselors seem to frame questions as dichotomies that yield either affirmative or negative answers. The questions are: Are school counselors obsolete or not? Relevant or irrelevant? Likely to survive or to disappear?

Given the complexity of the roles and functions of school counselors in diverse urban, suburban, and rural settings, variations in affluence in school districts and among those served, and variety in the need for mental health services in and out of schools, yes or no answers about the relevance and suitability of school counseling as a profession seem to oversimplify the factors involved. It might be possible to reduce the status of school counseling in a particular school district or school building to criteria that yield yes or no answers, but the status of school counseling across the nation is not so easy to describe in simplistic terms (Herr, 1986).

If the question for the profession of school counseling is not one of simple survival as a visible entity in the school, what is the question? It is more nearly: What models of school counseling roles and functions are most likely to be effective under different conditions of student need, educational priorities, and availability of resources? Such a question does not address whether school counseling is worthwhile or effective. It does not treat school counseling as a singular process or set of functions to be uniformly applied in all settings. Rather, it suggests that school counseling can take on different forms and has different purposes given different assumptions about its values and priorities.

In this sense, school counseling has different types of relevance depending on the needs of the nation or of a particular school district at a particular time. Such a perspective also indicates that because different approaches to and organizations of school counseling can effect varied outcomes, the expectations of different groups of students, parents, teachers, administrators, policymakers, or others involved are likely to be described differently. Indeed, as social and economic conditions change in their effects on children and youth, new expectations for counselor functions will continually emerge and be given varying levels of priority.

Examples of relatively recent areas in which various constituents have expected counselors to intervene by offering identification of problems, treatment, or support are single-parent families, chemical dependency, grief and bereavement, adolescent suicide, child sexual abuse, children with learning disabilities, and anger management. Of course, such foci for counselor involvement exist along with the traditional assumptions that school counselors will engage in developmental or remedial efforts on behalf of curricular choice and planning for postsecondary education, career development, education for decision making, job search and access, the transition from school to work, personal adjustment, and other related areas.

Neither the emerging nor the traditional expectations of school counselors are necessarily inappropriate. In schools across the nation, counselors undoubtedly get involved with every one of these problem areas and many others. The problem for counselors in such circumstances is not whether they are relevant or whether they are wanted;

rather, it is the need to clarify priorities given varying resources and multiple sets of needs.

In essence, the above observations suggest that some counselors may be asking the wrong questions. There is little evidence that school counselors are not wanted or are likely to become extinct as a profession. More positively, there seems to be considerable evidence that some observers view school counselors as quite relevant, even essential to achieving certain educational goals. A few examples of the many available national indicators of support for school counselors follow.

The Carl D. Perkins Vocational Education Act of 1985

The Carl D. Perkins Vocational Education Act of 1985 is literally filled with indications of the importance of counseling in meeting the Act's purposes. In each of its titles and sections, the Perkins Act assigns career guidance and counseling roles in dealing with such issues as the problems of special needs populations, sex equity, career choice, information about new and emerging occupations, and many other matters of importance to vocational education students and to the economic development of the nation.

What is perhaps most important, this legislation indicates that career guidance or counseling functions should be discharged by professionally trained counselors. Unless school counselors are aware that in the past the vocational education legislation identified career guidance functions as important but did not require certified counselors to do them, it is difficult for some people to know how important the current language is. Such legislative language affirms that school counselors are relevant to students' choice of and success in vocational education, to the transition from school to work, and to the nation's economic development, and it describes the specific functions of school counselors that are relevant to these goals.

In this sense, the question is not whether counselors are useful, worthwhile, or obsolete. Rather, the implied question is: What roles are important for them to play? The question to be debated, therefore, is not a dichotomous good or bad, but one of which functions under what conditions are priorities for counselors if they are to be most relevant to the educational goals supported by the Carl D. Perkins Vocational Education Act.

National Commission on Secondary Vocational Education

Still in the general realm of vocational and career issues is the affirmation of the National Commission on Secondary Vocational Education that school counselors are important to excellence in vocational education. Created as a response to the spate of national commissions on academic excellence in 1983, which essentially neglected the role of vocational education and school counseling in achieving academic excellence, the National Commission on Secondary Vocational Education was created to correct that imbalance in the views of American education.

Of particular importance to the discussion of the relevance of the school counselor are the findings of the commission regarding school counselors in relation to vocational education. For example, with regard to overall function, in the commission's report, *The Unfinished Agenda* (National Commission on Secondary Vocational Education, 1984), it was suggested that "school counselor functions need to include cooperative activity with teachers, the use of group guidance techniques, computer-assisted guidance, comprehensive career information systems, and related methods designed to provide career guidance to all students" (p. 24). The commission also recommended that counselor-student ratios should not exceed 250 students per counselor and that systematic programs of interest and aptitude assessment, career planning, and occupational information designed to facilitate student curriculum choices should be available to all students. At other places in the report, the commission suggested that all students should be able to choose from a comprehensive set of course offerings across academic and vocational areas.

In broad as well as in narrower terms, the commission's report supports school counselors in roles beyond those of importance only to vocational education students. This view is reflected, indirectly at least, in the following passages:

> Finally, inadequate student knowledge subtly but formidably constrains student access to vocational education. Students and parents need to be accurately informed about what vocational education is, how it relates to their personal and career goals, and how it can be used to help them achieve their goals. One does not choose what one knows little about or is constrained from choosing by unexamined social attitudes.
>
> We need comprehensive career guidance programs that will provide this information and remove some of the subtle status distinctions involving vocational education. Comprehensive guidance means counseling that is available to all students, covering all subjects, leading to all occupations.
>
> We cannot achieve this goal of comprehensive guidance when counselors must deal, on the average, with 400 or

more students. Nor can this goal be achieved unless counselor and teachers cooperate in new approaches to facilitate the career development of students, unless counselors expand their use of group techniques, computer-assisted guidance, comprehensive career information systems, and other methods designed to provide assistance to all students. Counselors must serve as a resource to integrate career guidance concepts and occupational information in the classroom. In addition, the amount of shared information between vocational educators and school counselors should be increased to reinforce the likelihood that counselors will effectively advise students to consider vocational education as an option. (p. 16)

School Counseling and Vocational Education

Part of the effect of both the Carl D. Perkins Act and the National Commission on Secondary Vocational Education's Report, *The Unfinished Agenda*, has been to remind school counselors that the effective selection of an appropriate pattern of vocational education courses, adjustment to and success in such courses, and a systematic transition from school to work embodies models and elements that fall within the purview of counseling, not vocational education. These transitional processes into and through vocational education and into the world of work are really manifestations of self-awareness, career planning, and decision making, parts of a guidance process within the context of vocational education, rather than vocational education per se. Thus, the role of school counselors and, perhaps more specifically, career guidance in relation to vocational education needs to be conceived in several ways.

One model of career guidance in vocational education is to see the former as a support to the latter. In such a view career guidance and counseling can play important support roles before and after vocational education instruction. As examples, school counselors, in implementing the career guidance process, can play significant roles in attracting, recruiting, or selecting students for vocational education options. This process can be instrumental in conveying information and positive images about the content and outcome of vocational education to potential enrollees, parents, employers, sending schools, and others to whom such information should be accessible.

School counselors also have a significant role in assisting in the selection of students for admission to various vocational education programs and in motivating them to take advantage of the courses chosen. Such a role involves, although it is not confined to, individual assessment of aptitudes and preferences and exploration of their relation to probabilities of success and satisfaction in vocational education options. It also involves helping students come to terms with their personal feelings of self-efficacy and enhance their readiness to commit themselves to the challenges presented.

School counselors interacting with students about vocational education have a role in direct support of instruction. Vocational education students, like other students, need the opportunity to learn employability skills and interpersonal skills with co-workers and supervisors. They need opportunities to understand stress, time, and anger management and ways by which to deal effectively not only with the technical content of work but with the psychological environments in which work expectations and interactions are played out. Because these skills are composed of attitudes, emotions, psychological factors, as well as cognitive and informational elements, school counselors have a significant role to play in providing such insights and skills. To discharge these roles may require school counselors to work with vocational teachers as collaborators or consultants to find ways to infuse and reinforce such learning in curricula. In some situations counselors may actually teach such insights in the same way as they would implement a psychoeducational model as discussed in the previous chapter—using small group work, role-playing, gaming, computer-assisted career guidance, or other techniques.

Finally, the school counselor has an important role in the placement of students. Increasingly such an outcome of vocational education is seen as a process that precedes the actual event of placement. Therefore, the intent is to create a sequence of experiences that help to enhance self-awareness; the commitment to educational excellence and technical competence; decision-making capacity; awareness of educational and occupational options and how to prepare for and gain access to them; and practice in job search and job interview behavior. As these unfold, students can be helped to see placement as a target toward which they are moved systematically and purposefully, not abruptly and apprehensively. In such a view career guidance and the functions of the school counselor are seen as central to the outcomes achieved in vocational education and in the placement of students, not as tangential and irrelevant.

The Carnegie Foundation for the Advancement of Teaching

Another major national report dealing with the current federal rhetoric about educational excellence is that of the Carnegie Foundation for the Advancement of Teaching entitled *High School, A Report on Secondary Education in America* (Boyer, 1983). This national study, unlike many others, is unequivocal in its support of guidance as a critical need. The report's conclusion states:

> The American high school must develop a more adequate system of student counseling. Specifically, we recommend that guidance services be significantly expanded; that no counselor should have a caseload of more than one hundred students. Moreover, we recommend that school districts provide a referral service to community agencies for those students needing more frequent and sustained professional assistance. (p. 306)

The report alludes to how busy school counselors are, to the multiple expectations others hold of them, to the lack of time to meet with all those who need to talk with them, and to the overloading of counselors with case loads of students of more than 600 to 1 in some schools. There is no implication in the report that counselors are obsolete, useless, or irrelevant. The plea throughout is for the need to expand guidance services to effectively reach those students who need assistance. Such a perspective is reached in the report after the emphasis turns from the needs of college-bound students for a more effective assessment and guidance program to the needs of students not going on to college:

> There is also an urgent need to help noncollege students figure out where they should go and what they should do. It is ironic that those who need the most help get the least. Frequently noncollege students get only snippets of information about job possibilities from family or friends or other students or counselors at school. It is unacceptable to focus our elaborate testing and assessment system only on those moving to higher education while neglecting the other 40 to 50 percent who even more urgently need guidance. (Boyer, 1983, p. 134)

Keeping the Options Open; the Report of the College Board Commission on Pre-College Guidance and Counseling

In 1984, the College Board established a 21-person commission consisting of school counselors, professors, industrialists, and administrators in higher education (i.e., presidents, directors of student financial aid or of admissions). The official report of this commission

(Commission on Pre-College Guidance and Counseling) was published in 1986. It is useful to cite briefly its areas of concern. In general, it is a study of how students receive information about opportunities and financial aid available to them in higher education. The commission is concerned about how early and in what forms information must be delivered to students and their parents to have the greatest effect on their academic planning, preparation, and achievement. Of particular interest is how information and support are provided to children from racial or ethnic minority groups. Among other issues of concern to the commission are when and how children develop feelings of self-worth and confidence and who is involved, what the preconditions for choice are, what the specifics of transition from high school to college are, and what elements need to be included in guidance programs in secondary schools to help ensure that once students have been admitted to a college of their choice they will be able to anticipate and cope with the requirements of college adjustment (e.g., time management, loneliness, and separation from home).

In the commission members' dialogues in cities throughout the nation one theme prevailed: School counselors are important in pre-college guidance and counseling at each educational level from elementary school through junior high school and into senior high school. The roles of counselors in fostering feelings of confidence regarding academic readiness, curriculum choice, and planning for higher education are not the same at each of these levels, but, in the aggregate, counselors at each educational level complement each other's efforts. The commission also found that in many places counseling is inadequate because too little is offered too late, and it is uneven for particular groups of students. Counselors should not be expected to do everything. Their role has been stretched so many ways that its essence is frequently lost.

It is important to note that the commission is cognizant that if greater numbers of minority children are to gain access to and succeed in college, effective counseling must begin at an early age, in the elementary school, and continue through high school. Although counselors are not the only individuals responsible for the effective academic planning and performance of children, they are key sources of information and support in this process. Ways must be found, therefore, to sharpen the counselors' role on behalf of such students' needs, to prepare students for their roles, and to reduce the unevenness in availability of guidance services across students and settings.

The report of the College Board Commission on Pre-College Guidance and Counseling was cited in the previous chapter in relationship to its strong statement in behalf of planning for guidance programs and in doing so on a building-by-building basis.

Frontiers of Possibility; The National College Counseling Project

Somewhat similar to the work of the College Board Commission on Pre-College Guidance and Counseling, the National Association for College Admissions Counselors published its report, *Frontiers of Possibility*, in 1986. The concern of this report was the quality of the college decision process for students and the role of counselors in that process. Among other things studied was the amount of time that the guidance staffs of schools spent on college counseling as a proportion of all of their activities, including personal and vocational counseling as well as noncounseling activities.

One of the most constructive perspectives of the contribution of the school counselor and counseling in the context of schooling was stated in this report as follows:

> Situated at the juncture of the academic and the personal lives of students, we found that the counseling office is central to the mission and life of the school. Looking more specifically at the college counseling process, we found that the counseling office is strategically located at the convergence of school, family, and societal aspirations. . . . There are several college counseling practices that are consistently associated with excellence, including a (college) guidance curriculum, networks of support, financial aid initiatives, and productive relationships with colleges. (pp. 49–50)

The report goes on to describe the college guidance curriculum as one that has an explicit sequence of activities designed to carry students through several years of high school experience. Accordingly, "The goals of the curriculum should include the enhancement of student self-esteem, the broadening of horizons and aspirations, and preparation to make sound decisions—especially decisions about college" (p. 39). In suggestions about the content of such a college guidance curriculum, included are effective study skills, clarification of values, writing and speaking, testing, the application process, career exploration, information about colleges, financial aid, criteria for decision making, work internship opportunities with local businesses and social service agencies, special workshops for women dealing with college issues, SAT preparation, and career counseling and transition workshops focused on coping with the transition from high school to college or work.

In addition to the above perspectives on the content of a college guidance curriculum, the report also identifies the characteristics of effective college counselors such as student advocate, effective manager, and effective leader. To discharge such roles, counselors need both a strong work ethic and political savvy. This report as well as the previous one acknowledges that minority students as well as nonminority students must be encouraged to prepare for higher education. The United States must expand its pool of skilled and educated people to provide leadership, research, and enlightened citizenship to the economic, social, and political structures of the nation as it moves toward the 21st century. School counselors are vital components of that process.

In one sense, the future role of school counselors is based upon several pivotal concerns:

1. The degree to which school counseling programs are systematically planned; tailored to the priorities, demographics and characteristics of a particular school district or building; and clearly defined in terms of the results to be achieved rather than the services to be offered.
2. The degree to which school counseling programs begin in the elementary school or in the secondary school. Thus, the degree to which school counseling programs can truly be longitudinal, K to 12, and are planned around major developmental tasks and the knowledge, skills, and attitudes they comprise; or are confined to crisis intervention activities and quasi-administrative functions such as testing and scheduling.
3. The degree to which school counseling programs are seen as responsible for the guidance of all students or for only some subpopulations of students such as those ''at risk.''
4. The degree to which school counseling programs include teachers, community resources, parent volunteers, and families as part of the delivery system.
5. The degree to which school counseling programs are focused on precollege guidance and counseling, counseling in and for vocational education, counseling for academic achievement, and counseling for students with special problems: bereavement, substance abuse, antisocial behavior, eating disorders, and family difficulties—single parents, stepparents, blended family rivalries.

6. The degree to which counselors should be generalists or specialists, members of teams or independent practitioners, proactive or reactive.
7. The degree to which counselors employ psychoeducational models or guidance curricula as well as individual forms of intervention to achieve goals.
8. The degree to which the roles of counselors can be sharpened and expanded while at the same time not holding counselors responsible for so many expectations that their effectiveness is diminished and the outcomes they effect are vague.

The Professional Identification of Counselors

Although considerable space was committed to the discussion of the changing expectations and views of the school counselor, many of the dilemmas and concerns of that professional group have relevance to the evolving professional identification of counselors in other settings. Reflecting both a recurring and an emerging issue, the status of professional counselors, clinical mental counselors, and other subsets of counselors (who have successfully obtained credentials as nationally certified counselors or licensure to provide independent counseling practice in a particular state) in comparison to other mental care providers is still problematic.

As a function of history, training, credentialing, and power, the mental health professions differ in their status, in their fee-setting ability, in their access to third party payments, in the techniques they are permitted to use, in the clients they may serve, and in other terms in relation to each other. Such differences describe the fact that the mental health professions independently and collectively play out various caregiver roles frequently defined in legislative statutes or in governmental regulations. Therefore, what they are permitted to do and to whom becomes part of a sociopolitical process that is partly scientific and to a much larger degree political.

In comparison to psychiatrists, clinical and counseling psychologists, clinical social workers, and psychiatric nurses, professional counselors (outside of either a school base or a setting concerned with employment or rehabilitation) are relatively new arrivals on the mental health scene, particularly as independent providers of such services. As the functions they perform are seen as overlapping with those of the mental health practitioners who have earlier established their legitimacy in the provision of such services, issues of professional identity are frequently proxies for issues of economics and political power.

In addition, as professional counselors lay claim to the legal sanction to obtain clients without either the referral of other mental health professionals—particularly psychiatrists and psychologists—or supervision by members of such groups, professional identification and competence as buffers against problems of territoriality and other assaults—legal, economic, political, ethical—need to be communicated and the access to clients refought across states and communities, through legislation, and regarding procedures for paying insurance or mental health care benefits.

These issues have been discussed at length elsewhere (Herr & Cramer, 1987; Weikel, 1985). Suffice it to say here that professional counselors' search for professional identification and sanction is not unlike the struggles that counseling psychologists had to engage in for recognition and social sanction. Professional counselors and counseling psychologists have both evolved from roots in the guidance movement, from origins in the practice of counseling in schools and universities, and, particularly, from historical commitments to vocational guidance as a technique in which they had obtained considerable expertise. In their evolution professional counselors and counseling psychologists have adapted many psychotherapeutic interventions, including psychotherapy, to the developmental and crisis needs of many of the essentially "normal" populations, perhaps better described as nonpsychiatric or nonpathological, with whom they have traditionally worked. As national mental health policies have increasingly shifted funding from institutional settings, particularly educational settings, to community settings, then to private practice, and now to such settings as health maintenance organizations (HMOs), professional counselors, clinical mental counselors, and counseling psychologists, particularly those who wished to engage in longer-term and more in-depth procedures with children, youth, or adults than educational settings permitted, sought other settings, including independent practice, in which to employ their skills.

Part of the recurring professional identity problem for professional counselors, clinical mental counselors, and counseling psychologists is the tension between the mental health services for which the society wishes to pay and what professional counselors have purported to be skilled in and to which they are committed. For example, as cited in previous chapters, the prevention of mental disorders and risk factors or the promotion of health and the quality of life have tended not to be targets of mental health funding. Mental health funds, including so-called third party payments, tend to be focused on the treatment of severe emotional or behavioral problems—those classifiable within the taxonomy provided by the American Psychiatric Association (1980) in its *Diagnostic and Statistical Manual of Mental Disorders, Third Edition* (DSM-III) or its subsequent revision (DSM-IIIR). Such disorders tend to be seen as more appropriately treated by psychiatrists or clinical psychologists whose skills and training have been oriented to the procedures and perspectives of the medical rather than the nonmedical setting in which professional counselors and counseling psychologists are usually trained.

The conflict between funding of treatment or the funding of prevention and the promotion of healthy behavior also gets caught up in the recurring debates about the nature of mental illness, problems in living, personal competence, and other areas of behavioral, psychological, or biological dysfunctions that cause personal distress or impairment. As these definitions blur and move increasingly from the realm of biological causes to those predominantly explainable by faulty learning, psychological distortions, inadequate socialization, behavioral skill deficits, or related phenomena, the clamor for parity ensues among a wider group of "mental health" professionals than among those with primary allegiance to the medial setting, the medical model, or the "cure" of pathology. Such notions lie at the base of the recurring issues of professional identification professional counselors face. These issues then become overlaid with questions of content and length of training, type and length of supervision, purpose, organizational affiliation, and related matters by which different groups of mental health practitioners might be differentiated.

The classic distinction between counseling psychology and clinical psychology promulgated by Super in 1955 continues to provide contrasting views of service delivery, values, and priorities relevant to the clients different groups of mental health providers might serve, and to what purpose. Super's definition was as follows:

> *Clinical psychology* has typically been concerned with diagnosing the nature and extent of *psychopathology*, with the abnormalities of even normal persons, with uncovering adjustment difficulties and maladaptive tendencies, and with the acceptance and understanding of these tendencies so that they may be modified. *Counseling psychology*, on the contrary, concerns itself with *hygiology*, with the normalities of even normal persons, with locating and developing personal and social resources and adaptive tendencies so that the individual can be assisted in making more effective use of them. (p. 5)

The two "windows" or anchor points provided by the distinctions cited by Super on the clinical psychology versus the counseling psychology approach to mental health delivery are both subsumed in the definition of the professional mental health counselor:

> The mental health counselor performs counseling/therapy with individuals, groups, couples and families; collects, orga- nizes, and analyzes data concerning clients' mental, emo- tional and/or behavioral problems or disorders; aids clients and their families to effectively adapt to the personal concerns presented; develops procedures to assist clients to adjust to possible environmental barriers that may impede self-under- standing and personal growth; utilizes community agencies and institutions to develop mental health programs that are developmental and preventive in nature; provides a wide variety of therapeutic approaches to assist clients, which may include therapy, milieu therapy, and behavioral therapy. (Palmo, 1981, p. 1)

This definition of the clinical mental health counselor shows a decided interest in the use of counseling (or psychotherapy) to promote self-understanding and personal growth, in development rather than pathology in behavior, in prevention, and in the use of psychoedu- cational models designed to build client strengths and teach them life skills as a major therapeutic tool. This view of the professional coun- selor is more likely to focus on helping clients achieve control over their lives than on excising pathology, on helping them deal with the emotional intensity of transitions and life crises than on restructuring personality, and on helping them master and maximize personal re- sources and strengths through growth and learning than on diagnosing and classifying symptoms.

Models of professional identity are always simpler than profes- sional reality where distinctions are less clearly defined and sharply drawn between pathology and hygiology, between treatment and pre- vention, between being in crisis and in transition. Nevertheless, the recurring problem of counselor professional identity seems to be mov- ing positively and constructively toward tentative resolution as profes- sional counselors are increasingly able to declare their purpose and their contributions to treatment, to education, and to prevention. These contributions serve populations that are chronically at risk, acutely at risk, or are in transition to a new life style through career choice or change or environmental or family change. They also serve those who seek a level of mentally healthy behavior or wellness they have not yet attained for themselves. These perspectives, as they organize broadly held views of professional counselors, mental health counselors, and counseling psychologists are likely to diminish the recurring problems of professional identity for counselors and, indeed, for other mental health professionals.

Testing

Another of the recurring challenges to counseling is the use of testing and assessment. Some theorists have argued that the use of tests violates the principles on which a nondirective or collaborative relationship between counselors and clients is based. Perhaps more emphatic is the concern of many observers that testing is sexually or racially biased and, indeed, penalizes rather than facilitates the growth of specific groups of clients. Still others argue that the reasons for testing during this century have changed, and that the purposes and uses of testing in contemporary counseling approaches must change accordingly.

Most counselors are familiar with these contentions about testing and their recurring nature. Therefore, because of space limitations, an in-depth analysis of each of these matters will not be undertaken. But, it is important to acknowledge the continuing challenge that the use of tests represents and summarize a few of the major themes underlying such concern.

Gordon and Terrell (1981) put the pro and con arguments for testing succinctly when they stated:

> Critics of testing argue from a sociopolitical context, and thus challenge the very purpose as well as the developed technology of standardized testing. Defenders of testing argue from a traditional psychometric context, with little or no concern for political or social issues. The arguments of the two parties cannot be understood and appreciated without reference to those contexts. (p. 1167)

Gordon and Terrell argued that the reasons for testing at the beginning of this century and for several decades afterward have changed and so must the purposes of testing. In their view, a meritocratic approach to testing designed to identify those few who deserve special attention is no longer viable in a period when the availability of human resources has increased. The meritocratic selection of a few as a goal has given way to a shift in the approach to allocation of opportunities in response to changes in the social and political environment. The assertions of group superiority on the basis of test scores and the subsequent control of the opportunity and reward structure to retain low-status groups in some socially assigned position has given way to an attempt to democratize access to opportunity; thus the use of tests also should change. As understanding grows about the pluralism in and diversity of the effects of ethnicity, sex, race, and social class upon cognitive and affective structures, learning styles, motivation, and related matters, these should be reflected in purposes for assessment. Gordon and Terrell (1981) contended that:

> The proper course of assessment in the present age is not merely to categorize an individual in terms of current functioning, but also to describe the processes by which learning facility and disability proceed in a given individual so that it is possible to prescribe developmental treatment if necessary . . . . The equalization of opportunity may require that intervention be responsive to the functional characteristics of the person to whom the opportunity is being made available. It must be determined where the examinee is in terms of function, how he or she got there, and how growth within the examinee's particular social and cultural environment can be enhanced. (p. 1170)

Underlying the concerns of both the critics and the defenders of testing, but not always well articulated, is the reality that any test, assessment, or other measurement procedure has many validities, not only one. In fact, it is not only the validity of the measure itself about which counselors must be concerned but rather the validities of the inferences from the measures that counselors make. Guion (1974) stated that, "The kind of validity statement we seek in any given measurement situation depends on the kinds of inferences we wish to make. This fundamentally is a value judgment" (p. 290). Thus, however scientific or empirical the development of any measurement instrument may be, its probable multiple validities and the inferences that can be made from it bring both the test and the inferences into the area of values and social contexts. Frequently, then, those who argue for or against tests, are really arguing about the different validities or inferences that can be assigned to these tests.

Haney (1981) studied the history of social concern over standardized tests and testing throughout this century. Although the content of the debate continues to change as more is known about the technical aspects of test construction and interpretation, Haney contended that social concerns about standardized testing tend to be as much matters of social and political philosophy as they are technical matters of scientific measurement. In this sense, the perennial controversy about the use of standardized testing can be dismantled into such issues as the construct or predictive validity of tests on the one hand, and such issues as the utility of test information or, perhaps more precisely, the social functions of standardized tests on the other.

Embedded in the ongoing debate about the social functions of testing is a major concern about test bias, particularly with regard to sex-related concerns or whether members of minority groups are being inaccurately assessed or otherwise disadvantaged by the use of tests. But test bias, like other aspects of test content and use, is more than a singular issue. For example, Flaugher (1978) observed that test bias consisted of at least the following elements: overinterpretation, sexism, content, differential validity, the selection model, the wrong criterion, and the testing atmosphere.

Other observers argue that the main features of test bias lie in content, modality, and structure as well as in application and interpretation. Therefore, standardized tests are inappropriate for use with populations whose cultural, linguistic, economic, or social backgrounds differ from those in the majority culture for whom the test was designed and validated (Garcia, 1981).

Cole (1981), Cronbach (1980), and other scholars of testing have differentiated between the technical aspects of test bias and the questions of proposed use of tests that are really ethical or policy questions. These scholars are concerned about whether or not a test accurately measures what it purports to measure. This is a scientific and technical question involving assessments of criterion-related or predictive, construct, or content validity, or, indeed, the more recent efforts to combine these three measures of validity into a broader understanding of the meaning of a particular score (Cronbach). In the latter view, the different types of information reflected in the various approaches to validating a test's accuracy are simply types of evidence that singly or in combination attempt to reduce the technical bias, the lack of accuracy in what is measured, the inappropriate interpretation of test scores, and the misranking of persons on the construct or content measured.

But the concern of counselors and the public about test bias is not a technical matter. For the most part, it is a question of ethics or values. Simply stated, the questions are: Regardless of the technical validity or accuracy of the test, should it be used for the proposed purposes? What are the potential consequences of testing or the effects upon social values inherent in a particular type of test?

In essence, a test can be designed to accurately predict performance in some educational or occupational set of tasks. Indeed, it may accurately indicate that Whites or men are more likely to be successful than Blacks or women on these tasks. Thus, in its predictive validity it is unbiased in its technical or psychometric qualities, but the social and ethical questions begin where questions of technical bias stop. The question arises in this example: Should the test be used for selection purposes? If it is, Whites or men will continue to gain in access to opportunities and Blacks or women will continue to be impeded in this quest. Is such a result ethical? Does it represent an appropriate social policy? Does the test accurately reflect the social history of the groups? For example, even though the test accurately differentiates the groups on the basis of their potential performance, it is not able to factor in the fact that Blacks and women have been penalized in their current performance on the basis of previous inferior educational opportunities, limited developmental experience, or lack of encouragement. What part should the causes of different types of test performance play in using the test results? These are not issues of test validity per se but rather of policy, ethics, and values. They raise policy questions about "differently weighting" the characteristics of applicants to attempt to compensate for past social wrongs, or the use of quotas in selection of applicants. They also raise other questions of ethics or policy. For example, should tests be used to select or facilitate access to opportunity?

Anastasi (1985), after reviewing trends in psychological measurement over a 50-year period, extended to test developers and counselors the challenge that results from the interaction between the individual and the social contexts in which he or she has developed and in which tests are given. These two contexts may be dramatically different in cultural and in other terms. Different cultures provide different opportunities or reinforcements to learn or to implement different cognitive skills, form particular concepts, participate in logical analysis, or engage in abstract thinking. These cultural contexts are also likely to differ in the affective variables they reinforce relative to test performance and test taking generally. Counselors must understand and appreciate such differences and transform the information tests provide into what is relevant to the counseling purposes at hand—to modify and extend behavioral options not simply to classify people in fixed categories of high and low—and to the growing understanding of the effects of cultural diversity on test performance.

The recurring challenges to testing specified above are not likely to abate for the foreseeable future. Counselors will continue to need to understand and be able to respond to such challenges. But, counselors also need to see the new possibilities in the use of and the purposes for testing. One of these is reflected in the growing need for informed personal excellence.

Since 1983, the United States has been the focus of many reports calling for a renewed national effort to attain educational excellence.

The impetus for this pursuit is the rapid application of advanced technology in the home and in the office, in government and in industry, in the armed forces and in education. According to this perspective, the technical requirements of new industrial processes and of international competition will set excellence in basic academic skills as a requirement for larger numbers of youth and adults than ever before. People lacking such knowledge and skills, those who are functionally illiterate, or those who possess other major academic deficits are likely to be left in the wake of technological applications to more and more occupations, work places, and settings. Thus, educational excellence must surely embrace the teaching of basic academic skills to children and youth of different learning styles and motivations, to diverse populations of new immigrants, to adults who need retraining, and to those who have been on the margins of society with jagged work histories and assorted limitations on their ability to perform consistently and effectively in the work place. Each of these groups will require different forms of educational excellence to equip them with the requisite skills and attitudes necessary to compete in an economic environment of rapid occupational change.

From an assessment perspective, however, educational excellence is an unattainable abstraction without personal excellence and the individual's ability to use fully the educational opportunities available. The mechanism pivotal to effective use of educational opportunities is accurate self-knowledge and intelligence about one's strengths and one's purposes. Such self-knowledge must, in turn, be embedded in the personal confidence that using one's skills or talents constructively will lead to meaningful and desired outcomes. Thus, assessment cannot stand alone but must be integrated with other dimensions that provide motivation and direction to individual purposefulness. In the case of children and youth, such self-knowledge must be available as early as possible so that students can use it before making curriculum choices that restrict their future access to advanced education or occupational mobility. To assist students in making effective use of the educational reforms manifested in improved academic standards and courses, schools must help students acquire a base of personal information capable of providing purpose and direction to their schooling, and monitor their progress toward goals. In a large measure, the vehicle for such personal information is a comprehensive testing program.

Within such a comprehensive testing program, in addition to monitoring academic progress in various clusters of academic skills—mathematics, science, reading, etc.—and to flagging the need for remedial education where necessary—it is equally important to use assessment to help students decide upon and adjust their decisions about which academic patterns of coursework to pursue. This type of testing is important not only in pursuing educational or personal excellence but in career guidance as well. Curriculum decisions are not trivial. They are, in fact, intermediate career decisions. By their content, they open some doors and close others. The degree to which individual course selection includes mathematics and science determines whether or not one will enter specific college majors, which are also intermediate career decisions, or specific occupations or careers.

Thus, within a comprehensive testing program there must be at least two major types of assessment: aptitude and interest. Aptitude assessment measures what is variously called "developed abilities" or "learning potential." These are the individual traits that comprise maximum performance, potential for vertical mobility, competitiveness, and trainability at different levels of intellectual or cognitive rigor.

In interest assessment, the focus is not on maximum behavior but on one's typical behavior relative to those attitudes and preferences that mediate job satisfaction or feelings of similarity in values and goals with others in a work place, occupational group, or curriculum. Related to interest assessment is values assessment and other measures of motivational direction. Whether the focus of such assessment is interests, values, or satisfaction, the content is not so much cognitive or performance-based but, rather, oriented to identifying preferences. Such data help the individual to define goals, purposes, and settings in which performance aptitudes might be applied.

Aptitude assessment and interest measurement combine in various combinations with other measures of career planning and decision making to help students make informed choices, set personal standards, chart progress, determine areas of performance in which they are likely to succeed, and career fields in which they might feel comfortable. The self-knowledge from these assessments permits the student to approach educational opportunities and challenges with a sense of personal commitment and anticipation. It permits the student to view educational opportunities as avenues leading to personal goals rather than hurdles over which to leap without a clear sense of where the finish line is or what the rewards awaiting one's finishing the course are.

We have lingered over the notions of an informed commitment to personal excellence as fundamentally important to a national quest for educational excellence. This commitment is no less vital given the competitiveness of the international economy. In the corporate world also there is an increasing shift of emphasis from personnel management to personnel development. For broad national goals as well as for individual adults seeking a midcareer change or contemplating retraining, the assessment of occupational potential, personal preferences, and ability to choose becomes an important factor in facilitating employability, commitment, satisfaction, and goal direction.

In such views assessment procedures and testing are not simply classification devices. Rather they represent information resources by which clients can plan changes in their commitments, in the options they wish to pursue, or in other aspects of their environment. Such information is not seen as a static or fixed characterization of individuals but rather a "snapshot" of a point in time of potential modifiability in goals and behaviors. This information can be used to educate people for choice and to celebrate diversity, not slot people into roles defined by some cultural criteria. Implementing different perspectives on testing and articulating its meaning to the public and, indeed, to clients will be a recurring challenge.

Emerging Challenges

Because of the interplay between external events and people's feelings about themselves, the information they possess, and the knowledge and skills they have acquired, the content of counseling is, in some sense, always changing. Although underlying issues of lack of self-efficacy, misperceptions or mislabeling of events, inability to make commitments, stress, depression, anxiety, or uncertainty may be present in any problem brought to counselors, the precipitants of the counseling problem or its overt classification may change. Thus, although the fundamental elements of the problems counselors help clients solve may remain relatively constant, the causes of the problems or the interactions between clients and economic, social, or psychological environments constantly undergo change.

Although it is not possible to consider all the emerging challenges of concern to counselors and clients, several deserve special note. They include: AIDS; alcohol and substance abuse; the importance of self-esteem, personal responsibility, and control; and the variety of issues associated with counseling for an older or elderly population.

AIDS

One of the most feared of contemporary health problems is AIDS. A result of a human immunodeficiency virus (HIV), sexually transmitted or borne by blood through shared needles among intravenous drug users or by adventitious events, AIDS is a terminal disease for which there is currently no cure, only prevention. The Medical authorities typically view prevention as either complete abstinence from sexual activity, monogamous sexual relationships with partners free from AIDS antibodies that signify the presence of the virus, the use of a condom to keep bodily fluids from being exchanged by sexual partners or, in the case of intravenous drug users, not sharing needles. Indeed, the sharing of intravenous drug apparatus is now seen as the most likely conduit of AIDS to the heterosexual population (Bridge, Mirsky, & Goodwin, 1988). AIDS is also a highly emotional disease in respect to the fact that many of the public have overlooked current medical research that suggests that a person who tests positively for AIDS antibodies may not necessarily progress to the terminal and malignant disease itself nor to the Aids Related Complex (ARC). Obviously, however, testing positively for AIDS antibodies is a precondition for acquiring the symptoms and the degenerative course of the disease itself to a terminal result. The only two current uncertainties in the matter are whether an individual who has the AIDS antibodies will also acquire the disease and, if AIDS is acquired, how long it will take for the person to die as a result of the disease.

The extensive and recent media attention to the AIDS epidemic within the gay community and users of intravenous drug apparatus poses major challenges to the counselor in any setting. For example, how does one work with an AIDS victim who is by definition experiencing a terminal illness that will result in death in the foreseeable future, possibly months to not more than 2 to 5 years? Or, how does one inform students about AIDS and its prevention? Or, what responsibility does the counselor or psychologist have to notify individuals at risk for exposure to the HIV virus because of their relationship with a carrier of the virus such as a wife who the counselor knows is married to a client with AIDS? Are counselors who help AIDS victims to practice stress management and other forms of health psychology able to assist AIDS victims to slow the course of the disease?

Answers to the above questions are not yet clear or complete. Both the American Psychiatric Association and the American Psychological Association are developing policy guidelines to identify psychotherapists' responsibility for notifying individuals at risk for exposure to HIV (AIDS virus). The complexity of that responsibility has been debated in an important article by four attorneys (Girardi, Keese, Traver, & Cooksey, 1988). The thrust of their analysis of therapist responsibility is the degree to which the so-called Tarasoff (1976) decision in California is applicable in the case of knowledge of an AIDS carrier. Essentially, in the classic case of Tarasoff versus the

Regents of the University of California, a patient confided to his psychologist his intention to kill his ex-girl friend, Tatiana Tarasoff. The psychologist notified the campus police of this threat but did not notify or warn Tatiana Tarasoff of the known and pending danger posed by his patient. The patient eventually brutally murdered Tatiana Tarasoff, and her parents brought a claim against the Regents of the University of California (employer of the psychologist). The question with regard to AIDS is whether a counselor or psychotherapist who knows that a client is an AIDS carrier should consider that person's sexual activity a "lethal threat" and thereby warn any known sexual partners. Thus, in respect to the principal outcome of the Tarasoff decision, public policy in favor of protecting confidential communication must yield to the extent to which disclosure is necessary to avert danger to others. The application of this concept to the therapist's or counselor's responsibility in AIDS has not yet been clearly drawn by the courts, but its presages the complexity of the challenges the presence of AIDS holds for counselors.

Beyond the legal implications for counselors, AIDS also holds other concerns. For example, there is the question of the counselor's role in educating people about AIDS. One recommendation is that programs should stress behavioral strategies for preventing AIDS. "The development of skills in decision making, assertive communication, stress management, and self-esteem will empower students to take control of their lives and practice healthy behavior. . . . Students must understand that AIDS is a disease for which one chooses to put oneself at risk" (Sroka, 1988, p. 36).

One of the important findings about AIDS is that it is not only an immunodefective disease, it is also a neuropsychiatric disease. The HIV viral infection proceeds rapidly to the brain and begins to generate central nervous system manifestations. These include cognitive impairment (forgetfulness, poor concentration, confusion, slowed thinking), motor symptoms (loss of balance, poor handwriting, leg weakness) as well as affective problems (depression). Among the treatments of promise, beyond those of treating the viral infection itself, are processes familiar to or available to counselors: stress management techniques, social support systems, and classical conditioning to combat depression, stress, and other psychosocial factors that make the AIDS victim more susceptible to secondary infections and other forms of physical vulnerability. Enough research is now available to suggest that there is a direct relationship between heightened stress and less effective performance of the immune system. There is also significant evidence that personal attitudes of "hardiness," willingness to fight against the disease by positive personal attitudes, and similar expressions of "control'' may delay, it not prevent, the deterioration associated with many progressive diseases, including AIDS (Temoshok, 1988; Cohen & Adler, 1988; Glaser & Kiecolt-Glaser, 1988). These findings do not suggest that AIDS is acquired because of stress-induced problems; rather they suggest that psychological attitudes, positive or negative, influence the course of the disease. Counselors using cognitive behavioral therapy, stress and anger management, and related techniques are likely to provide important help to AIDS patients as they attempt to improve the quality of their life, reduce depression and anxiety associated with having the disease, and exerting as much control as possible over the progressive deterioration expected.

Finally, counselors are likely to come into contact with terminal AIDS victims and their relatives. In such instances, the role of helping the terminally ill and those who remain to work through the Kübler-Ross stages of loss is similar to that in the case of other terminal illnesses. These methods are discussed elsewhere in the book.

Alcohol and Substance Abuse

In other chapters of this book, alcohol and substance abuse were identified as major risk factors for different populations, conditions related to family violence, and the seedbed for children of alcoholics who themselves are likely to become alcoholics or to reflect other types of addictive or codependent behavior. The challenge for counselors regarding the prevention or treatment of alcohol and substance abuse is likely to continue into the future. Thus, this challenge is described as an emerging one only in terms of the growing recognition of the magnitude of the problem.

For example, the National Institute of Mental Health (Taube & Barrett, 1985) has indicated that of all mental disorders, the most prevalent for men is alcohol abuse/dependence and the third most prevalent is drug abuse/dependence. Using the very conservative figures of the 1980 census, 6.4% (10 million) of the population aged 18 and older experience substance abuse disorders. These figures include 7.8 million who abuse and are dependent on alcohol and some 3.1 million who use and are dependent on drugs. Of admissions to inpatient psychiatric services in the United States in 1980, 22% of those entering state and county mental hospitals had alcohol-related disorders and 5% had drug-related disorders; 34% of the people entering Veterans Administration medical centers experienced alcohol-related disorders and 5% had drug-related disorders. Indeed, alcohol-related disorders represented the most frequent primary diagnoses among admissions to

VA medical centers and state and county mental hospitals. In some contrast, affective disorders (e.g., manic episode, depression, dysthymia), followed by schizophrenia were the most frequent reasons for admission to private psychiatric and nonfederal general hospitals but within the latter, primary diagnoses for alcohol-related disorders still represented about 9% of all admissions.

Alcohol is a drug and it can be addictive. The use of alcohol, particularly drunkenness (being under the influence), is implicated in perhaps the majority of traffic accidents in the United States. It is also implicated in a range of interpersonal problems including child abuse, spouse abuse, and difficulties at the work place. Overuse of alcohol is implicated in cirrhosis of the liver, which occurs six times more frequently among alcoholics than among nonalcoholics, heart disease, and other cardiovascular problems. Alcohol use is also related to symptoms of depression when people are not drinking (Parker, Parker, Harford, & Farmer, 1987).

The actual number of alcohol-related deaths is hard to estimate but the true figure is likely to be close to 200,000 deaths per year. According to national polls, there are now about 28 million alcoholics in the United States and 32% of homes have someone with a serious drinking problem. Put another way, 1 out of every 5 people who drinks alcohol has a serious problem with its effects. According to the National Highway Traffic Safety Administration, in 1985 more than 22,360 people were killed in alcohol-related traffic accidents involving either primary drivers or pedestrians. This figure does not include all the people injured, broken families, or those who suffer as a result of such accidents (Alcohol Research Information Service, 1987a). In addition, 1983 data from the U.S. Department of Justice on alcohol use among convicted offenders just before committing an offense indicate that the percentage of people convicted of violent crimes found to be using alcohol at the time of the offense was 54%; of people convicted of property crimes, 40%; of people convicted of drug traffic or possession, 29%; of people convicted of violating the public order, 64% (Alcohol Research Information Service, 1987a). In collective terms, the cost to the U.S. economy for alcohol problems was estimated by the Alcohol Research Information Service to be $128.3 billion for 1986. This amount includes the costs of treatment, health support services, mortality, lost employment, reduced productivity, crime, social welfare, incarceration, and motor vehicle crashes.

Alcohol is a mood altering drug and one that has been called "the most dangerous and debilitating of all the common drugs" (Glasser, 1984, p. 127). However, chemical dependency, or drug abuse, also includes a variety of other substances that cause their consumers pain and problems. These mood altering substances include amphetamines, barbiturates, cocaine, inhalants, LSD, opiates, PCP, tranquilizers, marijuana, quaaludes, valium, and heroin. One might also include tobacco and even caffeine in this list. All of these substances change current physical, social, or psychological conditions in ways that stimulate, tranquilize, or energize behavior, or increase personal feelings of control for short periods. These drugs are both psychologically and physically addictive for regular users. They become psychologically addictive because the mood alteration that occurs feels good or gives sufficient pleasure to the user so that he or she wants to experience it as often or as intensely as possible. They are physically addictive because the body accepts them, integrates them into normal body chemistry, and begins to crave them in increasing amounts.

Alcohol and substance abuse are problems for all age groups, and they are a major concern for children and youth. Because alcohol and drugs are so widely available and adolescents are so susceptible to peer pressure, it is estimated that over 90% of high school seniors have tried marijuana and many have tried other drugs such as cocaine and, particularly its smokable form, "crack." Alcohol is believed to be the drug most widely abused by youth in binge drinking, particularly on weekends. Because adolescence is a period of considerable confusion about personal identity, career directions, sexuality, self-esteem, and many other matters, teenagers may decide to turn to drugs to mask their emotions and their insecurities as well as to feel a part of their peer group. Although it is very difficult in the early stages of drug use to separate the signs of normal fluctuations in adolescent behavior from those associated with incipient drug use, the following signs are likely to be present: increasingly secretive behavior, isolation, change in friends, depression or mood swings, change in interests or family involvement, school problems (grades, attendance, etc.), the presence of drug paraphernalia (pipes, rubber tubing, razor blades, cigarette papers, etc.), money problems, and physical symptoms (needle marks, changes in weight or dress patterns) (Krames Communications, 1987).

Half of all teenagers treated for alcohol and drug abuse started using alcohol by age 12 and marijuana by age 13. In a recent study conducted in 13 treatment centers in 5 states it was found that many addicted teenagers have problems at home or at school. For example, 60% of the teens reported that someone else at home also abuses drugs or alcohol. Of the addicted teens, 45% of the girls and 35% of the boys reported having experienced physical abuse; 45% of the girls and 11% of the boys reported having experienced sexual abuse. About 11% of the girls and 25% of the boys who were addicted to alcohol or drugs were identified as suffering from learning disabilities; 30% of the girls and 10% of the boys had attempted suicide; 44% of the girls and 60% of the boys had been suspended or expelled from school; and 15% of the girls and 33% of the boys had been arrested. Other underlying problems found among the addicted teenagers included poor self-image, troubled relationships with parents, sleep disorders, and depression. Moreover, in most instances, the teenagers reported experiencing three or more of these problems (Alcohol Research Information Service, 1987b). This study advocated a multidimensional approach in which teenagers are treated for personal problems at the same time they are treated for alcohol and drug abuse problems. They also need to be helped to acquire the social or job skills necessary to cope with life events after their chemical dependency is terminated.

Other researchers suggest that one can use "peer cluster theory" to understand why adolescents use drugs as well as how to provide treatment or preventive approaches (Oetting & Beauvais, 1986). Peer cluster theory suggests that "small subsets of peer groups, including pairs, dictate the shared beliefs, values, and behaviors that determine whether, when, and with whom drugs are used and the role that drugs play in defining cluster membership" (p. 17). From a treatment standpoint, the premise is that unless the influence of the peer cluster in determining adolescent drug use can be changed, there is little likelihood that one can change the drug involvement. Thus, the counselor may need to help the client dissociate from the drug-using group and strengthen ties with another peer cluster. Or, the counselor may work directly with the drug-using peer cluster in applying techniques analogous to those in family or systems therapy in order to try to change the collective reasons for drug use and to find alternative methods of filling the needs to which drugs are related. Finally, in addition to working with the peer clusters that support drug use, it is important for the counselor to deal with whatever underlying psychosocial problems clients experience that sustain their drug use such as needs for self-confidence or social acceptance, anxiety, unhappiness, social isolation, anger, or feeling blamed. Peele (1986) contended, in responding to the peer cluster theory, that society and, indeed, counselors

> . . . give children the competencies, values, and opportunities to find superior alternatives to drug use for relating to their world. . . . The mission of those concerned with adolescent drug abuse is to create a cultural climate that encourages children to value and to achieve independence, adventure, intimacy, consciousness, activity, fun, self-reliance, health, problem-solving capacities and a commitment to the community. . . . There is no better antidote for drug

abuse than adolescents' beliefs that the world is a positive place, that they can accomplish what they want, and that they can gain satisfaction from life. (p. 24)

With respect to adult alcoholics, there are many treatment formats in which counselors are likely to be involved. Among them are brief inpatient treatment (approximately 30 days), day treatment programs, or halfway houses. Extended outpatient psychotherapy rather than brief counseling with alcoholics is believed to be an effective intervention, particularly with people who have neuropsychological limitations. Out-patient group counseling, counseling approaches that emphasize role-playing, behavioral rehearsal of appropriate actions in stressful situations that are known to contribute to relapses, and psychoeducational approaches targeted to helping alcoholics acquire new behaviors that improve interpersonal skills and self-efficacy each represents an important approach to counselor intervention for particular types of alcoholic clients, depending on whether or not they experience cognitive deficits or other neuropsychological problems (Clifford, 1986). In addition, family education and counseling, built around basic family systems concepts, is now a component of most alcohol treatment programs (Goodman, 1987).

Before leaving the multifaceted challenges for counselors reflected in alcohol and substance abuse, two related phenomena need to be noted. One is the growing national concern for children of alcoholics and the other, the related issue of codependency. Problems of and approaches to dealing with children of alcoholics have been discussed in chapter 3 and mentioned in other parts of the book. Nevertheless, it will be useful to revisit this matter briefly.

Children of alcoholics. Current estimates suggest that there are approximately 12 to 15 million minor children of alcoholics and between 15 to 18 million adult children of alcoholics (Black, 1981), or in all perhaps as many as 34 million children of alcoholics (Black, 1986) now living in the United States. Whether or not genetic connections or environmental factors are involved, research has found an array of negative outcomes associated with being raised by an alcoholic parent. These include being too self-critical, serious, responsible, and controlled. Such children may have difficulty with intimacy, honesty, and commitment. They may reflect a tendency to ignore their own needs, possess a poor self-concept or low frustration tolerance, and experience poor academic performance. They may experience a high incidence of depression, hyperactivity, emotional and behavioral disorders, sexual confusion, and a variety of somatic complaints. Also implicated is a tendency to deny parental alcoholism, difficulties in trusting others, compulsive behavior (workaholism), and a tendency to chemical dependency themselves (Goodman, 1987; Downing & Walker, 1987).

The treatments proposed for children of alcoholics include family counseling and therapy, intensive group psychotherapy, support groups, and psychoeducational groups. The latter tend to focus on reducing feelings of isolation and decreasing denial; confronting denial and learning about alcoholism and codependency; and recognizing and recovering feelings. This final phase tends to include structured group exercises and group discussions of such topics as difficulties in trusting others, emotional awareness and expression, responses to the alcoholic, reactions to drinking, and valuing of personal needs (Downing & Walker, 1987). Lewis (1987) contended that counseling for young children who still live in the home with the alcoholic parent should concentrate on providing empathy and support and on developing coping skills useful in the current situation and in the future. The latter would be likely to include helping them reach out to others, recognize and express their previously forbidden emotions, and possibly participate in a structured group that allows them to experience peer support and learn about substance abuse, families, feelings, and coping with problems and choices. There is also a growing body of self-help materials that younger children and adult children of alcoholics can use to try to understand and cope with their experiences.

Codependency. Implicit in the work with children of alcoholics cited above is concern about the notion of codependency. Codependents may be children, spouses, or other intimate partners of alcoholics who have behavior problems or exhibit violent behavior. Codependency has come to have different definitions. But, one definition that synthesizes such elements is: "A codependent person is one who has let another person's behavior affect him or her, and who is obsessed with controlling that person's behavior" (Beattie, 1987, p. 31).

Thus, codependents, although not the primary victims of a life of mental disorder, substance abuse, or other behavior problems, are nevertheless victims in comprehensive ways. They are the caretakers of troubled people and get caught up in their problems. As Beattie (1987) suggested:

> . . . codependents are reactionaries. . . . They react to the problems, pains, lives, and behaviors of others. . . . Many codependent reactions are reactions to stress and uncertainty of living or growing up with alcoholism and other problems. . . . Codependency is progressive. As the people around

us become sicker, we may begin to react more intensely. What began as a little concern may trigger isolation, depression, emotional or physical illness, or suicidal fantasies. . . . Codependency may not be an illness, but it can make you sick. And, it can help the people around you stay sick. . . . Whatever problem the other person has, codependency involves a habitual system of thinking, feeling, and behaving toward ourselves and others that can cause us pain. Codependent behaviors or habits are self-destructive. (pp. 33–34)

Codependency, like other human behavior, is learned. Sometimes it is learned early in life; sometimes later in life. The roots of codependent behavior may come from religious interpretations or from socialization of nurturance in sex-related differences.

In general, codependent behaviors surface as the individual tries to cope with an environment where a "significant other" is troubled, ill, alcoholic, or a problem for him- or herself and others. In this context, children, spouses, friends, and parents take on self-protective adaptations that may become self-destructive if perpetuated beyond their time of primary usefulness. According to Beattie (1987, pp. 37–45), such self-protective adaptations may involve caretaking (e.g., thinking and feeling responsible for other people's feelings, thoughts, actions, choices, wants, needs, well-being, lack of well-being, and ultimate destiny); low self-worth (e.g., blaming themselves for everything); repression (e.g., being afraid to be authentic or to be themselves; pushing thoughts and feelings out of awareness); obsession (e.g., constant worry about minor things and about problems and people); controlling (e.g., trying to control events and people through helplessness, guilt, coercion, threats, advice giving, manipulation, or domination); denial (e.g., looking for happiness outside themselves and centering their lives around other people); poor communication (e.g., frequently having a difficult time expressing their emotions honestly, openly, and appropriately or asserting their rights); weak boundaries (e.g., letting other people continue to hurt them as they increase their tolerance of negative behavior from others); lack of trust (e.g., not trusting their feelings, decisions, or other people); anger (e.g., having a lot of anger but being afraid of it and of other people's anger); and sex problems (e.g., reducing sex to a technical act or losing interest in sex).

Character, Personal Responsibility, and Self-Esteem

Clearly, codependent behaviors take on many different patterns. Many people, probably millions, could be described as in some stage of codependent relationship in which they feel trapped, helpless, to blame. Undoubtedly, a major emerging challenge to counselors will be helping such people recognize their codependency, find ways to be responsible for themselves, not others, and to adapt more personally healthy behavior. This involves helping codependents to detach themselves from the intense involvement and, indeed, entanglement with the person with whom they have been codependent, and assisting the codependent to come to terms with the reality that he or she cannot solve problems for others and that worrying about the situation will not change it.

Self-esteem, personal responsibility, control. At the root of many of the emerging challenges discussed in this and in previous chapters, particularly in sections dealing with changing family structures and people at risk, there are recurring allusions to self-esteem, personal responsibility, and control. In some sense, these terms are interactive. When individuals feel good about themselves, they are able to accept their characteristics, and systematically attempt to understand and improve selected ones; these people are likely to experience high self-esteem and to love themselves in healthy and wholesome ways. In such a scenario, people of high self-esteem are also likely to exhibit personal responsibility toward self and toward others. They are able to exert control over their lives.

Self-esteem can be defined in many ways. It is basically a judgmental process about one's personal worth. As Coopersmith (1967) suggested, it is a judgmental process in which individuals examine their performance, capacities, and attributes according to their own personal standards and values and reach decisions about their personal worth. Ford (1987), in his application of the Living Systems Framework (LSF) to the notion that humans are self-constructing living systems, placed self-esteem within a broader notion of human governing functions composed of regulation, values, and evaluative thought. In particular, he noted that humans must regulate their internal functioning, their functioning in relationship to the environment, especially the interpersonal environment, and their functioning in the relationship between their internal states and environmental transactions. In his view, there are two methods for accomplishing these tasks: biochemical regulation, and cognitive regulation.

In Ford's (1987) perspective, self-esteem falls within the category of cognitive regulation. He stated:

> Every problem-solving activity, decision, or choice requires
> selection from among options representing alternative goals

or means for controlling behavior. This implies that there must be criteria for making such selections. Evaluative thoughts provide such criteria. . . . Three major kinds of evaluative thoughts have been studied. One kind is self-evaluative thoughts. Every behavior episode provides people with information about themselves. From such information people develop concepts and propositions about themselves as parts of their behavior episode schemata. These concepts and propositions are often termed the *self-concept* or *self-system*, of which self-evaluations are components. Self-evaluations of one's ability or opportunity to function as a causal agent are sometimes called *self-efficacy expectations, causal-attributions*, or *control beliefs*. Self-evaluations of one's self- or social acceptability are often termed *self-worth or self-esteem*. (pp. 31–32)

Ford and Ford (1987), in a second volume describing the theoretical perspectives discussed above, further discussed self-esteem as follows:

. . . self-esteem refers to evaluations of one's personal and social worth, rather than to evaluations of one's competence. It may be constructed, in part, from evaluations of performance feedback. . . . Self-esteem appears to be significantly influenced by the actual or anticipated social evaluative feedback provided by others. . . . This has led some to propose that one's self-concept is largely a social product. . . . (p. 476)

Obviously, dealing with issues of self-esteem may involve the counselor with the application of cognitive behavior therapy as described in chapter 6. Because a lack of self-esteem frequently stems from negative evaluations of one's worth, such evaluations and the bases for them may need to be confronted and alternative ways to viewing oneself must be examined. Because self-esteem is so fundamental to one's way of viewing others, the world, and the utility of one's continuing to live and being purposeful, the counselor must create in his or her communication with the client a relationship that is characterized by caring, trust, understanding, honesty, sincerity, acceptance, liking, and interest. These relationship variables may sound so familiar to the reader that they are passed over lightly in the reading; the point is, however, that these kinds of interpersonal elements are precisely what has been missing from the client's life and have brought him or her to a lack of self-esteem or self-worth. These types of counseling variables are the healing ingredients by which people can be helped to self-disclose, exhibit trust in another, and communicate the feelings of pain and loneliness that underlie and presage dealing with problems of self-esteem. Frankl (1963) observed 25 years ago that the salvation of humankind is love. It is in loving and being loved that individuals find a sense of self-worth, self-respect, and dignity. The counseling relationship should help the individual to restore the ability to love and to feel capable of being loved.

Johnson (1986) indicated that "the human species seems to have a *relationship imperative*: we desire and seek out relationships with others and we have personal needs that can be satisfied only through interacting with other humans" (p. 1). Johnson extends the point to suggest that the basis for personal well-being is effective interpersonal skills. In his view human development follows a pattern of expansion of interdependence with others; individual identity is built out of our relationships with other people; psychological health depends almost entirely on the quality of relationships with others. Johnson also contends that each of us needs to be confirmed as a person by other people. "Confirmation consists of responses from other people in ways that indicate we are normal, healthy, and worthwhile. Being disconfirmed consists of responses from other people suggesting that we are ignorant, inept, unhealthy, unimportant, or of no value, and, at worst, that we do not exist" (p. 3). In a world of loneliness, rapid change, discrimination, complex stressors, and psychological or physical abuse, many have never learned nor have been systematically exposed to interpersonal skills that allow them to develop self-worth, identity, or effective relationships with others. Thus, their behavioral repertoire may be very limited in how to act in an interdependent world, or they may feel so limited in their internal locus of control, their ability to manage their lives, that they attribute everything that happens to them to fate or external control by other people. The sense of stress, powerlessness, frustration, and lack of personal worth that results may frequently be manifested in vandalism, aggressiveness, uncontrolled anger, violence, bullying, chemical abuse, and other self-destructive or antisocial acts.

Among people for whom life is a negative experience and relationships with others do not lead to feelings of personal confirmation or a sense of community, a major counselor role is to help such people acquire the basic interpersonal skills by which to initiate, develop, and maintain caring and productive relationships. Included among these sets of basic skills are those listed by Johnson (1986, pp. 7–8) that relate to:

1. Knowing and trusting others;

2. Communicating with other people accurately and unambiguously;
3. Accepting and supporting oneself and others; and
4. Resolving conflicts and relationship problems constructively.

The learning of interpersonal skills is typically accomplished by the application of a psychoeducational model such as that described in chapter 6. Whether implemented on an individual basis or in a group context, clients have to be helped to understand why the basic skills to be learned are important in alleviating the problems they are experiencing, what the basic components of the skills are, the need to practice such skills and get feedback about their progress in implementing the skill, and, ultimately, the persistence to make it an authentic part of their personal behavior. In implementing such a psychoeducational approach to interpersonal development, the counselor will have to use modeling, reinforcement, homework, and other techniques to sustain the client's motivation to learn these skills in order to alter the feelings of poor self-esteem and unworthiness that are central motivations for whatever self-destructive or antisocial behaviors are exhibited. Counselors obviously cannot change the world, but they can help people understand what they are experiencing and equip them with the skills by which they might become more positive about themselves and enhance their ability to gain access to and cope with interpersonal, family, and career opportunities that validate them as persons.

The elements of building self-esteem, according to Johnson (1986), which in essence become the goals of the counseling relationship, a psychoeducational model, or a cognitive behavioral approach, include the following in somewhat abridged form:

1. Control your self-esteem through how you see yourself. Changing the way in which you think about yourself will change your self-esteem.
2. Set your own standards for evaluating yourself. People with low self-esteem tend to be particularly susceptible to persuasion and too readily accept others' standards as their own.
3. Set realistic goals. Do not demand too much of yourself.
4. Modify negative self-talk and attributions. Individuals with low self-esteem tend to think in counterproductive ways and make negative statements to themselves. In essence, they do not take credit for the good things they do nor talk to themselves in self-enhancing ways.

5. Emphasize your strengths. Accept your personal shortcomings that you are powerless to change and work to change those that are changeable.
6. Work to improve yourself. Efforts at self-improvement can be used to boost your self-esteem.
7. Approach others with a positive outlook. Negativism toward yourself can result in negativism toward others. When you approach people with a positive, supportive outlook, you will promote rewarding interactions and gain acceptance. (pp. 288–289)

The lack of self-esteem or effective interpersonal relationships, in addition to resulting in self-destructive or antisocial acts, may also be reflected in such emotional manifestations as shyness, anxiety, and a reluctance to risk. These and similar feelings restrict people from being who they want to be. The way to control such feelings is to take charge of behavior that will alter these feelings or stimulate action that is managed and self-directed. Every individual operates within the limits of time, resources, and other restrictions on what can be done. But, the only limits on attitudes or purposeful behavior within whatever external constraints exist are those that are self-imposed. "Doing" changes attitudes. This perspective, too, becomes a major ingredient of building self-esteem. It is the essence of what Glasser (1984) calls "Control Theory."

The central notion of control theory is that regardless of how people feel, they have some control over what they do. The underlying perspective is that "Nothing we do is caused by what happens outside of us. If we believe that what we do is caused by forces outside of us, we are acting like dead machines, not living people" (Glasser, 1984, p. 1). Thus, people have the opportunity to choose how they will feel and how they will react or behave in response to life's unfolding events. If, then, individuals want to change a total behavior, they must choose what to *do* and what to *think* differently. As they do so, their *feelings* about themselves, about the situation, and about others are also likely to change.

Much more deserves to be said about the promotion of self-esteem, personal responsibility, and control as a major emerging challenge for the foreseeable future. Space does not permit a fuller elaboration of these matters here. Suffice it to say that although the terminology has been used differently, much of the content of this book has been about the variety of ways counselors can add a personal dimension to an otherwise impersonal and, perhaps, hostile environment whether in the family, the school or university, or the work place. As the counselor helps clients of any age to consider alternatives, sharpen values, deal with their individual quests for meaning or spirituality, understand more about their strengths and their possible application in social and work situations, and identify and learn the skills sets (e.g., interpersonal, problem-solving, communication) likely to permit them to live a more purposeful and productive life, the probable outcome for clients is increased self-esteem, personal responsibility, and control. By helping clients to free themselves from the negative attitudes, pictures, and information deficits by which their previous existence has been shaped and stifled, the counselor, through personal caring, commitment, and expertise, is acknowledging the worth of the clients and their potential to alter the conditions that brought them to counseling. The efforts of counselors who understand and provide the conditions to enhance individual self-worth, positive self-attributions, and respect for oneself and others are powerful ingredients in combatting the need for chemical dependency, sexual exploitation, child and spousal abuse, suicide ideation, and other self-destructive or antisocial behaviors. Building character, personal responsibility, and self-esteem is obviously a major emerging challenge for the future.

Counseling With Older Americans

It is probably fair to suggest that counselors and counseling psychologists have, for most of their history, been more identified with youth and young adult populations than with older Americans or the elderly. Indeed, as recently as 1984, a special issue of the *Counseling Psychologist* devoted to counseling with the aging indicated that people who are old or concerned specifically with matters of later life are basically a new clientele for counseling psychologists (Ganikos & Blake, 1984). That perspective is beginning to change as more insight is gained in research and in theory about the variety of transitions and changes older Americans experience. As life circumstances change, so do identity, marital, and career issues. Life after young adulthood is not stable and stress-free. It is dynamic and filled with questions and uncertainties just as are other stages of life. The implementation of counseling responses to the needs of older citizens represents a major emerging challenge to counselors in the years ahead.

But the challenge of counseling with older Americans is not solely a matter of new and comprehensive insights about the needs of this population. It is also a function of the demographics of the matter. Americans are a "graying" population. In 1985, older people outnumbered teenagers in the United States. Some statistics will put the situation in perspective.

According to the American Association of Retired Persons (1987), the following are paraphrased and selected highlights describing the older populations as these are reflected in census data and other resources:

- People 65 years or older constituted 12.1% (26.2 million) of the U.S. population in 1986 or 1 in every 8 Americans. The number of older Americans has increased by 14% since 1980 compared to about 5% in the under-age-65 population.

- The sex ratio of older women to older men increases with age. In 1986, there were 121 women for every 100 men in the age group of 59–65, and that ratio increased to 253 women for every 100 men at ages 85 and older.

- Since 1900, the percentage of people 65 years and older as a proportion of the total population has tripled (4.1% to 12.1%) and the actual number in the population has increased by nine times (3.1 million to 29.2 million).

- Within the older population, the ages of the subgroups are getting older. For example, in 1986 the number of people in the United States 85 years of age and older (2.8 million) was 22 times larger than the same age population in 1900; the 75–84 age group (9.1 million) was 12 times larger than in 1900 and the 65–74 age group (17.3 million) was eight times larger than the same age group in 1900.

- In 1986, the average life expectancy for people who had reached age 65 was 18.6 years for women and 14.8 years for men.

- By the year 2030 it is expected that the older population will number 65 million older people or 2½ times the number in 1980. Given current fertility and immigration levels, it is expected that the only age groups to experience significant population growth in the next century will be those beyond age 55. Indeed, by 2030, the population aged 65 and beyond may climb to 21.2% of the total population.

- In 1986, older men were twice as likely to be married as older women (77% men, 40% women). Half of all older women in 1986 were widows and there were five times more widows (8.1 million) as widowers (1.5 million).

- In 1986, about 30% (8.3 million) of all noninstitutionalized people aged 65 and above lived alone (6.6 million women and

1.7 million men). The number of older people who lived alone increased by 68% between 1970 and 1986. The majority (67%) of older noninstitutionalized people lived in a family setting in 1986, often with children, siblings, or other relatives.

- A small number (5%) of the 65+ population lived in nursing homes in 1985 with this proportion ranging from 1% for people 65–74 years of age to 22% for people 85+.

- By racial and ethnic composition, approximately 90% of those over 65 were White, 8% were Black, and 2% were of other races. Those of Hispanic background represented 3% of the older population.

- Approximately one half (49%) of the population aged 65 and above lived in eight states. Those having over 2 million older citizens were California, New York, and Florida. States having over 1 million older citizens included Pennsylvania, Texas, Illinois, Ohio, and Michigan.

- In 1986 some 3.5 million elderly people were below the poverty line and another 2.8 million were classified as near-poor. The median income of older people in 1986 was $11,544 for men and $6,425 for women. About one of every seven (15%) families with an elderly head had incomes less than $10,000 and 38% had incomes of $25,000 or more. Elderly people living alone or with nonrelatives were likely to have low incomes in 1986 with nearly half (44%) reporting incomes of $7,000 or less. In 1986, the median income for this classification of individuals was $7,731 ($8,098 for Whites, $4,974 for Blacks, and $5,291 for Hispanics).

- In 1986, 3 million older Americans (11%) were in the labor force. They constituted 2.6% of the U.S. labor force. About half of the workers over 65 in 1986 were employed part-time and one-quarter of older workers were self-employed.

- Most older people have at least one chronic health condition and many have multiple conditions. In 1984 about 6.0 million (23%) of older people living in the community had health-related difficulties with one or more personal care activities and one or more home management activities. In 1984 the 65+ group represented 12% of the U.S. population but was projected to account for 31% of total personal health care expenditures.

Within these statistics describing the older population there is obvious variance across many categories of concern. Not all older people have health problems or economic difficulties. Not all older people are lonely or alone. However, that does not mean that the elderly who do not fit such descriptions are without mental health issues related to identity, self-worth, employment, interpersonal conflicts, parent-child or grandchild concerns, or other topics that matter to them. There are also preretirement issues and issues of how to begin to taper off, which concern people from 55 to 65 years of age, that need to be addressed in counseling availability and response.

Given the size and variation of the older population and those around the age of 50 who begin to contemplate retirement and its attendant issues, the need for access to comprehensive counseling responses will be an increasing challenge. The Office of Technology Assessment (OTA) of the U.S. Congress (1985) stated that "A major challenge stretching well into the 21st century will be to maintain the health and functional ability of America's rapidly growing older population." Among the responses OTA recommends to meet the needs of the older population are: programs designed to help older people acquire behaviors that promote health and thereby prevent or delay the onset of various chronic diseases (even at the oldest ages, the positive effects of such behaviors can be realized in relatively short time periods); supportive services and settings; work-place technologies that may improve performance, efficiency, and safety for many older workers; the use of telecommunications to enable older people to take advantage of new home-based work arrangements; and retraining of older workers to encourage continued employment or provide new employment possibilities. In one way or another, most of these recommendations have been addressed in other parts of this book with other populations. Thus, in essence, many of the counseling techniques or approaches described in chapter 6 and elsewhere are applicable to older populations. However, there are additional possibilities.

Waters (1984), for example, contended that in counseling with older clients "new knowledge must be acquired and although basic counseling skills apply across the life span, adaptations frequently must be made to meet special conditions or counseling needs that an older person may bring to the helping encounter" (p. 63). For example, "As people reach more advanced ages the basic goal of maintaining independence and control over one's life often becomes increasingly threatened and at the same time increasingly important to the individual" (p. 64). Within such a context, group work can be a helpful modality by which to assist older people to improve their social skills, discover resource sharing and increase self-esteem, reduce loneliness, facilitate catharsis, and discover commonalities with their peers. Such approaches might include preventive mental health or enrichment groups designed to enhance self-esteem and communication skills; assertion training groups to help with the improvement of interpersonal communications skills and direct expression of feelings to help older people cope with bureaucracies and significant others; retirement planning groups to help older citizens anticipate and adjust to retirement; and self-help groups for widows or widowers or other special populations of older citizens for whom support, sharing, and structured opportunities to communicate with other older citizens would be particularly useful.

Frequently, agencies for the aging, senior citizens groups, and counseling centers providing counseling to older citizens are using older people as peer counselors and group leaders. This trend is occurring for several reasons: a gross lack of counseling services for older people, an insufficient number of counselors trained in gerontological mental health issues, the high cost of providing traditional mental health resources to older citizens, and the reluctance of older people to avail themselves of mental health services because they think that doing so denotes a lack of ability to manage their own affairs or solve their own problems. On the more positive side, older people serving as peer counselors have a measure of instant credibility to other senior citizens because of their comparable age and experience; they also can serve as role models for other older persons in their willingness to be useful and other-directed. Regardless of the potential benefits of using older persons as peer counselors, it is also important to train them in effective listening skills and in other behaviors that will be of therapeutic use to others. Age itself is an insufficient criterion for selecting peer counselors. Systematic screening, training, and ongoing support are essential for using peer counselors at any age.

Waters (1984) suggested that some specialized counseling procedures are particularly useful with older people. The techniques Waters suggested are additions to and not replacements for more general techniques useful with any age population. Examples are life review, reality orientation, and remotivation. Life review is a technique that focuses on the tendency of older people to engage in reminiscence and reliving the past. As a therapeutic device, this life-review process can help older people take stock of their lives, survey and resolve past conflicts about which they have been troubled, complete unfinished business, reintegrate past experiences, and think through how they want to use whatever time is left to them. Life review as a counseling technique for older citizens is consistent with the observation that throughout life the questions people ask have different orientations depending on where they are on a continuum of time from birth to death. For example, youth tend to orient their questions to the future; people in midlife are oriented to the present; older citizens are concerned about the past.

Therefore, "Young people ask: Who am I becoming? People in mid-life ask: Who am I? Do I want to remain this person for the time I have left? Old people ask: Who have I been? What has been the meaning of my life?" (Waters, 1984, p. 70). Life review processes may help older people identify recurring themes in their lives, rediscover coping mechanisms they used at earlier times that may still be useful, and rediscover already-developed skills that may be valuable now in different applications. Such a review may broaden the range of alternatives they might consider for the future.

Reality orientation as a therapeutic approach to working with older people is a technique designed to hold or reverse "the confusion, disorientation, social withdrawal, and apathy so characteristic of in-stitutionalized elderly patients" (Waters, 1984, p. 71). At its simplest level, reality orientation reinforces the repetition and learning by older patients of the basic facts of their existence: their names, the place where they are living, date, time and day of week, or when the next meal or bath will be. Beyond these routine matters, the principle is to show personal respect to older patients and thereby provide social reinforcement in order to reduce dependency and deterioration.

Reality orientation as a technique is frequently an antecedent of another technique used with older citizens—remotivation. The latter is an attempt to get moderately confused elderly patients to renew their interest in their environment by engaging them in the objective features of everyday life. Using a structured program of discussion topics, pictures, music, and other stimuli, the elderly can be encouraged to focus on such matters as sports, gardening, pets, work, and how these topics relate to their former roles, functions, and likes and dislikes as ways to bridge their current status to the larger "reality" of their present and past lives.

Many other techniques may be especially useful in working with older citizens. For example, in milieu therapy elderly patients are encouraged to try new skills in a safe and supportive environment. Or, analyses of support systems help older people identify support systems present in their lives, or those available to them if they learn certain accessing skills.

Sargent (1980) identified what he termed nontraditional therapy and counseling with the aging. Some of these methods have already been described briefly. In Sargent's view, such approaches to providing counseling services for senior citizens would include assertiveness training groups, widows groups and emeritus classes, adult day-care centers (that allow the frail elderly to remain in their own or children's homes rather than nursing homes), new directions workshops for senior citizens, therapeutic efforts to facilitate the transition to nursing homes, creative aging workshops, and behavioral approaches to therapy with the elderly.

On balance, the nontraditional therapies Sargent advocated are in group formats and are skill-based in order to reduce the well-documented resistance of older citizens to use traditional mental health services and change their perceptions that being seen at the locations of mental health services advertises their distress or incompetence to handle their own problems. Nontraditional therapies are, nevertheless, responding to the magnitude and range of mental health problems many older citizens experience. Estimates by professional organizations such as the American Psychological Association are that at least 15% of the older population need mental health services. Other observers feel that such an estimate is much too conservative because of the combination of poor economic and interpersonal factors that put so many of the elderly at risk of significant emotional breakdown or decline (Butler & Lewis, 1977). Other statistics that affirm the older citizens' needs for mental health services are the large number of suicides among people over age 65, some 25% or more of those in the total population (Butler, 1976). Thus, although the need for mental health services among the older population is great and older citizens' resistance to availing themselves of traditional mental health services is high, one of the answers is to provide increased opportunities for therapeutic activities in settings where senior citizens may come together but that are not themselves traditional sites for mental health services (e.g., day-care centers, long-term care facilities, senior citizen centers, churches, housing settings, malls, etc.) (Myers & Salmon, 1984).

To move from the notions of nontraditional therapies for older citizens to the more traditional, several final comments are in order. Because of the comprehensiveness of the needs of older citizens, it is necessary to recognize that for some groups of older citizens remediation or rehabilitation will be important; for others, preventive approaches; and for others, educational or developmental orientations. In some instances, the application of family theory and family counseling will be extremely useful as an elderly parent is moving to an intact family of his or her child. The need to look at the alterations of family dynamics and how such matters can be anticipated and reduced in their effect upon the various family members will be helpful. Similarly, family counseling is likely to become important in the situation when an elderly parent is contemplating moving from either his or her home or the children's home to a nursing home.

Whether traditional or nontraditional therapy is used with the older population, several dimensions have been found from syntheses of the research literature to be important considerations in counseling with the older population (Wellman & McCormick, 1984).

1. The relationship between the counselor and the client is important in the change process.
2. Brief therapy is somewhat more successful than long-term therapy.
3. Interventions that are experiential, participatory, and encourage a high degree of client involvement are more effective than more passive interventions.
4. Cognitive/behavioral interventions tend to be effective.
5. The success of treatment is related to the client's mental and emotional resources.
6. Group interventions are helpful for those elderly who are not severely disabled.
7. Although team approaches look promising, more research is needed with this modality.

One of the "new" groups to whom counselors will need to give particular attention in the future is the "children of aging parents." An increasing number of middle-aged people are finding themselves in the situation of parenting their own children while at the same time taking on a parental role for their elderly parents. Such a condition can cause stress, anxiety, financial burdens, and uncertainty for all concerned. As a result, a large and increasing need for help for the adult children of aging parents has become apparent in the past decade, and its importance is likely to increase dramatically in the future. Frequently, a group format can be useful to help adult children of aging parents to share their concerns with others experiencing the same circumstances. The counselor is likely to share information about the aging process to help these adult children understand what is happening with their older parents as their needs and behaviors are changing. Information is typically shared about the availability of community resources. Helpful books about the aging process are frequently identified and their use reinforced.

In most such situations, a group environment needs to be created in which these adult children of aging parents are able to examine their personal feelings of guilt, unfinished business, financial or communications problems with their aging parents and with their own children, and alternate ways of responding in the areas identified. These middle-aged parents/children are sometimes called the "sandwich generation" because their needs are sandwiched between those of their adolescent children, who seek increasing independence, and those of their aging parents, who are facing a loss of independence (Myers, 1988). Many people caught in these multigenerational responsibilities find themselves losing their own independence at a time in their life when they had anticipated such freedom as their children leave home, their career is well advanced, and they have an opportunity to reestablish intimacy with their spouse. They lack role models for caring for aging parents and also maintaining their own quality of life. Role changes and role strains occur in unanticipated and frustrating ways and may in fact put the adult child and caregiver of aging parents at risk of ill health. When adult children have siblings, either near or distant to the aging parent, rivalries and tensions can arise about how contributions to the aging parents will be made and by whom.

Myers (1988) suggested that in working with adult children of aging parents counselors may engage in individual counseling, family counseling, or group work with any of the actors in the situation. Given the complexity of the interpersonal and family dynamics involved, it may be difficult to know clearly who is the client and whose needs are preeminent at different points in time. Within such circumstances, counselors need to help both adult children and their aging parents to achieve a balance between their needs, to identify future solutions, and to reestablish and maintain the level of emotional relationships and communication important to each of them.

Many other trends reflect needs for counseling responses to aging populations that deserve to be mentioned but for which space is limited. One of these has to do with counselors working with older workers. Obviously, older and elderly workers are in the work force. Although the number of such workers had been decreasing, that situation is likely to change because of the relative lack of young workers available to enter the work force. Rather than continuing to encourage older workers to retire early, prior to age 65 or even 60, an increasing emphasis on retaining older workers is likely. Other factors that might reinforce this trend are federal legislation prohibiting age discrimination in the work place, continuing efforts to reduce "ageism" and the stereotypical and demeaning effects upon older people, and, certainly, the economic aspects associated with proposals to raise the eligibility age to receive social security benefits to age 67 or beyond. Aside from these factors many older or elderly workers remain in the work force beyond normal retirement ages for personal reasons such as income. But work also provides other important life satisfactions for older people that for many constitute reasons to continue in the work place: status, personal achievement, social relationships, and the structure of time (Ginzberg, 1983).

Older workers who remain in the work force, retire from one career and return to the work force in another part-time or full-time role, or who modify a long-time career pattern are likely to seek and benefit from counseling (Hitchcock, 1984). These people are likely to need counselor help to evaluate their strengths, interests, and transferable skills, and to learn how to cope with salary or age discrimination, how to market themselves, or how to implement job search skills. They may need assertiveness or communications training. They may profit from peer support or other therapeutic interventions designed to increase their self-esteem and their feelings of self-efficacy.

Smyer (1984), in noting the large amount of within-group variance in the development of biological and psychological variables among the older population, advocated three major counseling tasks with this population:

1. Help the client differentiate normal aging from pathology.
2. Help the client assess his or her resources and deficits.
3. Explore the reality of aging and its social consequences.

Sterns, Weis, and Perkins (1984) acknowledged a major concept that receives little attention in the literature: Most of the problems of older workers are not unidimensional, they are multidimensional. They suggest that different personal needs require different forms of intervention. For example, using Blocher's model of human effectiveness (1966), they suggested that if the client's issue is mastery, then an educational intervention is most appropriate; if coping, then peer support; if striving, then group counseling; if inertia, family therapy; if panic, individual counseling. Whether or not one agrees with these particular problem/treatment interactions, the important issue is that the older worker or older client needs to be understood holistically and treatments need to be matched to whatever set of needs the client has.

Conclusions

As suggested in other chapters, the content with which counselors deal is dynamic. The unfolding of social, political, and economic events creates new and different stressors and these, in turn, are reflected in the anxieties, uncertainties, confusion, information needs, or the perceptions of self-worth and potential, accurate or inaccurate, that people bring to counselors. But, the changing psychological, political, and economic environments within which people negotiate their identities, attempt to resolve personal and social conflict, or forge careers also affect the methodology and the professional identity of counselors.

In this chapter, several recurring challenges have been identified that reflect perennial concerns for counselors. They include the appropriate role of school counselors, the credibility and opportunities of professional counselors to deliver mental health services compared to those of other mental health providers (e.g., psychiatrists, clinical psychologists, counseling psychologists, marriage and family therapists, etc.), and the social implications of testing and assessment of individual differences. Each of these challenges surfaces regularly as a focus for debate and for new syntheses of concepts and purposes.

In part, the recurring challenges identified above are affected by the emerging challenges described in the chapter. AIDS; alcohol and substance abuse; the importance of self-esteem, personal responsibility, and control; and the growth and needs of the aging population are either new challenges or challenges about which new insights have suggested much greater importance than was previously understood. AIDS, for example, is a terminal disease that did not affect Americans until the last decade. Its presence has spurred threat, anxiety, probable changes in the sex habits of many Americans and, potentially, a growing recognition of the part that stress plays in increasing the vulnerability of the immune system to hastening the course of HIV infection. These considerations, in turn, have reinforced the role that counselors can play in helping people deal with stress management and with other corollaries of the disease: grief, bereavement, anger, and rejection.

Certainly, a second major challenge is the rapidly expanding knowledge of the destructive effects on personal health, social relationships, family integrity, and work productivity from alcohol and drug abuse. Although general knowledge of such effects is not new, the pervasiveness and the intensity of the effects of these substances has brought new levels of concern to policymakers, educators, employers, and the public at large. The victims of substance abuse and their codependents have come to be a more visible clientele for counselors in all settings. An emerging result of the AIDS epidemic and the widespread concern about alcohol and substance abuse is the dawning recognition in many sectors of the society that the basic antidote to such problems lies in personal responsibility, feelings of self-worth, control, and personal character. Helping people to deal with the emotional aspects and stress of AIDS and the problems represented by alcohol and substance abuse will be formidable challenges for counselors far into the future. In addition, however, counselors will increasingly be involved with helping people develop the attitudes and behaviors toward themselves and others that foster personal responsibility, acceptance of one's internal behavioral control, and related ingredients of mental health.

Finally, the shifting demographics of the American population to one which is, on average, becoming older and experiencing the wide-ranging needs for information, support, opportunities, and quality of life associated with the elderly constitutes a new frontier for counselors. Such challenges will require counselors to develop new techniques and modify existing ones as they work comprehensively with the aged and their families, with those approaching retirement, and with those who create barriers for the aged through attitudes of prejudice and discrimination.

References

Alcohol Research Information Service (1987a). *Monday Morning Report, 11*(24), 2.

Alcohol Research Information Service (1987b). *The Bottom Line on Alcohol in Society, 8,* 3.

American Association of Retired Persons. (1987). *A profile of older Americans: 1987.* Washington, DC: Author.

American Psychiatric Association. (1980). *Diagnostic and statistical manual of mental disorders, third edition.* Washington, DC: Author.

Anastasi, A. (1985). Some emerging trends in psychological measurement: A fifty-year perspective. *Applied Psychological Measurement, 9*(2), 121–138.

Beattie, M. (1987). *Codependent no more: How to stop controlling others and start caring for yourself.* New York: Harper/Hazelden.

Black, C. (1981). *It will never happen to me.* Denver: Medical Administration Company.

Black, C. (1986). An interview with Claudia Black. *Changes, 1*(4), 4–18.

Blocher, D.H. (1966). *Developmental counseling.* New York: Ronald Press.

Boyer, E.L. (1983). *High school; A report on secondary education in America.* New York: Harper & Row.

Bridge, T.P., Mirsky, A.F., & Goodwin, F.K. (Eds.) (1988). *Psychological, neuropsychiatric, and substance abuse aspects of AIDS.* Volume 44, Advances in Biochemical Psychopharmacology. New York: Raven Press.

Butler, R.N. (1976). An interview with aging's best advocate. *APA Monitor, 7,* 14.

Butler, R.N., & Lewis, M.I. (1977). *Aging and mental health; Positive psychosocial approaches.* (29th ed.). St. Louis, MO: Mosby.

Clifford, J.S. (1986). Neuropsychology: Implications for the treatment of alcoholism. *Journal of Counseling and Development, 65*(1), 31–34.

Cohen, N., & Adler, R. (1988). Immunomodulation by classical conditioning. In T.P. Bridge, A.F. Mirsky, & F.K. Goodwin (Eds.), *Psychological, neuropsychiatric, and substance abuse aspects of AIDS* (pp. 199–202). Volume 44, Advances in Biochemical Psychopharmacology. New York: Raven Press.

Cole, N.J. (1981). Bias in testing. *American Psychologist, 36*(10), 1067–1077.

Commission on Pre-College Guidance and Counseling. (1986). *Keeping the options open: An overview.* New York: College Entrance Examination Board.

Coopersmith, S. (1967). *The antecedents of self-esteem.* San Francisco: Freeman.

Cronbach, L.J. (1980). Validity on parole: How can we go straight. In W.B. Schrader (Ed.), *New directions for testing and measurement: No. 5, Measuring achievement, progress over a decade.* San Francisco; Jossey-Bass.

Downing, N.E., & Walker, M.E. (1987). A psychoeducational group for adult children of alcoholics. *Journal of Counseling and Development, 65*(8), 440–442.

Flaugher, R.L. (1978). The many definitions of test bias. *American Psychologist, 33*(7), 671–679.

Ford, D.H. (1987). *Humans as self-constructing living systems: A developmental perspective on behavior and personality.* Hillsdale, NJ: Erlbaum.

Ford, D.H., & Ford, M.E. (1987). Humans as self-constructing living systems. In M.E. Ford & D.H. Ford (Eds.), *Humans as self-constructing living systems. Putting the framework to work* (pp. 1–46). Hillsdale, NJ: Erlbaum.

Frankl, V.W. (1963). *Man's search for meaning.* (Rev. ed.) New York: Washington Square Press.

Ganikos, M.L., & Blake, R. (1984). Guest editor's introduction. *The Counseling Psychologist, 12*(2), 13.

Garcia, J. (1981). The logic and limits of mental aptitude testing. *American Psychologist, 36*(10), 1172–1180.

Ginzberg, E. (1983). Life without work: Does it make sense? In H.S. Parnes (Ed.), *Policy issues in work and retirement* (pp. 37–39). Kalamazoo, MI: Upjohn Institute for Employment Research.

Girardi, J.A., Keese, R.M., Traver, L.B., & Cooksey, D.R. (1988). Psychotherapist responsibility in notifying individuals at risk for exposure to HIV. *The Journal of Sex Research, 25*(1), 1–27.

Glaser, R., & Kiecolt-Glaser, J. (1988). Stress-associated immune suppression and acquired immune deficiency syndrome. In T.P. Bridge, A.F. Mirsky, & F.K. Goodwin (Eds.), *Psychological, neuropsychiatric, and substance abuse aspects of AIDS* (pp. 203–215). Volume 44, Advances in Biochemical Psychopharmacology. New York: Raven Press.

Glasser, W. (1984). *Control theory: A new explanation of how we control our lives.* New York: Harper & Row.

Goodman, R.W. (1987). Adult children of alcoholics. *Journal of Counseling and Development, 66*(4), 162–163.

Gordon, E.W., & Terrell, M.D. (1981). The changed social context of testing. *American Psychologist, 36*(10), 1167–1171.

Guion, R.M. (1974). Open a new window. Validities and values in psychological measurement. *American Psychologist, 29*(5), 287–296.

Haney, W. (1981). Validity, vaudeville, and values. A short history of concerns over standardized testing. *American Psychologist, 36*(10), 1021–1034.

Herr, E.L. (1986). The relevant counselor. *The School Counselor, 34*(1), 6–13.

Herr, E.L., & Cramer, S.H. (1987). *Controversies in the mental health professions.* Muncie, IN: Accelerated Development.

Hitchcock, A.A. (1984). Work, aging, and counseling. *Journal of Counseling and Development, 63*(4), 258–259.

Johnson, D.W. (1986). *Reaching out: Interpersonal effectiveness and self-actualization*. Englewood Cliffs, NJ: Prentice-Hall.

Krames Communications. (1987). *Chemical dependency: Kids and drugs*. Daly City, CA: Author.

Lewis, J.A. (1987). Children of alcoholics. *Counseling and Human Development, 19*(9), 1–9.

Myers, J.E. (1988). The mid/late life generation gap: Adult children with aging parents. *Journal of Counseling and Development, 66,* 331–335.

Myers, J.E., & Salmon, H.E. (1984). Counseling programs for older persons: Status, shortcomings and potentialities. *The Counseling Psychologist, 12*(2), 39–53.

National Association of College Admissions Counselors. (1986). *Frontiers of possibility*. Report of the National College Counseling Project. Burlington: University of Vermont.

National Commission on Excellence. (1983). *A nation at risk*. Washington, DC: Author.

National Commission on Secondary Vocational Education. (1984). *The unfinished agenda*. Columbus, OH: National Center for Research in Vocational Education.

Oetting, E.R., & Beauvais, F. (1986). Peer cluster theory: Drugs and the adolescent. *Journal of Counseling and Development, 65*(1), 17–22.

Office of Technology Assessment, U.S. Congress. (June, 1985). *Technology and aging in America*. OTA Report Brief. Washington, DC: Author.

Palmo, A.J. (1981). *Mental health counselor*. Unpublished manuscript prepared for the Board of Directors of the American Mental Health Counselors Association, Washington, DC.

Parker, D.A., Parker, E.S., Harford, T.C., & Farmer, G.S. (1987). Alcohol use and depression symptoms among employed men and women. *Brown University Digest of Addiction Theory and Application, 6*(4), 48–51.

Peele, S. (1986). The cure for adolescent drug abuse: Worse than the problem. *Journal of Counseling and Development, 65*(1), 23–24.

Sargent, S.S. (Ed). (1980). *Nontraditional therapy and counseling with the aging*. New York: Springer.

Smyer, M.A. (1984). Life transitions and aging: Implications for counseling older adults. *The Counseling Psychologist, 12*(2), 17–28.

Sroka, S. (1988, April 27). Planning effective AIDS-education programs. *Education Week*, p. 36.

Sterns, H.C., Weis, D.M., & Perkins, S.E. (1984). A conceptual approach to counseling older adults and their families. *Counseling Psychologist, 12*(2), 55–61.

Super, D.E. (1955). Transition: From vocational guidance to counseling psychology. *Journal of Counseling Psychology, 2,* 3–9.

Tarasoff v. Regents of the University of California. (1976). 17 Cal. 3d 425, 131 C.R. 14.

Taube, C.A., & Barrett, S.A. (1985). *Mental health, United States 1985*. Rockville, MD: National Institute of Mental Health, U.S. Department of Health and Human Services.

Temoshok, L. (1988). Psychoimmunology and AIDS. In T.P. Bridge, A.F. Mirsky, & F.K. Goodwin (Eds.), *Psychological, neuropsychiatric, and substance abuse aspects of AIDS.* Volume 44, Advances in Biochemical Psychopharmacology. New York: Raven Press.

Waters, E.B. (1984). Building on what you know: Techniques for individual and group counseling with older people. *The Counseling Psychologist, 12*(2), 63–74.

Weikel, W.J. (1985). The American Mental Health Counselors Association. *Journal of Counseling and Development, 63*(7), 457–460.

Wellman, F.E., & McCormick, L. (1984). Counseling with older persons: A review of outcome research. *Counseling Psychologist, 12*(2), 81–96.

CHAPTER 8

FUTURE CHALLENGES FOR COUNSELING

A persistent theme of this book, expressed in many different ways, is that counseling content, counseling processes, and counselors' and counseling psychologists' roles are shaped by events—political, economic, and social—external to the client. Such external events shape behavior as they are filtered through clients' perceptions, information processing, feelings of self-efficacy, and other intrinsic mechanisms by which possibilities are translated into actualities. How the client interprets and acts upon these external events becomes the content of counseling. Put somewhat differently, the term *psychosocial* is frequently used in the counseling literature to imply "that at all stages of the life cycle, healthy development represents an interaction among the individual and his or her psychological dynamics, and the larger social world in which the individual is living" (Kiunick, 1985, p. 126). Thus, human development does not occur within a cocoon that is independent of the environmental influences within which an individual negotiates his or her identity, forges a career, and plays out the life cycle. The forms, directions, and substance of people's lives are interactive with political, social, and economic environments.

In the previous chapters, we have examined four major challenges and several recurring and emerging challenges that counselors need to consider and plan for as they look to the remainder of this century and the beginning of the next. Other future challenges tend to be more vaguely defined, more abstract in their possibilities than those discussed up to this point. These represent projections, estimates, and extrapolations that have been promulgated by individuals and groups

369

who term themselves "futurists." Although not all the trends they foresee are directly relevant to counseling and counselors, they represent the future psychological, sociological, and organizational topography in which future clients will grow and develop and by which counseling and related mental health processes will be shaped, supported, and delivered.

The following sections will discuss some of the future trends to which counselors will need to become increasingly alert and informed and to which they will need to be able to respond. The chapter will conclude with specific recommendations for counselor function in the future.

Perspectives on Future Challenges

The Views of Oxford Analytica

Oxford Analytica is a multidisciplinary research and consulting firm based in Oxford, England, that engages in worldwide studies of stability and change for corporations and governments. For much of the 1980s this team of researchers and scholars has been engaged in seeking new insights and approaches to America's near-term future, particularly the 1990s. Under the sponsorship of three major U.S. corporations, Oxford Analytica has been engaged in formulating reliable projections of the social, economic, political, fiscal, and psychological trends that are likely to characterize American society into the 1990s and beyond. The results of these massive studies were distilled and released to the public in 1986 (Oxford Analytica, 1986). These projections, and the others examined later in the chapter, are not to be thought of as inevitable blueprints of the future, but rather as outlines of probabilities in selected areas of American life. The themes that follow do not include the full effects of international influences on America in the next decade nor of major changes in political ideology or policy. Obviously, either of these dimensions can alter the themes discussed dramatically. Nevertheless, the themes that follow are seen as concepts with continuity, as threads running out of the past into the future.

The eight themes of major importance to the United States in the rest of the century, according to Oxford Analytica, are the following:

1. The resilience of the American dream;
2. Diffusion;
3. Precarious conservatism;

4. Europeanization;
5. The household frontier;
6. A high-risk and high-stress society;
7. Limits of technological life; and
8. Testing confidence.

The combination of these themes brings together the seeds for new metaphors of American life, new visions of personal opportunity or constraints upon it. In the following sections some of the elements constituting these eight themes, their connections to other content discussed in this book, and the author's interpretation of the importance of these themes for counseling are identified.

The resilience of the American dream. Many observers of the United States have expressed concern that the vision of abundance, openness, and opportunity to which Americans have subscribed for 200 years is in its twilight. These observers assume that there will be significant decreases in the quality of life and that the standard of living the majority of Americans enjoy will soon erode under the pressures of the growing national debt, an aging population, and international competition. The researchers from Oxford Analytica suggest otherwise. They believe that the relative abundance of food and energy resources in America and the underlying drive and energy of the American enterprise system will enable the nation to adjust quickly and flexibly to the inevitable global economic and structural change likely to occur in the future. In economic terms, America is now more open to global forces and shifts than ever before in its history. This openness should continue to provide opportunity and economic viability, with only temporary problems, into the next century.

Another aspect of the resilience of the American dream lies with the continuing openness of the United States to immigration and to the absorption of immigrants into the mainstream of the United States. The levels of immigration to America are again approaching the numerical peaks that occurred in the great immigrant waves between 1900 and 1910. But whereas the major flow of immigrants at the beginning of this century was from Europe, the current waves of immigrants are predominantly from Hispanic countries—Mexico and Central and South America—and from Asia. As discussed in chapter 4, America is taking on a more Latino or Hispanic character in many parts of the nation. Spanish will be a major language of commerce and business; Hispanics are moving increasingly into the political structure at local, state, and national levels. These characteristics are likely to intensify in the future. Among many other possibilities, the growth and influence of Hispanic and Asian American groups in the United States will foster an increase in economic activity and other types of interaction with the nations of the Pacific basin and Latin America. The notion of America as a "melting pot" will be replaced by metaphors expressing pluralism and cultural diversity as the American reality.

Also of increasing interest to the resilience of the American dream is the rise in entrepreneurial behavior, self-employment, and the informal economy. Many of the recent immigrants to the United States are survivors of war, political conflict, or harsh economic conditions. They have learned to cope with such circumstances, support each other, and become self-reliant. They see America as a "second chance," and they have brought to it a renewed spirit of initiative, resourcefulness, and determination. "America's specialty has been to include foreigners, to welcome, to offer a chance. Labor shortage might account for some of this historic acceptance, but not the openness to foreign culture, a willingness to be influenced. America will remain the land where ideas, novelties, people can have another chance. Technology, sense of progress, size and complexion of the populace make it so for the next decade" (Oxford Analytica, 1986, p. 328).

In such a context, the increasing need for counselors to be bilingual and sensitive to cross-cultural needs is self-evident. So is the need for counselors to be brokers of training and encouragers of opportunity in many nontraditional areas of employment.

Diffusion. With the increasing waves of immigration and cultural pluralism, there is a growing likelihood of more fragmentation in politics, economic policy, and social characteristics. The roles of special interest groups will probably grow and replace the power traditionally ascribed to such social institutions as major political parties. Governing America and finding ways for government to meet the common needs of people will be more difficult. Deregulation in economic policies will continue to disperse power from governmental institutions to corporations and other private sector entities. Some historically governmental functions such as welfare, health, and education provisions may be increasingly decentralized to state and local units and possibly not performed at all in some parts of the nation. Such circumstances might exacerbate the social contrasts among different population groups and intensify the poverty of people now captured in its web. These conditions are likely to increase the need for self-help groups in local communities, for more attention to the possibilities within the informal economy, such as self-employment within the legal and illegal economies, and, perhaps, for structured community programs to provide specific training and guaranteed employment to people who would otherwise qualify for welfare. Because such people might have to deal with multiple barriers to employment—skill training, child care, management of resources, self-efficacy issues, becoming personally responsible in taking control of their life and family rather than depending on government programs—counselors and counseling are likely to become essential support elements.

Issues related to diffusion and fragmentation in personal lives will expand counselor roles as divorce, illegitimate births, demands of dual-career families, sexual choices, family configurations, and diverse social values increase as part of the culture. Although it can be argued that a "multiple option" society will increase creativity, liberation, and personal fulfillment, such a society will also increase confusion, alienation, stress, and the loss of purpose and judgment for many. As traditional values and behavioral anchors erode, many will feel adrift and find difficulty defining personal norms that are secure and satisfying. Counseling will be a valuable sanctuary and a process by which to sort out such feelings, clarify their meaning, establish reference points, and develop plans of action.

Precarious conservatism. According to the findings of Oxford Analytica, a deep stream of conservative values (e.g., retreat to the household, reaffirmation of the importance of personal and family success, personal fulfillment, security over change) characterizes large segments of the American population, particularly those numbered among the massive baby boom generation now approaching 40 years of age. Perhaps out of frustration, cynicism, anger, or sheer practicality, this group seems to be rejecting ideas of "big government" and its ability to solve major social problems. As a result, there is a turning inward to personal achievement, local programs, and the importance of the family as antidotes to what are perceived as governmental extravagances, wrong national priorities, falling national prestige, and the excesses of the counterculture. For members of the economic and social groups who share such convictions, counseling will be an important mechanism to help them clarify their commitment to family role integration, personal fulfillment, career paths that allow accommodation of parenting, and family achievement.

Europeanization. As America matures and moves into the next century, it is expected to acquire certain characteristics Americans typically think of as European. For example, smaller families are becoming the rule rather than the exception. The rural past of the United States is merging into the suburban and urban reality of contemporary America. Religious belief, as in Europe, may become more personal and less collective, and religious impulses may be transferred to substitutes such as traditions, culture, home, family, and the nation. On a structural level, running against the tide of a united European community are the continuing and strengthening national differences among European nations. Similarly, as was suggested strongly in chapter 4, in the United States regional differences in attitudes, resources, life styles, and occupations are becoming more visible. It is possible that those differences will be reflected in more clearly defined ethnic identities from region to region, differences in economic and political life, and divergent relationships with other nations or areas of the world: "The East will look to Europe, the Sunbelt to Latin America, and the West Coast to Asia and the Pacific rim" (Oxford Analytica, 1986, p. 334). Such trends may also be translated into the structural equivalent of "walled cities" where special groups are likely to seek protection, security, and the companionship of those like themselves: senior citizens, students, ethnic minorities, young married couples, the wealthy retired. Such enclaves might potentially harden class lines and reduce social mobility, although the resilience of the American vision of equal opportunity and access is not likely to permit widespread class consciousness.

Counseling in a context of growing Europeanization will probably require counselors themselves to be more specialized in the questions and developmental tasks of particular importance to special groups. Cross-cultural counseling may have increasingly important parallels in cross-generational and cross-socioeconomic status theory and practice.

The household frontier. Chapter 3 and other parts of this book have discussed at length the effects of the changing family structure in the United States, and chapter 2 has talked about the growing numbers of women in the labor force. Even so it is projected that the household, however it is defined, will become more central as a private world of support to develop and reaffirm values and to provide leisure and intimacy, and, indeed, as a center of part-time work as telecommuting by computer will permit working at home rather than going directly to the office or work place. There is as always a paradox. As the household increasingly becomes the center for activities that have typically occurred outside the home—paid work, entertainment, religion—increased stresses and strains among family members may arise as tensions develop from being so totally immersed in each other and the possibilities offered by the household.

In a somewhat different perspective, as the work place becomes sensitive to the total—not only the economic—needs of workers, it is likely that there will be more "home at work." For example, child care, health care, fitness programs, employer educational assistance programs, family counseling, and related programs will grow. These employment-based activities will blur the lines between home and work and personalize the work environment in new ways. Concern for the geographic transfer of family units and their adjustment to new regional or national cultures will become routine. Counseling and counselors will be central ingredients of such corporate strategies, and, outside of such settings, their importance will grow in response to the needs for family counseling and therapy.

High-risk and high-stress society. A United States in major transition in values, opportunities, work, family structures, cultural diversity, and political and social institutions is also a society of potentially great stress and strain within families, communities, and population groups. Although opportunities to choose may be greater for most, people are also likely to have to pay penalties for choosing wrongly or be traumatized into indecision or indecisiveness because of "overchoice" (Toffler, 1970). Toffler's "future shock" with its dilemmas of novelty, rapid change, frustration, and violence is now upon us, and its symptoms are obvious. As some ethnic groups resist assimilation into the national mainstream and regional differences in structural unemployment prevail, individual quests for fulfillment and achievement are likely to be frustrating and confusing. The increasing need for America to become a major player in the global economy is to risk giving away some control to achieve interdependence with others. Such conditions are likely to involve compromises that suggest confrontation and unease.

On the one hand, people seeking to relieve their personal anxiety are likely to generate various forms of social and political or collective tension. On the other hand, people who are highly stressed and unable to deal with the rapidity or magnitude of change or the shifting social and value systems are likely to be major consumers of mental health services of all kinds, including counseling.

Limits of technological life. As discussed in chapter 2, technology of many types has pervaded American life. The influence of technology has changed the content of the occupational structure and the way much of work is done. It has changed the effects of health care and altered personal longevity. Home entertainment, transportation, retailing and wholesaling, chemicals, agriculture and fishing, and manufacturing has each experienced dramatic modifications as technology has been introduced and adopted. Americans have frequently exhibited almost a "childlike" belief that know-how and technology can resolve any problem, keep the nation competitive, and deter economic and military aggression.

But, creeping into the national consciousness is ambivalence about some of the ethical and political dilemmas certain forms of technology pose (e.g., genetic engineering, "Star Wars"). Concern about ecological disasters like Chernobyl, Bhopal, and Three Mile Island have sobered and frightened many people about the price that needs to be paid for technological advances or international competitiveness. Such concerns—when added to the stresses and strains of individual worries about being swept up in a technological juggernaut that requires retraining, requires changes in personal identity, creates underemployment for some and unemployment for others, and potentially widens the gap between the rich and the poor and the skilled and the unskilled—creates an environment that is intensely psychological in its influence on personal responses.

Thus, the next decade or so is likely to test the limits of national and individual confidence in technological solutions to social, political, and human problems. Concerns about the economic insatiability of investment in technology, as well as concerns about whether the human price exacted by technological advancement is equalled or exceeded by the benefits derived, will be apparent at many levels of society.

Chapter 2 identified some of the ways counselors can engage the implications of advanced technology as they affect exploration of work, education and lifelong learning, work adjustment and retraining, and unemployment and underemployment. Within such areas, counseling is also likely to be important in helping people deal with their hopes for and skepticism of technology, their views of the life styles and habits generated by technology, and their worries about the limits to which technology can revitalize their future.

Testing confidence. As the United States moves through the multiple transitions described above, the level of confidence about the future of the nation, whether its institutions are working properly, and the security of its place in the global economy are likely to ebb and flow. The likelihood of blaming other nations, institutions, or elected leaders and the potential for internal conflict between subgroups of the population will be high. People will search for reassurance that existing problems can be fixed and that everything will ultimately come out all right. Counselors will have important roles in helping people identify the sources of the ambivalence, ennui, and uncertainty they experience, the steps they can take to create a more manageable environment, and the areas in which they can exert personal control.

Such challenges will require a large repertoire of counselor knowledge and skills that can be differentially applied to meet purposes of development, exploration, prevention, remediation, and treatment.

Megatrends

Another important projection of trends that are likely to characterize the United States during the rest of the 20th century are the forecasts of Naisbitt and his associates (1984; 1986). Because of the widespread popularity of the book, *Megatrends*, in which these forecasts were first published, many readers will undoubtedly be familiar with the content of these trends. Indeed, many of the trends identified are already established and their influence has already been identified in other parts of this book. Nevertheless, they are likely to continue to be important to counselors and to their clients and deserve brief elaboration here.

Basically, Naisbitt described 10 transformations that are now occurring in American society. Each of these transformations speaks to the context in which job paths, educational content, and interpersonal circumstances are likely to be shaped and sustained. In many cases these transformations have been ongoing for 30 years or more, but their subtle influence has become more visible and powerful as they have become more pervasive in the society. Using the headings by which Naisbitt describes his transformations, shifts, or trends, the following discussion will connect these to other parts of the book and to some implications for counseling.

From an industrial society to an information society. As suggested in chapter 2, both agriculture and industry continue to be extremely important to the American occupational structure, but both sectors are increasingly influenced by the adaptation of advanced or high technology to their processes and technical content. More importantly, perhaps, these changes reflect an economy built on information generation and application rather than on the production of goods per se. Even within the rapid rise of so-called "service jobs" in the economy, most of the new jobs created are concerned with the creation, processing, and distribution of information. In contrast to 1950, when about 17% of Americans worked in information jobs, in 1984 more than 65% of the American labor force was involved with "information work" as programmers, teachers, clerks, secretaries, accountants, stockbrokers, managers, insurance agents, bureaucrats, lawyers, bankers, technicians, and those in information jobs in manufacturing companies.

From forced technology to high tech/high touch. Naisbitt's basic point in this transformation is that "whenever new technology is introduced into society, there must be a counterbalancing human response—that is, *high touch*—or the technology is rejected. The more high tech, the more high touch" (Naisbitt, 1984, p. 35). In essence, the pervasive application of technology in the work place and in the home can lead to feelings or forms of interpersonal isolation to which people react negatively. In response, people seek new ways of being with others, bringing a personal touch to their environment, and finding interpersonal contact. As "high technology" tends to invade more sections of work life and the home, people tend to expend more energy in spirituality, religious orientations, and ways to expand their personal human potential. They seek new forms of leisure that allow the use of hands and bodies, physical activity, to balance the constant use of mental energies work and many other daily routines require.

From a national economy to a world economy. The United States is no longer the only dominant player in the world economy. We do not include within our continental borders the tools, physical plants, or labor to maintain industrial supremacy. Instead, the United States has become an interdependent player in a world economy in which Japan, Europe, and many Third World nations each participates in increasingly strong, decisive, and vital ways. As most of the major industrial nations are deindustrializing as part of their movement into an information society, they are shifting durable goods production—steelmaking, shipbuilding, automotive manufacture—to other less developed nations—South Korea, Brazil, Taiwan, Singapore, Hong Kong—that are now entering major cycles of economic growth. Major manufacturers of electronic products and automobiles, for example, are entering into new cooperative arrangements and joint ventures that are increasing the tendency to globalize specific forms of production. Different national groups are contributing different pieces of a finished product that may appear under the label of a U.S. or Japanese corporation but, in fact, is the hybridization or production sharing of many national efforts in providing raw material, design, assembly, and distribution.

Although the globalization of the economy has many ramifications, at the very least it will reinforce the importance of more Americans becoming bilingual or trilingual if they are to be fully successful in business and industry or in government. It will also require a modification of the vision of America's place in world society as portrayed in education at all levels. The sense of individual identity promoted by social institutions in the United States will need to be increasingly oriented to Americans' place in a world order, not simply confined to a domestic or nationalistic view. From a counseling perspective, the need for cross-cultural understanding and sensitivity will be a growing imperative.

From short term to long term. American institutions of all types— business, education, government—will need to adopt a longer term plan to achieve their goals. Seeking short-term rewards to the long-term detriment of results, whether in terms of profit-taking or character-building or the nurturance of personal commitment and responsibility, is inconsistent with international trends in long-range planning. The needs for systematic and continuing research and development, risk taking, and viewing problems in whole terms will require people who are generalists, who are able to see the big picture, who understand and accept change, and who can be secure with systematic planning to change their priorities and techniques to keep pace with a shifting environment. People and institutions will need to be able to rethink their roles and to reintegrate new visions of themselves in a form of dynamic equilibrium, a sense that their core values remain intact but that their application needs to be reconceptualized in an environment of inevitable change.

From centralization to decentralization. Corporate structures of all types are moving from power concentrated in a home office or central group of executives to more decentralized networks of power and control. Career paths and career mobility are being altered, flattened out, and are less hierarchical in their patterns. Business and industry tends to be downsizing its physical plants and dispersing them geographically. Part of this diffusion is a function of the changing types of work to be done. Information production, generation, and distribution, for example, do not require the massive capital investment and raw materials that steelmaking does. Therefore, the work sites can be smaller and more diffusely located. In addition, communication links from site to site or nation to nation can be so instantaneous as to substitute for the need for consolidating all activity and power in one geographical area. In government, the political principles embodied in the presidential administrations since 1980 have contended that big government is wasteful, inefficient, and essentially anathema to the American notions of democracy, local control, and citizen participation in the political process. Within such contexts, the characteristics of leadership are being redefined and more locally applied; political power has and is shifting from the national government to the states, cities, and small towns. These entities, by default or intent, are dealing with the social issues of local concern and empowering the types of services and specialists needed to respond to those issues. One result is increased diversity and unevenness across the nation in the character and content of opportunity, life styles, and services available. National standards and mandates erode in favor of more regionally tailored and delivered policies and practices.

As suggested in chapter 4, the regional differences apparent in the United States in traditions, attitudes, and ethnicity have not yet been integrated into perspectives on cross-cultural counseling, but the transformation of centralization to decentralization in political power, economics, job availability, and related phenomena is relevant to this issue. One can foresee that current attempts to strengthen the national credentialing processes for counselors and accreditation of counselor preparation programs is running against a national tide of sentiment for more state and local control of such matters. On the other hand, decentralization of people and power from urban areas to suburbs, small towns, rural areas, and across the nation also may spread certain problems across wider populations: how to choose from more diverse opportunities and life styles, how to rationalize the availability of poorer education in a particular geographical area with less stress on children and families, how to acquire skills and access to make a difference at a particular local level, how to find outlets or remedies for the feelings of isolation occasioned by working on a computer terminal at home or from moving from an urban to a rural area, or how to learn the ways regional values and transitions in one geographical location differ from those one has now left. In their own way, these issues may be the antecedents of new forms of stress or information deficits likely to become the concerns for many counselors.

From institutional help to self-help. As institutional decentralization tends to energize local control and management of social problems rather than dependence on remote and large collective institutions, there seems to be a parallel in a revitalization of self-reliance in individuals. Rather than being passive bystanders dependent on government or specialists, more people are taking personal responsibility for their own health, well-being, education, sense of self-worth, and social contacts. Self-help is apparent in virtually all areas of life. More people are concerned about fitness, wellness, controlling personal habits, the integration of mind and body, natural birth, and the rejection of medical technology that prolongs life in favor of the acceptance of death and its management in hospices. More support groups and, in essence, peer counseling are emerging as people attempt to cope with and master issues related to mental health problems, retirement, obesity, alcohol and substance abuse, divorce, grief, and loss. Obviously, such trends affect how counselors as professionals and counseling as a process are being seen and used by those seeking help. As chapter 5 suggested, counseling is becoming briefer, more goal oriented, and increasingly directed to specific skill development through the use of psychoeducational models. Counselors and clients are engaging in more collaborative definition of problems and needs for treatment. Moreover, clients are participating more actively in their own treatment and in the use of homework and self-directed materials to augment and perhaps accelerate the insights and planning gained from counseling.

From representative democracy to participatory democracy. Basically, the people of the United States are pushing for and gaining increased participation in all sectors of life. Quality circles and worker teams are engaging in planning for increased productivity, better quality, and mutual problem solving in the work place. Husbands and wives are participating on a more equal basis in parenting, in covering household chores, and in other facets of marriage and family development. Local citizens are participating more fully in the decisions affecting the quality of life, taxes, and other political issues important to them. Simply electing representatives and then turning over political or economic decisions to them without any participation is eroding in favor of more individual involvement. Individuals are becoming independent and assertive about their needs and the responses they seek to these needs. Consumer rights groups, activism in the church and other social institutions, and employee-rights advocacy is each a part of the transformation from representation to participation. In such contexts, leadership cannot be autocratic, tyrannical, aloof—it must be facilitative. In the same sense, counseling must be facilitative and collaborative, a maximizer of opportunity, not a cold and distant evaluator and interpreter.

From hierarchies to networking. In traditional work organizations, the metaphor of "getting to the top" is a symbol of achievement and success. In the emerging work environments, the pyramidal hierarchy is becoming increasingly viewed with disdain as inefficient, ineffective, and out of step with an information economy. Indeed, bureaucracies and hierarchies tend to stifle information flow and the quick decisions that reflect the instantaneous communication now available in work settings, political structures, and other social institutions. Emerging in the place of hierarchies is networking, structures by which people can share information and resources in rapid and more egalitarian ways. Power is shifting to a more participative structure away from a centralized form. The leadership of such organizations needs to be facilitative, not controlling.

There are a number of implications for counseling in such transformations. One is that people considering preparing for or entering occupations may be well advised that career paths in the future may not be vertical but horizontal. In other words, as hierarchical pyramids are flattened out and decentralized, fewer people will move to the top of some executive form of leadership, and more people will move across work clusters to facilitate problem solving and planning in decentralized forms of facilitative leadership. The latter type of leader is less likely to be narrowly trained as a technical specialist and more likely to be a generalist who is able to see problems whole, reason, and facilitate the participatory problem solving. In such a situation, the assessment challenge for counselors is not how to identify the maximum levels of performance of which a person is capable, as measured, for example, by aptitude tests. Rather it is to assess how capable a person is of behavior that can be described as evidencing "complementarity," facilitation of groups of people and empowering them to participate and give their personal best to a project, as measured, for example, by interpersonal and communication skills.

From North to South. By the beginning of the 1980s, the regional differences of the United States about which remarks have been made in several other places in this book were also changing in dramatic ways regarding population and economic activity. By 1980, for the first time in American history, the South and the West combined had a larger population than the North and the East. A similar result was found in the location of wealth and economic activity. In relative terms, these two indicators had shifted from North to South. The result is regional differences in the number and types of jobs created, unevenness in opportunity, economic decline in many parts of the North and East while the South and West were in an economic boom; crises in the availability of infrastructures (water, sewer, roads), education, and other services available to meet the burgeoning populations in the South and West. These shifts, because of migration, redefined where the largest percentages (although not the largest numbers) of the best educated of the population live (the West). The decaying of outdated industrial plants and warehousing facilities in many of the old industrial cities of the North and East contrasted with an explosion of "sunrise" corporations (e.g., electronics, information generation and distribution, customized manufacturing) in the South and West, a shifting of the young in search of jobs from the Northeast to the Southwest with older, less mobile, less educated populations remaining in the Northeast. The problems that these shifts entail for counselors in the different regions of the nation are not clear, but at the least they suggest important issues of career planning, cultural adjustment, family counseling, and preretirement and retirement planning.

From either/or to multiple option. In the United States as it is emerging there are few dichotomies—either one thing or the other—in the choices available to people. As indicated in chapter 3, family structures are increasing in number and type. In chapter 4, we talked about the expanding range of cultural diversity in the country. In chapter 5, we talked about the range of risk factors in the society. In chapter 2, we discussed the major shifts in the occupational structure. Whether in religion, education, work, or self-expression, the options available to youths and adults in America are wide, accessible, and virtually unencumbered by values of good or bad. However, such a multiple-option society also poses problems of overchoice, ambiguity, and information deficits for many. Sorting these out and matching the possibilities to individuals' levels of interest, commitment, ability, and values is a major counseling challenge.

Implications for Counselors of Emerging Challenges

The perspectives of "futurists" about the projected characteristics of American institutions, people, and resources could be extended into a multivolume set of books. The two major sets of trends identified here, however, are sufficient to make the point that has been reiterated throughout this book: The content of counseling and its importance is a function of political, social, and economic events in the larger society. The effects of these events—whether psychological or literal—upon individuals may shape the questions of self-efficacy, purposefulness, social value, access, and performance with which counselors must be prepared to deal. Given such a reality, it is obvious that counselors cannot be "encapsulated" (Wrenn, 1962) by a limited understanding of the contexts, images, events, or cultural traditions within which people negotiate their identity, security, and goals and, in some instances, find themselves "at risk." Counselors must be able to help clients separate the general effects of events from their specific effects, if any, on themselves as individuals. They must help clients anticipate the timing and the meaning of their experiences and of plans of action to modify or strengthen their ability to deal with such matters.

A decade ago, several observers began to apply "futuristic perspectives" to the changing place of counselors in society and to the emerging social images from which these changes would be derived. For example, Walz and Benjamin (1979) suggested several emerging images of the behavioral and social consequences of change that had particular meaning for counselors. They saw these as "beacons of future developments and as priorities which may be instrumental in shaping future counselor roles and functions" (p. 8). Many of these perspectives have become increasingly likely as the past decade has unfolded. They include the following, with some updated commentary by the author of this book:

- *Individuals will place an emphasis on role before goal.* The essence of this image is that in a society with the intense psychological quality of contemporary America, individuals are increasingly likely to give primary priority to finding themselves as human beings and seeking to clarify their own personal identity before identifying their goals or professional identity. Such a perspective seems to be consonant with the growing development of self-help materials and groups, the quest for lifelong learning opportunities, and the attention to personal fitness and control that seem to describe many people in the American society. Issues of role integration, blurring of sex-related division of labor or education, and balance in family life, leisure, and commitment to work each suggests that many Americans in the 1980s are intensifying their attention to who they are, who they want to be, and how to exert as much control as possible given the instability of a changing world.

- *Hostility, polarization, and aggression will become more commonplace.* Fortunately these societal situations have not become generalized across communities and states in the past 10 years. It is clear, however, that many occasions can be cited to suggest that hostility, polarization, and aggression are only slightly below the surface in many localities and present dangers in some urban areas. Gang wars, racially inspired violence, and other forms of prejudice and discrimination symbolize the psychological economic realities with which many Americans live on a daily basis. They reflect feelings of need to protect "me and mine," to fend off perceived incursions by other groups into what is already a fragile economic situation, and "to do unto others before they do unto me." For many swept up in such environments, counselors will be engaged, on the one hand, in conflict resolution, and, on the other, in dealing with people whose priorities are personal satisfaction and survival rather than contributing to a more abstract "common good" or even achievement as defined in broad social terms.

- *Knowledge will become the most eagerly sought-after resource of the future.* As suggested in many parts of this book, the United States is in transition from an economy and an occupational structure based on industrialization and the production of goods to one based on the generation, distribution, and application of information. Some 65% of jobs in the American work force now deal with information as a major aspect of the work content. Obviously, then, the wedding of science and technology, which is a central aspect of the American economy, has also made knowledge, trainability, ability to retrieve and use information, and lifelong learning essential elements of work access and mobility. For those not interested in or prepared to deal with these realities, opportunities for work will shrink in demand and in reward. The role of counselors will increase, not only in schools, but in other contexts as specialists who help people with educational planning, analyzing and engaging in retraining programs, anticipating needs for remediation of skill deficits, and keeping their career options open as long as possible through deliberate choices of curriculum and course content with the greatest elasticity.

- *The transitional dynamics in personal and social change will increase in importance.* The American society, as are most of the world's nations, is in the process of major transformation of its social and economic institutions and probably in its national metaphors. Change swirls throughout the society and pervades all of the systems, from the macrolevel to the microlevel, with which individuals interact. Although this comprehensiveness of change is inevitable and, indeed, in a conceptual sense understandable, it also generates feelings of stress, anxiety, uncertainty, and information deficits in individuals and organizations. Thus, counselors increasingly need to be able to understand and interpret change processes, the characteristics of and intervention in crises and transition, and the procedures for planned choice and planned change.

- *Attitudes and values in relation to work will change.* Interestingly, a decade ago, it was assumed by many, including Walz and Benjamin (1979), that the midterm future would bring an increasingly jobless society. It was assumed that within 20 years 15% of the population would be able to provide all of the necessary goods and services for the total population. As this book is being written, we are only halfway through the midterm future that Walz and Benjamin were projecting in 1979, but rather than being in the throes of a jobless society, there has been a continuous decrease in unemployment. The rate in late 1988, 5.3%, is one of the lowest since World War II. Rather than joblessness, there seems to be, as described in chapter 2, a continuing movement from agriculture and manufacturing to service; there is lower unemployment but higher underemployment; those who are unemployed tend to have the most jagged employment histories and multiple problems that require comprehensive remediation; the United States has a new and less dominant role in the global economy, but one that creates employment opportunities for workers, although they may not be as good or well paid as the jobs that have been eliminated; and the demographics of a smaller youth cohort entering the labor force permits other population groups (e.g., immigrants, women, older people) to find employment with less competition than is true in a time of a population bulge. The implications of many of these trends for counselors have been discussed elsewhere in this book and will not be repeated here. It remains clear, however, that changes in attitudes and values in relation to work as well as in the content of work available will be major issues for counselors as they deal with youth in the process of exploration and preparation for work, with adults contemplating retraining and midcareer change, with dislocated workers who are unemployed because of structural changes in their work, with women intending to reenter the work force, with dual-career couples deciding on how to synchronize the best opportunities for each partner, or with immigrants trying to gain entrance into the American work force.

- *Depersonalization will be a common response to viewing the future.* Depersonalization in the face of change can take many forms. One is acting as though it will not affect the individual personally and therefore does not require planning for change. Depersonalization might also mean withdrawing into an insular existence with interpersonal contacts limited to people who share one's views. Counselors in a depersonalized world need to help people find relationships between external events and personal plans of action that are as accurate as possible and that reinforce personal control. In the case of other forms of depersonalization, counselors can help people to connect with self-help, support systems, and volunteer opportunities that allow them to reach out, be less insulated, and gain increased sensitivity to the needs and aspirations of other people for communication and social interaction.

- *Future images act to control present behaviors.* Walz and Benjamin suggested in 1979 that one's view of the future "can have a direct effect on how one behaves in the present" (p. 13). That insight has been reinforced in the past decade as the growth of cognitive psychology has acknowledged that feelings and actions follow one's thoughts about a situation. Therefore, if individuals believe that they can master the challenges of the future, they are likely to attempt to understand the emerging trends and opportunities as the bases for personal plans. If they think that the future is frightening and beyond their ability to cope, they are unlikely to plan for it. Such people are likely to seek immediate, short-term gratification rather than longer term gain and to behave as though life were a function of external control and fate rather than a context in which they can maximize an internal locus of control or develop an evaluative center from which to define opportunities for choice and personal action. In such situations counselors will need to be able to teach people about planning, about the relationships between the future images they hold and current behavior, and about general coping skills that can be used to anticipate and deal with both potential problems and potential opportunities in the future.

In response to the seven topical areas Walz and Benjamin identified in 1979, they suggested four roles counselors could play in "helping individuals to create a future that is positive both for the person and for society" (p. 15). The four roles in paraphrased form are:

- *Facilitator of caring and sharing.* Counselors can help people strengthen their own sense of self-worth and the need to achieve that self-concept through expressing their interdependence, caring for, and sharing with others.
- *Facilitator of life transitions.* Counselors increasingly will be called upon to assist individuals understand and acquire the skills by which to move in and out of different life roles and activities.
- *Broker of vital information.* Counselors will be sought out as "resource linkers," professionals who can help people locate, interpret, and use information and data relevant to their specific

needs and interests and who can help them implement a systematic decision-making process.

- *Facilitator of change.* Counselors can assist people to "acquire the skills of effective change agents, to be authors of change rather than passive or frantic responders to it. Specifically, they can help their clients to develop criteria for identifying when a change is needed, to learn a process for making the change happen, and to develop guidelines for determining whether the change is a successful and adequate response to their particular needs and wants" (p. 17).

One can use other terms such as "maximizer of resources" or "broker of opportunity" or "facilitator of self-actualization" to describe images to which counselors might aspire. However, when combined with the array of central challenges portrayed in this book—the effects of advanced technology and a changing economic climate, a shifting family structure, rising cultural diversity, and growing concerns about "at risk" conditions among youth and adults—the essence of the counselor roles projected by Walz and Benjamin a decade ago—facilitator of caring and sharing, life transitions, and change, and broker of vital information— continues to have currency as the content of a metaphor counselors can embrace as they turn their vision to the 21st century.

If such counselor roles are to become a reality across settings and populations, however, they must be reflected in a national agenda of research, professional, and legislative action that was outlined in 1979 (Herr & Pinson, 1979). This agenda remains incomplete and is in need of a comprehensive reevaluation. The issues for the profession of counseling, now as then, continue to include planning needs, shifting concepts of professional identity and practice, and the importance of cooperation and deliberate networking of related groups of professionals (e.g., school, employment, mental health, rehabilitation, counselor, marriage, and family therapists; social workers; and members of the psychiatric community) to create a mental health delivery system that defines credentialing mechanisms that are inclusive and oriented to the quality of the competence of each of these groups to provide services, prevention, promotion, development, remediation, and treatment—across the spectrum from mental disorder to mental wellness.

Conclusions

The future challenges for counselors are diverse and, in some cases, vague, but they are rooted in the multiple social, economic, and political transformations that the United States is now undergoing. These structural, regional, sociological, and psychological changes are likely to have different effects on different groups in the society, and the timing and intensity of such changes are not fully predictable. Even so, counselors cannot be insular or encapsulated within limited models of individual-environment transactions. They must develop for themselves a "meta-language" of likely change in the various environments their clients occupy (family, work, social, leisure, educational, training), an understanding of how people may be affected by such changes, and how they can behave to make the best of the options available. Counselors will need to help people understand that they can be instrumental in creating "reality" for themselves if they are aware of the available options, the tangible and intangible investments required, as well as the risks and commitments of which they are personally capable.

Counselors must also be attentive to the constant refinements and reformulations of the possible interventions in client behavior they might use for different categories of presenting problems, and to the changing insights into behavior that continually emerge. Both the repertoire of treatment-problem interactions and the available conceptualization of different expressions of behavior are dynamic. They change as understandings of stressors, risk factors, physiological deficits, or psychosocial influences change. New interventions emerge as research on cognitive structures, value systems, and information processing mechanisms is linked to experimental evidence showing how and under what conditions these structures, systems, or mechanisms can be modified.

Perhaps, in the last analysis, the ultimate challenge to counselors will be that of continuing self-definition as professionals, commitment to lifelong learning to constantly hone and add to their competencies, and the willingness to read widely and experience life fully to stay current with the trends and conceptual models that signal the need for and the processes of behavioral change. The future will require that counselors sharpen their professional self-concepts as applied behavioral scientists, as technologists, as program planners, as facilitators of caring and sharing, and as maximizers of opportunity for others. Counselors of the future will need to think much more conceptually about the outcomes and results they can and do achieve rather than confining themselves to implementing a set of processes and services without a clear sense of the behavioral outcomes they intend to produce. In the future, counselors will need to give more attention to who they are and the influence they have as professionals in a nation of growing pluralism, changing family structures, shifting work conditions and technostress, as well as a society abundant in risk factors and conditions that create personal vulnerability.

References

Herr, E.L., & Pinson, N. (Eds.). (1982). *Foundations for policy in guidance and counseling*. Falls Church, VA: American Personnel and Guidance Association.

Kiunick, H.Q. (1985). Disability and psychosocial development in old age. *Rehabilitation Counseling Bulletin, 29*(2), 123–134.

Naisbitt, J. (1984). *Megatrends: Ten new directions transforming our lives*. New York: Warner Books.

Naisbitt, J., & the Naisbitt Group. (1986). *The year ahead 1986; Ten powerful trends shaping your future*. New York: Warner Books.

Oxford Analytica. (1986). *America in perspective: Major trends in the United States through the 1990s*. Boston: Houghton Mifflin.

Toffler, A. (1970). *Future shock*. New York: Bantam Books.

Walz, G.R., & Benjamin, L. (1979). *A futuristic perspective for counselors*. Ann Arbor, MI: The University of Michigan, ERIC Counseling and Personnel Services Clearinghouse.

Wrenn, G.G. (1962). *The counselor in a changing world*. Washington, DC: APGA Press.

APPENDIX

Trends in Science and Their Technological Applications

As described in 1985, the "25 discoveries that could change our lives" include the following (Science 85, 1985, pp. 2–3).

Biomedical Science

Biology of birth—Scientists are exploring the cytoplasm of maternal molecules and the interaction of the egg with the sperm. As a result, information is accruing about how fertilization occurs and how it malfunctions.

Egg development—Genetic mapping of the egg is performed as the egg is transformed into an organism. Based upon embryology, molecular biology, developmental biology, and genetics, scientists are researching the "fate map," the sequence of switches or triggers that cause a single fertilized egg to become the complex and multidimensional organism that represents the diversity of life.

Gene therapy—A so-called third revolution in medicine, after the first in the 19th century when physicians stopped bleeding, purging, and blistering sick patients, and the second in this century when physicians were enabled to cure some infectious diseases with antibiotics, the third revolution requires "the mapping, cloning, and studying of thousands of human genes to understand the body's normal functions at the molecular level" (Anderson, 1985, p. 49). As a result, the practice of medicine will become more precise as physicians should be able to treat many disorders by inserting a normal gene into the cells of a patient. Obviously, many empirical, ethical, and religious questions accompany such scientific breakthroughs as diseases that require and are amenable to gene therapy are identified and treated.

Drug therapy—Through the use of recombinant DNA joined with genes from different species in units called recombinant plasmids, scientists can program the synthesis of a variety of therapeutic proteins to make vaccines and other agents from sources other than human plasma. A further approach to drug therapy is the creation of monoclonal antibodies, antibodies that come from white blood cells primed by foreign substances for use in inactivating viruses that cause some diseases or for diagnosing infectious diseases.

Farm productivity—Genetic engineering, plant breeding, and the insertion of one or two genes from one organism into another are increasingly producing plants that resist major diseases and some insect pests. Scientists are working to enhance the desirable characteristics of plants such as drought resistance on poor farmland, increased nutritional quality, and changing growth cycles to provide more crop yields per growing season, and to produce plants useful in the chemical industries and for fuel.

Creating cancer—In efforts to decipher the sequence of cellular processes that are shortcircuited in cancer or result from mutations in genetic material, scientists are creating cancers in order to understand what causes them (e.g., viruses, proteins, genes) and how to develop treatments.

Replacement body parts—As a function of activity and longer life expectancy, a large number of people experience arthritis and other musculoskeletal problems. Increasingly the treatment is joint replacement or other forms of orthopedic implants. Such treatments involve many scientific and technological breakthroughs. They involve the modeling of necessary joint replacements through the use of special three-dimensional computer graphics and radiographic techniques. They also involve the combination of super-strength composite materials such as velours or carbon fibers (which can be manufactured to tailored specifications quickly in the hospital), special cements, and other techniques to develop the implant, as well as the use of microcomputers to guide robotic surgery to precisely locate the implant. In addition such approaches will include finding new ways to use the body's ability to heal so that natural tissue and implants can grow together or certain body parts may be naturally regenerated. Also, this blend of science and technology might enable implanting computer-driven prostheses into the body to reduce the paralysis caused by spinal cord injuries and increase mobility, stimulate muscles, or provide other forms of treatment. Such computer-driven prostheses would move limbs or provide energy or signals to various parts of the body to initiate action.

Physical Science

Space and matter—Physicists are now engaged in revising the theory of gravity and integrating it with quantum mechanics. Such an effort is part of a larger effort to create a unified field theory from all that is known about the fundamental forces of nature. Another new perspective, the Superstring Theory, includes the possibility that space is composed of nine dimensions rather than three, and that the geometry of space and matter is more complex than current theories suggest.

Space telescope—The new Hubble space telescope placed in orbit gives astronomers the capability to look deeper into space and therefore into time. The astronomer will be able to see galaxies as they were billions of years ago, compare new ones with old ones to see how they form and change, more accurately measure distances from earth to other galaxies as a way to measure the size and age of the universe, better understand the composition of the variety of astral bodies in space, study how stars form and develop, and conduct other inquiries of interest to space travel and related phenomena.

Quarks—Quarks are subatomic elements of protons, one of the most elementary forms of matter, and are important ingredients of the building blocks of matter in the universe. To understand the variety and role of quarks, extraordinarily high levels of energy are required to reveal their form and substance. This will be one of the roles of the Superconducting Super Collider to be built in the near future. A giant circular underground tunnel up to 60 miles in circumference, the SSC will allow proton beams to be brought together to collide head on at near the speed of light. This will release incredible amounts of energy to drive extraordinarily powerful electron microscopes and will enable the study of matter 40 trillion times smaller than a human hair.

Evolutionary Science

Evolutionary revolution—Scientists are rapidly calling into question several of the basic notions that underlie Darwinian concepts of evolution. Traditionally species have been thought to evolve over time, moving toward species perfection and adapting to their environments through survival of the fittest members of the species. Implicit in such a perspective is linear and gradual change toward optimal adaptation to environmental change. Current studies suggest that such a view is flawed. Fossil data, according to Bakker (1985) and others, suggest that species in general resist change even when habitats change. These scientists are suggesting that adaptive evolution is a rare event even when such structural modifications would make a species better fitted to environmental needs. Thus, species frequently operate at a suboptimal level for long periods of time. New perspectives suggest that adaptive change occurs abruptly in episodes created by the immigration of other, better adapted species into a habitat, or that a new daughter species suddenly buds off from an isolated population of the parent. Then the newer, daughter species tends to spread and exterminate the parent over most of its range. In such a view, "long-term evolutionary trends aren't produced by continuous adaptive honing of one evolving lineage; rather they are produced by pruning away entire species—the daughter, granddaughter, and great-granddaughter—so that the best applied species survive the longest and bud off the greatest number of new species" (Bakker, p. 74). Bakker (p. 80) suggested that these findings in evolutionary science have several implications for changing views of nature:

> The surgeon ought not to assume that the healthy human organ is the optimal piece of machinery that could be designed for its task. Environmentalists shouldn't assume that every habitat is a perfect and fragile balance of irreplaceable species. And the eugenicists are simply dead wrong when they think that selective breeding can produce a better human race—evolution is too rare an event.

Evolutionary biology—In addition to studying changes in species through fossil records, geneticists are attempting to learn about evolution and the differences between species by studying differences in their genes. How and which genes cause different species to look different or to behave differently? Why do species that look alike have different genetic characteristics? How many and which genes need to be manipulated in a species to produce a new species or to change the traits of that species? What are the practical effects of transferring genes between species to improve the productivity of animals or plants for foods or for other commercial benefits?

Mathematics

Experimental mathematics—Given the capability of computers to visually or graphically display geometric or mathematical formulae, the science of mathematics has become increasingly experimental. As a result, mathematical approaches have increased in their intent to explain dynamical systems—electrical fields, quantum theory—that evolve in a well-defined way over time. Such systems are linear, cause and effects are identifiable, and they are generally amenable to precise mathematical analyses. Experimental mathematics are also being applied to nonlinear dynamical systems—weather, fluid dynamics. Although cause and effect for these systems is also known, they are functions of such contingent factors that they are less predictable, but theoretical progress is being made. One such new breakthrough in experimental mathematics is the use of "fractals," geometric constructs that can model clouds, the topography of a mountain, and other aspects of nature through mathematical equations that can be converted into computer graphics, permitting the scientist to test various theoretical propositions. Obviously in such circumstances, as new computer programs are developed and as attempts move forward to make mathematics understandable to computers, new mathematical concepts and better algorithms result.

Geometry unbound—As scientists continue to probe the mysteries of space and of nature, the levels of abstraction increase. In response, new notions of geometry, dimensionality, and mathematical formulation need to be developed. To this end, added to the traditional concepts of three dimensions of space and one of time, is a new kind of space-time called superspace with its own form of geometry called supergeometry. Such notions are being used to probe the beginnings of the universe when space-time, matter, and energy were all a single state with such symmetry that mathematicians and other scientists view it as supersymmetry. They are now able to construct mathematical models of that world, of the dimensions that composed it, and of the forces that have changed it. As such conceptualizations occur and are applied to other phenomena, hidden symmetry becomes apparent in physics and in number theory that may in time lead to other manifestations of the knowledge of supersymmetry in the universe (Manin, 1985).

Neuroscience

Biochemistry and behavior—Researchers studying the links between genes, cellular and molecular biology, brain chemistry, and behavior are beginning to map the origins and mechanisms that trigger or sustain our most basic emotions, drives, and behaviors from the level of genes and molecules to specific nerve circuits and brain systems. They are finding biological underpinnings of thirst, hunger, pleasure, pain, stress, sexual arousal, and learning (Baskin, 1985). As this research unfolds, scientists are examining the interactions of nerve cells, hormones, transmitters and receptors, genes, neuropeptides, and the circuitry and the chemistry of brain organs to further their understanding of questions such as: What are the chemical thresholds and how are they set/reset for pain, pleasure, depression, anger, or even memory? Do people differ in their biochemistry relative to their susceptibility to stress or anxiety or depression? Are hormonal states flexible or stable? As such questions are addressed, treatments emerge that can affect individual behavior to enhance certain types of outcomes (e.g., memory) and inhibit others (e.g., depression, aggression). These treatments may stimulate the alteration of the individual's physiology to heal or otherwise behave more effectively, or to use drugs that can treat mental illness by mimicking or blocking natural transmitters. At the very least, as such understandings about the brain and behavior unfold, they have the potential to modify the practice or even the likelihood of the use of psychotherapy in certain mental disorders that are basically organic or chemical in their etiology and structure.

Brain drugs—As the chemical and neural mysteries of the brain are plumbed, drugs follow to address neurological or psychiatric problems. Drugs such as monoamine-related drugs can correct the responsiveness of transmissions within the nervous system even when it is not the original cause of the problem. Other drugs work directly on the transmitters or hormones that inappropriately trigger the endocrine system or cause hypertension. Molecular biology is identifying the causes of inherited disorders, isolating gene defects, screening susceptible individuals, and informing them of environmental factors that can be modified to ease the condition or providing direct treatment through some form of gene therapy. In the future, it is expected that "the combination of chemical, physiological, and psychological diagnostic tests could define—and perhaps alter—the limits of an individual's stress tolerance and help clarify the role of the brain in causing diseases now attributed to cancer or heart and lung problems" (Bloom, 1985, p. 101).

Included among the 25 discoveries suggested are several that are more directly technological. They include the following:

Parallel computers—Concurrent or parallel computers is not a new idea. However, to date, most computers, even the so-called supercomputers that can make millions of arithmetical operations per second, have operated as single units. Indeed, some scientists believe that as fast as they now are, these high-speed computers have about reached the limits of their speed and capability. The alternative is to figuratively start over with computer technology by redesigning their structures and capabilities. One way to do this is to create a machine with multiple processors (computers) that are able to work simultaneously on many different parts of a complex task to reduce the total solution time. The process involved would actually "rip a problem to shreds, deal one piece to each of hundreds or thousands of processing units that will chew away simultaneously, and spit the answer out in a fraction of the time of today's machines. It will be the computational equivalent of barn raising" (West, 1985, p. 102).

Although today's minicomputers used in business are frequently networked in such a way that they shift back and forth between tasks very quickly or they vectorize, perform identical operations on a large list of similar tasks or different data very quickly, computer scientists now believe it is less expensive to have a large number of less powerful processors working at the same time on a problem that has been divided into as many parts as possible. In essence, each processor would be assigned a single operation. There is much work yet to be done on the architecture and use of parallel computers, but the time when a billion calculations per second are possible is not far away.

Fiber optics—The use of lightwave communications through glass fibers rather than traditional electrical, electronic, or radio transmission has increased communication speed and bandwidth dramatically in the past 10 or so years. Currently, optical technology is moving to include collections of light wave modules on a single fiber that is also integrated with microcircuit chips. "If the capacities of optical fibers were fully exploited, the entire present telephone voice traffic in the United States could be carried on a single fiber. The contents of the Library of Congress could be transmitted in a few seconds" (Lucky, 1985, p. 112). The potential of this technology in the home and the work place has not yet begun to be exploited, but it will revolutionize communication and information processing, television delivery, two-way video-telephones, and many other applications as the economics of fiber optics catch up with technology.

Space transportation—Although the space shuttle has become familiar as a means of carrying equipment, satellites, and people into space, it is a very costly venture. The amount of propellant to get it into space is 85% of its lift-off weight, thus reducing the size of its payload to 1.5% of that weight. In the future, the economics of such a situation require other solutions. Among them are new propulsion systems such as solar power, electric and magnetic thrusts, and nuclear power. Also possible are larger but less complex vehicles made of extremely light, advanced structural materials (aluminum-lithium alloys and various types of composite materials like graphite, fibers embedded in epoxy, etc.) that can reduce structural mass by 30% or more. Experiments with these technologies indicate that they might be applied to earthly forms of transportation and to other uses.

Composite materials—As natural raw materials are exhausted or become inadequate for many uses, new materials are being developed from polymers to form synthetic fibers and plastics. These composites made of fibers of carbon or aramid embedded in plastic are stronger and lighter than steel or ceramics. They also require less energy to make than does steel. Thus, for reasons of economics, strength, weight, and other factors, such composite materials will be increasingly important for space structures, machinery, robot arms, boats, small aircraft, automobile bodies, housing, and bone and joint replacements.

Chips—As computers, integrated circuits, transistors, and other electric and electronic devices have been miniaturized so that the equipment in which they are located can become lighter, smaller, faster, and more powerful, scientists are working on developing "superchips" capable of storing 10 million bits of information, the equivalent of 800 typed pages, on areas much smaller than a fingernail. Such engineering challenges include determining how to interconnect millions of tiny circuits and transistors on a single chip. Even now, it is possible to create situations in which 150 or more integrated circuit paths are located in spaces smaller than the diameter of a human hair. But, the problem is not only making such circuits small, but being able to interconnect levels of wiring to provide the types of input and output information sources that need to be connected to other superchips as major systems of information processing are assembled. Another problem still to be solved is how to manufacture these complex devices of such small size without contamination from dust or other foreign substances. Accomplishing these tasks will require new robots and guided vehicles that can operate with precision in the small scale and "clean" environment that humans cannot.

Ceramics—Ceramic science has been important to industry for hundreds of years as it has sought to provide new materials (e.g., firebricks for ovens, abrasives for grinding, containers, building materials) for new manufacturing and building requirements. But ceramic science is also intimately involved with developing key components for computers, electrical insulators, optical communications, cutting tools, engine parts, and capacitors. The use of raw materials such as sand and clay and other fabricated synthetic materials allows ceramic scientists to develop ceramics that are strong, light, anticorrosive, and also are useful for different purposes requiring sensitivity to changes in temperature, humidity, pressure, and sound intensity. Ceramics in different forms are used for electronics, optical, mechanical, or medical purposes. They also frequently replace natural raw materials that are in short supply across the planet.

Catalysts—"Simply stated, a catalyst is a substance that accelerates the rate of a chemical reaction to a desired product without itself undergoing change" (Cusumano, 1985, p. 120). Catalysts are important in the manufacture of drugs and vitamins; fuels such as gasoline; fertilizers, pesticides, and herbicides; plastics and adhesives; and every man-made fiber (e.g., polyester, nylon, and rayon). Currently $750 billion worth of products manufactured each year require the use of catalysts. Scientists are now searching for new catalysts to create specific chemical products or reactions. Combined with molecular engineering, catalytic design is being used to make drugs specific to treating selected mental or physical illnesses; to produce high-octane gasoline directly from natural gas, methane; to develop commercial fuel cells that convert chemical energy to electricity; and to produce hydrogen fuel or electricity from solar energy more effectively. In the future, it is likely that revolutionary reactor systems will be produced that will be the chemical analog of computer circuiting and systems; a hierarchy of cells that recognize, store, and treat information at the molecular level to selectively produce novel and complex chemical products: advanced drugs, plastics, fibers, composite materials, and fuels (Cusumano, 1985).

Software—The computer as hardware is guided by a script typically called software. The latter tells the computer what to do and how. Although miniaturization has made computers and the internal components smaller, more powerful, and less expensive, the next decade is likely to see large and dramatic changes in computer software. Software, as script, will be written increasingly in natural languages, such as English, which will be much easier for users to understand and implement. Software will also be constructed to extend both the representation of information on the screen (e.g., 3D graphics, speech generation and recognition, music synthesis, etc.) and the ability to tailor responses to examples of needs much like a human programmer now does. Perhaps the most dramatic achievement of the near future will be constructing software able to engage in some learning and artificial intelligence that will create qualitative differences in the capability of computers that parallel the quantitative leaps of the past two decades.

Space butterflies—By wedding engineering principles and biology, it is likely that in the next decade, some spacecraft used for space exploration will be miniaturized and propelled into space in the form of a cocoon from which, when in orbit, a spacecraft will emerge that will spout solar sails (wings); telescopic eyes; gossamer-fine antennae for receiving and transmitting radio signals; long springy legs for landing and walking on small asteroids; chemical sensors for tasting (analyzing) the minerals and other elements on planets, asteroids, and solar winds; electric-current generating organs for orienting its sails (wings) to the interplanetary magnetic field; and a high quality brain (computer) to enable it to coordinate its activities, navigate, and report back to earth.

References

Anderson, W.F. (1985). Beating nature's odds. *Science 85*, *6*(9), 49–50.

Bakker, R.T. (1985). Evolution by revolution. *Science 85*, *6*(9), 72–80.

Baskin, Y. (1985). The way we act. *Science 85*, *6*(9), 94–100.

Bloom, F. (1985). Brain drugs. *Science 85*, *6*(9), 100–101.

Cusumano, J.A. (1985). Designer catalysts. *Science 85*, *6*(9), 120–122.

Lucky, R.W. (1985). Message by light wave. *Science 85*, *6*(9), 112–113.

Manin, Y.I. (1985). Geometry unbound. *Science 85*, *6*(9), 89–91.

The next step: 25 discoveries that could change our lives. *Science 85*, the sixth anniversary issue, *6*(9), 2–3.

West, S. (1985). Beyond the one-track mind. *Science 85*, *6*(9), 102–109.

INDEX